Deviance in Soviet Society

DEVIANCE IN SOVIET SOCIETY

CRIME, DELINQUENCY, AND ALCOHOLISM

WALTER D. CONNOR

New York and London 1972

COLUMBIA UNIVERSITY PRESS

Walter D. Connor is Assistant Professor of Sociology and an associate of the Center for Russian and East European Studies at the University of Michigan.

Copyright © 1969, 1972 Columbia University Press
Library of Congress Catalog Card Number: 71-180044
ISBN: 0-231-03439-3
Printed in the United States of America

To my mother and father
Edward and Mary Connor
and to
Paul W. Facey, S.J.
Teacher, counsellor, and friend

ACKNOWLEDGMENTS

I have received generous assistance from many sources, both institutions and individuals, at various stages in the preparation of this book; it is a pleasure to acknowledge their help.

Along with many other authors in the field of Soviet studies, I owe a great debt to the Russian Research Center of Harvard University, which for two years provided me with the facilities and atmosphere that made possible the completion of a doctoral dissertation similar in topic but much narrower in scope than the present work. Special thanks are due to Mrs. Helen Parsons, then administrative assistant at the Center, and its director during my "tenure," Professor Abram Bergson.

The Inter-University Committee on Travel Grants (now the International Research and Exchanges Board) made possible a semester's sojourn at Moscow State University. Without that time to examine Soviet sources unavailable elsewhere and to consult with Soviet scholars, this work would have been impossible to complete.

To the University of Michigan's Center for Russian and East European Studies go my thanks for financial support during much of the period of preparing the final draft. Professors Morris Bornstein and Alfred G. Meyer, as Directors of the Center, deserve special acknowledgment. Coleen Glazer, Janis Perlman, and Adaline Huszczo were cooperative and tolerant in the face of an often rushed typing schedule.

Scholarly debts are due to a number of individuals, who bear no responsibility for whatever inadequacies this work may contain. Allen Kassof provided the right mix of encouragement and criticism when some of the ideas herein were formulated at the dissertation stage. Mark G. Field was a friendly and perceptive critic in the early stages. Conversations in Moscow with Peter Solomon, a fellow student of Soviet criminology, were stimulating. Paul W. Facey, as the mentor and friend who first aroused my interest both in sociology and the study of the USSR, deserves his own share of credit for whatever merit this book contains. My thanks go as well to those scholars and researchers in the criminal law department of Moscow State University, the All-Union Institute for the Study of the Causes of Crime and Elaboration of Preventive Measures, and other Soviet institutions who helped the project on its way. They may find here much with which they will not agree, but hopefully something of interest as well.

John D. Moore and Karen Mitchell of Columbia University Press provided a good deal of encouragement, and can claim a large share of credit for suggestions and criticisms which have eliminated rough spots in the original manuscript.

Greatest thanks go to my wife, Eileen, whose patience in the face of the frequent isolation this work demanded of the author was unfailing, and whose perceptive criticisms have greatly improved the readability of the result. Thanks are really inadequate; the debt itself is beyond sufficient acknowledgment.

Finally, thanks are due to the publishers who kindly granted permission to quote from the following sources: Kai T. Erikson, *Wayward Puritans: A Study in the Sociology of Deviance* (New York, John Wiley and Sons, © 1966); "An Observer," *Message from Moscow* (New York, Alfred A. Knopf, © 1969); M.N. Rutkevich, ed., *The Career Plans of Youth*, translated and edited by Murray Yanowitch (White Plains, New York, International Arts and Sciences Press, © 1969); Marshall B. Clinard, ed., *Anomie and Deviant Behavior* (New York, The Macmillan Company, © 1964); translations © 1958, 1961, 1965, 1966, 1968, 1969 by *The Current Digest of the Soviet Press*, published weekly at The Ohio State University by the American Association for the Advancement of Slavic Studies.

CONTENTS

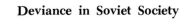

Deviance in Soviet Society

1

INTRODUCTION

ALL SOCIAL SYSTEMS have rules: the small system of the family as well as the large nation-state, the fraternal lodge as well as the military unit. And in all these systems, there occur violations of the rules. This is a no less universal characteristic. As a large and complex social system, the Soviet Union is not immune.

This book is a study in the sociology of deviance. It is concerned with deviance in one society—the contemporary USSR. The size and complexity of that society render the study of any of its aspects a formidable task, and one which demands a clear definition of subject. We will not be concerned with all forms of deviance in Soviet society. Deviance of a directly political nature—the composition and circulation of dissident manifestoes, petitions, and creative writings through the medium of *samizdat* ("unauthorized" writing, circulated generally in typed copies) and the increasingly open protests of scientists, students, and intellectuals against numerous aspects of regime policy, both of which have claimed increasing Western attention in recent years—however interesting, will not be the object of our attention.

The types of deviance that concern us here are apolitical, although the specific shapes they take in the Soviet context may have indirect political relevance. They are juvenile delinquency, drunkenness and alcoholism, and crime, "aberrant" rather than "nonconforming" behaviors, in the sense Robert K. Merton attaches to these words.[1] Their perpetrators, in breaking the "rules," are unlike the nonconformist political dissidents: they do not announce their offenses but seek to conceal them and avoid punishment; they do not question the legitimacy of norms prohibiting their acts,° but violate them by way of expediency or out of impulse; and, illustrating clearly the gap between principled nonconformity and their own deviation, they present no arguments for an alternative set of moral and legal priorities to replace the one which proscribes their acts.

We are, then, interested in deviance of the common sort as it occurs in Soviet society. Special problems are involved in studying the topic and some words about the aims and the necessary limitations of this book are in order. My objective is to present a picture, as coherently as possible, of these forms of deviance: what sorts of offenses criminals and delinquents typically perpetrate, what forms alcohol problems take, and the characteristics of the deviants themselves. The limits involved in doing this are formidable, for unlike many other nations, the USSR does not publish its nationwide statistics on crime or other forms of deviance. Nor does it seem that the near future will witness any break from what is now a forty-year tradition of relegating such data to the "classified" category. Crime statistics, in most societies, are among the most problematic and the least accurate of all statistics collected, and there is no reason to assume that the Soviet Union fares any better than average in this regard. The inaccessibility of such statistics, however flawed they might be, makes it impossible to render precise judgments about the incidence of criminal and other deviant behavior.

The fragmentary statistics the reader will encounter throughout the book (generally percentage distributions which leave us in the dark as to the integers they represent) are not, however, without some value. While they are mute on the matter of *how many* offenses are

° A limiting case to be discussed later may be the heavy drinker, who may feel that such behavior causes no great harm and that he should not be subject to disapproval.

committed, *how many* offenders there are, they do suggest what types of offenses predominate and something about the characteristics of those who commit them. No single Soviet study reveals any great amount of information: but when several such studies examined together give a relatively consistent picture of, for example, low average educational levels among offenders, they deserve careful attention.

But further qualifications are necessary if the reader is not to be led astray in viewing the statistical data presented. It would be most accurate to characterize statistics on deviance, assembled and produced by agencies of social control, as reflecting the activities and foci of attention of those agencies themselves, not the deviants who are both their clients and their "targets." Not all crimes are "known to the police"; yet out of such information, as well as arrest records, is much of the American crime rate manufactured. Soviet sources most frequently talk of "convictions," the numbers of which represent an even smaller proportion, presumably, of all crimes. Virtually all American criminologists acknowledge flaws in our own statistics, but there is substantial disagreement over whether the statistics are so flawed as to be useless. Some find it difficult to comprehend how their colleagues can "cling to the belief that information collected by social control agencies is a rough index of the extent and patterning of delinquency." [2]

Without taking sides on this specific issue, we acknowledge that our Soviet statistics, such as they are, presumably reflect law enforcement more closely than criminality. How rough an index these statistics provide of the patterning of deviance, if they provide any index at all, we cannot answer except to note, where necessary, what types of offense seem likely to be underrepresented in official statistics. The statistics provide some ideas about what offenses are typical—at least in the sense that these offenses are typically the ones law enforcement agencies deal with and record. About the "atypical" we have little information and can only conjecture from impressionistic evidence.

To those who reject statistics on deviance *in toto,* who deny that they provide even rough indices of behavior, the use of Soviet statistics here will seem unwarranted. Nor will all the qualifications satisfy them. In answer it can only be said that the statistics are presented with caution, in the knowledge that they can be *only* the roughest indices at best, whether of deviant behavior or of the behavior of social control agencies. It would have been simple to exclude them entirely and base parts of this book on fewer sources. But interpreting the subject at hand seems to demand that we make maximum, if careful, use of all the materials available. The reader himself, it is hoped, will be careful as to how much significance he attaches to the statistics, even if the rhetoric of the author's arguments may sometimes stray beyond the limits I had intended to impose on my own use of them.

Consequently, nothing of a rigorous nature said in the following chapters can be regarded as absolute: the statistics must be viewed in the broader context of other, nonquantitative information. It would be most correct to say that the picture of deviance and its "processing" presented here is one which, while not limited in its bases to statistical information, is not inconsistent with that information. Where Soviet sources themselves are inconsistent, this is pointed out. Proceeding thus involves the assumption that the quantitative information at hand, however poor its quality (due to relatively unsophisticated sampling and data collection methods), is not the product of conscious falsification. This assumption seems warranted: the data are drawn from legal journals and other Soviet sources, the very sources upon which Soviet legal scholars, practitioners, and researchers depend for much of their own information. Some of the sources are accessible to the broad Soviet public, while others are "restricted." In any case, to publish false rather than merely limited information in such sources would be to compromise seriously the work of those in the criminal law and public order fields. It is extremely unlikely, then, that our information represents a concoction designed to mask the real situation. The difficulties and expense of keeping two sets of figures, one false, one true, would be enormous. We lack access to the whole picture—but then, so do many university-located Soviet researchers, who only get access to particular statistical series on a "need to know" basis.[3] The circle of those Party and government officials and researchers in institutes subordinated to the organs of justice and public order who have general access is a relatively small one.

Beyond the portrayal of deviance itself, I am concerned with the Soviet explanation for it. What factors or causes are seen by Soviet scholars and practitioners as accounting for the existence of crime, delinquency, and alcohol problems in the contemporary USSR? The answer to this question tells us something about theoretical orientations shared among Soviet criminologists and will illustrate the constraints Marxist-Leninist ideology imposes on the process of explanation. No less interesting are the points of divergence between Soviet criminological perspectives and those of what may be loosely called "Western" criminology, and the question of how the different perspectives fit the information we have about deviance in the Soviet context. But some words of caution are also necessary here.

First, it need be said that the present work does not and cannot provide a "test" of the validity of Western theories of crime and deviance. It would be both valuable and interesting were we able to hold up against the Soviet facts any of a number of Western theories in order to measure their cross-cultural validity. But unfortunately the data at hand are not sufficient in quantity to meet the requirements of any such test. Nor are the data we have qualitatively fit for such purposes: the research of Soviet criminologists has thus far been mainly a matter of assembling statistics on various aspects of lawbreaking and lawbreakers and has not been designed for the empirical testing of hypotheses on the causes of criminal behavior, whether Soviet or Western in origin.

Nor in any case is it clear whether many Western theories which have enjoyed a vogue are formulated in such a way as to render them testable. A certain plausibility attaches to, for example, theories which would explain crime and delinquency in the United States by recourse to "criminogenic" elements in American culture itself. Dynamism, complexity, materialism, and a persistent tradition of self-sufficient individualism are put forward as basic roots of American criminality. From another point of departure, "subterranean" values of hedonism, "smartness," and corner-cutting, in conflict with but held as surely as are the values of work, thrift, and honesty that make up the "Protestant Ethic," are seen as finding their reflection in delinquency.[4] Subterranean values are seen to be as much part of the American value complex as those on display "above ground." There is, one feels, something in these conceptions; they strike a responsive chord in many thoughtful persons. Yet they elude attempts to confirm or disconfirm them. They resist "operationalization." To say this is not to dismiss them, but only to note that these, and similar theories presenting such general explanations of deviant and criminal behavior, raise problems of validation that cannot be resolved in the context of this work, however interesting the effort might be. This does not mean that Western theory is of no interest here. Some striking parallels and convergences between Soviet criminological thought and other varieties may be emerging, and of these due note will be taken.

A third major concern of this book is the approach the Soviet Union has taken in attempting to prevent the sorts of deviance enumerated here and in rehabilitating, curing, or correcting the deviants themselves. Here again, within the limits imposed by the often fragmentary quality of our information, the goal is a coherent description of the structure and operation of delinquent and criminal corrections systems, and the institutions and modes of treatment aimed at drunkards and alcoholics. Soviet concern with the effectiveness of different types of rehabilitative techniques—"in-society" forms of punishment, probation, imprisonment—has fostered a number of informative studies which occasionally provide surprising amounts of useful data on institutional success in preventing recidivism. Less clear, and in any case difficult to convey, is the "feel" of Soviet correctional institutions, the texture of the daily life of inmates. But here, too, certain Soviet sources are helpful in illuminating what hitherto have been dark corners in our knowledge. From the time of the purges of 1936–1938 to the present, former political prisoners have communicated some of the aspects of their life in confinement, but relatively little has emerged from these sources on the life of the common criminal or delinquent prisoner. This is one of the gaps the study tries to fill, with information frequently gathered from those journals and monographs that are the professional reading matter of administrators and staff in the corrections system.

The foregoing is a very general statement of this book's objectives. The following chapter specifies in greater detail the questions posed in each area of concern. Chapter 2 is intended not so much as an analytic framework as an attempt to orient the reader to some important issues inherent in deviance as a social phenomenon, criminology as a social science, and preventive and corrective strategies and tactics as techniques of social intervention.

It is probably a hope common to all authors that their writings will be useful to members of different audiences: that their thoughts and findings will be valuable or, at least, informative beyond the merely interesting. This is the case here. For the reader from whatever discipline whose main interests lie in the area of Soviet and communist studies it is hoped that this book will provide a helpful picture of one of the least-examined aspects of Soviet life. Much has been made recently [5] of the desirability and necessity of integrating "Soviet area" and communist studies more tightly with the increasingly sophisticated concepts and methodologies of the various social science disciplines. Generally, this is all to the good. Stress on the uniqueness of societies typically characterized in the past as "totalitarian" has led to disjunction between the methods employed by economists, political scientists, sociologists, and others engaged in the study of communist societies and those employed by their disciplinary confreres whose interests lie elsewhere. But the question of adopting particular methodological approaches, in the author's opinion, is one that must be resolved on a case-by-case basis. The problems of information and access which distinguish the study of the USSR, for one example, from that of many other societies of similar complexity and a similar level of development are very real ones. No mechanical imposition of a particular analytic framework can resolve them. In the present case, the nature of both the topic and the data seemed to rule out any major analytic design. Where relevant, as at many points they are, the concepts of sociology and political science are employed— fruitfully, it is hoped. At some period in the future, when the problems alluded to have been overcome, a book on this topic may emerge which more fully reflects the impact of the "behavioral revolution" in the study of communist social systems. Then, I hope, the undeniable gaps in this work may be filled.

Some readers whose interests are not specifically in the Soviet area—sociologists, criminologists, specialists in criminal law and corrections—may find much of interest here as well. While the data assembled do not permit any tests of the validity of theories of deviance causation, those that refer to corrective and rehabilitative strategies and tactics may throw some light on the successes and failures of another society's attempts to deal with its more recalcitrant members. At a time when modes of correction and rehabilitation in the United States are undergoing deep reexamination, such information may be valuable in calling attention to the pitfalls as well as to the promise in as yet unexplored alternatives to our present techniques. Finally, what is written here should make clear, to those who doubt, that a different social system and a different mode of economic organization promise no "total cure" for the problems of crime, alcoholism, and delinquency.

2

ISSUES AND QUESTIONS

ONE MAJOR LINE of inquiry in this study concerns the "criminological enterprise" in the USSR: to what levels of explanation do Soviet criminologists have recourse in explaining the acts of offenders? What *specific* causes are adduced to account for such acts? What influence is exerted by Marxist-Leninist ideology on criminology's theoretical perspective?

Deviance prevention and the "correction" of deviants is another area of concern. In addition to the questions of specific forms and mechanisms of prevention and correction and why these and not others are chosen, the issue of responsibility for activating and administering such mechanisms must be explored. Here, the degree to which such responsibility is centralized in a relatively narrow group of professionals in law enforcement and correction or, on the other hand, diffused among broader categories of the Soviet public is important. No less important is the congruence (or lack thereof) between the reactions of state and public to the forms of deviance to be described. Do state and public view specific types of deviance with equal concern? If so, or even if not, how salient are problems of deviance to their "audience"? What priority does deviance of this apolitical variety possess, among other challenges and problems with which both state and public must deal?

Though generally stated, these questions are relatively specific ones —which is not to say that they can all be answered unequivocally. When the topic of deviance is seen in a broader perspective, other issues crop up. An important one relates to the general adequacy of Soviet explanations of deviance. "Adequacy" here is seen as a matter of being in accord with the realities of Soviet life; determining it is clearly a matter of judging those explanations in the light of both data from Soviet sources and other data and interpretations gleaned from non-Soviet investigators. The judgment rendered can only be the observer's and of necessity reflects his own view of Soviet reality. Yet it can be based as well on more generally accepted criteria of theoretical adequacy or "worthwhileness" in a heuristic sense.

Still another issue relates to deviance as a challenge to the problem-identifying and problem-solving capacities of the Soviet state and Party apparatus. How has deviance rated among other challenges during the period under consideration, and what sorts of evidence may be found which indicate rises and declines in its relative priority as a problem?

Some of these questions will be answered directly by the data assembled in chapters 4 through 9. Others, not so readily answerable, will be taken up in chapter 10. It remains for us now to look in somewhat greater detail at the questions just summarized and to comment on the sort of answers we may expect.

Identifying and explaining the causes of deviant behavior has been, for society, a difficult undertaking. The *apparent* difficulties, however, may be many or few depending on the presence or absence of consensus on a number of basic theoretical and metatheoretical issues. If some issues are beyond debate, the task of explanation may appear simpler than it would otherwise.

What then is the impact of Marxist-Leninist ideology on Soviet theorizing about deviance? Marxism-Leninism in its "official" Soviet version *is* an orthodoxy, with elements impinging directly on issues in the social sciences. Indeed, its supporters offer it as a "science of society," as the only truly "scientific" one. Two elements of its model of man are of particular importance here: first, the claim that man is more-or-less "perfectible" in his earthly existence, and second, that he is basically a social being. These views imply that deviance is not a necessary or eternal phenomenon and that, as a social being, man's tendencies toward deviance are *socially* induced: the conditions of his social existence determine his behavior, for good or ill, and modification of those conditions will in time change his behavior.

The two elements need not be indissolubly linked. To those who might believe in perfectibility but who see man himself as less social and his behavior primarily as a product of individual, organic properties, a commitment to reaching that state of perfection might mean genetic or psychiatric manipulation. To those who discount perfectibility but who do see man as a creature social in essence, there are no easy answers to the problems engendered by the imperfections of both man and the society that shapes him. The latter position might be said to characterize with rough accuracy the presuppositions of many Western theorists of deviance.

But when the beliefs converge, as they do in the Soviet model of a social and perfectible man, they would seem to close off certain channels of inquiry on the one hand, and on the other open up the prospect of an "optimum" resolution of the problem of deviance through the manipulation of man's social environment. To what degree the explanations advanced by Soviet writers on crime, deviance, and alcoholism for these phenomena do or do not reflect both the "closed" nature of certain issues and the ideological positions just discussed is a question yet to be answered.

Other questions about Soviet approaches to deviance are also of importance. Different levels of a social system may provide the major foci for inquiry into the causes of deviance. To which level or levels does Soviet theorizing turn? Ideology may influence the choice of level. Are broad societal characteristics (modes of organization, cultural belief systems, etc.) looked to to provide explanations? Or is the focus on the "infrastructure"—on the dynamics of family life, on peer and reference groups, on those social contexts which make up the immediate milieu of the individual? Or, finally, is the target of inquiry the individual himself and the basic assumption that "something" deep-rooted in him can account for his deviant behavior?

Among sociologists of deviance in the West, recent years have witnessed controversies about matters so basic as the choice of subject matter itself. Which actors, which processes may most properly claim the attention of whoever seeks to investigate the social phenomenon of deviance? Without doing too much violence to subtle distinctions among the many contributions to the discussion, one can identify two basic tendencies and some variations or differences of emphasis. Of these two basic tendencies in explaining deviance, the "determinist," as we shall call it here, has by far the longer history. Determinism focuses attention on the deviant actor, viewing him as constrained in such a manner that he, unlike the conforming "majority," breaks society's rules in matters of serious import. The sources of the constraints have been very different according to different theorists. At the turn of the century, Lombroso's "positive criminology" located them in the organism itself: some men, he argued, were "born criminals," destined to be criminals because of physiological properties which prevented them from bending to the demands of society's discipline. They were profoundly "different" from noncriminal individuals.

No less "different" for analytic purposes are those violators of norms whom modern sociologists and psychologists see as determined by *social* circumstances, whether by experiences within the family or by the broader circumstances of poverty, discrimination, or nurture in delinquent or criminal subcultures. Though this is a softer determinism, it too views the deviant as one made "special" through a set of experiences and links his behavior to his special qualities. As the sociologist David Matza has put it, from biological to sociological determinism, the explanation of deviance has rested in the "radically different circumstances" experienced by the deviant on the one hand and he who abides by the rules on the other.[1]

The "interactionist" approach challenges the assumptions of determinism. To the determinist model of an actor motivated or constrained to act in a deviant manner, and to determinism's assumption that agencies of social control primarily *react* to deviance, it counterposes an alternative model, a

view of deviation as a consequence of the extent and form of social control. [It] rests upon the assumption that social control must be taken as an independent variable rather than as a constant, or merely reciprocal, societal reaction to deviation. Thus conceived, social control becomes a "cause" rather than an effect of the magnitude and variable forms of deviation.[2]

The interactionist model, as developed by Becker, Lemert and others,[3] moves the deviant out of center stage and places him in the position of one among many actors, all of whom contribute to the phenomenon of deviance. In this view, the deviant need not be motivated to act in any particular way—he may violate a rule because he is unaware of its existence, or, knowing it exists, may misinterpret its applicability to his own action. He may, thus, "wander" into deviance.[4] More important in identifying him as deviant, in recruiting him to play the role of deviant, is the treatment society accords him. A deviant act may go undetected and unpunished; conversely, an "innocent" may be mistakenly identified as deviant. Identification is crucial, since the imputed initial act (or "primary deviation," to use Edwin Lemert's term), may become the basis for a reaction by society, or some segment of it, which forces the new-labeled deviant into "secondary deviation," a

means of defense, attack or adaptation to the overt and covert problems created by the societal reaction to primary deviation. In effect, the original "causes" of the deviation recede and give way to the central importance of the disapproving, degradational, and isolating reactions of society.[5]

Here then the "cause" of deviance may be sought in the rules men make that separate out a category of behavior to be classified as deviant, in the way the rules are enforced, and in the consequences of such enforcement for its targets. The interactionist perspective makes problematic the enactment of certain laws and not others, the differential enforcement of different laws, and the differential deployment of enforcement resources toward different components of the population. It seeks answers to questions about what *interests* make some persons assume the mantle of "moral entrepreneur" and push for the elaboration of new prohibitions,[6] what differential distributions of resources render certain persons less liable, others more, to damage in their careers from the application of a "tag" of "deviance."[7]

These two approaches look in different directions, not necessarily completely denying each other's validity but parting company on the matter of where attention should be concentrated. Further development of some themes in the interactionist perspective, primarily by Kai T. Erikson,[8] may allow us to speak also of another variant—a "neo-functionalist" approach. Within a functionalist framework, deviance has more often than not been consigned to the category of dysfunctional phenomena—those that lessen societal integration and stability. As such, it is seen as a problem to be controlled and, if possible, eliminated. Erikson, however, drawing in part on Durkheim's view of deviance as providing occasions for the affirmation of common norms and beliefs among the conforming, and thereby *promoting* solidarity,[9] sees an important element of utility in it as a marker of societal boundaries.

To begin with, the only material found in a society for marking boundaries is the behavior of its members—or rather, the networks of interaction which link these members together in regular social relations. And the interactions which do the most effective job of locating and publicizing the group's outer edges would seem to be those which take place between deviant persons on the one side and official agents of the community on the other. The deviant is a person whose activities have moved outside the margins of the group, and when the community calls him to account for that vagrancy it is making a statement about the nature and placement of its boundaries.[10]

Seen from one side, deviance is a "problem" to be eliminated. From another, however, it is a *resource*, which the forces of social control husband, in a sense, for society's benefit.

If we grant that human groups often derive benefit from deviant behavior, can we then assume that they are organized in such a way as to promote this resource? Can we assume, in other words, that forces operate in the social structure to recruit offenders and to commit them to long periods of service in the deviant ranks? [11]

If the neo-functionalist view casts deviance in a rather novel light, one other view, still very much alive, contains elements of a markedly traditional nature. This might be called a "voluntarist" view of deviance: contrary to determinist views which minimize the deviant actor's choices and interactionist views which minimize the relevance of the deviant's acts themselves, voluntarism sees the deviant act as at least significantly if not totally the product of a choice. "Free will" comes in and out of vogue among social scientists, and there is little of voluntarism in criminological theories today: [12] yet it is alive in the criminal legislation of virtually every nation, which provides punishments for presumably responsible actors, and it lives also in those ar guments for the deterrent effect of punishment which presume that the actor calculates the probable costs and benefits before embarking on a particular path. The free will model was a part of that classical criminology to which Lombroso's biological positivism was a "scientific" response: elements of both remain with us, whether in theoretical criminology or in practical strategies of coping with deviance.

This digression into different perspectives in Western (essentially American) views of deviance may seem rather wide of the mark in the present context. Yet, the questions posed by these diverse views and the differences between them are important ones, and not evidently culture-bound. They might be asked in any society, in the form presented here or under other terminology. It shall be one aim of the present inquiry to determine what elements of these perspectives on deviance are present in Soviet approaches, and why some others may be missing. The answers are important, for choices so basic as the adoption, in whole or in part, of one or more of these perspectives have strong implications for the way deviance is handled.

To return to the realm of the ideological: if inquiries about the impact of ideology on positions concerning the causes of deviance are proper, it is no less proper to ask about the functions, beyond the strictly scientific, that such positions or theories perform—functions of a basically political nature. Theories may serve and have served many purposes for their supporters and others. Theories purporting to account for the existence of specific "evils" such as those that concern us here may represent not only explanations, but attacks upon the legitimacy of a specific social order—"radical critiques" aimed at unmasking elements of that social order which may be seen as inevitably producing the evils under examination. Such, indeed, is the Soviet explanation of crime, alcoholism, and delinquency, as well as other social evils, in *capitalist* society.° All these are seen as flowing, in ac-

---

° In line with this reasoning, criminal deviance, alcoholism, etc. in the contemporary USSR are viewed as "survivals of capitalism," in the sense that the *socialist* system contains none of the "inevitably" deviance-generating elements of the capitalist social order which preceded it. A major component in the explanation of why deviance and the attitudes underlying it "survive" so long is the Marxist-Leninist notion of the "lag in consciousness." "Life" (the realities of social and economic organization) determines consciousness, but only in the long run.

cordance with the objective "laws" of capitalism, from the nature of capitalist society itself: that set of arrangements marked by private property in the means of production. Nor have some American radicals in recent years hesitated to borrow virtually the same critique.

Theories, on the other hand, may serve to exculpate a particular social system, to excuse it from responsibility for those gaps between the "real" and the "ideal" that exist within it. The causes of crime and other ills may be externalized, spatially or temporally: the influence and machinations of other societies or the weight of past history may be cited to show that the *present* social order in a particular nation-state bears no responsibility for such problems, since its ability to control other nations and past history is of necessity quite limited. By selection of a particular focus, theories may also deflect attention from the macrostructural properties of a society and turn criticism instead toward less general characteristics, labeling these as departures from the ideal blueprint and blaming them for deviance.

To what uses have explanations of deviance in the USSR lent themselves? Are there elements of critique of the Soviet system in them, as well as "conservative" exculpation? In what proportions? These are important questions for criminology and for other branches of Soviet social science as well. They are particularly sharply posed in the Soviet case because of the demands made of social sciences there: demands for "utility" and "congruence." [13] Utility is providing something of practical value—information upon which decisions may be made, data indicating the success or failure of programs, justifications for decisions and actions. The production of knowledge for knowledge's sake, the raising of "significant" questions, does not suffice to legitimate the existence of a discipline. The demand for congruence requires that a social science, in seeking results, must remain ideologically compatible with Marxism-Leninism. In the interpretation of data and the treatment of its subject matter, it must neither operate from nor arrive at positions varying from official ideology. These de-

---

Hence, while the transition from capitalism to socialism has changed consciousness in some areas, in other areas consciousness "lags" behind life, and old attitudes, including many of those which foster deviance, "survive." No extended discussion of these concepts is intended here, but some further comments on them and their application in causal analysis are provided in chapters 4 and 8.

mands are imposed, directly or indirectly and with greater or lesser vigor, by the regime itself. To what degree they have met with resistance or with willing accession is a matter still to be determined, as is the implied question of how "useful" and "congruent" a social science Soviet criminology is.

A different set of issues surrounds the matter of "diagnosing" and attributing significance to different forms of deviant behavior. Power is differentially distributed in societies: not all persons have the same amount, nor do all roles afford their incumbents equal access to it or its exercise. This is true also of that type of power which involves the determination of what types of behavior are to be regarded as deviant, the relative seriousness of each type, and what is to be done about them. The opinions of some on these matters have greater impact than those of others. Even in political systems that may be described as liberal-democratic, legally defining deviance is a matter for courts and legislators; it is not done by plebiscite. To the degree that jurists and legislators emerge from social backgrounds dissimilar to those of many of their constituents and members of the society at large, their priorities and views may diverge from those of the latter. Public control over the deviance-defining process, or at least over its *legal* variant, is indirect and intermittent. Generally it amounts to the power of either re-election or rejection at the polls.

The tighter centralization of effective power in the USSR and the absence of the ballot as an effective, if indirect, means of control raise questions about the "non-plebiscitary" determination of deviance in a particularly interesting way. First, do the state and the public view the types of deviance that concern us in the same way, or do their reactions differ? For our purposes, "state" may be taken roughly as signifying the official sector of Soviet society, especially those Party officials, police and court functionaries, and public health personnel whose main concerns impinge on or are directly in the area of maintenance of order and management of deviance. The "public" is, by implication, the residuum—the rest of Soviet society. These definitions are, of course, exceedingly loose, and in present form leave unconsidered the possibility of differences within each sector. But they focus attention on an important issue. In determining whether state and public responses are parallel or divergent, we have evidentiary problems: the public's reaction is not so clearly expressed as the state's (the latter having, at least, declared a formal position on the issue). Yet occasional readers' letters to the Soviet press, expressing opinions on certain issues, are of some value: "deviant" opinions are sometimes printed, if only to be "refuted." Similarly, complaints in specialized periodicals and monographs about the *lack* of public response to campaigns against one or another type of offender may point indirectly to areas where state and public diverge. Such materials must be used with care, but they should not be ignored.

Two particular characteristics of the Soviet system should be noted in connection with the issue of parallelism or divergence between state and public reactions to deviance. The Soviet Union, first of all, is a society in which everyday life is highly "politicized," in which

the elite is concerned not merely with the "commanding heights," but also to an overwhelming degree with the detailed regulation of the entire range of social life, including those institutions which, in the West, typically have been regarded as lying beyond the legitimate scope of public authority and political intervention.[14]

Attribution of such significance to this broad range of behavior increases the potential scope for applying the label of "deviance" to certain types of behavior. Over the course of fifty years, certainly, a majority of Soviet citizens have come to accord legitimacy to a government which sees itself as "governing best," among other reasons because it "governs *most*." State intervention in many everyday affairs may not be seen by much of the public as objectionable in principle. But for some types of deviance, and in particular instances, the tendency (often complained of in the Soviet press) of many citizens to think of their everyday affairs as personal matters may well come into conflict with state interventionism. If such attitudes are widespread, the struggle against a variety of forms of deviance may involve the state in combatting not only the deviants themselves but also a relatively tolerant or unconcerned public, little interested in taking either side.

Important as well is the question of whether, given the present stage of modernization in the USSR, there is not a sufficient "reservoir" of traditional values, attitudes, and behavior patterns among some segments of the population to bring them into conflict with the present-day heirs of the Bolshevik modernizing elite, specifically over such matters as what kinds of behavior should be classified and treated as deviant.

Unquestionably, there exist gaps between the values of modernizers and those of the populations in the traditional societies they seek to transform. Typically, the modernizers seek to substitute for a system of particularistic and parochial loyalties the organization of such loyalties around a national focus. The scope of the peasant's world widens, and he becomes a "citizen." The preoccupation with *growth*, with the translation of available resources into national power, normally involves industrialization, a process with profound implications for predominantly peasant populations. Adaptability, order, work habits responsive to man-made schedules rather than to those dictated by nature, "rationality," and universalistic orientations—all these are valued by the modernizer, but it is in all these that traditional societies seem most deficient. The strains of industrialization are immense. As numerous historians and social scientists have observed, such transformations are *imposed* on societies: history provides no clear example of a *nation* having willingly opted for industrialization.

Our question refers to specifically Soviet modernization and its ultimate effects. In holding out the model of the "new Soviet man" for mass emulation, the Bolsheviks were basically demonstrating a commitment to transforming the traditional Russian peasant into a Soviet counterpart of the Western industrial worker—a disciplined, predictable, rational producer, at home in the environments of factory and city. Here special problems arose. The industrial working class was minute, compared to the masses of peasantry. The commitment to rapid industrialization meant that, in a very short time, millions of peasants would be "transformed" into urban workers. By comparison, the industrial revolutions of Western countries had been gradual processes, with intermediate phases in which peasants moved from the land to employment in crafts and trades, frequently in small enterprises—not to the giant factories and plants of the Five-Year Plans. The transition from farming to full industrial work was a matter of more than one generation. In the Soviet Union, one generation was all the time many had to make the move.

That Soviet modernization was generally successful is beyond question. But the very speed and intensity of the process, as well as its ongoing nature (for it is not yet completed) pose particular problems. Many Soviet urban workers of today come from rural, peasant backgrounds. Probably most are only one generation away from the land. And a substantial portion of the population, larger in percentage terms than in other comparable societies, remains on the land. How "modern," then, is the Soviet citizen? How congruent, after fifty years, are his attitudes with those of a regime which demands of him orderliness, competence, and predictability? Individual labor productivity, for example, depends on such characteristics, as well as on material supply and efficient organizational formulas: to what degree can the relatively lower productivity of the Soviet worker be attributed to things about himself rather than to material and organizational factors? To pose such a question is not in any way to rate Soviet workers as "inferior" but only to raise the question of how well many of them fit their urban industrial environment and its demands. This is a question of some currency today, as in the past, since much urban growth in the USSR is still attributable to migration from the countryside to the cities. Large numbers are still undergoing the transformation, often a difficult one, from the traditional life of the countryside to that of the cities. And if, in the cities as well as the rural areas, attitudes toward daily life and leisure persist which diverge from official attitudes, the implications of such a divergence for official and public definitions of deviance may be great.

This argument may seem a tenuous one, and it is fully realized that it is difficult to establish a linkage between attitudinal cleavage on a modern-traditional dimension and differential assessments of deviance. But some previous research, of a "characterological" type, *does* suggest that a large gap existed for some time between the Bolshevik-modernizer's view of the world in general and the view of the population at large. On the basis of a clinical study of some Russian displaced persons, Inkeles and his collaborators noted the "poor 'fit' between the personality patterns of many Soviet citizens and the 'personality' of the leaders as it expressed itself in the institutions they created . . ."[15]

The general expansiveness of the Russians in our sample, their easily expressed feelings, the giving in to impulse, and the free expression of criticism, were likely to meet only the coldest reception from the regime. It emphasized and rewarded control, formality, and lack of feelings in relations. Discipline, orderliness, and strict observance of rules are what it expects. Thus, our Russian subjects could hope for little official reward in response to their normal modes of expression.[16]

We do not assume that these gaps in attitude, widened and intensified by the real privations and strains of industrialization, collectivization, and the construction of a totalitarian social order, exist in the same form or degree today. But it would be equally wrong to assume that no gap exists, or to ignore its implications.

Finally, we reach the question of what is done about deviance, and to the deviant. Chapters to follow will focus on the types of punishments and corrective techniques, the sorts of institutions, and varieties of post-treatment supervision the Soviet system has available for different categories of transgressor. Within the limits imposed by scarcity of information, some observations on their effectiveness are also offered. Beyond these matters, there remains the question of how the whole enterprise of deviance management, punishment, and correction fits into the broader context of Soviet life. Emphasis on public involvement in controlling and reforming the deviant, a frequent theme in Soviet writing, turns our attention to some specific issues. First, to what degree *is* the public given real responsibility in this area (realizing that law enforcement and corrections "professionals" also have large roles) and to what degree does it exercise such responsibility and actively participate in control and correction? In the midst of their other daily concerns, do many Soviet citizens allocate any time and energy to such activities, or even desire to do so?

Second, what of the fact that, in the USSR as in other societies, the public is an "audience" in relation to the deviant "performer"? The Soviet press, unlike much of its American counterpart, does not engage in sensationalist crime coverage. Its interests lie in other areas than the titillation of readers. Yet deviance *is* publicized, and the public exhorted not to be indifferent to it, in posters, through display boards in factories, on farms, and in other institutions showing pictures and names of offenders, and in popular pamphlets. For "educative" purposes, criminal trials may be held in visiting sessions, with the whole process taking place in an auditorium or assembly hall at the offender's place of work in front of an audience composed of his fellow workers. What are the aims of this type of publicity accorded the deviant? If the aims are to intensify sentiments against deviance among the conforming population and to deter the "unstable" who might transgress the rules in the future, to promote "solidarity" among the righteous in the face of the unrighteous, how well do the mechanisms employed serve these aims?

These, then, are the questions we ask as we begin to examine three varieties of deviant behavior in Soviet society. There are difficulties in answering them in similar form for each variety, especially since much of the problem of "alcoholism and drunkenness" involves behaviors not strictly illegal, as are crime and delinquency. But, taken together, it is hoped that they provide a suitable framework for the inquiry we are about to undertake.

3

HISTORICAL BACKGROUND

CRIME IN THE
USSR, 1917–1936

AMONG THE PROBLEMS faced by the new Soviet government when it came into power after the October revolution of 1917 was that of crime, in both its adult and juvenile variants. Reliable data on the fight against crime in the immediate post-revolutionary years is scarce, and the data for the 1920s and 1930s up to the period of Stalin's purges is not much more confidence-inspiring. However, some general trends marked by Soviet scholars are worth mentioning, to place our main concerns in perspective.[1]

The Soviet characterization of crime in the years 1917–1921 reflects both the unsettled nature of those years, when "Soviet power" was only tenuously established in many areas, and the final judgment that victors render on the vanquished. The most serious crimes are political—the military activities of foreign interventionists, the "Whites" and other anti-Bolshevik forces, "banditism," etc. Also widespread were speculation and trade in prohibited goods, theft, robbery, and other property crimes. (In the period 1918–1919, according to Soviet sources, of 2,458,800 tons of bread delivered to the population, only 40 percent came through legal government channels, the other 60 percent being funneled through illegal trade.)

A chronicler of these years sums it up:

For crime in the period of the October revolution, the foreign intervention and the civil war, the following were characteristic: a) a high rate of crime; b) predominance . . . of especially serious crimes; c) the political, counter-revolutionary character of the majority of serious crimes; d) the significant specific weight of professional and recidivist crimes; e) a general growth of crime.[2]

General growth was indeed a hallmark of the period—robberies, assaults, and other crimes against the person are said to have soared ten to fifteen times above their 1917 rates by 1921. The introduction in 1921 of Lenin's New Economic Policy, under which a good deal of private enterprise was tolerated in the interests of restoring the ruptured economy, saw armed, violent resistance to the Bolsheviks give place to what is described as "economic counterrevolution." Diversion of government goods, sabotage, embezzlement, trade in contraband, and counterfeiting drew much of the attention of the organs of law and order in the period 1921–1926. Along with these property crimes, crimes against the person (predominantly "hooliganism," which at the time fell into this category) and illegal manufacture of liquor were the most common offenses appearing in criminal statistics.

While the crimes were, in general, of a less serious nature in this period than in 1917–1921, they were sufficient to keep courts occupied. In 1923, the courts of the USSR convicted 575,761 persons—in 1924, 1,021,032 persons.[3] By 1926, however, the number of crimes, according to Soviet sources, was showing a marked tendency to decline.[4]

By the mid-1920s, juvenile delinquency[5] had become a serious problem. Children orphaned or displaced by the civil war, the *besprizornye*, wandered the land, living by theft and taxing the resources of law enforcement agencies. An estimated 6 to 7 percent of all criminal convictions in the period involved juveniles; one cannot estimate the number of delinquent juveniles the courts never reached.

The later 1920s, the period of the first Five-Year Plan for industrialization and of the beginnings of collectivization, tended toward a further drop in crime, according to Soviet sources. From 1927 to 1929, the number of cases instituted by investigative organs dropped 15.5 percent.[6] Yet other figures cause one to wonder: in 1928, the courts of the Russian Republic *alone* convicted 955,629 persons.[7]

As the USSR underwent the massive upheaval of collectivization, the liquidation of the kulaks (rich peasants) "as a class," it becomes evident that the courts themselves must have stood aside from much of the "criminality" associated with resistance to collectivization. In 1928, it is reported that only 0.12 percent of criminals convicted had been convicted of "counterrevolutionary crime," and only a relatively small share of these for terrorist acts. (But of these, according to a Supreme Court report of the time, 95 percent were rich peasants and 5 percent "middle" peasants.) The share of terrorist acts among all counterrevolutionary crimes grew, and then fell again, tracing the intensification and final completion of collectivization: 29.9 percent in 1928, 52.4 percent in 1929, 35 percent in 1930, and 22.5 percent in 1931.[8] We do not know how many convicted kulaks these figures reflect—but it seems safe to observe that many more faced summary justice than reached the courts to appear as statistics. At the same time, the courts concerned themselves to a large degree with what has become their standard fare—property offenses and offenses against the person, generally it seems of a non-extraordinary nature. The courts of the RSFSR in 1928 handed down 70.1 percent of their convictions for "petty crimes."[9]

From 1929 into the mid-1930s, the era of "socialist reconstruction of the economy and the triumph of socialism in the USSR," crime was again on the increase, as the social changes taking place were reflected in new legislation and intensified campaigns against certain types of offenders. The large increase in cases of offenses against socialist property, abuse of office, and other related crimes was, as one observer notes, "a direct indicator of the offensive policy of the Soviet state on all fronts."[10] According to the doctrine that the class war intensified as the USSR came closer to achieving socialism, the law enforcement organs intensified their own activity, often beyond the limits later Soviet observers have seen as reasonable.

There were districts in the country where from one-fourth to one-half of the chairmen of collective farms and rural soviets were convicted for official crimes, mainly for negligence, where in a majority of instances [these offenses] could have been handled with measures of a disciplinary type.[11]

While crimes of this sort grew, or appeared to, due to intensified enforcement and the legislation that, in effect, created new crimes, offenses against the person declined in conviction statistics by about 3 times from 1929 to 1934.[12]

By the mid-1930s, the Soviet Union was in the period of the "cult of personality." Stalin had emerged as undisputed leader, and the "great terror"—the purges of 1936–1938—were soon to follow. Given the massive impact of the purges on Soviet society, when millions of innocent persons suffered arrest, imprisonment, and death for offenses they had not committed, the tracing of nonpolitical criminality through these years becomes for Soviet scholars a difficult and even a trivial matter, and the fate of the "politicals" a sensitive topic. Soviet writers generally limit themselves to a statement of the following sort: "In the years 1934–1938 extremely gross violations of socialist legality were permitted in the area of the fight with counterrevolutionary crimes, [and] by indictments for such, many innocent people were convicted." [13]

For the years of World War II and the postwar period up to 1956, the picture of crime is an even more incomplete one—the surveys upon which this account is based have virtually nothing to say about it. We can only note the Soviet summary for the whole period from the revolution to the mid-1930s, characterizing crime at that time as follows:

. . . 1) crime—for this period a necessary massive social phenomenon, had in all its forms the character of a class struggle of the exploiting classes with the worker-peasant power; 2) crime was distinguished by a rather high rate; 3) less serious crimes [began] to predominate in the structure of crime; 4) the crime rate, from the middle of the 1920s, is characterized by a general steady decline, with occasional, sometimes sharp oscillations in the curve of crime, in view of frequent legislative change and elements of campaign-ism (*kampaneishchina*) in the struggle with crime; 5) a high specific weight of professional and recidivist crime was retained as a heritage received from Tsarist Russia, the basic contingent of which was composed of de-classed elements and unemployed; 6) organized forms of crime, in the form of bands and gangs, were widespread, especially in the period of the civil war and the rebuilding of the national economy, with a subsequent gradual reduction of this type of dangerous crime; 7) convictions of minors at first were high, on account of displaced children, and later with the economic and political consolidation of Soviet power, relatively low . . .[14]

What is to be made of this account? We have an exceedingly rough picture with many unfilled spots. The statistics upon which it is partially based are inadequate.[15] They refer to numbers of convictions and, less frequently, numbers of criminal cases instituted. They reflect, then, the activity of courts, and only courts—not the number of crimes committed (a dark figure in any society), nor the number known to the authorities, nor even all cases "disposed of." Soviet justice in the 1920s was frequently summary and was dispensed by "revolutionary tribunals" which did not keep statistical accounts. Changes in legislation, variations in court practices, shifts in the targets of police work, upsurges and declines in the work of investigative agencies —all these, in the unsettled state of Soviet society in the early post-1917 period, and again during collectivization at the end of the 1920s and the beginning of the 1930s, probably had as much (or more) effect on the rough "crime rates" of the time as did actual variations in the incidence of criminal acts.

The account is, however, the official one, and therein lies a good deal of its significance. It is against this period, using it as a base, that Soviet jurists and criminologists at least partially judge their work today. Such as it is, the picture does correspond, although roughly, at most points with the realities, the main social forces of the time. It should be kept in mind as a yardstick for judging the post-Stalin period which is our main concern.

THE PROBLEMS OF
CRIMINOLOGY, 1918–1935

No less important for an understanding of Soviet attempts to explain and cope with problems of deviance in the post-Stalin era is some understanding of the early phase in the development of criminology in the USSR, the period extending roughly from 1918 to the mid-1930s.[16]

The new social order the Bolsheviks sought to create—one purged of poverty, injustice, the exploitation of man by man, and private ownership of the means of production, the "basic root" of the first three—had no place for crime as a persistent phenomenon. But since the new order was born out of the old, crime and other forms of deviance admittedly could not be eradicated at once. Lenin gave his blessing to the study of crime and penal practices, in the apparent hope that progress would result from such study.[17]

The first steps in what was to be a relatively uncoordinated but widespread study of crime were taken by the courts, the police, and the Cheka (the state security body). While such activities suffered from limited resources, on the national level support for the criminological enterprise was extended through publication of conviction statistics by the Central Statistical Administration, established in 1918. To promote some measure of uniformity in the reporting of data, the CSA designed in 1922 a standard form to be filled out by the court for each criminal case heard, containing data on the offense and characteristics of the offender.[18] While the accounting systems had many evident deficiencies, they provided a good deal of information which was eagerly consumed by scholars and "practitioners" alike.

The early to mid-1920s saw a rapid growth of institutions devoted to studying crime. Offices (*kabinety*) for the study of crime and criminals were established in Leningrad, Saratov, Odessa, Kiev, Kharkov, Minsk, Rostov-on-Don, Irkutsk, and Baku, as well as in Moscow. The Moscow office was established after the publication of a collective volume, *The Criminal World of Moscow*,[19] a product of the researches of social scientists at Moscow University under the direction of the City Soviet. The offices, in whose work both scholars and professional law-enforcement officials participated, were not under any single administration and often took different theoretical directions in their studies.

On the national level, the Communist Academy's sector on law and state was engaging in criminological work, but the largest step came in 1925 with the establishment of the State Institute for the Study of Crime and the Criminal, subordinated to the NKVD of the Russian Republic. The Institute was comprised of four sections: socioeconomic, penetentiary, bio-psychological, and criminalistics (techniques of crime detection and prevention).

During these years, there was no question of Soviet criminologists speaking with one voice. Disagreements were rife over the causes of crime, the proper subject matter of criminological investigation, and the nature of the criminal offender himself.

The polyglot tone of Soviet criminology was due to at least two factors. First, as contemporary Soviet writers have noted, the leading positions in criminology were occupied by members of the "old professoriate," such as S.V. Poznyshev and A.A. Zhizhilenko, many of whom had established their positions and reputations before the revolution.[20] These scholars, often with little knowledge of or concern with Marxism, pursued the same courses in the 1920s as they had in pre-revolutionary times.

Second, and probably more important, Marxism-Leninism had not yet become concretized into a dogmatic system offering only one "correct" answer to questions about the nature and causes of social phenomena such as crime. There were at the time two trends in Marxism, one of which was mechanistic, deterministic, and materialistic in a thoroughgoing fashion. Its conception of causality was rigid, emphasizing inevitability. In short, it placed narrow limits on the possibilities of successful intervention in social processes, stressing instead the operation of immanent laws which might be discovered but not modified. There also existed a voluntarist trend, more sanguine about the effectiveness of human intervention, about the role of consciousness and ideas in goal-directed behavior. This trend emphasized not the "spontaneous" unfolding of social development according to Marxist laws, but the necessity of intervention and action to achieve results, and the danger in a semi-quietistic attitude of waiting for "inevitabilities" to come into being. On the one side, mechanistic science, stressing "genetics"; on the other, dialectical materialism, emphasizing "teleology." Both in social theory and in practice, these trends were to struggle for supremacy in the USSR of the 1920s,[21] and criminology was not to remain uninvolved. The spirit of controversy permeated discussions to a much greater degree than is observed in later Soviet history. What Bauer wrote of psychology might equally be applied to criminology:

An over-all characteristic of this period, and one which distinguishes it markedly from the era after 1930, is a fundamental faith in free scientific debate. This meant that a far wider variety of psychological views were expressable in the twenties than was permitted later.[22]

The schools of criminology were diverse. "Biocriminology" occupied many scholars, who sought the roots of criminal behavior in genetically and organically conditioned individual disorders. Psychiatrists, psychologists, and biologists formed, in many cases, large segments of the staff in the institutions for the study of crime. E.K. Krasnushkin, who headed the bio-psychological section of the NKVD's Institute, argued that the majority of criminals were either mentally retarded or psychopaths.[23] S.V. Poznyshev argued the relevance of the criminal's physical constitution in determining the roots of criminal behavior.[24] Others, too numerous to cite here, viewed crime from similar perspectives,[25] and whole institutions followed the bio-psychological orientation.[26]

These directions of research, of course, fit the mechanistic, determinist side of Marxism, presenting the criminal as a special type of person, his behavior determined by forces over which he had no control. The language of Soviet criminal law at the time, substituting "measure of social defense" for "punishment" and "socially dangerous act" for "crime," similarly reflected a move away from "idealistic" and voluntaristic conceptions of guilt.

Other criminologists, less positivist in persuasion, pursued the explanation of crime from the perspective of the "theory of factors," [27] or from combined approaches admitting basic social and bio-psychological influences on the criminal.

Against these tendencies were arrayed a number of scholars and practitioners.[28] The actual content of their views, aside from opposition to the bio-psychological, is not easy to determine from contemporary Soviet accounts of the period.[29] A.A. Gertsenzon, D.I. Kurskii, V.I. Kufaev, D.P. Rodin, M.N. Gernet, and others have fared better in these accounts. The greater emphasis in their works on social determinants of criminal and delinquent behavior, and their opposition to biological determinist views of crime, fit better with the variety of Marxism that was to gain ascendancy as the 1920s came to a close.[30]

For Soviet criminology, the 1920s were a period of free, and often acrimonious, debate between scholars and researchers who in their basic positions reflected the two trends in Marxism already noted.

Throughout the period, it appears that the "biologists" had the advantage. However, as the 1920s came to a close, the situation began to change. The Soviet Union under Stalin was gathering its forces for the long-range industrialization and collectivization campaigns to come, and the choices made in the wake of the debates on economic development in 1927–1928 [31] reflected the rise of a voluntarist, teleological trend, and a move away from what was later to be castigated as "vulgar" determinism. "Dialecticians" began replacing determinists as the commanding figures in philosophy,[32] law,[33] and psychology.[34] The Soviet leadership was in the process of liberating itself from the doctrinal shackles of determinism, as a prelude to a period of extreme "interventionism." The support this provided to antideterminists pointed the direction in which criminology was to go.

A large-scale attack was launched on the "biologists" and on all those who argued that criminal personalities were of a different type from those of normal citizens; on those who held that some antisocial tendencies were neither created by social influences nor amenable to basic modification by social influences, as well as on adherents of "bourgeois sociological" positions. In January, 1929, S. Ia. Bulatov's article, "The Resurrection of Lombroso in Soviet Criminology," appeared.[35] At a debate soon afterward (organized by the section on law and state of the Communist Academy, whose journal, *Revolution of Law*, had published Bulatov's attack on "Lombrosianism"), the issues between the bio-psychological criminologists and what may loosely be called the "dialecticians" were joined, and, riding the crest of a favorable wave, the latter won.[36] A contemporary Soviet author reviews the conclusions that emerged:

Social phenomena, to which crime belongs, cannot be explained by the methods of the natural sciences, in particular psychiatry. Therefore any attempts to show that crime is explained by the biological constitution of the individual are doomed to failure.[37]

To the present time, the majority of Soviet criminological writing reaffirms the justice of the verdict rendered on the losers in the 1929 debate, and those who show signs of continuity with the bio-psychological ideas of the twenties are frequently criticized, as we shall see. But 1929 was not the beginning of a period which would see increased study of crime and related phenomena from a social and dialectic, nondeterministic perspective. It was, rather, the beginning of the end for Soviet criminology. For a generation, criminology would virtually disappear.

It is difficult to trace the death-throes of Soviet criminology, in a period when it became increasingly inadvisable to investigate undesirable social phenomena closely. Institutions hitherto engaged in criminological studies began to be disbanded, or to change their emphasis. The "offices" in many cities ceased to operate. In 1931 the Institute for the Study of Crime and the Criminal was transferred to the People's Commissariat of Justice; its auxiliary institutions were closed and its empirical research activities curtailed in favor of work on the "analysis of legal norms." [38] In 1933 it was further subordinated to the *Prokuratura* and the USSR Supreme Court, and further "practicalized." Theoretical matters were to be handled by organs of the Communist Academy, itself subordinate to the Central Committee of the Party.

By 1935 open research and publication in criminology had come to a virtual halt. Teaching of criminology and criminological material in textbooks disappeared from universities and law institutes. The "moral statistics" division of the Central Statistical Administration, which had ceased publishing nationwide conviction statistics, was disbanded. Criminology was, along with much of Soviet natural and behavioral science in general, a victim of the "cult of personality," and "Mistakes [in criminological research] were taken advantage of by the people who determined the direction of policy during the period of the cult of personality. Work on the study of crime and its causes was broken off." [39]

CRIMINOLOGY'S POST-STALIN REBIRTH

Criminology remained effectively proscribed until after Stalin's death.[40] The criminologists went various ways, some presumably victimized by the purges,[41] some dying natural deaths, and some surviving, after having bent their efforts to more abstract areas of criminal law, to see the Twentieth Congress of the Soviet Communist Party in 1956 give the green light to criminology once again, at least in a qualified way. The party's theoretical journal, *Kommunist,* pointed out to jurists the weak state of the study of crime,[42] and soon a process of institutional redevelopment was under way. The criminal law section (established in 1957) of the All-Union Scientific Research Institute of Criminalistics began studies based on case records, personal files of offenders, and inmates of corrective-labor colonies. Also involved, from 1958 on, was the Scientific Research Institute of the Militia (police).[43]

The early investigations (and, indeed, later ones as well) were sparse on statistics and often suffered from methodological weaknesses when reported in published form. This situation reflected the generation-long gap in formal criminological training, which limited resources in the late 1950s to survivors of the earlier period, such as A.A. Gertsenzon and B.S. Utevskii, and to relatively untrained newcomers. As publications in the area increased, and as a series of conferences met to discuss the lines of development of criminology, concern over the quality of investigation increased as well. A team of scholars, headed by A.A. Gertsenzon and working under the sponsorship of the Institute of Criminalistics and the Institute of State and Law of the Soviet Academy of Sciences, produced a "program" volume, *Problems of the Methodology of the Study and Prevention of Crimes.*[44] Monographs and articles dealing with the causation and prevention of crime and delinquency, among which A.B. Sakharov's *On the Personality of the Criminal and the Causes of Crime in the USSR* [45] deserves special mention, appeared with increasing frequency.

The year 1963 marked what was perhaps the most important step in the relegitimation of criminology as a "policy science" deserving governmental support—the founding of the All-Union Institute for the Study of the Causes and Elaboration of Measures of Prevention of Crime (hereafter, to be referred to as the Institute of Criminology), under the USSR Prokuratura. The new institute's staff was drawn from the relevant sections of the Institute of Criminalistics, the

Academy of Sciences' Institute of State and Law, and the All-Union Institute of Legal Sciences. It embarked on a program of research, publication, and training of new specialists in a number of areas and in 1966 published the first edition of a new criminology textbook for use in university law faculties and legal institutes. The new text provided a vehicle for introducing criminology in all the nation's law faculties.

Publication and dissemination of research and theoretical materials continued as the 1960s progressed. In 1964 the Institute of Criminology began the twice-yearly publication of a selection of its papers, *Problems of the Struggle with Crime*,[46] which continues to the present (1971). During the same period, two relatively large collective volumes, with contributions from "practical workers" as well as theoreticians, were published under the Institute's sponsorship: *Problems of the Eradication of Crime* (1965) and *The Prevention of Juvenile Delinquency* (1965).

Thus, at present, the study of crime, delinquency, and related forms of deviance, such as drunkenness, is a going concern in the USSR. Although, as the reader will see, the publication of comprehensive crime statistics is not yet permitted as it was in the 1920s, and although the debates among criminologists concerning the causes of deviance have taken place, for the most part, within the framework of an orthodoxy that reflects the triumph of one trend in Marxism in 1929, the debates and the increased information available about crime are themselves exceedingly informative and valuable in gauging the significance of problems of deviance in the USSR.

4
ALCOHOL PROBLEMS

LESS OFFICIAL DATA are available about the magnitude of alcohol problems in the USSR than are open to the investigator of similar problems in societies that are freer with their statistics and generally less secretive about social data. We can, however, learn a good deal about the concern alcohol problems cause Soviet authorities from statements like the following, made in 1965: "It turned out, as everybody had long suspected, that . . . drinking was, and still is, very much of a problem in the Soviet Union, as it is in other countries." [1] This statement, remarkable for the fact that it appeared in *Soviet Life*, a magazine published for American consumption, has been reaffirmed many times since in the Soviet domestic press, by party and government officials, and through legislative activity. Whatever the situation may be in the "other countries" referred to, claims are no longer advanced that in the Soviet Union drunkenness is just another social evil whose eradication is around the corner. Since 1965, this type of evidence has increased to the point where, even in the absence of nationwide statistics on numbers of diagnosed alcoholics or chronic drunkards,° we are justified in regarding the Soviet alcohol problem as a severe one.

While national statistics from any country on production and consumption of alcohol are frequently fraught with inaccuracies, and their interpretation is risky,† the scanty figures for the USSR are worth investigating.

"Official" Russian and Soviet consumption in 1948–1950 (the most recent figures available) was behind most Western European nations and the USA and had been so since before the Revolution, as table 1 shows. Soviet writers in the 1950s frequently alluded to the success of official temperance policy, reflected in the drop from 3.41 liters an-

TABLE 1 ANNUAL PER CAPITA CONSUMPTION FOR SELECTED NATIONS, IN LITERS OF ABSOLUTE ALCOHOL

	1906–1910			1948–1950	
1	France	22.93	France	21.5
2	Italy	18.29	Spain	10.0
3	Spain	14.02	Italy	9.2
4	Greece	13.87	Switzerland	9.0
5	Switzerland	13.71	Belgium	6.5
6	Belgium	10.58	Great Britain	6.0
7	England	9.67	USA	5.1
8	Germany	7.56	West Germany	3.75
9	USA	6.89	Sweden	3.6
10	Denmark	6.82	Denmark	2.85
11	Sweden	4.33	Norway	2.2
12	Russia (Eur.)	3.41	Holland	2.0
13	Norway	2.63	USSR	1.85
14	Finland	1.54		

Sources: 1906–1910: *Alkogolizm—put' k prestupleniiu* (Moscow, "Iuridicheskaia literatura," 1966), p. 65. 1948–1950: *Bol'shaia meditsinskaia entsiklopediia,* Vol. 1 (1956), col. 727, fig. 1.

° Most Soviet sources make no clear distinction between "drunkenness" and "alcoholism," the drunkard and the alcoholic, and seem to use the terms interchangeably. The reader should be aware of this as he reads these chapters.

† Official statistics generally do not reflect private or illegal distilling. Nor is there a direct equivalency between total alcohol production and domestic consumption. In addition, national figures are usually couched in terms of annual per capita consumption of the whole population, including infants, children, and others who, for whatever reasons, do not consume alcohol.

nual per capita consumption in the 1906–1910 period to 1.85 liters in 1948–1950. This is certainly a sizable decrease. Yet, as the figures show, all nations reporting for both periods experienced a decline in reported consumption (and Italy, an even greater percentage decline). Official statistics also reflect a Russian preference for alcohol under strong (100 proof) forms. Though twelfth in general consumption in 1906–1910, Russia was fifth in consumption of 100-proof liquor [2] and in 1948–1950 remained ahead of the other reporting countries in percentage of total alcohol intake consumed in 100-proof form.[3]

Forgetting for the moment the impact of illegal distilling on this picture, we find in official Soviet figures on alcohol production some indirect indications of probable increases in consumption. Table 2

TABLE 2   PRODUCTION OF ETHYL ALCOHOL, BEER AND GRAPE WINE IN THE USSR, 1940–1965 (IN MILLIONS OF DECALITERS)

	Ethyl Alcohol	Beer	Grape Wine
1940	89.9	121.3	19.7
1950	73.0	130.8	23.8
1958	163.9	199.1	61.8
1960	170.7	249.8	77.7
1964	213.1	283.0	127.1
1965	236.0	316.9	133.9

Source: Narodnoe khoziaistvo SSSR v 1965 godu: Statisticheskii ezhegodnik (Moscow, "Statistika," 1966), p. 240.

shows a pattern of steady growth in all forms of alcohol production since 1950.

Somewhat over 60 percent of all ethyl alcohol production goes to industrial uses.[4] Let us assume the figure to be as high as 65 percent, and the remaining 35 percent of ethyl alcohol to be used in the making of vodka and other liquors, with an average 80-proof (40 percent alcohol) rating. Disregarding beer and wine completely, this would represent 3.57 liters of 80-proof liquor and 1.43 liters of absolute alcohol per capita for 1950 (with an estimated population of 178,547,000). The gap between our estimated production and 1948–1950 reported consumption can be fixed at 0.43 liters per capita. Given the possibility that our estimate of alcohol produced for beverage use may be low by almost 5 percent, and given the exclusion of wine and beer from the calculation, this estimate would not be out of line with the reported figure of 1.85 liters of absolute alcohol consumed per capita in 1948–1950.

A glance at the table will show how the situation has changed. Ethyl alcohol production had climbed to 236 million decaliters, while the official estimate for 1965 puts the Soviet population at 231 million. Going on the assumptions made above, we arrive at an estimate of 3.57 liters of absolute alcohol and 8.9 liters of 80-proof liquor available for each Soviet citizen in 1965. In addition, the 1950–1965 period had seen total grape wine production increase from 23.8 to 133.9 million decaliters, and beer output from 130.8 to 316.9 million decaliters. Although these figures do not specify how much of total beverage alcohol production is exported, they give a picture consistent with complaints that domestic alcohol sales are growing rapidly, and in some regions had grown by more than twice in the ten-year period 1955–1965.[5]

No contemporary Soviet estimates have been published on that very dark figure, total annual output of illegal distilling; but indirect evidence indicates that it is quite large. A study of rural areas in the Russian Republic (RSFSR) in 1927 revealed that residents consumed, on the average, 7.5 liters of *samogon* (home-brewed spirits) annually per capita, and that this accounted for 80 percent of their yearly consumption.[6] Statistics on registered crimes in a district in the Belorussian SSR show a fluctuating pattern of growth in the share of cases of illegal distilling, among all criminal cases—from 12.47 percent in 1953 to 34.07 percent in 1963.[7] Complaints about the social costs of illegal distilling in rural areas are, as we shall see, frequent and sharp.

What all this amounts to is an increase in alcohol consumption and an increase in habitual drunkenness and alcoholism among Soviet citizens, the latter increase strongly indicated by the mounting level of official concern over the negative consequences of this trend. As a noted Soviet clinical specialist observes, the situation "gives no foundation whatsoever for reassurance."[8]

SOCIOCULTURAL
PATTERNING

For a nation or a group to have a high per capita rate of alcohol consumption does not necessarily mean it has high rates of drunkenness and alcoholism. Thus, an increasing production of alcohol in the USSR does not dictate a rise in the incidence of alcohol problems. Yet increasingly frank Soviet discussions point to the existence of a problem which, whatever its rate of increasing seriousness, is already regarded as massive, in a country which by world standards falls (or fell) behind a number of nations in per capita consumption. What are the roots of this problem?

In answering this question, one must go beyond the obvious fact that alcohol *is* available and examine evidence on the attitudes of Russians toward drinking, and on the patterns of behavior these attitudes foster—what we may call a Russian "drinking culture." °

One of the most striking elements in Russian drinking behavior is the multiplicity of occasions with which drinking is associated. In the sphere of popular, unofficial values, alcohol appears as a virtually indispensable adjunct to many pleasant events and as a refuge from stressful or painful situations. A medical specialist on alcoholism sums it up thus:

People drink when they meet, when they take leave of each other; to quiet their hunger when they are hungry, to stimulate their appetite when they

° While we are dealing here with alcohol problems as a *Soviet* phenomenon, the use of the adjective "Russian" with "drinking culture" is advisable. The republics of the Caucasus, the Moslem areas of Central Asia, differ widely from Russia in history and traditional culture. The lack of Soviet data on ethnic differences in drinking behavior makes it difficult to estimate how characteristic of other areas the Russian drinking culture may have become, due to population migrations and other influences, or how uncharacteristic it may remain. Impressionistic evidence from travel by the author suggests, however, that high degrees of alcohol consumption may be diffusing to non-Russian populations, even to Moslems, espe-

are satisfied. They drink to get warm, when it is cold, to cool off when it is hot. They drink when they are drowsy, to wake up, and when they are wakeful, to bring on sleep.[9]

Persistent complaints in the press about the practice of payday drinking bouts by factory workers, which often end in brawls with co-workers and family scandals when the intoxicated worker returns home minus some of his wages, indicate one of the most frequent occasions for "convivial" drinking.

Important events in family life provide another stimulus for the sort of excesses deplored by those who write about the problem of drunkenness. *Pravda* noted on two separate occasions the large amounts of money spent, and work-days lost, as a result of large wedding celebrations on collective farms, which entail "drinking bouts lasting many days and involving large numbers of people and in which . . . an unhealthy competition in plying the guests with liquor has been conducted." [10]

All this is regarded as deviant behavior by Party and government writers and propagandists. Yet such patterns are supported by unofficial values. It comes as little surprise, then, to learn that Soviet non-drinkers often find themselves in difficult social situations. The teeto-taler, or even the person who is unshakable in his resolve to drink only moderately, does so at the risk of offending his companions, of being considered something less than a "real man." Obstinate refusal to indulge in the company of drinkers is often regarded as insulting as well as peculiar behavior. He who abstains may be seen as "stupid" in foregoing one of life's pleasures.[11] Strenuous also is the route of the reformed drinker, whose friends and relatives may provide the push to send him off the wagon.[12] One of the leading Soviet medical specialists in alcohol problems notes that, in one survey of alcoholic backsliders, 42.2 percent of the cases were attributable to the influence of companions or relatives who convinced the patient to have a drink.[13]

Drinking remains, by and large, a male activity (cases of alcohol-

---

cially in areas like Kazakhstan, where some Islamic prohibitions have always been relatively weak. Certainly, native populations in larger Uzbek cities do not seem to be consistent abstainers from alcohol.

ism are "still encountered" among women, but "very seldom" [14]), and socialization into drinking practices often begins early. A father who, over his wife's objections, gives his five-year-old son a glass of wine argues, "let him get used to it . . . he's got to be a real man." [15] Teenage factory workers soon become accustomed to payday drinking with "veterans" in their shops—a refusal to participate is often viewed as "bad form." The intoxication which often follows the "workers' baptism" accompanying the first payday occasionally lands the youth in the arms of the police.[16]

Practices such as these reflect the existence of a Russian drinking culture—one which, because of its extreme permissiveness both on quantity to be imbibed and on the situations and locations in which drinking is accepted or encouraged, leads to heavy drinking and frequent drunkenness. Studies of drinking culture among other ethnic groups (where a great deal more data is available than in the Russian case) have demonstrated the impact of norms and attitudes about drinking on rates of alcohol pathology.[17] When drinking is closely linked to religious ritual and hedged with strong prohibitions against drunkenness, as among Orthodox Jews, or an integral part of meals, a *food* substance, as the consumption of wine is among Italians, it takes on pathological dimensions comparatively rarely, even when the population shows a high annual per capita consumption rate. The relatively high rate of alcohol pathology among the Irish, on the other hand, has been at least partly explained by citing the *absence* of contexts integrating drinking with moderating elements of ritual, nourishment, or stable family life, and a conception of drinking as a masculine activity, something which affirms one's manhood and solidarity with one's fellows, and as an approved means of increasing one's gaiety or deadening one's sorrow.

Much the same may be said of the Russian drinking culture. Beyond the evident fact that in both Irish and Russian cases, there is a preference for consuming alcohol in relatively concentrated forms (whiskey, vodka), both cultures share a definition of drinking as "man's work." While Russian women do drink, there is no linkage between drinking and any demonstration of attributes considered essential to femininity, and women constitute, apparently, a negligible portion of all alcoholics.° In neither the Russian nor the Irish case is drinking integrated with religious ritual observance, cases of widespread drunkenness in rural areas of Russia on government holidays, saints' days, and other special occasions notwithstanding. (In these cases, the "event" provides an occasion for heavy drinking, but nothing about the event itself is so ritualized as to enforce limits on alcohol consumption.) Moreover, the de-emphasis on the significance of alcohol that seems to attach to its definition as a food substance (e.g., wine in Italy) and promotes a low incidence of pathology in the face of high individual rates of consumption is foreign to both Irish and Russian drinking cultures.

It would not be wise, however, to go too far in arguing parallelisms between Russian and other drinking cultures. For the Soviet case, both ethnographic and statistical material is too scanty to allow detailed and precise description. It is possible only to touch on some of the readily observable elements of this culture and to fit them into the picture of heavy and excessive drinking that Soviet sources themselves present. While it "proves" little directly, the following passage by a writer in *Literaturnaia gazeta* shows that some Russians concerned with the problem are beginning to see it in cultural terms:

One must admit that in Western Europe, while they drink more than we, they drink wisely, devil take them! They drink most often on a full stomach, and mainly less-strong or mixed drinks, and drink their fill little by little, in the course of a whole evening.

We Russians, however, drink without fail on an empty stomach, and don't hurry to fill it up until we have drunk our full portion of vodka. . . . Such a tradition must have been historically established. But to fight with traditions is difficult, and eradicating them demands much time.[18]

OFFICIAL VALUES AND
PUBLIC OPINION

The writer quoted above does not underestimate the difficulty of fighting "historically established" traditions. In no other case of deviance

° There is, however, a strong possibility that female alcoholics are underrepresented in the USSR, as in the USA. They have a greater probability of escaping diagnosis, since less of their drinking will be done in public.

is the gap between official and unofficial or public attitudes so great as in that of drunkenness. The contemporary situation is an example of what one student has called an "ambivalent" drinking culture; one in which "the cultural attitude toward beverage alcohol usage is one of conflict between co-existing value structures." [19] In the Soviet case, the value structures are, on the one hand, the traditional drinking culture just described, and on the other, an official value structure in which a citizen is found "good" to the degree that he embodies the qualities of the new Soviet man—sober, methodical, industrious, committed to productive work and participation in the public life of Soviet society. Though these value structures coexist, they do so with a good deal of friction.

Increasingly, representatives of the official value structure are coming to recognize how serious are the problems presented by public attitudes which range from indifference toward alcohol abuse to positive approval of heavy drinking in a broad range of circumstances. Data to support this diagnosis are not lacking. A Moscow University law professor, in a pamphlet entitled *Crime and Alcoholism*, complains that the struggle against alcoholism would enjoy greater success "if there were not connivance and an indifferent attitude toward it on the public's part." [20] The belief that alcohol is an indispensable element in celebrations, inculcated early in life, is seen as a major cause of alcoholism. A doctor reports two pertinent studies.[21] Of a group of chronic alcoholics, 70 percent reported that they had been raised in families where "moderate drunkenness" was not frowned upon, 10 percent reported the encouragement of serious drunkenness, and for the remaining 10 percent drinking was disapproved. In a group of less serious drunkards, 11.7 percent recalled family attitudes as anti-alcohol, while the families of 75.9 percent had held "moderate drunkenness" acceptable on holidays and paydays, and 10.6 percent had accepted *any* form of drunkenness.[22] The absence of a control group of persons without drinking problems makes it difficult to assess the meaning of the results—we cannot really tell how typical or atypical such families may be.[23]

Still, the public as a whole seems to regard the struggle with drunkenness as a matter of low priority. Factory managers, when informed by the police that their workers are being apprehended for public intoxication, often take no measures against the offenders. (In the Pacific coast city of Khabarovsk, an official of the *Prokuratura* [the Soviet procurator's, or state's attorney's, office] complains, "several thousand" such notifications were sent to managers. Only 634 reports of measures taken were received by the police.[24]) Frequently condemned by the government is the feeling that drinking is part of one's private life and not to be interfered with. In the case of a worker whose constant drinking had dissolved his family life, a manager is quoted disapprovingly as saying, "Well, so the man drinks. It's his money he spends, nobody else's. He beats up his wife? Well, she's his wife!"[25] Even the police are criticized for inadequate displays of intolerance and enterprise in clearing the streets of drunkards.[26]

Complaints from official sources seem well founded and show how wide and persistent is the gap between official and public appraisals of the situation. Whether this gap is narrowing or growing wider is a question that may be deferred until later. It is clear, however, that since the late 1960s the state has been entertaining the possibility of newer and more stringent anti-alcohol measures, including the revival (see chapter 5) of some form of prohibition law and the organization of temperance societies on a national level.

Who are the drunkards, the alcoholics, to whom so many complaints refer? While Soviet sources do not provide a clear statistical portrait of the average public drunkard or alcoholic, fragmentary data points to the working class as the main source of problems.* Studies of the clientele of "sobering-up stations" (*meditsinskie vytrezviteli*) show a majority of manual workers and an average educational level that rarely rises above incomplete secondary schooling. (Of 1815 clients brought to sobering-up stations in the city of Gorky in the fall of 1965, 79.7 percent had no more than seven years of

---

* There is, of course, a danger that the data itself may reflect middle-class "observer bias" in the Soviet sources. An executive with a drinking problem is more easily able to hide it and more likely to segregate the contexts in which he drinks and works. The personal observations of the author and some other visitors to Soviet cities, however, would tend to confirm the image of the "working-class drunkard." It is not particularly difficult, at any time of day, to find intoxicated persons lying on the sidewalks of major streets. External appearances, dress, and the like, as observed in this rough "sampling," indicate that the majority of the intoxicated are workers.

schooling.[27]) While education figures for drunkards are sometimes said to diverge little from those for the population as a whole, even within the working classes, where seven years of schooling at most is typical, it is the unskilled who provide a large share of the clientele of sobering-up stations. So large was the proportion of unskilled workers in one instance that, as an author noted, it was "unrepresentative of the contemporary working class." [28] By and large, public drunkards start drinking young (before 15 or 16), rarely visit theaters and museums, or otherwise take part in "cultured" recreation, and spend their leisure time passively, frequently citing boredom as a reason for drinking.

Substandard and crowded housing, low incomes, shortages of goods, and the general drabness of working class life in Soviet cities have seemed to Western observers adequate reasons for escapist use of liquor in the USSR; but this view finds an unenthusiastic reception among Soviet writers, who do cite such conditions, however, to explain alcoholism in capitalist countries and in pre-revolutionary Russia.[29] Yet, while they deny any direct connection between dissatisfaction with living conditions and drunkenness, concern with the latter increases the probability that the linkage of drunkenness with other elements of the working-class life-style will receive further study. With what results, it is difficult to say.

THE SOCIAL COSTS OF ALCOHOLISM

Fifty years after a revolution designed to do away with the poverty, injustice, and deprivation which "naturally" drove him to drink, Soviet man has not been cured of the habit. This in itself is vexing to the regime but not, in practical terms, the main cause of their concern. The abuse of alcohol has more evident and more easily calculated costs.

At the center of official concern is the relationship of drunkenness and crime,[30] especially violent crime. Soviet statements attribute startling percentages of crime ("more than 80 percent of hooligan acts," [31] "70 percent of all crimes" [32]) to drunkenness. Violent crimes, especially, are regarded as products of drunkenness.

S., in a drunken state, slashed her husband's face with a knife. . . . Citizen N., in a state of intoxication, slashed his wife with a knife. . . . K., father and son, had a falling-out during a drinking bout and dealt each other serious knife wounds. . . . There is no need to demonstrate that in a sober state nothing similar would have happened.[33]

Premeditated offenses as well are sometimes traced to alcohol, especially embezzlement and theft by employees who seek funds to finance their drinking.[34] Jurists show special concern with the numbers of juveniles who commit crimes while intoxicated, or who steal in order to get liquor. A study of 450 juveniles in the Kazakh SSR revealed that 41 percent had committed offenses while intoxicated, and that 72 percent of these had been habitual heavy drinkers before their arrests.[35] Another study notes that 32.3 percent of juveniles convicted of theft were drunk at the time of offense, and that many of those who were sober stole either alcoholic beverages or money to buy them.[36] Adults are frequently responsible for getting juveniles intoxicated and have been threatened with equal penalties if such juveniles break the law.[37]

The role of alcohol as the final link in a chain leading to a criminal act, typically the escalation of a quarrel into violence when the parties are intoxicated, is not disputed. But concern goes beyond this. The long-term effect of "systematic drunkenness" on a person's conformity to the basic norms of acceptable behavior is also emphasized.

It is necessary to see that the linkage between alcoholism and crime is not exhausted by the fact that a state of intoxication facilitates or directly calls forth the commission of socially dangerous acts, thanks to the peculiarities of the psychic activity of the person in such a condition.

The negative activity of alcohol on the person consists also in the fact that systematic drunkenness deeply affects the general spiritual and moral make-up of the person. It narrows significantly the scope of his intellectual interests, coarsens his feelings and morals, activates and strengthens individualistic, anti-social, base desires and strivings, leads to the tearing away of the individual from the *kollektiv*, and not infrequently to the complete moral destruction, the degradation of the human personality.[38]

This represents an even more negative view of the alcoholic offender than do the cases cited earlier where, without the element of drunkenness, "nothing similar" to the crime would have occurred. This is more than saying that an offender would not have committed his act *were it not* for his having been intoxicated, or that such an act can only be explained in terms of his temporary intoxication. On the contrary, crimes committed in a state of drunkenness are claimed to demonstrate something wrong with the offender beyond the incidental fact that he happened to be intoxicated.

Alcohol . . . facilitates the release and manifestation of the *actual* antisocial essence of the given subject, those negative moral qualities present in him, individualistic and egoistic impulses, base feelings, etc.[39]

Thus, alcohol reveals qualities the offender, when sober, has managed to control or to hide. Conversely, this means that a "morally stable" person, while his drunkenness is no less reprehensible, will not behave as a criminal even if he is not fully conscious of his acts.

Even in a state of intoxication, a person does not do that which is utterly foreign to his nature; possessed of high and strong moral principles, he even under the influence of alcohol, does not commit an immoral act.[40]

These statements represent both an official position on the boundaries of criminal responsibility and a conclusion about the moral characteristics to be deduced from the fact that a person is a habitual drunkard. At least some Soviet data tend to support the assertion that the main problem in the drunkenness-and-crime phenomenon is the chronic or habitual drunkard. Forensic psychiatry studies are cited as showing that only 17 percent of a number of persons studied who had committed crimes while intoxicated did *not* have long alcoholic periods before their offenses. The other 83 percent were "chronic alcoholics." [41]

In particular categories of crime, high degrees of association between drunkenness and offense are reported. For example, the association between drunkenness and homicide appears greater in the USSR than in other countries for which data are available.[42] A report by the Supreme Court of the USSR attributes 90 percent of the homicides which developed out of fights, quarrels, and "hooliganism" to intoxication. In Gorky *oblast'* (province), 83 percent of all persons convicted of homicide, infliction of serious bodily injury, and rape committed their offenses in a state of intoxication; in Yaroslavl' *oblast'*, the parallel figures for homicide and rape were 85 percent and 76 percent, respectively.[43]

Hooliganism, the general category for offenses against "public order," is also closely related to alcohol. For the whole USSR, Supreme Court data indicate that "over 90 percent" of such offenses are linked to intoxication. A sampling of Ukrainian cases yields a figure of 92 percent, a Latvian study, 96.7 percent, and one in Lithuania, 93.7 percent. In Yaroslavl' *oblast'*, 96 percent of all cases of hooliganism were attributed to drunkenness.[44]

Another alcohol-related offense—illegal distilling (*samogonovarenie*)—bulks especially large in rural crime statistics. Data from one area in the Belorussian SSR (noted earlier) show that every third offender brought to criminal responsibility during the years 1961–1963 was apprehended for illegal distilling.[45] The holiday use of alcohol in the countryside and the high price of legal, state-produced spirits probably account for much of the vitality of *samogonovarenie*, which has remained characteristic of rural life since Tsarist times.[46] Even given the apparently high number of arrests, complaints about law enforcement in this area seem to indicate either inefficiency or tolerance on the part of local officials. Probably, inefficiency and tolerance are both involved. Observing that steps are normally taken to deal with moonshiners only in connection with some other offense or when their apparatus is discovered during other investigations, one author appeals for a wider involvement of the public, especially the Komsomol or youth organizations, to conduct propaganda work against this "survival" of capitalism. He calls also for an expansion of the competence of comrades' courts to make examples of offenders through such measures as "public destruction of the distilling apparatus and confiscation of the products" in addition to the imposition of fines and corrective labor.[47]

Other costs of drunkenness are manifold and provide an apparently inexhaustible source of grist for the mills of the Soviet press. While comprehensive figures are not available on time lost and industrial accidents caused by drunkenness during working hours, comments indicate that alcohol plays an important role in these areas. The *Izvestiia* weekend supplement, *Nedelia*, reports that a study in Gorky showed violations of work rules to be connected with drunkenness "in

66 instances out of a hundred." [48] In March 1964, the Party secretary of a lathe-building plant complained that workers' and technicians' drinking sprees had caused the loss of over 1000 man-hours—"enough for six new lathes." [49] Workers tempted to drink at lunch time are continually warned that anything but complete sobriety in operating large machines can lead to serious injury,[50] and anti-alcohol writers also strive to convince the many who feel they work better after a drink that this sense of increased capability is not matched by any increase in productivity and often leads to a higher rate of spoilage.[51] In the agricultural sector, rural illegal distilling with stolen sugar, grain, beets, and potatoes exacerbates the already-serious problem of lagging farm output, as does the working time lost as a result of drunkenness among collective farmers.[52]

A host of family problems are attributed to drinking excesses of husbands and fathers. Iu. M. Tkachevskii, a Moscow University professor and frequent writer on crime and alcohol problems, claims that "40% of all divorces are caused by the drunkenness of one of the spouses." [53] Mistreatment of children is another major problem. In 1965, a letter from a 12-year-old whose father's habitual drunkenness had made home life unbearable was the starting point of a readers' discussion in *Izvestiia* that went on for many issues.[54]

As Soviet writers become less reticent in discussing sexual matters, they find alcohol connected with many of the problems in this area. Prolonged impotence from habitual "overdosing" with liquor is noted as a source of marital tensions,[55] and a noted Soviet clinician cites his own research to show that heavy-drinking husbands become gross in their approach to intercourse and decrease the pleasure of both partners.[56] The evils of casual sex under the influence of alcohol are pinpointed for youth; [57] and the author of a book aimed primarily at members of the armed forces cites in a warning tone the words of a Soviet venereologist, 90 percent of whose syphilis patients and 95 percent of whose gonorrhea patients contracted the diseases while drunk.[58]

The growth of leisure time which has accompanied the recent shortening of the work week and the institution of the two-day weekend has given rise to concern that the time might be used unprofitably.[59] Among "unprofitable" uses, heavy drinking is paramount.

Rather than using the added time to participate in "amateur arts or study circles," to read, or to visit theatres, many apparently continue with the leisure activity they are most accustomed to—drinking with neighbors or fellow-workers. After the establishment of the five-day work week, weekend liquor sales were reported to have increased by as much as 25 percent in Moscow.[60] Even those who engage in "healthy" athletic activity, such as swimming, may endanger their lives by combining it with drinking—Tkachevskii notes that 63 percent of all individuals who drowned in Moscow *oblast'* in 1968 (which should include a large number of swimmers) were intoxicated.[61] The peril to sports careers from drinking is detailed in a number of Soviet books and pamphlets, with stories of the moral and physical downfall of athletes who develop a taste for alcohol.[62]

THEORIZING ABOUT CAUSATION

In chapter 2 the concept of capitalist "survivals" was introduced briefly, and its implications for Soviet theories of deviance causation were discussed. As the basic label, the tag which defines the place of deviant social phenomena within the perceptual framework of Soviet Marxism, the "survival" label is, of course, applied to alcoholism. "Alcoholism under [Soviet] conditions is, above all, a survival of capitalism. [The capitalist] social structure creates the most favorable conditions for the most serious and widespread forms of alcoholism." [63] But if, as it is said, alcohol's function under capitalism has frequently been to dull proletarian perception, inhibit the formation of a revolutionary consciousness, and thus facilitate exploitation,[64] how can one explain its persistence under socialism, where exploitation itself is avowedly a thing of the past? At the most elementary level, explanations can be framed in terms of the "lag in consciousness" discussed in chapter 2. In the face of large-scale social change, such as that from capitalism to socialism, man's consciousness and behavior change. But some elements of consciousness and behav-

ior, especially those connected with family life, leisure, and personal
conduct, change at a slow rate relative to changes in political attitudes. Thus, the traditions which inhabit the popular consciousness,
socialism's legacy from capitalism, are bound to persist. With respect
to alcoholism, most frequently blamed are religious traditions in the
countryside that support the celebration of numerous religious holidays with heavy drinking and workers' traditions in urban areas that
see drinking as one of the manly arts. Historically, these are viewed
as reflections of the brutalized life of the industrial proletariat and the
extreme poverty and deprivation of the rural peasantry in pre-Revolutionary times, which necessitated some escape from misery. The lag
in consciousness is invoked to explain this persistence of tradition.

To explain, however, is not to condone. While the ideas of survivals and the lag in consciousness provide a rough social-psychological
explanation of why drunkenness persists, the phenomenon itself remains something to be deplored and struggled against. *Izvestiia* publishes with approval the complaint of a veteran miner who is perplexed by the vitality of old customs among his coworkers.

"Our life changed very much indeed after the revolution," Nikolai Savvich
said. "The mines became completely different, and so did mining work and
life. The miners changed, too. Now one often meets people at the coal faces
who have a secondary education. There is only one thing I don't understand, and that is why they think that even now miners just have to drink
vodka, and that drunkenness is practically an occupational disease with
them.

"It makes you ashamed when you still hear the same old thing: 'He
drinks like a miner,' 'a miner's shot' and other idiocies." [65]

Survivals provide an explanation of sorts, but it is not an explanation which gives clear guidelines for the state's fight against alcohol
abuse. Thus Soviet authorities have increasingly turned to rather
frank examinations of existing social and economic patterns in their
search for the roots of the problem.

Prime importance as a cause of drunkenness is attributed to early
socialization of young men into the view that "to be a real man," one
must drink. Such socialization, deviant in terms of the regime's expectations, takes place mainly in primary-group settings—that area of social space Soviet writers have come to call the "micro-environment"

(*mikrosreda*). The family and work environments provide the two main contexts for this socialization. Fathers press wine and occasionally stronger drink on young offspring at the table, referring to the necessity that their sons grow into "he-men." While the amounts may be relatively small, worried doctors and officials trace many alcohol problems to this early introduction.[66]

Entry into the labor force and hence into the primary group made up of one's fellow workers and foreman in a factory department provides another occasion for transmission of the drinking culture. A young worker will find that his older comrades expect him to treat them all from the proceeds of his first pay envelope, to the point of emptying it. Paydays in general are a time when communal drinking for many workers is *de rigueur,* and the 16-year-old worker who refuses to go along may find himself isolated from his workmates.

Another major element contributing to drinking as a social problem, and one about which official sources have become increasingly frank, is the lack of any widespread public intolerance or condemnation of drunkenness. The oft-cited failure of schools to indoctrinate students sufficiently against drink and the tolerance shown by public organizations and even the police reflect and contribute to this continued tolerant attitude, which the regime has had little success in eliminating. Finally, the volume of alcohol production and the great number of trade outlets for its sale receive their share of the blame for the persistence of drunkenness and alcoholism. The latter is an obvious point, yet one which, as we shall see, has led to little decisive action in the face of another state interest—revenue from the sale of alcoholic beverages.

What this brief catalogue of social causes amounts to, of course, is recognition that a drinking culture persists and is passed on within primary-group contexts with relative ease, since public opinion by no means views drinking as so serious a problem as does the state. A Soviet doctor sums up the situation:

In socialist society [all the following] lead to the diffusion of alcohol abuse: alcoholic traditions in the micro-social environment, a lenient-complacent attitude toward drunkenness on the part of a significant portion of the population, defects in explanatory and cultural work, which sometimes has a formalistic-bureaucratic character, insufficient inculcation in the young generation of such characteristics as self-discipline, a sense of duty before the family and society, [and] an inability to organize its leisure interestingly and direct its interests correctly, thanks to which young people frequently turn out to be unable to use their free time wisely.[67]

Virtually all parties concerned with alcoholism—state and Party officials, jurists, propagandists, journalists, and doctors—participate in the identification and description of what are taken to be the causes of alcoholism as a social phenomenon. The other aspect of causal inquiry, the mechanics of the process whereby an individual becomes an alcoholic, lies largely within the province of doctors.

Before getting into the matter of the etiology of alcoholism in the individual, we would be well advised to pause on another point: the conception of the alcoholic (or habitual drunkard). Is he regarded, in the USSR, as a "sick" person, or as a culpable deviant? The answer to this question is important, for to a large degree it determines the approach that will be taken by medical specialists to resolving questions of etiology and to coping with the alcoholic in therapeutic situations.

The preponderance of medical opinion regards the alcoholic as a deviant, as someone who is responsible for the condition from which he suffers. Physicians and psychiatrists, in striking similarity to their American counterparts,* are reluctant to treat alcoholism strictly as a disease. Medical treatment enters *post factum*, when alcoholism-induced complications such as delirium tremens are present.[68]

It would, of course, be extremely difficult for the Soviet medical profession, whatever its collective private conviction, to fly in the face of the state with a definition of the alcoholic as sick when the state is engaged in an attempt to stigmatize him as a deviant deserving of condemnation. But relative shares of power in defining the status of the alcoholic do not explain the matter fully. The dominant orientation of the medical profession toward the alcoholic seems to be a matter of professional conviction. Some doctors have attempted to draw a line between drunkards on the one hand and chronic alcoholics on the other, putting the latter in the category of the sick and arguing that they are unable to help themselves.[69] They have been met with

* We are not speaking here about American psychiatric specialists in alcoholism, virtually all of whom support the "disease" concept of alcoholism in one form or another.

criticisms that such an attitude is "unscientific" and "misleading to public opinion." The medical critics sometimes assert that neither drunkenness nor alcoholism (the distinction is often unclear) are ill-nesses, though illness may come as a result of alcoholism.[70] At other times, alcoholism is accepted as illness, but distinguished from other illnesses in that it is one for which the sufferer himself is responsible —a position which preserves the idea of the sufferer's moral culpabil-ity.[71]

This orientation, which has been characterized as "moralistic and punitive," [72] affects many doctors' attitudes toward therapy. It is not surprising to hear the complaint of a secretary of a factory Party or-ganization that "many drunkards are corrupted by our superfluous humanism and encouraged by lack of punishment," [73] nor a Moscow prosecutor's claim that "drunkards are spoiled by our excessive humaneness." [74] It is somewhat more interesting, however, to read a psychiatrist's recommendation of "universal censure and contempt, not solicitude" toward the alcoholic, or the words of another psychia-trist, who argues that the

usual psychiatric hospitals and dispensaries are not suitable for curing chronic alcoholism. It is necessary to create special medical establishments with special conditions and regime; and they must be set up not in the health system, but in the system for maintenance of public order.[75]

The generally accepted Soviet etiological explanation of alcoholism is a simple one: alcoholic behavior is learned behavior. Alcoholism is, in this sense, a habit, and one develops this pathological habit by drinking, especially when one increases his intake of alcohol over time.[76] Such a position is at variance with the views of many Western specialists that drinking itself does not provide the explanation for eventual alcoholism. Soviet psychology and psychiatry, eschewing "Freudism" and relatively unconcerned with problems of the uncon-scious elements in human behavior, do not seek for explanations in unresolved childhood dependency needs, repressed homosexual ten-dencies, or any of the other possible sources to which Western psy-chiatry frequently has recourse. In answering the question, "What causes an individual to become an alcoholic?" medical literature puts forth such statements as "Most often, the regular consumption of not-large doses of alcohol brings one to chronic alcoholism" [77] and

The peculiarity of alcohol consists in the fact that one beginning to drink it may soon become a drunkard, a chronic alcoholic. As any serious illness begins from a trifling one, often with a slight indisposition, so chronic alcoholism begins from a harmless overindulgence, from a glass of vodka or a glass of beer.[78]

While it is acknowledged that persons with certain types of psychological disturbances may be poorer risks than others in their propensities to become alcoholic, the Soviet view is that the alcoholic is usually a normal person, like any other, who has drunk systematically for a long enough time to become an alcoholic.[79] This is not to say, however, that some medical specialists do not make further distinctions among drinking personalities. The possibility of different roads to alcoholism is taken into account, even though their relation to diagnostic and therapeutic questions may not be clear.

The more, and in more detailed manner, you study alcoholics, the more you are convinced how unequal may be the predisposition of people to drunkenness, i.e., how differently their organisms react to the action of liquors and how varied and complex [are] the causes that lie at the base of a person's predisposition to alcoholism.

One, for example, very easily gets drunk with very insignificant amounts of alcohol, and those around him consider him a person whose tolerance to alcohol is low in the extreme, but in return he runs less risk of becoming an alcoholic, if he possesses a sufficiently strong will and above all if a passion for wine does not arise in him. Another manages a large enough amount of alcohol, as it seems, without special excesses, but in return he very soon gets a real passion for it, i.e., there swiftly develops in him an unconquerable craving for alcohol. This is the most dangerous category of alcoholic, who can only be compelled to relinquish [his] weaknesses after long and serious treatment.

A third does not get drunk quickly, holds himself well after a drinking bout, and is not consumed by a sick craving for liquor, but by the very nature of his own weak character, he is careless and easily gets accustomed to vice. Serious danger threatens him too, that he may get habituated to alcohol by his own weakness of will or the insistence of comrades.[80]

Allowing for such differentiations, the theoretical orientation remains focused on alcoholism as the product of a learning process, in which the drinker finds drinking rewarding and pleasurable and thus is likely to increase the dosage (hence the position of some, but not all, doctors that initial moderate drinking generally leads to heavier drinking, just as "rivers flow from streams" [81]). The "unlearning" process, as the next chapter will show, is based in part on Pavlovian conditioned-reflex therapy—the extinguishing of a positive reflex toward alcohol and its replacement with a new, negative one. Such therapy makes sense in the context of the etiological position Soviet physicians and psychiatrists generally seem to accept.

Noteworthy for its absence from Soviet discussions of the causes of alcoholism is a concern with dependency conflicts in the male life-cycle, a concern reflected in much Western research on the topic.[82] For a variety of reasons, "dependency needs" (for maternal warmth, response, nourishment, protection) acutely felt by male children may be inconsistently and sporadically fulfilled in the family setting. While "legitimate" for young children, such needs conflict with elements of the "model" image of the adult male—in the USSR as well as in the West—as a mature, productive and independent person, whose duties revolve to a large degree around satisfying the dependency needs of wife and children. For those whose childhood dependency needs are satisfied, the transition to the adult male role is relatively easy. For the unsatisfied, the transition is fraught with difficulties. Consciously or subconsciously, dependency needs, now regarded as "illegitimate" and "feminine," are suppressed and disavowed through adoption of decisively "masculine" behavior patterns —in some cases extremely aggressive behavior and in other cases, where the culture makes it available, heavy drinking, a "man's prerogative." The warmth, solace, and dulling of worry that for many accompany drinking provide a means, if a dangerous one, of satisfying the dependency needs still felt.

While Soviet research is not conducted from this perspective, its relevance to the Soviet case is quite arguable. Problems of divorce, desertion, parental conflict, and the like are widespread in Soviet as in American society and presumably have an important impact on parental abilities to satisfy dependency needs. Given the existence of some segment of the male population whose childhood needs remain unfulfilled, and given the demands on them, as on other Soviet men, to provide support for dependents in much the same manner as in the West—to be, within the scope of their jobs, "achievers"—it is not difficult to imagine some seeking the refuge that a manhood-affirming drinking culture offers.

Unavailability of statistics, lack of access to clinical and other forms of data, and a general Soviet reluctance, even in a time of increasing frankness, to disclose as much about social problems as some other nations do limit the picture of alcoholism and drunkenness in the USSR that we can present here. But some points may be made in summarizing.

Alcoholism and drunkenness are large-scale problems and, according to changing Soviet perceptions, on the increase, rather than decreasing toward eventual disappearance. While those who represent the concerns of state and Party view heavy drinking as a serious social evil and deplore the drinking culture that in many cases sets the pattern for alcohol pathologies, they have yet to convince Russian adult males (or those of other nationalities to whom the Russian drinking culture has been diffused) that temperance and sobriety are dictated by their own personal interests, as well as that of the state. The public's response to drunkenness, with the exception of the wives of drunkards, whose complaints to the press seem genuine, is relatively tolerant and shows little of the condemnation the state wishes to mobilize.

From the perspective of the non-Soviet observer, the widespread nature of drunkenness and alcoholism seems inextricably connected to the vitality of the historically conditioned and culturally transmitted patterns of drinking, which assures it a place in the behavioral repertoire of many Russian men. The apparently high incidence of drunkenness among working-class males with little education and medium to low skills suggests (though here better statistics would be desirable as a foundation for any firm conclusion) that certain forms of alcohol pathology may be connected with the deprivations and boredom of Soviet lower-class life.

Although Soviet writers tend to soft-pedal the latter explanation, they are aware of the role alcoholic traditions play and view the transmission of these traditions in primary-group contexts as one of the major sources of their problems, along with public tolerance or indifference toward drunkenness. They also attribute a significant role to institutional malfunctioning—the failure of the schools, youth organizations, and state-sponsored public organizations, as well as the police, to perform effectively as agencies of persuasion and control.

On the individual level, alcoholism is viewed as learned behavior, as a product of largely free choice by the drinker, whose culpability for his condition is reaffirmed. The Soviet view on etiology is relatively straightforward and couched in "commonsensical" terms. While it leaves out many of the possibilities Western theories explore, the lack of success in effecting permanent cures of alcoholics in many other societies, whatever the complexity of theory and its relation to therapeutic measures, does not permit us to reject the Soviet position solely on the basis of what might appear to be an over-simplicity of its content.

5

ALCOHOLISM: THERAPY AND PREVENTION

THE SOVIET CAMPAIGN against alcoholism and drunkenness takes a number of forms. Some have as their primary target the restoration of the alcoholic or chronic drunkard to a stable working life. They are modes of treatment which necessarily begin after the fact and their preventive thrust is limited to keeping the reformed alcoholic away from his old habits. Primarily medical in nature, these types of treatment will be relatively familiar to those concerned with therapeutic approaches to alcoholics in the West. On the other hand, among its stock of armaments against alcoholism, the Soviet Union has some primarily preventive weapons, less familiar to outside observers, anti-alcohol "propaganda" being one of these. Within the limits that space and available information impose, they will all be discussed in this chapter.

Roughly, five classes of measures can be distinguished: (1) medical and psychotherapeutic treatment, applied to alcoholics in medical institutions; (2) "mixed" measures, combining treatment of some sort with labor and confinement, the archetype here being the "treatment-labor" institution (*lechebno-trudovoi profilaktorii*); (3) anti-alcohol propaganda aimed at educating the public to the dangers of drinking and thus preventing alcohol problems; (4) a category we may call "public pressures," wherein the aim is the mobilization of public opinion and action against drunkards on a face-to-face basis; and (5) pricing and trade regulations aimed at controlling the amount of alcohol available to the public.

MEDICAL APPROACHES

Medical measures in the treatment of alcohol problems differ primarily according to the stage of affliction at which they are aimed, from casual public drunkenness to chronic intoxication. The initial encounter of many urban alcoholics and drunkards with the control and treatment apparatus occurs in the "sobering-up station" (*meditsinskii vytrezvitel'*). These institutions, under the supervision of the militia, receive drunkards picked up on the streets and provide them with a hot shower or steam bath and a bed for the night. For this service, a charge is made, usually about 10 rubles. While they are generally spartan establishments, a hospital-like atmosphere in some stations has evoked complaints about "coddling" of drunkards and about the inadequacy of the fees they pay in light of the operating expenses of the stations.[1] There have been overreactions to the latter problem. In the Turkmen SSR, sobering-up stations were put on a cost-accounting basis and thus given a "plan," which resulted in the necessity for 3,300 people to be serviced by the stations in the capital city of Ashkhabad in order to fulfill the 1962 targets. This sort of social planning for a necessary minimum of deviance was, as one might expect, sharply criticized.[2]

Of course, what the sobering-up stations offer is not really treatment but only short-term custodial care. The more serious and habitual offender needs and will be given further aid, depending on how far his problem has progressed. Generally, for diagnostic purposes, three types of alcoholics (or stages of alcoholism) are distinguished in order of increasing severity. The first type includes those who are conscious of the dangers of their alcoholic state and wish treatment. These may be treated with supportive and psychotherapeutic measures, generally as outpatients. Alcoholics unconscious of their problems and not seeking treatment, who are thus on the verge of "deterioration," make up the second category. Psychotherapy may be tried here, but the main effort is devoted to setting up a negative conditioned reflex toward alcohol with the use of emetics, and sometimes hypnosis, in a hospital setting. Finally the third category includes deteriorated cases who, lacking the desire for treatment and subject to "psychotic episodes," need prolonged care in work-colony treatment institutions.[3] The more serious cases, where long-term alcoholism has resulted in frequent delirium tremens or hallucinations and where the person could not function in the treatment-labor institutions, are sent to large psychoneurological hospitals or "psychiatric colonies." [4]

The treatment needs of these various categories are filled by a number of institutions,° which are specialized according to the characteristics of their clientele.[5] The front line of Soviet institutions catering to the alcoholic includes the system of district polyclinics (*raionnye polikliniki*) and the alcoholism departments of the psychoneurological dispensaries (*psikhonevrologicheskie dispanseri*). In the great majority of cases, these are outpatient treatment centers, using psychotherapeutic and pharmaceutical as well as physiotherapeutic measures. Strong emphasis is given to their "explanatory-educational" work with the families and associates of outpatients. As the local link in the complex of treatment institutions, the polyclinic's functions include dealing with family and work problems, organizing and conducting anti-alcohol propaganda, public lectures, and film showings, and in general mobilizing public opinion against "drunkenness and debauchery." Milder cases of alcoholism are generally treated here.

The significance of the dispensaries is magnified by the Soviet preference for outpatient treatment of illnesses whenever possible.[6]

Dispensary treatment is to be preferred (though more difficult) . . . because it is important to achieve results not in a closed treatment institution,

---

° Recent years have seen many changes and reshufflings in the special tasks of institutions, especially since the 1967 decree on compulsory treatment, which demanded the organization of treatment-labor institutions. While the picture given here is accurate for now, it will probably undergo modification.

where the sick person is naturally located for a limited time, but in the circumstances of regular social life.[7]

When the seriousness of the case makes outpatient care impossible, a number of other institutions provide inpatient care for varying lengths of time. The "narco-admitters" (*narkopriemniki*), sometimes merged with the sobering-up stations, provide up to ten days of care to restore a measure of health to victims of drawn-out binges whose nutrition and bodily functioning have been disturbed. They possess basic facilities for hydrotherapy and work therapy. More serious cases whose needs still fall short of total institutionalization are cared for in psychoneurological treatment centers, with "all treatment methods" at their disposal, for periods of from one to three months, and usually continue to work during their stay.

Finally, for those whose cases resist one of these levels of treatment, for alcoholic "recidivists," and for deteriorated cases, longer stays in institutions which combine medical treatment with work are prescribed.

Three major forms of treatment are provided by these institutions: (1) work with drugs and hypnosis to induce negative conditioned reflexes toward alcohol; [8] (2) "rational psychotherapy" on an individual or collective basis; and (3) work therapy. The latter two are also employed in the treatment-labor institutions.

Rational psychotherapy, as employed in the Soviet Union in the treatment of alcoholism, is a process of explanation and persuasion, directed at the patient's consciousness in an attempt to make him forswear drink. Medical manuals dictate that "pedagogical," rather than purely psychiatric means, are to be used.[9] The doctor first attempts to establish contact with the patient (in individual therapy) and to gain his confidence. A "correct approach" to the individual patient is sought; a moralizing, didactic tone is to be avoided. Excessive familiarity, as in the use of the familiar (thou) form of address,[10] is not encouraged. Maintenance of a certain distance between therapist and patient, Soviet writers feel, will better preserve the atmosphere of seriousness necessary if the patient's resolve to avoid alcohol is to be kept firm.

Great importance is attached to convincing the patient that his cure depends largely on him, that it is not the doctor's job alone to

cure him. The middle stages of rational psychotherapy involve eluci-
dating the conflict situations and other factors that have played a role
in the development of the patient's alcoholism. This done, attempts
may be made to reestablish him at regular work and perhaps with his
family.[11] The goal of therapy, the restoration of the patient to effective functioning in society, should remain uppermost in the therapist's
and patient's minds. Doctor-patient conferences, while conversational
in form, are to be kept focused on the purpose of therapy.[12] Gaining
rapport is a precondition of therapy and is not to be regarded as an
end in itself. In the latter stages of treatment, the patient is encouraged to develop new tastes and pastimes so that his return to normal
social life is not accompanied by a return to old vices.[13] Interest in
sports, physical culture, and technical or creative hobbies is encouraged.

Collective rational psychotherapy, where doctors meet patients in
groups, is organized along the lines already noted, with the same end
in mind. The new element is one of limited mutual self-help, of *kollektivnost'* among the patients, leading to a form of guided group interaction. "Group psychotherapy makes possible the organization of
psychotherapeutic influence on alcoholics by the forces of other [al-
coholics] . . . a sick person often believes another sick person more
than the doctor." [14] These sessions should be kept purpose-oriented
and well controlled by the doctor leading them.[15] Reproduced below
is a list of topics suggested for discussion in group sessions, which
speaks for itself.[16]

1. Social causes of alcoholism. Alcoholism—most harmful survival of the
   past. Causes of alcoholism in our time.
2. Program of the construction of communism in the USSR. Moral code of
   communist society and the struggle with alcoholism.
3. Alcoholism—source of antisocial acts.
4. Effect of alcohol on the organism.
5. Alcohol and neuro-psychic illnesses.
6. Influence of alcohol on progeny.
7. Cure of alcoholism in hospital and dispensary conditions.
8. Work of the sick person on himself in the alcoholism-treatment process.
9. Role of work in the treatment of alcoholic illnesses.

10. Social-upbringing work—the main thing in the struggle with alcoholism. Significance of social pressure in the process of treatment and thereafter.

11. Concerning prevention of recidivism to alcoholism. What the sick person should know as he finishes the course of alcoholism treatment.

12. Conclusion.

Other forms of collective activity in line with the restorative purpose include group reading of letters from recovered patients and their families, discussions of anti-alcohol films and pamphlets, and lectures by former alcoholics.[17] In one institution, letters from "cured" former inmates generally expressed the opinion that lectures and films had been of greater efficacy in keeping them sober than drug treatments.[18] Social therapy, they felt, had had a more lasting effect than a purely medical approach.

Given the rather widely accepted definition of the alcoholic as a culpable deviant, it comes as no surprise that some collective therapy sessions do include a heavy dose of moralizing, with patients condemning their own and others' flaws in what amounts to a ritual of self and mutual criticism.

In one "model" institution, the newcomer is required to confess, in the presence of other patients, the worst drink-connected episodes of his past.[19] Those who break any of the institution's rules have their "cases" considered at a meeting of the other patients.[20] One institution proudly claims that its patients are dismissed, without the right of readmission, for the "smallest infraction" of the treatment regulations.[21]

Socially useful work in the form of labor therapy is calculated to give the patient a sense of self-sufficiency and effectiveness, the feeling of "mastery" he needs in order to reenter the world and be effective there.

It cannot be doubted that the stimulation of productive activity is a most important matter; in this connection not simply the regular fulfilling of labor obligations but the maintenance of a perspective of creative growth (improvement of job, technical learning, rationalizing ability, the mastering of a new profession, etc.) with the purpose that the sick person really feels the results (including material results) of a new mode of life.[22]

One may ask whether, given the regime's concern with financing the treatment of alcoholics, work would not be required in the treatment institutions even if its therapeutic effect and place in the treatment process were not such articles of faith. The cost to the state for the containment and treatment of alcoholics is a matter of mounting concern, and where possible, patient contributions toward defraying operating costs are welcomed. Still, it is unlikely that this is the sole explanation. Maintenance of the inmate's involvement in productive work is viewed as essential, and the negative effects of exclusion from working life during an otherwise beneficial term of treatment are combated through involving the inmates in collective work in the institution.[23] Specifically, physical work is intended: not necessarily heavy labor, but skilled hand-work. The insistence on physical work is extended even to those patients whose normal work is mental. Sometimes, persons in this category refuse to engage in physical work and are given explanations complete with data said to show the beneficial effects of labor therapy.[24] In such institutions, the patient's first few days are taken up with whatever physical recovery may be necessary. He is then gradually brought into the labor process, until an average of six or seven hours of work per day is reached.[25]

Post-release supervision and treatment, when carried on, is handled by the local dispensary [26] on an outpatient basis. Public organizations may provide assistance, as in the case of a hospital in Novoshaktinsk which utilizes local Komsomol members to maintain monthly contact with its discharged patients.[27]

Little information is available on the success of these therapeutic approaches. In general, however, the Soviet experience seems similar to that of other societies with large-scale alcoholism. B.M. Segal, one of the leading Soviet medical specialists on alcoholism, notes that, on the average, remissions are not prolonged. In close to one-third of all cases, recidivism to alcohol comes early, and strict avoidance of alcohol is observed relatively rarely.[28]

COMPULSORY TREATMENT: THE PROFILAKTORII

With the exception of the sobering-up stations, the institutions just discussed are essentially medical in their orientation, generally under the control of republican Ministries of Health and staffed by doctors and paramedical personnel. Most of their clients are voluntary, but not all. The Criminal Code of the Russian Republic [29] and parallel provisions in the codes of other republics provide for compulsory treatment in cases of confirmed drunkards who committed crimes under the influence of alcohol. Until relatively recently, it appears that compulsory treatment was carried on in various types of institutions. This no longer seems to be the case.

A decree of the RSFSR Supreme Soviet on April 8, 1967 [30] provided for changes in the applicable legislation that simplified significantly the procedural requirements for committing a person to compulsory treatment and specified a new variety of institution for the containment of alcohol offenders. Previously, an offending drunkard had to be on trial for a crime before the People's Court in order for the question of compulsory treatment to be raised (by way of petitions from "public organizations, workers' collectives or state agencies"). Now, those who violate "labor discipline, public order and the rules of socialist communal life" (varieties of deviance frequently not containing the elements of crime) are similarly liable. The decree provides for no appeal from the court's decision to compel treatment, and specifies a one- to two-year period in treatment-labor institutions, with a mandatory stay of one-half the sentence period before release of cured inmates can be contemplated. Escape from the institutions, a criminal offense, is punishable by imprisonment (see chapters 7 and 9).

The treatment-labor institution, or *profilaktorii*, to which offenders are sent under the new legislation falls under the jurisdiction not of the ministries of health, but of the Ministry of Internal Affairs (MVD). Prior to the creation of this new variety of institution, compulsory treatment was generally carried on either in special sections of psychiatric hospitals (for convicts who had not been sentenced to deprivation of freedom for their crime, or who had received a suspended sentence) or in treatment-labor divisions of corrective-labor colonies (for those who had been sentenced to deprivation of freedom).[31] The new *profilaktorii* are intended to serve, in addition to this clientele, a whole new class of noncriminal but socially disruptive alcoholics, and represent a tougher attitude toward the alcoholic than any yet taken. Though undoubtedly not so harsh in many aspects as corrective-labor colonies for criminals, the new institutions operate on the same cornerstones as the colonies (with the exception of medical treatment)—a "regime" of confinement, compulsory labor, and political-educational work.[32] From the wages paid inmates, deductions are made for their food, clothing, and other expenses.

The get-tough attitude clearly manifested in the creation of these institutions reflects long-term concerns of both medical and public order officials. The punitive attitude of one doctor, who suggested that something very much like the *profilaktorii* be established, was noted earlier (chapter 4). Jurists and police officials have been asking for such institutions for some time.[33] Apparently, there will be no lack of clientele for the institutions. Even after the 1967 decree went into effect, complaints were still being voiced about habitual drunkards who commit themselves voluntarily, sometimes as often as once a year, to psychiatric hospitals for treatment and resume their old habits when released. They receive their medical care free, do not work in the hospitals, and receive sick-leave pay in addition. A psychoneurologist describes one in this category:

After drinking up his last kopeks, a drunkard is placed in the comfortable conditions of a psychiatric clinic . . . After a few days of treatment with modern medicines the alcoholic's symptoms of psychic derangement disappear, as a rule, and he is transferred to the category of the so-called "conscious ill." And then a perfectly healthy lug begins literally making fun of people who are really sick. As soon as he is discharged, the drunkard "washes off" his sick leave payments, and everything starts all over again.[34]

Since the 1967 RSFSR decree, and similar decrees in other republics, expand greatly the potential pool of candidates for compulsory treatment and labor-reeducation, it is probable that many of these "lugs" can now be classified as violators and removed from the hospitals where they are treated completely at state expense.

The success or failure of the *profilaktorii* is not, as yet, clear. Organization of the new institutions has been slow (as early as March 18, 1968, *Pravda* was already complaining about slowness in implementing the decree [35]), and it seems that a nationwide network of institutions is still to be established. By late 1968, a legal journal was already dealing with the problem of escapes from the *profilaktorii*.[36] Problems have also arisen in the relatively large periods of time that may elapse between a court commitment decision and actual entry into an institution—a period the alcoholic spends in police preliminary confinement along with accused criminals.

Among the very few statistics on cures reported are figures which claim a 77 percent success rate for institutions in the Ukraine, with only 7.9 percent of graduates returning to the *profilaktorii*. Published figures for repeaters in Latvia and Belorussia are even lower.[37] It is difficult to evaluate these figures, since the criteria for a "cure" are not specified. We do not know how long released inmates need avoid further encounters with alcohol to be considered successes. The figures given, however, may well be inflated by the lack of adequate success criteria. In what is probably the most comprehensive Soviet treatise on alcoholism, B.M. Segal cites results of compulsory treatment of a group of alcoholics in a psychiatric hospital, where a variety of medical measures and facilities greater than are likely to be encountered in a *profilaktorii* were available. Fifty-five percent of the released patients stayed away from liquor for over a year. This is apparently regarded as a rather high success rate, and application of such criteria to the *profilaktorii* might provide a somewhat different picture.[38] At present, one can only say that it is too early to render judgment on the *profilaktorii*, even if adequate statistical data on their operation were available. They have not been part of the Soviet scene long enough. In a sense, they are a logical outgrowth of concern with costs to the state of maintaining alcoholics in hospital surroundings and of a punitive attitude toward those whose drinking leads to disorderly conduct. Whether they will have a sufficient payoff remains to be seen.

ANTI-ALCOHOL PROPAGANDA

The old adage about an "ounce of prevention" is reflected in what has been for some years the main preventive thrust of Soviet anti-alcohol forces—"propaganda" against drinking, aimed at the public at large. In a society where communications media are under strict government control, propaganda against any designated social evil assumes special significance, and such is the case with anti-alcohol propaganda.

In the face of the traditional Russian drinking culture, anti-alcohol propaganda is charged with two tasks: the formation of public opinion and attitudes that view drunkenness as a phenomenon foreign to Soviet society and life, with harmful consequences for the individual, the family, production, and the "whole work of communist construction"; and the involvement and organization of the public in an "active struggle with alcoholism." [39]

This commission is executed through various media—press, radio, television, lectures by Party activists and medical workers to groups assembled in factories, schools, and apartment buildings—but the content is consistent. Drinking is dangerous; excessive drinking harms the individual, and through him, society as a whole. Readers and listeners, the public as a whole, are the targets of a multilevel appeal. The drinker's concern with his health, with the welfare of his family, with job security, with respectability in the eyes of his peers, and finally with remaining on the right side of the law is exploited on the level of personal concern. On another level, he is reminded altruistically that, as a Soviet citizen, he should have nothing to do with pernicious survivals like drunkenness, which hamper his participation in public affairs, his productivity, and his total contribution to the progress of Soviet society toward communism.

The propagators of anti-alcohol messages aim at a wide audience. "Popular-scientific literature" is printed in large editions for purchase by the general public at low prices. After work, a homebound Muscovite can purchase a pamphlet demonstrating how "Drink Corrupts Man" at a subway station kiosk. Propagandists employ lectures and discussions, radio and television broadcasts, "popular-scientific" films, the press, wall newspapers, placards, exhibits, and a number of other media to put across their message.[40] Both the Central Scientific Research Institute of Sanitary Education of the USSR Ministry of Public Health and the USSR Ministry of Culture, provide a number of films for mass exhibition. Titles such as "Villainness with a Label" [41] and "I Don't Remember Anything" (the oft-quoted statement of the drunkard when accused of committing an offense while under the influence of drink) are supplemented by lectures to the audiences after the films have been shown.

Pamphlets and newspaper articles frequently rely upon the shock effect of detailed accounts of the dangerous consequences of heavy (or even long-term moderate) drinking. Vivid descriptions of degenerative changes in one's internal organs as a result of overindulgence are presented in many pamphlets. Concrete examples, the tragic case histories of drinkers, receive a great deal of space. Accounts of broken families, lost jobs, crimes committed and lives ruined are typical of this approach. "Uplifting" stories of occasional comebacks emphasize the ever-present possibility of successful treatment and the paramount importance of the patient's persistence and desire to be cured.[42]

Some of the recurring claims made by propagandists prove unconvincing. One of special importance is the oft-repeated observation that moderate drinking leads almost inevitably to heavy drinking [43] —to many audiences, this claim is hard to believe, and even those specializing in propaganda work find themselves complaining about it.

"Rivers begin from a stream"—they repeat, in every way, this favorite proverb. The numerous exceptions to this rule compel one to have doubts about its infallibility . . . the majority of those who have gotten used to contenting themselves with small doses, despite the "prognosis," don't change for the rest of their lives.[44]

Soviet doctors themselves express doubts about the factual basis of the assertion, frequently encountered in popular literature, that drunkenness and alcoholism have a direct physical influence on offspring —accounting for the birth of many weak-witted and physically handicapped children.[45] The possibility that academic and emotional problems of children of alcoholics are attributable not to direct physical consequences but to early home environments reflecting parental pathologies is taken into account by some medical specialists,[46] but propagandists continue to rely on the scare value of the direct biological nexus.

From general indications, it appears that much of the face-to-face propagandizing in factories, apartment complexes, and the like is done by low-level Party activists who have no medical knowledge or by lower-echelon medical workers who themselves may find the content of their message difficult to believe. Segal notes that the low effectiveness of propaganda in combatting the deep-rooted pro-alcohol traditions of the population may be traced in part to the lack of "internal convictions of the correctness of their appeals" among the propagandists themselves.[47]

The supply of anti-alcohol reading material falls below the level of demand—at least, the regime's demand. *Pravda's* Leningrad correspondent complained that there were only 22 prints of anti-alcohol film shorts in the city and the surrounding province and that "feature-length popular science and art films" were totally lacking; he asked why the Leningrad division of the Medical Literature publishing house, which published 125 titles in 1963, devoted none to alcoholism.[48]

Making lectures and film showings concrete through the use of scientific data, specific examples, and the like [49] has sometimes led to a depopularization of the material aimed at mass audiences. Thus, doctors who make use of pictures of healthy and enlarged hearts in before-and-after demonstrations are reminded that such demonstrations only make an impression on those with medical training and merely puzzle laymen.[50] Other shortcomings often criticized are failure to compose lectures or pamphlets with specific appeal to particular audiences, like youths, workers, or soldiers, and propagandists' unfamiliarity with local conditions and infrequent use of local examples, where such highlighting of drunkards known to particular audiences would increase the impact, as in lectures delivered in factories or on collective farms.[51]

In addition to the dangers of saturation inherent in presenting the same material to the public over and over again, the Soviet regime faces three major problems in its attempts at anti-alcohol persuasion. The first is the inherent difficulty of attitude change itself. It is hard to penetrate the web of popular attitudes which define drinking as manly and a necessary adjunct to conviviality. An individual's conviction that drinking is an acceptable activity is likely to be supported by his friends. Pro-drink attitudes, as one doctor notes, "are extremely hard to overcome in an adult, especially when the majority of those around him also use alcoholic beverages." [52] Nor has anti-alcohol propaganda linked itself effectively to *other* positive values in the drinker's consciousness. Rhetorical appeals on the basis of patriotism and civic dignity are remote from everyday, pressing concerns. Warnings based on the negative effects of drinking, the dangers of illness to oneself and genetic harm to one's offspring, are closer to the individual's concerns but are met in many instances with disbelief that such can happen in one's own case.[53] (Such scare tactics are, in the opinion of many Western specialists on alcoholism, unlikely to produce positive results.[54]) Appeals to the drinker not to jeopardize the happiness of his home life may confront a feeling that, at home at least, he should be allowed the mode of relaxation he wishes.

The second major problem in convincing the public is that the picture of drinking presented by the electronic and printed media and in lectures is by no means always consistent. Most anti-alcohol tracts deny positive functions to any sort of alcoholic beverage. Yet, apparently regarding the preaching of total abstinence as a mission doomed to failure, they often make a distinction between beer and wine on the one hand and stronger drink on the other, thereby, tacitly legitimating the use of the former in the minds of anti-alcohol hard-liners. In view of the counterproductive experience of both the Russian Empire and the Soviet state with "dry laws," prohibition has been rejected, at least until recently, as a way of handling the problem.[55] Yet such a refusal may be somewhat hard for Soviet citizens to comprehend, accustomed as they are to governmental readiness to intervene in many aspects of private life; as an occasional drinker's wife in a letter to a Soviet editor may ask, "if alcohol is so bad, why isn't it prohibited?" [56]

Despite state commitments, a pro-alcohol message seeps through controlled entertainment media. Cinema heroes are frequently criticized for the amounts they drink on screen and the gusto with which they do it.[57] Critics question the need for such scenes, considering them both harmful to the "struggle" and, in any case, often extraneous to the development of the plot. But even the guardians of youth are seemingly not untouched by the association of drinking with manliness. In a discussion of the problems of heavy holiday drinking and proposals to enact some sort of prohibition to curtail them, the Young Communist League paper, Komsomol'skaia pravda, turns down the suggestion on the grounds that it would be "inconceivable" to "emasculate our holidays and ceremonies." [58]

The third obstacle the anti-alcohol forces face lies in the quality of Soviet life as it is experienced by that segment of the "audience" who are problem drinkers. These are frequently said to be those with "little culture" and little formal education, often working in relatively unskilled jobs. Such persons are not great consumers of printed media and are unlikely to be reached by the anti-alcohol message. Many cite boredom as a reason for their drinking. And indeed, crowded housing, low incomes, shortages of goods, and the like still render Soviet working-class life relatively drab (though in material aspects it continues to improve). The tendency to use liquor in an escapist manner must be taken into account in any assessment of the alcohol problem, at least until Soviet working-class life itself has undergone some fundamental improvements.[59]

MOBILIZING PUBLIC PRESSURES

In a nation where pro-alcohol attitudes and a relatively permissive view of drinking are so deeply ingrained, it is not surprising that the government and Party attempt to enlist the aid of willing members of the public to carry the message of sobriety to their fellow citizens on a face-to-face basis. Nor, however, is it surprising that this effort meets with many obstacles.

In the 1920s, an All-Union Council of Anti-Alcohol Societies coordinated the state-sponsored public effort on behalf of sobriety and abstinence. This organization ceased to function in 1930, and until recently,[60] the idea of a new national anti-alcohol organization received little attention, the involvement of the public being primarily local in nature. Although the situation is subject to change, as of early 1970 no national coordinating body had been established.

The responsibility of those in close contact with an individual at school or work, and the duty of the public at large, to show an uncompromising attitude toward drunkenness as a whole and to prevent alcoholic excesses by exerting pressure on the drinker in a stern but comradely way is continually reaffirmed as a central part of the total anti-alcoholism effort: "Obviously, this is not the business of doctors alone: without public organizations, in the first place without party and Komsomol organizations, we cannot manage here." [61] Instances of indifference or tolerance present a reverse mirror-image of the "correct" approach. The fellow workers of a youth who wound up in the prisoners' dock for offenses committed while drunk are condemned for their "indifferent attitude" which left him "outside the *kollektiv*." [62] The press carries many such accounts.

As an example of the sort of activity called for, the case of the public organizations in the Minsk Motor Plant is instructive. As it was one of the newest plants in the war-devastated city, its management had been forced to hire many workers whose credentials would have meant their rejection in a time when labor shortages were not so acute. The factory was required to take on what were referred to as "notorious 'drifters' and 'hair of the dog' enthusiasts." [63] After some complaints about their behavior and suggestions that they be fired, it was decided by management, Party, trade union, Komsomol, "leaders of production," and "public activists" that they be reeducated. Writes one of the latter: "The advocates of educational measures were in the majority, and we did not hasten to give up on a man while there was still hope of awakening his conscience." [64] "Guardians" were appointed for the offenders, who were kept in view by these companions during and after work-hours. Shaming techniques, such as criticism in the factory wall newspapers and display of offenders' pictures in showcases with appropriate comments, were also among the means used. Finally, particularly recalcitrant offenders were subjected to the trial-style "workers' circle." The example of a worker named Vladimir follows.

One day when he appeared in the shop drunk he was put into the "workers' circle." At first Vladimir was cocky.

"I got drunk; so what? I did it with my own money, not yours. What business is it of yours?"

But the workers began to speak, one after another. The "circle" came to life and got excited, and it was as if a refreshing wind were blowing around Vladimir. He began to sober up right before their eyes. His arrogance vanished as if by magic. He began to defend himself, then to make excuses, then to repeat, and finally he broke down and burst into tears. He swore on his honor that he would never do it again, and he has kept his word. He is now on a par with the leading production workers.[65]

The workers' circle can operate in other ways as well. Arrangements may be made whereby the circle gives the drunkard's wages directly to his wife. In the case of a childless person, it may recommend his transfer to a lower-paid job. Sometimes, loss of place on housing or nursery priority lists are proposed as penalties, or wage cuts are suggested even for those with dependents. But the negative effects of these measures on the families of the offenders are usually cited as reasons why their application should be avoided. Those who favor their imposition argue that, rather than excusing the drunkard from punishment, their dependence on him should cause wives, mothers, and fathers to assume more responsibility in keeping him from excesses.[66] Such broad measures are justified by noting that, since Soviet wives generally are earning an income, and since the state provides various forms of child-care assistance, reduction of the husband's salary need not have unwanted effects. Such collective responsibility is given even broader meaning by those who propose that "whole brigades and collectives be deprived of prizes and even fined for winking their eyes at drunkards, debauchers and slackers." [67]

Komsomol organizations, comrades' courts, and people's volunteers (druzhiny) are commissioned to wage the fight against drunkenness on the streets and condemn those who appear in public intoxicated. How much enthusiasm they show in their work (it will be recalled that not only the public but even police on the beat have been criticized for indifference to and tolerance of public intoxication), and to what degree the public supports them, is difficult to determine. But, on balance, their overall impact is questionable. These are unpaid, volunteer operations. Frequently, "volunteering" means being assigned by the Party (for rank-and-file members) or by one's trade union to a particular variety of public work—so that the organization may demonstrate how active its members are. Conversely, one who seeks the benefits of Party membership may volunteer for public work solely to produce a good record and hasten admission. Given these circumstances, and given an apparently inadequate system of rating the performance of public organizations, a lack of interest in certain types of public work, such as the fight against drunkenness, is not surprising. In fact, by the late 1960s Soviet sources seemed notably less enthusiastic about such organizations as semiformal social control mechanisms than they were at the beginning of the decade, when peoples' volunteer squads, comrades' courts, and the like had Khrushchev's enthusiastic backing.

TRADE REGULATION

As in other nations where state authority has defined abuse of alcohol as a problem, Soviet officials have concerned themselves with regulating the retail distribution of alcoholic beverages. In this area, more perhaps than in the other approaches to the drunkenness problem, there have been numerous ups and downs.

Reductions in the price of vodka between 1949 and 1955, coupled with a rise in average real income, encouraged use of strong spirits. In the same period, and extending through the end of the decade, the number of establishments selling liquor increased greatly, even while heavy drinking was deplored by official sources. Vodka, brandies, wines, and beer might be purchased not only in restaurants, public dining rooms, and other eating establishments, but also in produce stores and in sidewalk stands. In 1957, a visitor to Moscow observed that "Vodka can be bought almost any place; it is easier to obtain than a newspaper." [68]

The late 1950s saw the beginning of a spate of regulating activity, generally undertaken on the local level, aimed at curbing the number of trade points and limiting the hours of sale for alcoholic beverages. The regulations have been, however, primarily administrative in nature (i.e., not criminal laws), with fines the main sanction and enforcement a nagging problem. In a letter to *Izvestiia* in 1958, a doctor praised the Moscow City Soviet for an ordinance prohibiting the sale of vodka in market stalls, but he also complained about frequent violations and weak enforcement.[69] By 1961 fairly widespread regulations prohibited the sale of alcoholic beverages in dining rooms and snack bars (where the customer remains generally a short time for a quick meal—restaurants, where one is likely to remain a few hours, are still authorized to sell all alcoholic beverages). However, this failed to produce any drastic decline in consumption; patrons began to bring their own liquor.[70] Enforcement of the trade regulations continued to be less than complete, as *Vecherniaia Moskva* noted in September 1963.

Unfortunately, alcoholic beverages, although they are prohibited, are being sold as before not only in specialized meat and fish stores as well as in certain milk and dietetic stores, but also in restaurants, cafes, snack bars and refreshment rooms.[71]

The same article goes on to state that alcoholic beverages could also be obtained at various points near factories, schools, hospitals and theaters and in public parks. In larger cities, wine-vending machines in automated snack bars were doing a thriving business.[72] In 1965, violations of time and place regulations persisted and *Izvestiia* noted that wine was even being sold in a secondary school cafeteria in the North Ossetian ASSR.[73]

The difficulty of enforcing such regulations inheres in the structure of consumer trade and in the fact that retail enterprises as well as factories have plans to fulfill. Price increases in the 1960s, reversing the previous trend, have made liquor a high-profit item; and restaurants, snack bars, public dining rooms, delicatessens, and all sorts of stores find it the best and simplest means to fulfill and overfulfill their economic targets. (The price increases have not deterred consumption.) The same demands for plan fulfillment on higher levels in the retail trade trusts result in pressures to exceed the limit on alcohol in the "mix" of food and drink to be sold. A dining room manager complains, "According to the limit we should sell only six tons of wine, but the trust sets the plan so high that we have to buy twelve tons on the side. What can you do?" [74] To remedy this problem, a number of proposals have been made: for example, "Things should be so arranged that the index of a waiter's work is not based on the amount of liquor he sells. Nor should a restaurant's or dining room's earnings from liquor serve as an index of the quality of its work." [75]

The absence of any coordinated regulatory effort on the national level virtually guaranteed that the situation as the USSR entered the 1970s would be much the same as that over the preceding decade. *Komsomol'skaia pravda* on January 9, 1970 complained that, despite a regulation against the sale of vodka before 10:00 A.M., drinking of other potent mixtures such as fortified wines was under way, in all sorts of public places, from 8:00 A.M.[76] On the same day, *Sovetskaia Estoniia* noted that a railroad station buffet in Rakvers, Estonia was doing a profitable trade in vodka and other drinks, despite the provision, almost general for the whole USSR, that prohibits sale of alcohol in railway stations and in shops and kiosks near such stations.[77]

Obviously, one decisive step within the competence of the state would be to curtail the production of alcoholic beverages, especially stronger liquors. But such a move would cut at a source of considerable state revenues. The legal production of liquor remains a state monopoly under the Soviet, as under the Tsarist, regime, and Soviet officials have obviously been reluctant to disturb the present situation. Whether interest in public health and order will eventually prevail over economic interests is difficult to determine. The specialists at the All-Union Institute for the Study of the Causes and Elaboration of Preventive Measures of Crime, who produced the volume *Alkogolizm—put' k prestupleniiu (Alcoholism—path to crime)*, recommended that the state consider seriously cutting back production and find a new source of revenue.[78] While this recommendation provoked no notable response for some time after its publication in 1966, by 1970 indications of some support for a prohibition law, aimed at vodka and fortified wines and brandies, began to appear in the Soviet press.[79] This, however, is a larger step than the state is probably willing to take. A more likely response, in line with the sharpening concern over the effects of workers' drunkenness and absenteeism expressed by Brezhnev in early 1970, is further tightening of trade regulations, a move supported by B.T. Shumilin, Deputy Minister of the Interior, in an article * in *Sovetskaia Rossiia*.[80]

The frequent calls for construction of cafes and other facilities serving only beer and light wines and offering food and an environment in which moderate, "cultured" drinking will become the norm have apparently run afoul of construction costs. Where such facilities have

---

* It has been suggested that press "campaigns" against drinking, such as the one in early 1970, tend to backfire. *Komsomol'skaia pravda* (January 6, 1970, p. 4) claims that vodka sales climb drastically after articles against alcoholism appear, and that store managers thus increase their stock when such articles are published. Whether this is a common phenomenon is questionable; but it does suggest a "stockpiling" response on the part of drinkers who may fear that tighter regulations will follow such articles.

been built, often they soon progress to trading in hard liquor, vitiating the original purpose. At present, there are few places outside of relatively expensive restaurants where one can buy liquor by the drink and consume it on the premises. This lack of Western-style bars, pubs, or other drinking establishments contributes to the frequency with which one encounters small groups drinking on the street. In many cities, one frequently sees "troikas" (threesomes) sharing a half-liter of vodka. The price is about three rubles, and a drinker with one ruble may stand by a store with two fingers extended over the front of his coat, signaling to any potential sharers that two more rubles are needed. A great number of drunken street brawls might be attributed to fallings-out over "equal shares" among three persons, unknown to one another except for their common interest in vodka.

How effective, as a whole, is the complex of approaches that make up the Soviet anti-alcoholism program? Even were statistics available in much greater quantity than they are, this would be a difficult question. The complaints voiced over difficulties in implementing virtually every measure in the arsenal lead one to conclude that they are generally ineffective. While the absolute incidence of alcoholism and related disorders remains unclear, one can easily gain the impression that the problems are on the increase.

But measuring or estimating effectiveness is a tricky business. With all the problems and shortcomings in the application of the measures we have discussed, we cannot be sure that the Soviet alcohol problem would not be much greater in their absence. How many potential heavy drinkers are affected by anti-alcohol propaganda? How many are influenced by the attitudes of that portion of the Soviet public, however small it may be, which is really "anti-drink"? How many alcoholics, having undergone treatment, remain sober indefinitely? Such questions are often practically unanswerable, and Soviet specialists lack the answers as much as non-Soviet observers. In the absence of answers, one can only say that the program has its successes, but also its failures. We can expect further experimentation with new measures in the future, but for the present, no summary verdict is possible.

6

JUVENILE DELINQUENCY

WHILE MANY WESTERN CRITICS of Soviet policies see the institutions and organizations that surround Soviet youngsters in their formative years—day-nurseries, kindergartens, schools, state-controlled youth organizations—as mechanisms designed to produce technically qualified but politically orthodox and conforming adults, usually, whether grudgingly or not, they will make one concession. This is that the techniques of manipulation and control have at least left the Soviet Union by and large free of the problems of juvenile delinquency which plague policy makers and law enforcement officials in so many industrial societies. Deductively, such a concession can make sense: should one not expect less juvenile misbehavior in a society with so many instruments of control at its disposal? In fact, however, things are not so simple.

. . . The people's court of Chilin district, considering the criminal case of N. and others, established that the students at Kuram secondary school, where the accused studied, systematically organized group drinking-bouts, to which they also invited girls. And on November 7, 1966 the ninth-grader A., born in 1950, organized such an evening, to which he did not invite his acquaintances N., M., and others. The latter, being drunk, came up to A. to express their insult at this. Then a fight broke out between them, and N. mortally wounded A.[1]

The juveniles P., M. and Ia., were convicted of having, jointly with others . . . attempted on January 24, 1965 to rape Z. and, on the same day, O. The crime was committed with unusual roughness. . . . By the [court's] sentence, P. received four years, M., three years, and Ia., two years' imprisonment.[2]

Such cases are not necessarily typical. The Soviet delinquent is more likely to be involved in property offenses or in a variety of public order violations which the law lumps together under the term "hooliganism." But the N.'s, the P.'s, the M.'s, and their fellow delinquents amount to a sizable problem for Soviet society. If, given the lack of statistical data, we cannot say precisely how large the problem is, the concern Soviet officials and criminologists show in writing about it allows us to regard it as "large enough."

That delinquency should exist in the USSR today is not surprising, for it has been a persistent phenomenon throughout the Soviet period.[3] The social upheavals of revolution and civil war left many children homeless and abandoned in the 1920s, and they roamed the countryside and cities, frequently in bands, stealing and occasionally killing in order to survive. They numbered in the millions and presented a public-order problem of massive dimensions.

Bringing these bands of homeless youth under control was scarcely accomplished when, at the end of the 1920s, new social upheavals came with Stalin's programs of forced collectivization of the countryside and rapid industrialization; and in their wake delinquency was again on the increase. Migration from the countryside to newly developing industrial centers strained the capacities of formerly peasant families to survive as functioning units in the new surroundings and to control the behavior of their children. The severe economic deprivations of the first Five-Year Plan increased these pressures, and the delinquency rate, especially in the large cities, continued to rise.[4]

A harder legal line taken toward delinquents and their parents in the mid-1930s [5] may have had some deterrent effect, but World War II with its aftermath of destruction and chaos once again produced large numbers of homeless, unsupervised adolescents, who taxed the control capacities of the state. While the period since 1953 has been marked by general social stability and relatively constant, if modest, increases in the standard of living, delinquency today is still far from that point of final liquidation which, according to Marxism-Leninism, is to be expected as socialism gives place to its final stage—communism.

In fact, references to the "liquidation" of delinquency in current Soviet writing seem to be little more than rhetoric. The professors and researchers, prosecutors and police officials who occupy themselves today with the study and control of delinquency are concerned with more mundane tasks of explaining how and why various adolescents become delinquent and how to cope with the offenses they perpetrate. Since the late 1950s much (but by no means all) of the reticence about displaying dirty linen even to the domestic public, characteristic of Stalin's time, has been overcome. Delinquency is a problem of significant dimensions, and is recognized as such by those who write about it in the national press, as well as in specialized legal journals.

One does not observe in Soviet treatments of the delinquency problem any of the tone of panic sometimes encountered in Western, and particularly American, writings on the subject. This is, to some degree, a matter of style—on such matters, the Soviet press is nothing if not unsensational. It also probably reflects a delinquency problem which, while serious, is not (or is not perceived as) *so* serious as that in some other modern societies. But Soviet concern with delinquency is deep, and with good reason. Insofar as delinquency persists, it represents a series of failures on the part of institutions and activities which the state itself, to a greater or lesser degree, sponsors and regulates. While the family has not been in any sense completely replaced in Soviet society by other instruments of socialization and control, it is seen, ideally, as working toward the goals the state desires—the creation of orderly, law-abiding citizens. Its failures, then, are matters of official concern. The same may be said more directly of the schools, the youth organizations, and the factories which employ young workers. All of these are charged with moral upbringing as well as with other tasks. When they fail, as often enough they do, it means that the whole network of institutions which surrounds the Soviet adolescent is not working as it should.

In attempting to understand the malfunctions of this network, Soviet researchers have investigated the characteristics of its substandard products, the delinquents, and sought, in a more general way, for the sources of imperfection in its operation. These two topics—the nature of the delinquent and his activity and the factors which produce delinquency—will occupy us for the remainder of this chapter.

JUVENILE OFFENSES AND OFFENDERS: STATISTICS

While there are severe limitations on the degree to which we can present a statistical portrait of Soviet delinquency, data from Soviet sources, when assembled and cross-checked for consistency, do allow some generalizations to be made.° The generalizations are far from final, but should aid in an understanding of the nature of delinquency in the USSR and its similarities and differences to delinquency in other industrial societies.

Information regarding the types of offenses most often committed by juveniles is surprisingly sketchy, given the developing Soviet tendency to report a good variety of information, as long as the information is confined to percentage distributions of unknown raw totals. For example, a survey of court practice relative to juveniles conducted in Archangel *oblast'* yielded the data for a three-year period presented in table 3. Despite the missing data reflected in the low column totals, some points of interest emerge: first, the heavy weight of property offenses (the last three categories), which in no case fall below half of the total number of convictions; second, the relatively low incidence of convictions for crimes against the person (first three categories) and public-order offenses (hooliganism). While other articles on delinquency support these limited figures and affirm that a quite large percentage of all juvenile offenses fall in the property

---

° These generalizations, however, do not include any concerning the overall dimensions of delinquency. Data that would allow us to gauge or even estimate the incidence of delinquency among age-eligible juveniles remain, at least at present, closed to Western researchers.

TABLE 3   TYPES OF JUVENILE OFFENSE AS PERCENTAGES
OF ALL JUVENILE OFFENSES, ARCHANGEL OBLAST', 1961–1963

	Year		
Offense	1961	1962	1963
Homicide	1.1%	0.8%	0.9%
Infliction of serious bodily injury	2.2	3.1	2.9
Sex offenses	8.3	8.5	8.7
Hooliganism	4.9	7.0	6.8
Open stealing	11.7	13.7	12.7
Assault with intent to rob	6.5	7.7	7.2
Concealed theft	36.0	32.7	32.0
Totals	70.7%	73.5%	71.2%

Source: V.S. Karasev, "Nekotorye dannye, kharakterizuiushchie primenenie mer ugolovnogo nakazaniia k nesovershennoletnim prestupnikam," in *Preduprezh-denie prestupnosti nesovershennoletnikh* (Moscow, "Iuridicheskaia literatura," 1965), p. 225.

crimes category,[6] hooliganism is usually better represented than in these figures. In other aspects, the Archangel data are rather typical, especially in the low incidence of homicide and in the high proportion of theft among all property crimes.

These court statistics reflect the main business of the courts in the delinquency area—more serious offenses. Less serious violations such as truancy, running away from home, and various types of "mischief" are handled, by and large, by the Commissions on Juvenile Affairs,[7] in whose records offenses against the person and the graver varieties of property offense appear with notably less frequency.[8]

Why, however, the missing numbers in the table presenting the Archangel data? Given the focus of this section, such a question is worth some consideration. First, since Soviet tables are often only vaguely labeled, these *totals* may reflect cases carried through to a conviction, and the missing percentages, more than one-quarter of the total for all three years, cases which *reached* the stage of judicial consideration but which were transferred on remand to a Commission on Juvenile Affairs. It may also be, however, that older delinquents (toward whom courts tend to be less lenient), who committed less serious offenses and were convicted of them, make up the missing percentage, due to the compiler's decision not to include numerous lesser offenses either by name or in a large "other" category. The latter possibility seems more likely, but there is little basis for certitude about either explanation.

Data on ages of delinquent offenders are somewhat problematic, since the division of responsibility between the Peoples' Courts and the Commissions on Juvenile Affairs involves, to a degree, a specialization of work according to different age groups. Courts are empowered to try cases of juvenile offenders of age 16 and over, whatever the offense, and from age 14 on for more serious offenses. The commissions, on the other hand, have original jurisdiction over law breakers under the age of 14, and over those 14- and 15-year-olds whose offenses are not serious enough to warrant court proceedings. In addition, the commissions receive cases of juveniles 14 through 17 years of age on remand from the courts, when the offense or offender can, in the court's opinion, better be handled by the noncriminal sanctions of the commission.

What this leads to is a heavy representation of younger offenders in data from the practice of the commissions, and correspondingly heavy representation of older juveniles (legal majority in the USSR comes with the age of 18) in court statistics. However, variations in commission practice make for a picture that is not altogether clear. Table 4 presents data drawn from a number of commissions.

By area, the operations of the commissions appear to vary greatly. In Dushanbe, fully 61.3 percent of the offenders appearing before the commissions were under 14, and hence ineligible for court processing. The Proletarskii district commission, in Riga, transacted much less (30.3 percent) of its business with offenders under 14, but still exceeded the totals of the Sverdlovsk and Krasnopresnensk (Moscow) commissions. One cannot conclude that there are, proportionally, many times fewer 16- and 17-year-old delinquents in Dushanbe than in Moscow or Sverdlovsk, nor that the behavior of those under 11 years of age is especially turbulent in Riga and Dushanbe. Different degrees of preoccupation with younger (under 14) offenders, and the varying propensities of the courts to transfer cases on remand (very low in Dushanbe [9]), as well as desultory record-keeping by the commissions,[10] do much to influence the age distribution of their clien-

TABLE 4   AGES OF DELINQUENT OFFENDERS IN CASES HANDLED BY COMMISSIONS IN 1963

Age	Krasnopresnensk dist. Moscow 1963	Sverdlovsk 1963	Proletarskii dist. Riga 1963	Dushanbe 1963
Under 11	3.1%	0.7%	10.2%	8.0%
11	4.4	4.0	3.3	14.5
12	1.4	6.0	6.6	11.3
13	4.4	8.8	10.2	27.5
14	12.5	14.1	11.2	32.3
15	19.1	19.0	20.4	3.2
16	24.2	22.1	13.2	1.6
17	30.9	22.0	8.2	1.6
18	. . .	. . .	. . .	
No. infor.	. . .	3.3	16.7	
Totals	100.0%	100.0%	100.0%	100.0%

Source: E.V. Boldyrev, *Mery preduprezhdeniia pravonarushenii nesovershennoletnikh v SSSR* (Moscow, "Nauka," 1964), p. 135.

tele. Further evidence of variations in commission practice in other Soviet studies underscores the need to approach such data with caution.[11]

Court statistics, on the other hand, reflect the different clientele processed there and the impact of the fact that all persons age 16 and over are eligible for criminal prosecution, regardless of offense. Table 5 gives data for two districts in Sverdlovsk, a large industrial city in the Urals, for the years 1960–1964 and similar data for Moscow's Pervomaiskii district in 1962. While the table shows reasonably large variations in court operations, the courts' heavier concentration of effort on 16- and 17-year-olds, relative to the commissions, is evident. Other, more recent Soviet statements confirm that courts are dealing increasingly with 16- and 17-year-olds. "On the average," up to 85–87 percent of the cases involve this age group,[12] and courts where persons under 16 account for more than 20 percent of cases are relatively rare.[13]

Earlier studies of court records, generalizing from data such as that in table 5, sometimes concluded that the ages 15–17 were the "high risk" years for delinquency. While there is a tendency for more serious offenses to be concentrated in these age groups, it is not clear that these groups are more delinquent. G.M. Min'kovskii, one of the most authoritative students of Soviet delinquency, notes that some studies have taken little account of the size of relevant age groups compared to the total population, and thus may see an overrepresentation of one age group in court statistics where none, in fact, exists.[14] However, although the situation remains cloudy, one can conclude that Soviet authorities view the delinquency of 16- and 17-year-olds as the most serious segment of the problem.

Data on the sex of offenders, while only fragmentary, shows the same underrepresentation of females observed in other societies. Gen-

TABLE 5 AGES OF DELINQUENT OFFENDERS IN COURT-HANDLED CASES, TWO SOVIET STUDIES

Age	Kirov dist., Sverdlovsk (1960–1964)	Ordzhonikidze dist., Sverdlovsk (1960–1964)	Pervomaiskii dist., Moscow (1962)
14	4.5%	5.0%	8.9%
15	19.6	9.3	
16	30.9	30.3	51.4°
17	45.0	55.4	39.7
Totals	100.0%	100.0%	100.0%

° Includes 15- and 16-year-olds.

Sources: cols. 1 and 2, M.I. Kovalev, "Izuchenie prestupnosti nesovershennoletnikh i ee preduprezhdenie," Sovetskaia iustitsiia, No. 3 (1966), p. 16; col. 3, O.I. Morozov, et al., "Opyt kompleksnogo obsledovaniia prichin i uslovii, sposobstvuiushchikh soversheniiu prestuplenii podrostkami," Sovetskoe gosudarstvo i pravo, No. 9 (1963), p. 111.

erally, girls make up less than five percent of juveniles handled by the courts.[15] Over the course of three years (1961–1963), girls constituted only 2.3, 2.4, and 2.7 percent, respectively, of convicted juveniles in Archangel oblast'.[16] Although greater police attention to males and a greater propensity to transfer girls' cases to the commissions are probably important here, the figures presumably reflect the generally less offense-prone character of females.

What of the family backgrounds of juvenile offenders? Soviet criminologists have shown a persistent interest in the structure and performance of the family as a context of socialization, as well as in the socioeconomic characteristics of delinquents' parents. Since the late 1950s, one of the prime areas of concern has been the "incomplete" family, and its relation to delinquency. As table 6 shows, the percentage of delinquents from incomplete families in the early 1960s was rather large. It has shown, in recent years, a tendency to decline. The table figures are far from the highest recorded: a study of convicted juveniles in Yaroslavl' *oblast'* in the late 1950s showed the 68 percent of the sample lacked a parent (in 55 percent of the cases, the father).[17] This study reflected, undoubtedly, the large-scale loss of male life in World War II, a circumstance to which Soviet writers attributed a great deal of the delinquency-linked problem of fatherlessness in the late 1950s and early 1960s. A decline in the incidence of family incompleteness was naturally to be expected after that time, since by 1963 persons born in 1945, the last year of the war, would have reached legal majority.

While it is apparently on the decline at present (of delinquents convicted by courts in the Belorussian Republic in 1966, 77.3 percent

TABLE 6 FAMILY SITUATIONS OF MOSCOW DELINQUENTS, TWO DISTRICTS

	Pervomaiskii district	Leninskii district			
Situation	1962	1962	1963	1964	1965
Lived with					
both parents	53.8%	56.0%	44.4%	53.9%	51.0%
mother only	31.1	34.7	47.9	30.7	31.0
father only	1.2	1.1	. . .	1.1	3.0
father and					
stepmother	2.0	2.3	2.2	1.1	. . .
mother and					
stepfather	3.2	5.9	4.4	7.7	12.0
others, though					
parents living	0.8	. . .	. . .	. . .	. . .
Orphans	2.8	1.0	1.1	5.5	3.0

Source: col. 1, O.I. Morozov *et al.*, "Opyt kompleksnogo obsledovaniia prichin i uslovii, sposobstvuiushchikh soversheniiu prestuplenii podrostkami," *Sovetskoe gosudarstvo i pravo*, No. 9 (1963), p. 114; cols. 2–5, S.S. Ostroumov, "Opyt provedeniia konkretnogo sotsiologicheskogo issledovaniia pravonarushenii sredi nesovershennoletnikh," *Vestnik Moskovskogo universiteta* (Series XII-law), No. 2 (1967), p. 31.

came from complete families [18]), the incidence of family incompleteness shows a tendency to stabilize and perhaps even a possibility of
future growth. First, the incidence of unwed motherhood remains relatively high in the USSR, and the adjustment problems of illegitimate
children are often great.[19] Second, divorce and desertion are serious
problems. With the liberalization of divorce laws in late 1965, the
supply of divorces came more into line with demand, leading to an 80
percent increase in divorces in 1966 over 1965. This demand level
was sustained in 1967.[20] Insofar as Soviet authors have been able to
judge, absence of a parent is proportionally greater among delinquents than among the population at large,[21] and current trends
would indicate little chance of this situation's undergoing substantial
alteration.[22]

While the USSR does *not* (as many Westerners assume) claim to be
a classless society, the categories in which Soviet statistics are often
expressed—worker, collective farmer, and employee—represent
rather gross distinctions,[23] and the relation of "class" to such phenomena as delinquency is a delicate matter for Soviet scholar and foreign
observer alike. Little has been published on this issue, and the studies
available present an unclear picture. A study of delinquency statistics over the period 1960–1964 in the Kirov *raion* (borough) of
Sverdlovsk [24] gave the following breakdown on delinquents' social origins: 73.0 percent from workers' families, 23.0 percent from employees' (i.e., general white collar) families, and 4.0 percent from collective farm families.[25] In judging the significance of this distribution,
we have available only the roughest sort of base figures: the percentage distribution of the total population of Sverdlovsk *oblast'* (including the whole city plus a number of smaller cities and rural areas) by
class from the 1959 census. According to these, the *oblast'* population
was 69.9 percent worker, 22.0 percent employee, and 8.0 percent
collective farmer.[26] The lack of a breakdown by percentage of families in each class and of data on average fertility by class further complicates the issue. One can only say on the basis of these data [27] that
the slightly higher proportion of worker-background delinquents and
lower proportion of those with collective farm backgrounds could be
expected naturally, when attention is concentrated, as here, on one
urban *raion*.

Another source gives the class distribution of inmates of the labor colony for juveniles in the East Kazakhstan *oblast'* of the Kazakh SSR in 1965. Of the inmates, 50.3 percent came from workers' families, 34.7 percent from those of employees, and 15.0 percent from collective farm families.[28] Parallel 1959 census data (the latest available) give this distribution for the total *oblast'* population: worker, 65.9 percent; employee, 18.9 percent; collective farmer, 15.1 percent.[29] While the Sverdlovsk figures were averaged over five years, beginning with the year after the census, the Kazakh figures are for only one year, six years after the census, and thus the picture given by the census may have undergone significant change over even the space of three or four years, modifying what seems roughly to be an *underrepresentation* of inmates from worker families, and an overrepresentation of those from employee families.

These figures, while in themselves not very informative, indicate the difficulty in attempting to relate delinquency to family background solely by using the measure of class. Parental educational level, while it does not determine class (many employees have lower levels of schooling than skilled workers, and many of the employees with more education have lower incomes than skilled workers who are less educated but in critical areas of the economy), may provide some hint as to whether delinquents tend to come from "disadvantaged" families. A Belorussian study [30] found markedly lower educational attainment among delinquents' parents than in a control group of adults. Of the latter, 41.6 percent had completed secondary school, while only 29.6 percent of delinquents' parents had. More notable was a large contingent of marginally educated delinquents' parents —22.5 percent of these had either *no* school or only primary (four years) schooling, while only 4.6 percent of the control group fell this low. The 1968 edition of the criminology textbook observes that parents of delinquents have educations generally "significantly lower" than the average nationwide for the adult population.[31] To what degree educational deficiencies of the parents are related to low income and general disadvantage, we cannot specify. Material deprivation is not often cited as a cause of delinquency. In the face of an undeniably sensitive issue, assertions are made that family incomes and living accommodations for delinquents are "average" by Soviet standards. While interpreting what "average" means in these circumstances would bring us into the complex area of assessing subjective feelings of relative deprivation, it is worthwhile, at least, to note two results of a study of juvenile recidivists: asked to evaluate their living conditions, 40.9 percent, the largest single contingent, rated them "unsatisfactory," and 51.8 percent, in explaining their motives for theft, said they stole to get money for "personal needs." [32] While there may be an element of rationalization in such responses, they are nonetheless interesting.

A related type of data—that specifying the occupations of delinquents at time of offense—is more readily available from Soviet sources. The official criminology textbook summarizes the results of research and review of court records by stating that between 15 and 27 percent of delinquents are drawn from students in day schools and other academic institutions, 13 percent from trade schools (under the direction of a separate ministry), 50 to 55 percent from working youth, and 12 percent from youth who "neither work nor study." [33] These figures, given their generality as national estimates, are roughly in line with less comprehensive Soviet studies.[34] In cases handled by the commissions on juvenile affairs, the different age profile produces, as might be expected, modifications in this distribution: students in academic tracks amount to 50 percent of cases, while workers decline to about one-fourth of all commission clients.[35]

Do these figures signify an overrepresentation of certain categories of youth among delinquents, or merely reflect the percentage of each category in the total population? Soviet sources themselves now affirm the former. According to the criminology text, workers are 2.5 times more likely to wind up in court than are trade school students, and 13.0 (!) times more likely to do so than adolescents in academic schools.[36] A study of the records of a commission on juvenile affairs in Sovetskii *raion* in Minsk, the capital of the Belorussian SSR, supports this trend. Taking delinquents by occupation as percentages of the totals of such occupational categories, 0.13 percent of "academic track" students, 0.53 percent of trade school students, and 4.10 percent of working youth were delinquent.[37] However, those without any occupation—the youths who "neither work nor study"—have, apparently, the greatest delinquent propensities. The study in Sovetskii *raion*, Minsk, found that 10.9 percent of this group were delinquent,[38] a finding supported by other studies as well.[39]

All these arguments receive further confirmation from a study conducted in the Estonian Republic (table 7) which, virtually uniquely among such studies, provides the occupational distribution of the entire age-eligible republican population as a control for the delinquent distributions.

The overrepresentation of young workers and those without occupation would lead one to expect that, as in many other countries, many Soviet delinquents will have learning problems and educational levels below those of their peers. Such does indeed seem to be the

TABLE 7   DELINQUENT FIRST OFFENDERS, RECIDIVISTS, AND
TOTAL AGE-ELIGIBLE POPULATION, BY OCCUPATIONS, ESTONIAN
SSR, 1964–1967

Occupation	All juveniles, 14–17	First Offenders	Recidivists
Studied	83.4%	24.4%	9.7%
Worked	6.4	47.1	58.3
Studied and Worked	8.2	10.9	7.7
Neither Worked nor studied	2.0	17.6	24.3
Totals	100.0%	100.0%	100.0%

Source: Adapted from Kh. A. Randalu, "Obrabotka dannykh statisticheskikh kartochek na podsudimykh," Sovetskoe gosudarstvo i pravo, No. 10 (1968), p. 92.

case. Soviet sources vary in their exact estimates but generally affirm that delinquents are from one or two [40] to three [41] years behind the average level of attainment of their age group. Frequently, the problem is complicated by the tendency of youths with academic and/or disciplinary problems to drop out of a school environment they find unrewarding, or to be, practically speaking, expelled by school administrators under the fiction of transfer to part-time evening schools for working youth.[42]

Readers familiar with juvenile delinquency in the United States and other Western countries will probably find that, despite its many gaps, the picture of Soviet delinquency presented here has many familiar elements, as well as some not so familiar. In general, the age, types of offense, educational experience, and family background of the Soviet delinquent do not appear strikingly dissimilar from his

counterparts elsewhere. This is true as well of the heavily urban concentration of delinquency; 75 percent of juvenile violations are said to
take place in cities, demonstrating an overrepresentation of urban
youth in such offenses by one and one-half.[43] (While well over half
the total USSR population now resides in urban areas, high rural
fertility produces a more even spread of children and adolescents
across the rural-urban line.) Soviet delinquents tend to commit their
offenses in groups. The proportion of such offenders among all delinquents, in numerous studies, seems fixed at around 75 percent.[44]
These groups, however, are generally rather small in number and
fluid in composition, bearing little resemblance to the organized fighting gangs of large American cities in the 1950s. On the whole, it
seems doubtful that we can speak of "gangs" at all in the Soviet case.
The instances of Soviet delinquents acting in concert frequently seem
to reflect a spontaneous and temporary coming together for the purpose of some relatively specific act.[45]

This, then, is a sketch of some aspects of Soviet delinquency, assembled from the statistical data Soviet sources make available. Despite the evident gaps, and despite the frustrations inherent in
dealing only with percentage distributions relating to unknown integers, such data are useful, both for the rough information they give us
on trends and tendencies within the structure of delinquency and as a
base from which to examine Soviet attempts to explain why delinquency still exists in a socialist state a half-century after its founding.
Such data may better serve illustrative purposes than attempts to
draw firm conclusions, but the possibilities of making any reasoned
observations about Soviet delinquency would be greatly reduced in
their absence.

WHAT CAUSES DELINQUENCY?
THE SOVIET VIEW

Isolating the causes of delinquency and other varieties of deviance is,
as Western social scientists well know, a knotty problem. Even as-

suming agreement on the content of the *notion* of causation, one can find students of delinquency parting company on what particular factor or factors explain its existence in a given social context.

While the concept of survivals of the past provides a frame in which Soviet scholars can place delinquency, it does not, as they now admit, explain the concrete aspects of its causation. At the most general level, the concept of survivals is an ideologically orthodox label and sets the limit for general characterizations of delinquency and other forms of deviance. Deviant behaviors are survivals of an outgrown but tenacious pre-socialist past; they are not, *cannot* be, symptoms of a "sick" society, for ideology decrees that Soviet society is not sick.

Despite the framework of orthodoxy in which discussions take place, there are, as we shall see, differences of emphasis in Soviet writings. They may not permit us to talk of fully developed schools of thought regarding Soviet delinquency, but they are nonetheless of considerable interest.

We may characterize Soviet thought on the causes of delinquency as consisting of two related trends. The first and most representative concentrates on examining institutional malfunctioning. It seeks the sources of delinquency in the failure of various concrete social institutions, such as the family, school, factory, and youth organization, to socialize and control youth. Prevention of delinquency is thus primarily a matter of increasing the effectiveness of these institutions. Such an approach involves, essentially, a denial that there are delinquency-provoking factors inherent in Soviet society and also denies that the delinquent is, *ab ovo*, a special type of person (he is made, not born). It seeks explanations in the workings of the infrastructure of Soviet society. Thus, it maintains ideological acceptability while admitting, as a practical matter, that the performances of concrete institutions of control and socialization both can be and are frequently flawed.°

The second trend, while not denying the impact of institutional

---

° Such an approach is, in effect, implied in the sort of data Soviet researchers collect, surveyed in the preceding section. Much of it (family background, school achievement, occupation, etc.) describes the linkage of the individual to institutions (or the lack of such linkages) that presumably affect his behavior.

malfunctioning, explores in greater depth the dynamics and characteristics of the adolescent male personality. It emphasizes the importance of the adolescent's spirit of adventure, self-assertiveness, and desire for independence from parental authority. Tensions generated by necessary limits on the gratification of such impulses may find their outlet in delinquent solutions, given certain peer-group and other influences. Without claiming that any adolescents are "born" delinquents, this approach raises the question of whether adolescence *itself*, especially as experienced by males, contains certain definable risks of deviance. Defenders of such an approach see the adolescent as a person not yet fully formed—one who is more pliable and susceptible to bad influences from other persons than a morally upright adult.

The significance of the difference between these approaches should not be overestimated. In one sense, the difference is mainly a matter of the relative attention given to factors of one order—institutions of socialization and control—rather than factors of another—personality characteristics—within a framework where the latter are seen largely as a product of the former. Delinquency remains a socially caused phenomenon rather than one biologically or psychologically preordained in some persons, and its social nature does not imply a diminution or denial of the delinquent's responsibility for his acts.[46] In another sense, however, the difference grows more significant, depending on the interpretations Soviet writers themselves make of it. Those who lean toward personality-related explanations risk the accusation (mainly from those of the institutional persuasion) that they are moving too close to the bio-psychological positions and concepts of criminal (or delinquent) types that were discredited at the end of the 1920s. Whether this is, in fact, true is another question.* At present, one can say that these two trends coexist as elements in Soviet thought on delinquency.

* We postpone consideration for the moment (see chapter 8) of a position taken by a few Soviet criminologists which *does* seem to flirt with some earlier ideas about psychological predispositions to deviance and which raises sensitive questions about the relationship between mental illness or abnormality and crime. This position, identified mainly with the Saratov jurist I.S. Noi, is not taken with regard to delinquency per se, but to crime as a whole, and will be considered in that context.

INSTITUTIONAL MALFUNCTIONING

The concerns of those who view delinquency as a product of institutional malfunctioning are many. One writer enumerates the following "direct causes": negative influences in the family (egotism, cynicism, irresponsibility, and apoliticism); similar influences from peers and superiors in school and factory; the effect of films and books with criminal or sexual themes; the influence of bourgeois propaganda aimed at the corruption of unstable youths; and tourist and trade contacts, one of whose purposes is moral and political subversion of youth. To this list he adds a number of "conditions," second-order factors which facilitate the operation of the direct causes: unnecessary absence of parental supervision; shortcomings in adherence to the eight-year compulsory education law and in securing employment for youths who have finished school; insufficient "upbringing work" (moral education) in schools and factories; failure to take account of the growth of the youth population and thus to plan ahead for increases in construction of schools, clubs, youth cafes, and other institutions; and ineffective work by law enforcement agencies and the courts.[47] From this long list, particular institutions are selected for more lengthy examination.

Most discussions of delinquency begin with the family. Despite many shifts in policy since the Revolution,[48] the family remains a vital institution in Soviet society. In the care, feeding, and basic socialization of children, it is the regime's junior partner, and it is as a partner, to whom certain rights and duties have been delegated, that the family is evaluated.

Shirking of parental duties and lack of concern with children's behavior are often attacked. Typical targets for the press are those indulgent parents said to assume unfoundedly that all is right with their children. The case of a youth who participated in several gang-rapings, and escaped the death penalty only because he was a minor, caused *Komsomol'skaia pravda's* commentator to warn parents of the "boomerang of permissiveness."[49] Upper-class parents who use their influence to spare their wayward offspring the attentions of the police are also condemned. An illustration is provided by an *Izvestiia* story: among other youths appearing one evening in a militia station in the city of Magnitogorsk on an assault charge was the son of the vice-chairman of the city Soviet's executive committee. The father intervened, bringing pressure to bear on the militiamen, with the result that the boy escaped with the lowest possible fine (15 rubles). The captain of the local militia called the newspaper's attention to the events, and the paper responded, not unexpectedly with a strong condemnation of the behavior of father and son.[50] In a later issue, the paper reported the measures taken. The intervening father received a "strict reprimand" from the city's Party committee and was relieved of his vice-chairmanship, while the delinquent son was ejected from the Komsomol and from the metallurgical institute at which he had been studying.[51]

Another problem stems not so much from unconcern as from parental readiness to grant their children anything they wish in the area of material goods. "Irresponsibility and egotistical attitudes" manifested by some youths are seen as unwanted consequences of increases in upper-class living standards, ". . . creating objective conditions for some parents to satisfy their children's immoderate demands, which in turn stimulates similar demands on the part of their classmates at school and their comrades at work and at home." [52] Even in families not so well off, as one writer observes, parents stretch their resources and "deny themselves much, if only their daughter or son may live no worse than many others." [53]

On the other hand, families where the discipline is *too* strict, where minor peccadilloes are met by disproportionate punishment, are also to be encountered, and take a share of the blame.

. . . Beating children unmercifully for any cause, and even without cause, . . . they do not understand or, more truthfully, do not wish to understand, that it is impossible to raise a human being in the family while not respecting him . . . they achieve nothing good in this way, nor can they achieve it.[54]

Attention should be drawn here to the role attributed to drunkenness in the failure to discharge fatherly duties. A letter to *Izvestiia* [55] from a 12-year-old whose father was a habitual drunkard provoked a flood of letters, many undoubtedly genuine, from all manner of Soviet citizens. Ensuing round-table discussions in the paper's pages generated sympathy for the complaining boy and expressions of stern condemnation for the father's behavior. Here, clearly, was an "unhealthy" family—an example of the environment which may cause children to turn to the street and eventually to delinquency. There is also concern over the *direct* bad example such fathers may give, as was voiced in a report from the prosecutor's office in Mogilev *oblast'* about a father and his teen-age son who caroused together in the streets until they came to the attention of the police.[56] Such parental behavior is viewed as a serious matter, and has provoked Soviet legal scholars to argue the necessity of simplifying the procedures for deprivation of parental rights by the courts, a penalty which, despite its availability, seems to be used relatively seldom.[57]

But not all parental failure is culpable, and the problem of *beznadzornost'* (lack of supervision) is larger than the number of negligent and irresponsible families. The Soviet emphasis on drawing women into the labor force and the economic necessity that impels them to enter it mean that the average Soviet family is one in which both parents work, a fact which Soviet writers increasingly recognize. Even good parents may lack time to give their children sufficient attention. Such writers propose more state and public aid to these average families and point out the need for reduction in mothers' working hours. The working wife, however, will remain; and it is unlikely that an achievement on which the regime prides itself—the guarantee of women's "right to work"—will be compromised by being linked with what may be an unwanted consequence, delinquency.

We have already noted above the high incidence of incomplete families in the histories of delinquents. This is a final point of concern for those who look to the family as one of the contexts in which forces promoting delinquency may arise. The one-parent family, whether it arises through death, legal divorce, or simple desertion, is viewed as a problem.* While nationwide figures are not available, it seems notable that a large number of divorces occur in families which already have children,[58] who may suffer from parental breakups. As one Soviet jurist writes:

* A fourth variant of the incomplete family, that of unwed mother-cum-child, is presumably also a contributor to problems of child supervision. Such families are not infrequent in the USSR, where the incidence of illegitimate births remains high.

The breakup of the family, whatever its causes, is similar to a serious infection. . . . [Its] consequences are expressed in the consciousness of the children, they influence the long-term formation of their character and often serve as the psychological basis which, in the presence of other unfavorable conditions leads to antisocial behavior.[59]

Next on the list of institutions whose failure to perform their tasks adequately is connected, in Soviet thought, to the causation of delinquency is the school system—the general academic schools as well as the trade schools, which produce, as we saw earlier, a healthy percentage of delinquents.

One of the most common complaints (and one hardly unique to Soviet society) concerns narrowness on the part of school administrators and teachers in understanding their functions. Technical and cultural education are not enough, they are told; they must also make themselves responsible for the moral and ethical upbringing of Soviet youth.

The time has come, in our opinion, for a substantial reorganization of instruction and upbringing in the schools along the lines of thorough intensification of civic and legal upbringing, of molding a sense of collectivism and of responsibility for one's actions and of moral tempering of the personality. Without solution of these key problems it is impossible to complete the establishment of conditions for the eradication of juvenile delinquency.[60]

Teachers and administrators are taken to task for limiting themselves to instruction in academic matters and leaving the "private" matter of pupils' conduct to their parents and the police. Reluctance to broach some delicate topics to students lacking orientation is also criticized. Writing in *Izvestiia*, S. Kurashov, the Minister of Public Health of the USSR, took teachers to task for their failure to give frank instruction and advice to adolescents about sex and venereal disease, condemning this apparent squeamishness as "hypocrisy," [61] while a law professor complains that

the school, the teacher, as a rule, stand aside from [this] problem. On questions of sex young people do not have any contact with pedagogues. Pedagogical and other literature hushes up [sex] as though it were something shameful and forbidden.[62]

Soviet educators are admonished to see that their solicitude does not end at the school door. While it is recognized that teaching and administrative duties may leave a teacher little time for organizing extracurricular activities,[63] demands are made that schools, as well as other institutions, see that nonclass hours are spent in useful, worthwhile pursuits. Ideally,

the school should become the organizing center of all upbringing work with youth . . . [it] should become the organizer of youth's evening leisure, turn into a place of leisure, where youth might spend an evening, dance, play chess, occupy themselves in favorite hobby groups or meet with interesting people.[64]

The volume of complaints about shortcomings indicates that, on the whole, this ideal is far from being realized.

If apathy toward the inculcation of desirable moral and social attitudes on the part of teachers and administrators is viewed as a problem, even more serious is the tendency of some school personnel to meet the challenges posed by academic and disciplinary problem children by simply excluding them altogether from the academic track. What is described frequently as a dropout problem reflects in many cases a "force-out" procedure.

One of the widespread means of getting rid of so-called "difficult" pupils is transferring them to evening schools for working youth. In the majority of cases transfer to evening schools of students 12 to 15 years of age is accomplished directly on the initiative of teachers and school administration. Exerting pressure on parents or on the students themselves even without the consent of the parents, some teachers and school directors force them and others to submit applications for transfers to evening schools.[65]

In practice, this means that despite the eight-year compulsory universal education law, many such "transfers" leave school with fifth- or sixth-grade educations. The evening schools help little in such cases, for the transfers have even less motivation to study in lower-level evening schools. Many of them have no jobs at all, although one of the requirements of the evening schools is that one be, in fact, a "working youth." [66] Statistics indicate that approximately half of those in the evening schools drop out entirely in their first year.[67] Many such youth are thus added to the ranks of "those who neither work nor study"—the highest delinquency-risk category. Allowing (or forcing) youths to drop out is criticized as "prematurely releasing" them from school discipline and from "pedagogical demands which stimulate development of the habits of proper social behavior." The effects are seen as lasting, since

lagging behind in level of general education makes for impoverishment of the personality and a low cultural level, which in turn facilitates the assimilation of anti-social views and habits, breeds instability in the face of alien influences, and, in a dangerous situation, hinders self-control and the correct self-evaluation of motives and actions.[68]

To rectify this situation, it was suggested in the early 1960s that the power to transfer youths to evening schools be taken away from school administrators, and that they be empowered to effect transfers only with the consent of the responsible Commission on Juvenile Affairs.[69] Previously, such decisions required the *presence* of a commission representative, but not the commission's agreement: and this requirement was, in fact, frequently ignored.[70] The suggested change was made in a revision of the statute [71] on juvenile affairs commissions, but there are indications that the requirement is still being circumvented.

Other problems crop up in the trade schools—run by a separate ministry of professional-technical training—which many Soviet adolescents attend either after completing eight years of general schooling or, frequently, after having left short of that level. While some students enter these schools quite willingly, seeking to learn a skilled trade, many are simply the rejects of the system of general education.[72] The high concentration in these schools of what have been called "undisciplined and unsuccessful" youth raises particular problems in the areas of maintaining order and providing behavioral as well as technical guidance.

The trade schools, however, are notably short of the resources necessary to accomplish such a task. School personnel are not nearly so well educated nor so well prepared pedagogically as are the staffs of academic schools. The instructors themselves are frequently blamed for socializing their charges into such habits as heavy drinking and cursing or even involving them in thefts and other offenses.[73] In fact, some trade schools seem to be dumping grounds for undereducated or incompetent adult staff members as well as for students. "Many" of those engaged in teaching trades are "insufficiently qualified, with a low general educational level. Very often, by their level of development and education the students turn out to be above their teachers." [74] This general observation hardly overstates the case: sometimes the trade schools wind up employing extremely questionable characters. One press report reveals that two local party officials, apprehended for embezzlement and eased out of their positions, received jobs in the trade school system—one as director of a school training agricultural cadres, the other as head of the Marxism-Leninism department at a machine-building institute.[75] It is hardly surprising that shortcomings in the work of the trade schools are noticed and cited as contributing to delinquency.

Western students of delinquency may not be accustomed to thinking of the factory as an institution of general socialization; but such it is in the Soviet view, and its successes and failures are a matter of concern. In contemporary Soviet ideology, work is seen not only as a material but also as a *moral* necessity for man. "Socially useful labor," performed in cooperation with one's coworkers—the *kollektiv*—is viewed as playing a major, perhaps *the* major role in "making" men. Given this theoretical centrality of work in the human experience, it is logical that, in practice, the effectiveness of the factory in turning adolescent workers into productive and nontroublesome citizens is an important question. Management, factory-level party and trade union organizations, and the worker *kollektiv* as a whole are the state's "delegates" in the socialization of young workers. Yet the statistics on delinquency among young workers noted earlier testify to the well-founded nature of Soviet criminologists' complaints about how poorly these delegates sometimes discharge their duties.

When blame is being apportioned, management seems generally to come at the head of the line. Factory managers are castigated for assigning already-trained youths to jobs having nothing to do with their specialties,[76] for failure to organize on-the-job training programs for those who lack skills [77] (such persons are often used in unskilled, dead-end jobs), and for a general failure to perceive the importance of a young worker's early experiences on the job and their effect on his future behavior. Some managers are reluctant to hire young people at all, thus depriving them of "socially useful work and the beneficial influence of the workers' *kollektiv*," [78] and others fire young workers without sufficient justification.[79] Managerial indifference is held to cause young workers to feel "abandoned" before they have adjusted to jobs, to lose interest in their work, and thus to contribute to a high rate of job-changing among youth. Fledgling workers are also illegally exploited. A member of the Soviet executive committee in Riga reported frequent violations of labor codes which fix maximum working hours for minors, a complaint not unique to that city.[80]

While such conditions, fostering alienation of young workers, may well contribute to their relatively high rate of delinquency, management is unlikely to attempt or to be able to change them significantly. In the first place, hiring adolescents is generally economically disadvantageous. It seems probable that the great majority of 15- and 16-year-olds seeking jobs are unequipped with skills. According to one source, over two-thirds of the adolescents beginning work in 1964 lacked sufficient specialized training.[81] Labor laws make it relatively difficult to hire 15-year-olds who want work; they restrict the working day of 15-year-olds to four hours and that of 16- and 17-year-olds to six. These young workers, however, are to receive the same pay for the shorter day as an adult worker of the same specialty and skill rating.[82] But many of these restrictions, as well as others, are frequently violated by managers. "Instances are still not uncommon of giving minors overtime work, of using them in heavy or dangerous labor, in evening and night shifts, and then not for six, but for seven and eight hours, on the same level as adults." [83] Such attempts by management to get what they may consider a full day's work for similar pay complicate the lives of adolescent workers who may be attempting to upgrade their skills on the job [84] or to broaden their general education by attending evening schools. Combinations of unskilled work and illegally imposed overtime in the plant are conducive to neither. As a study of young workers in Sverdlovsk noted, their situations are in many cases unsatisfactory.

At most enterprises the working youngsters were found to be in difficult circumstances. Their conditions of work were characterized by the following: frequent changes in work place, turnover of instructors, lengthy stoppages associated with poor organization of work, and rush-work. Naturally all this cannot help but affect the quality of production training. As a result, after completing their training, many youngsters do not have the necessary theoretical knowledge and practical skills; they fail to fulfill their work norms for extended periods and permit considerable spoilage, which leads to low earnings and frequently to attempts to leave the job. This creates personnel turnover and a deterioration of the economic indices of the enterprise.[85]

Management is thus caught between two demands which often conflict: fulfillment of production targets and socialization of young and frequently unskilled workers. Given the pressures on managers to perform, to show consistent growth rates and efficient labor utilization, it can hardly be expected that they devote much energy to vaguely defined tasks of socialization when this energy could be applied to clearly defined production goals.[86] Criminologists seem better at stating the problem than solving it.

It is time to have done with the situation where at some factories and construction sites the administration . . . concerned with the fulfillment of the plan, looks through its fingers at [ignores] the task of the moral upbringing of youth.

Absolutely, the fulfillment of production plans is a first-order task. But here one cannot forget another side of the production process, which has no less important significance—how that generation which has been called on to complete the construction of communism will grow up.[87]

Youth's adult coworkers in the factory also receive a share of the blame, either for ignoring adolescents new to work or, on the other hand, for providing a sort of socialization not at all foreseen in the programmatic exhortations addressed to them. Although they are supposed to inculcate in their younger comrades a spirit of pride in their job, their shop, their factory as a whole, and bring them into the life of the *kollektiv*, the workers' traditions the newcomer learns may well be connected with heavy drinking on paydays and other occasions and lead to sorry consequences.

In an article entitled "Inciters," *Izvestiia* related the story of a young tinworker on his way to evening classes with his first pay envelope in his pocket. Accosted by an older co-worker, who cited the tradition of "washing down" one's first pay, the youth decided to skip class for the night. Later, after an evening of heavy drinking, the two reeled down the street insulting passersby until stopped by a member of the *druzhiny* (people's auxiliary militia). The drunken youth attacked him and ended the evening in custody for assault.[88] Such instances suggest that many Soviet blue-collar workers are still far from conceiving of themselves as responsible for providing moral guidance in behavior off the job to their young colleagues.[89]

Leisure is another problem for the young worker. Youths in the la-

bor force have a good deal of time, which need not be spent on home-
work or other activities that limit their student peers. Though their
incomes may be low, they have some money to spend. Whether they
use these resources constructively or not is of concern to the regime,
which demands that the factory see to its workers' leisure. Besides attending to the adjustment of young workers to adult responsibilities
on the job, management is exhorted to provide various extracurricular
activities for the young worker and to encourage him to continue his
education. But management has other, more pressing tasks, and
"uplifting" leisure activities may not attract much interest. Noting the
low educational and cultural level of many young workers, one Soviet
author writes that of a group of them who committed offenses in Leningrad in 1964 and 1965, "only 6 percent had attended technical
study circles and only 5 percent had taken part in amateur arts." [90]
While the state may consider that adolescents already out of school
may need the cultural influence of theaters, museums, and other
places of leisure, the young workers can be hard to motivate. On the
basis of data drawn from a poll of 4,000 young Leningrad workers, a
researcher observed that "the lower the general-educational and cultural level of those questioned, the more rarely does one come across
such words as theater, concert hall, exhibit museum, youth cafe." [91]
Nor do youth cafes and the like provide complete solutions, since

unfortunately, in their economic and organizational structures the youth
cafes are indistinguishable from public catering enterprises and continue to
be conventional "trade points." The cafes' workers are concerned about receipts, which here too are the decisive index. And the only way to increase
these receipts appreciably is to sell alcoholic beverages. In public catering,
alcoholic beverages account still for about one-third of the plan.[92]

Sporadic campaigns to exert greater control and improve the atmosphere in which working youth spend their free time seem to run
aground with monotonous regularity. This may be attributable to
lack of enthusiasm among working-class youth for "organized" leisure
in an already "administered" society, as well as to the conflict of social and economic motivations apparent in such enterprises as youth
cafes, where economic considerations most often prevail. The fact
that a juvenile offender may have had no access to the sort of leisure
facilities regarded as healthy, however, is not taken as an excuse for

his act. Those who would indulge him on this basis are accused of oversimplification and excessive "non-socialist" humanism.[93] But the high delinquency rate among those who live outside the school or work organizations which are supposed to influence behavior in the proper direction, among those "who neither work nor study," probably guarantees that organizing youth's free time will remain at least an ideal for some time to come.

Finally, the organs charged with direct moral training and political socialization of youth, especially the Komsomol, which accepts persons 14 years old and over, receive their share of criticism for shortcomings that reduce their effectiveness and contribute to delinquency. These shortcomings include lack of adequate training for those engaged in youth organization work, bureaucratic formalism and inflexible procedures that stifle enthusiasm, lack of understanding of youth problems by Komsomol administrators, and a general ineptitude in harnessing the energies of young people and directing them into creative channels. As Khrushchev remarked in his address to the 1958 Komsomol congress,

an inept, or, even worse, a bureaucratic handling of matters can seriously harm the upbringing of young people and drive them away from the League. Life in League organizations should literally seethe and initiative overflow. Then everybody will find something interesting to do and young people will not complain that life is boring in League organizations, whereas today you hear such complaints frequently.[94]

Little seems to have changed since 1958.[95] The youth organizations, we are told, show insufficient vigor in the struggle against "petty hooliganism"[96] and fail to provide the sort of preventive upbringing which would put an end to this phenomenon.[97] The root of the Komsomol's difficulties may, however, lie deeper than the shortcomings summarized above indicate. Active involvement in the Komsomol, or at least maintaining a clean record in it, is important for people in higher educational institutions, for the "upwardly mobile." It is not nearly so important, nor indeed attractive, to young workers or dropouts. Komsomol work is weak, and membership low, in factories and trade schools.[98] Whatever positive impact on behavior the Komsomol might have, the youth organization is not reaching those segments of the youth population from which the majority of delinquents are drawn.

There are other themes [99] frequently taken up by those who think mainly in the vein of institutional malfunctioning, but those just presented are the major ones. Though it may be belaboring the obvious, two points can be made in summarizing this perspective. First, the institutional malfunctions referred to are infrastructural. They represent deviations from the ideal in *particular* contexts—in *some* families, in *some* schools, in *some* factories. No attempt is made (or can be made, given the prevailing ideology) to knit these together into a picture of Soviet society problem-ridden as a whole. Soviet criminologists do not follow some of their Western counterparts in attempting to explain delinquency by endemic conditions, "criminogenic" factors that characterize the society *in toto*.[100] Ideologically and (as a practical matter) politically, such a characterization is not an available alternative.

Second, the institutional malfunction approach resembles many other theories of delinquency and crime causation in that it traces the problem at hand—delinquency—to other problems; it explains one deviation in terms of others that constitute its presumed cause. Putting it simply, "bad causes bad." Weak socialization in the family and unconcern by school personnel and factory management do not always cause an adolescent subjected to them to become delinquent; but they explain, it is argued, a great deal of the delinquency problem. This following of the principle that like causes like has an important effect: with few exceptions, it closes off the possibility of examining delinquency as an unplanned consequence of major social processes regarded as progressive—most notably for the USSR, industrialization and urbanization. While Western social scientists have tended, with various degrees of specificity, to link increases in various forms of deviance to pressures and strains engendered by rapid social change and by the quality of urban industrial life, Soviet writers have not gone along. Claiming that the processes of industrialization and urbanization as they took place under capitalism were indeed productive of crime and delinquency, they argue that the same processes under socialism are completely different in their effects.[101] There are recent signs that Soviet criminologists are coming to grips with the problems of urban life [102] (as they must if they are to provide a coherent explanation of the higher per capita rate of juvenile offenses in the cities); but it seems likely that, in accordance with the same logic which prompts many investigations of the causes of social problems, they will continue for some time to look most readily to other problems to explain delinquency.

THE PERSONALITY APPROACH

The other trend in explanations of delinquency, which focuses on adolescent personality characteristics, can be explained at lesser length than the institutional malfunctioning approach. (As will be seen in a later chapter, this personality-centered approach, when applied to explaining the criminal behavior of adults, received, and to some degree continues to receive, a very critical reception. But the fact that Soviet criminal law makes the distinctions necessary to separate juvenile delinquency from crime—and decrees different penal measures for delinquents—makes it logical that some theoretical explication of what the peculiarities of adolescence really are should be acceptable.) It is a basically social-psychological approach that considers the adolescent in the context of his environment, and how that environment may work on the adolescent personality to cause deviant behavior.

It must not be forgotten that due to such characteristics of the transitional age period as insufficiency of experience in life, the tendency to imitate, the inability to evaluate correctly one thing or another, weak development of the system of "restraints", etc., youths fallen into unfavorable conditions of life and upbringing, in a negative environment, may prove to be relatively susceptible to alien influences.[103]

Thus, the adolescent is seen as a less stable individual "system" than the adult. His equilibrium is more easily disturbed. Since the years of adolescence are seen as ones in which intellectual and moral development are still not complete, mistaken perceptions may also play a role in delinquent acts.[104]

In practice there are not a few cases known where the direct psychological cause of an adolescent's committing one crime or another was a distorted understanding of the basic ethical content of such categories as friendship, comradeship, treachery, courage, cowardice, etc. . . . often a juvenile decides to take part in a [crime] . . . to a significant degree [only] because he sees in this a manifestation of comradeship . . .[105]

Illegal acts may flow as well from a general striving on the part of the male adolescent to assert his independence and maturity.

In the most extreme instances, the striving for independence in combination with a craving for adventure, for the unknown, the heroic, pushes the adolescent to running away from home, in order to "see the world," "enjoy freedom." This running away may now and then be connected with law-breaking: theft of articles and money needed for the road, acquisition of weapons, etc. Not understanding and often not taking account of all these characteristics of growth, parents and teachers essentially deprive themselves of the possibility of influencing youth, guiding his moral development, and directing his behavior.[106]

Although they recognized the role a striving for self-assertion, natural to the adolescent, may play in precipitating delinquent behavior, Soviet writers give increasing attention to adolescent conformism and imitation—tendencies that condition the way in which this quest for self-assertion and independence from parents may be acted out. As the young adolescent becomes a member of groups and acquires non-adult "significant others," his behavior will be affected, for good or ill.

In the period of adolescence the direction of imitation is determined by the opinion of a group of companions, who are authoritative for and close to the [adolescent], with whom he shares general interests and opinions.[107]

In addition to being more easily led by his peer group than an adult, the adolescent may find models for imitation, new sources of behavioral cues, in persons who seem different from himself (and therefore interesting) or more experienced. Lacking the critical sense developed through experience, even "model" adolescents may thus be drawn into what is regarded as dangerous company.

Adolescents of weak-willed, indecisive character often strive for friendship with strong-willed, energetic persons. Such persons sometimes turn out to be experienced criminals (most often adults) or adolescents themselves, who appear in the eyes of their peers worthy of imitation, "heroic," etc., although possibly they also possess extremely low moral qualities.[108]

Adolescence is a time of testing, of measuring the degree to which one is esteemed in the eyes of others. Recognition of one's increasing maturity by parents, of one's developing capabilities by teachers, is important. For those who fail to gain recognition in these ways, other means may be sought, including antisocial behavior.

Chronic failure in school and at home promotes the formation of a feeling of [one's] own lack of worth. At the same time, this feeling is counterbalanced by the urge for self-assertion. This urge for even momentary recognition in the collective often takes the form of wanting to "make a showing," even though it may be a negative one.[109]

Antisocial behavior, then, may flow from motives far from antisocial in themselves. The delinquent may be acting out, in an easily available way, tensions whose roots may be relatively obscure. As the adolescent grows, he becomes increasingly interested in the world of mechanical objects, in the mastery of skills which are part of the adult world. While this shows his growth toward adulthood, it may, depending on the circumstances, take an unhealthy direction, as in the case of a teenage radio enthusiast.

Even basically healthy interests and fascinations may take on a distorted character. Valentine Levin was fascinated by radio from the seventh grade . . . [he] often hung around radio stores where he became acquainted with people who turned out to be "sharp dealers" and speculators. Gradually his occupation with radio from fascination became for Levin a profitable business. He began to construct receivers for sale, and was not squeamish about getting parts from clearly dubious sources, and began himself to speculate in them. This new activity hindered his normal study in the institute where he had enrolled after finishing secondary school. For failures and absences he was expelled from the institute. And soon he was . . . brought to responsibility for speculation. . . .[110]

The success of adult instigators or more experienced adolescents in drawing the young into illegal activity is attributed by some authors almost as much to "suggestibility," credulity, and "tendency to imitate" [111] as to deep moral flaws in young offenders. While the responsibility of the juvenile for his acts is not challenged as a legal matter, some formulations do tend to depart from a strictly free-will model of the actor.

[T]he peculiarities of adolescents in the emotional-volitional sphere lead not infrequently to the situation where the same persons, in different (and even sometimes the same) situations, conduct themselves in a completely different manner, alternating between sudden and sharp emotional outbursts and model restraints, a thoughtful approach to the selection of a pattern of action, etc. . . . The peculiarities of the adolescent's psyche may in a number of instances lower his ability to withstand harmful influences.[112]

Soviet writers recognize that adolescents differ from each other, just as adults, so that the characterizations of the adolescent personality presented here do not fit all with mechanical precision. The particular, widely shared characteristics of an age group should not obscure important individual differences which influence how adolescents act; and those who deal with delinquents, especially the judges who must settle the question of what is to be done with the offender, are advised to keep this in mind.[113] Seemingly similar adolescents may differ greatly in their levels of immaturity.

The degree to which this completely natural "defectiveness" is manifested is different, even among adolescents of the very same age. It depends on a whole set of factors of a social nature (level of education and training, upbringing, work, etc.).[114]

Thus, in the end, a great deal in the personality of the adolescent will depend on the institutions, educational and otherwise, that encompass his life. The personality-centered approach does not question the relevance of institutional malfunctioning for delinquency, but it differs in the subject that it places at the center of attention. It represents an attempt to supply a social-psychological model of the juvenile personality, filling a gap in the institutional malfunctioning perspective. The latter, working from a concept of deviant "immediate environments" created by family, school, or factory shortcomings and the like, linked these to delinquency rather mechanically, without any attempt to specify how their impact is mediated by the specific properties of the adolescent personality. Developing the concept of the personality was a difficult business (as some sharp criticisms of A.B. Sakharov's 1961 work, *On the Personality of the Criminal and the Causes of Crime in the U.S.S.R.*, a pioneering work in this area, showed), since it involved linking certain morally neutral personality characteristics (see chapter 8) of adolescents, albeit indirectly, with a potential for deviance. Some interpreted concentration on the personality of delinquents as a challenge to the thesis of the nature of delinquency and crime as socially caused phenomena and, as we have noted, saw dangers of a return to ideas of psychologically or organically conditioned criminal types. Nonetheless, the concept of the personality has established its place in Soviet criminology and, although supporters of different trends may disagree over its content and role, they all agree on the need for its further study.

This account of juvenile delinquency in the Soviet Union and the attempts of Soviet criminologists to explain its causes is inevitably incomplete. The USSR does not publish statistics on the overall dimensions of delinquency, nor do the statistics available allow us to make any worthwhile projections of the unknown overall figures. It has not been the author's intention to base this description of delinquency on statistics alone; but a survey of these statistics, in conjunction with other data provided by Soviet sources, yields a picture of Soviet delinquency that is at the same time both reasonably coherent and somewhat familiar. Delinquents (at least those who come to the attention of the police and criminologists °) seem to be recruited from relatively disadvantaged strata in Soviet urban society. While the distance from top to bottom, in terms of living standards and the like, may not be so great in the USSR as in some Western countries (though this in itself is open to some question), it is nonetheless hard to traverse. The adolescent from a working-class family will frequently find that, for a variety of reasons, he may not do so well in school as his peers from more culturally advantaged backgrounds. Dropping out after six or seven years of school with an indifferent or poor record, he finds only menial jobs available with little perceived opportunity for advancement; and even these jobs are scarce. Entering a trade school, he may find the instructors unqualified, uninterested, and incapable of dealing with a population of students similar in many ways to himself. Neither he nor his peers will find museums, theaters, or hobby circles—approved forms of leisure—very attractive. He has little to offer by way of marketable knowledge or skills to Soviet society, and it offers him correspondingly little. Is it going too far to speculate that his frustrations and boredom may find some outlet in delinquent behavior, whether aimed at the acquisition of goods he does not possess or violent, aggressive behavior with no particular aim in view? This, at least, must be a partial explanation. The Soviet delinquent's problems are not so acute as those felt by ghetto dwellers in the United States; nor, perhaps, does he suffer as much comparative disadvantage. But they are acute enough.

° Just as crime and delinquency statistics in the West reflect unequal access to resources such as legal counsel, informal influence, and the like (resulting in a probable underrepresentation of high-status offenders in official records), such may be the case in the USSR. Examples earlier in this chapter show that fathers are ready to use influence to hush up the deeds of their children, and it may be presumed that many of them succeed.

This is not, of course, the whole picture. Delinquency among upper- and middle-class youth must be explained in another manner. But the bulk of the problem, as it is presented in Soviet sources and as it appears to the outside observer, seems to be lodged in the urban working classes, much as it is in the West. While this is not the place to assess the adequacy of Soviet theorizing about the causes of delinquency, it can be said that the data they collect may be leading the theorists to a greater interest in this accumulation of disadvantage that characterizes many delinquents. Moves in this direction will proceed slowly, since theorists must contend with ideological rhetoric proclaiming that poverty, exploitation, and unemployment have been eradicated in the USSR. Such proclamations are of little help in fostering frank examination of those qualities of urban industrial life which seem to produce gradations of disadvantage, in the Soviet Union as well as in the West.

7

DELINQUENCY: PREVENTION AND CORRECTION

THE SOVIET RESPONSE to the challenge posed by delinquency includes both measures of intervention, aimed at preventing the occurrence of delinquent acts, and corrective measures which, through punishment and resocialization, aim at the rehabilitation of juvenile offenders. In their writings, Soviet specialists emphasize both preventive and corrective measures, while generally accepting the notion of ounces of prevention equalling pounds of cure. In the USSR preventive and corrective measures are closely linked, at least in theory. Preventive measures, as applied to youths whose deviant attitudes or lack of parental supervision make them appear as high delinquency risks, include corrective elements—attempts to change the attitudes or the situations which create the risk. On the other hand, "corrective" measures employed by the courts and the Commissions on Juvenile Affairs, whether they leave a juvenile offender at liberty or dictate his placement in an institution, also attempt to prevent further offenses —on his part and, by setting a deterrent example, on the part of others who thus become aware of the possibility of punishment for delinquent acts. Distinctions can, however, be made between measures in accordance with their *predominance* of "preventive" or "corrective" content, and it is in this order that we shall deal with them.

PREVENTIVE MEASURES

Measures aimed at delinquency prevention vary greatly in their degrees of specificity. Some reflect the general societal commitment to providing the environment and conditions for effective adolescent socialization *in toto,* while others are more directly geared to influencing youths already marked by some behavioral problem. Measures of the first sort can be summarized as:

1. "Increasing the material security, the cultural level and consciousness of citizens of the USSR" through "the construction of communism";

2. Inculcation of theoretical knowledge and "principles of a communist world-view, preparedness for productive work for the good of society" through the educational system;

3. Improving the conditions of adjustment to independent adult life for minors in the realm of work through setting up realistic hiring quotas, organizing production training, improving working conditions, facilitating continuation of education on part-time basis, and bringing young workers into the life of the *kollektiv* and under its patronage through ceremonies which foster pride in one's job and factory;

4. The work of youth organizations in organizing and administering facilities and programs which direct youths toward healthy interests and approved modes of utilizing their leisure time.[1]

As the reader will note, these measures are largely descriptions of the way various socializing institutions—the school, the factory, the youth organization—"should" operate. They are the reverse mirror image of the institutional malfunctioning Soviet writers cite as contributing to delinquency. Elimination of such malfunctioning is seen as bringing Soviet society closer to the point where delinquency will be "eradicated as a social phenomenon." At this point, delinquency will be so rare and random an occurrence that no talk of "rates" and their rise or fall will be necessary.[2] Whether such an optimistic prognosis is justified by Soviet reality is surely debatable. But it does illustrate two points extremely relevant to a discussion of delinquency prevention and correction: first, that delinquency is a socially caused phenomenon, to be coped with by manipulation and improvement of the social environment; and second, that the individual is, by and large, perfectible, given the proper social environment and a correct approach to influencing his behavior. Within this context, talk of ultimate eradication becomes more understandable.

Preventive efforts which focus more directly on youths with "problems" may be divided into three groups: first, "measures of aid to minors in harmful living and upbringing conditions"; second, "upbringing measures" to keep minors who have already committed petty violations from further progress along the criminal path; and third, "measures of correction and re-education" for those who have already committed more serious offenses, to insure their readjustment to society and to prevent recidivism.[3] (The last two anticipate the preventive content of corrective measures.)

Measures of the first type include the efforts of bodies such as the Commissions on Juvenile Affairs and the "children's rooms" of police stations to locate families that, due to illness, work schedules, divorce, or other reasons, cannot supervise their children and arrange for aid to them. Aid from these bodies may take the form of placing the minor in a boarding school, or under the wardship of a public-spirited citizen who volunteers for such duty, or of rendering some form of help to the family unit itself. The Commissions on Juvenile Affairs are also charged with arranging employment in local enterprises for youths who leave school, in order to insure that they do not join the ranks of those who neither work nor study.[4] In cases where the family problem is one of chronic drunkenness, cruelty, or criminality on the part of the parents themselves, commissions may institute proceedings for the legal deprivation of parental rights.

In another category we find the attempts of the bodies mentioned

above and their public auxiliaries to "detect and do away with conditions" contributing to offenses by minors.[5] Executing this general
commission involves locating the factors which presumably contrib-
uted to an offense: shortcomings in school, factory or youth organization, illegal sale of alcohol to minors, or some other deviation from
approved patterns. Here the targets are not predelinquent minors, but
those who have already committed violations and the conditions
which are supposed to have influenced their acts. For habitual petty
violators, police children's rooms may arrange, as in the case of predelinquent youth, to assign adult guardians to oversee their behavior. Alternatively, a case may be considered in the offender's presence
by the *kollektiv* of his school or factory. Upbringing work (*vospitatel'naia rabota*) may be conducted with him by a member of the
public auxiliaries of the local police.

Soviet sources make much of the "widespread participation" of the
public in delinquency prevention activities. The organizational forms
of this participation vary.

Parents' committees, organized on the basis of residence (parents
from the same block of apartment buildings) or place of work, are
among the forms most frequently encountered. These are led, for the
most part, by lower-level Party or Komsomol activists and work in
cooperation with school personnel. These are not parent-teacher organizations in the American sense. School personnel, as representatives
of the regime and as its agents in child training, enjoy certain prerog-
atives in the criticism of parental performance, and the flow of communication at meetings frequently tends to be one way. Two main
functions are entrusted to the parents' committees. First, they gather
to "exchange child-rearing experience" and to cooperate with authorities in the improvement of leisure facilities and the supervision of lei-
sure-time activities. Second, it is their duty to apply social pressure to
other parents who are not bringing up their children correctly. However, with the preponderance of families in which both parents work,
day-to-day participation in supervisory activities often falls to the
grandparent generation, pensioners and unemployed women who can
be present in apartment courtyards and other places where children
congregate during working hours. They supervise informal sports and
oversee the hobby circles organized to provide the young with con-

structive leisure.[6] Due to gaps in age and outlook, personality con-flicts occasionally develop between these senior citizens and their younger charges, which are reflected in press criticism of the offi-ciousness and inflexibility with which pensioners sometimes perform their tasks.

Parents' committees organized on a factory basis arrange after-work lectures by school personnel, local Party and state officials, and other figures, as well as discussing problems of child-rearing. In applying the aforementioned social pressures to negligent parents, both types of committee may convoke "courts" to discuss the cases before them. Penalties such as public reprimands or exhibition of one's picture, with appropriate caption, on a "board of dishonor" in factory or office are imposed.[7] Even the arena of "socialist competition" in the factory has been invaded. In some contests for honorary titles or bonuses, a shop or factory may lose points not only if output is low but also if the academic performance or behavior of workers' children gives evi-dence of parental negligence.[8]

The public *aktivs,* groups of unpaid auxiliaries attached to the chil-dren's rooms of the police and to the Commissions on Juvenile Af-fairs, discharge, on paper at least, a large variety of preventive functions. *Sovetskaia iustitsiia* [9] described in one issue what it appar-ently regarded as a model *aktiv,* working with the police. About sixty persons of various professions, including writers, doctors, students, and managers of apartment blocks, made up the *aktiv,* which was di-vided into four subgroups. The first worked with young offenders on suspended sentences, on parole, or recently released from correctional institutions. Its work involved monitoring the activities and associa-tions of its charges in order to prevent backsliding. The next group conducted preventive work in apartment blocks, organizing excur-sions, hobby clubs, and other leisure activities for children living there, and generally checking on their after-school and weekend be-havior. A third group cooperated with the schools in its district, and with parents' committees and teachers' councils, in helping children who were behind in their studies, as well as exerting influence on children whose behavior in school was disruptive. The fourth group investigated children's family situations in order to expose conditions which might contribute to delinquency and rendered aid to families that needed it.

Another model *aktiv* directed its attention to those who had just completed the compulsory eight-year school, locating those who were not continuing their formal educations. Local factory managers were informed of youths in need of job training and employment and were requested to take on their fair share of the contingent.[10]

Not all preventive activity on the part of the public, however, involves group action. During the 1960s, increasing attention came to be directed at individual work, through a system of wardship (*shefstvo*) aimed at establishing a more personal and permanent link in delinquency prevention—in a sense, the Soviet equivalent of a big brother program.[11] It involved the assignment of an adult or an older youth, usually a Komsomol member, to a minor from an incomplete or unstable family or to a person on suspended sentence or parole, in order to fill the gap left by parental absence or unconcern or to help with readjustment.[12] A veteran worker might be assigned to a young worker to help him adjust to adult status and the demands of factory life. The volunteer's work involved meeting with his ward two or three times a week, maintaining a friendly relationship, and avoiding lectures and reprimands. Personal example, encouragement of the youth's pride in his school or labor brigade, and a generally attentive concern with his ward's problems were seen as the means the guardian should employ in encouraging the ward to behave responsibly.[13] In the early to mid-1960s, this program of individual work with juveniles seems to have been largely a matter of "local" initiative on the part of juvenile affairs commissions, police precincts, factories, or other organizations. In 1967, however, the RSFSR Supreme Soviet approved a special "Statute on Public Guardians of Juveniles," [14] in an apparent attempt to give some formal clarity to procedures, rights, and duties of the guardians and to increase the status of such work. By the terms of the statute, the public guardians became arms of the Commissions on Juvenile Affairs.

There are other variations on the theme of public participation. Some involve specialized offshoots of the *druzhiny*. In one city, a special group of *druzhinniki*, made up of students from a pedagogical institute, specialized in street patrols. Armed with information about delinquency and specific delinquents in their area, they operated in cooperation with the children's room of a local police precinct.[15] In a Moscow district, a body of "young friends of the police" was formed from teenagers who helped "detect and prevent" delinquency by their peers.[16] For problem children, camps emphasizing physical work and sports participation are run during the summer vacations. In an attempt to emphasize the value of labor, a group of thirty problem youths was sent during the summer to work on the virgin lands under the supervision of Moscow University law students. The results were reported as "positive." [17]

Of course, it is not only the public that bears responsibility for delinquency prevention, nor even those responsible for schools, youth organizations, and the like. Judges, prosecutors, investigators, and other court personnel, who may enter a case only when a delinquent act has already been committed, are also viewed as important contributors to the prevention process. Judges and investigators especially, in view of the obligations imposed on them by the criminal procedure code to ascertain the minor's "conditions of life and upbringing" and the "causes and conditions facilitating commission of the crime," [18] have a preventive function, since such ascertainment may make possible intervention to change the conditions and prevent future offenses by others.[19]

How well do these preventive mechanisms work in practice? Soviet sources themselves point up many deviations from the ideal, both by the participant public and those whose full-time occupations involve responsibility for delinquency prevention. The parents' committees, for example, often fail to function as constant preventive forces. A complaint from the Belorussian SSR notes that parents' meetings are held "rarely"—on the average, four to five times a year—and then devoted more to academic questions than to topics relevant to delinquency prevention.[20] The pensioners and elderly women who work with children in the apartment blocks, as noted above, suffer in their work from a gap of many years between themselves and their charges and are frequently "inept" at the work.[21] The problems extend to the public auxiliaries of the police children's rooms as well.

Who works with children in the children's rooms of police precincts? . . . Basically . . . pensioners. . . . They are wonderful people, and we receive great help from them. But they are extremely old, and it is very hard for them to work with bright, energetic adolescents. They can talk with children, visit them at home, but to go with them to the stadium, on hikes, to compete with them on sports fields is clearly not within their powers. This work should be done by young men and women, our Komsomol members. But there are far from enough of them for us.[22]

While public work is supposed to be done on a volunteer basis, the obligation being moral rather than legal, social and indirect political pressures combine to subvert this principle and lower the quality of the work of *aktivs* and "guardians." Factory directors concerned about their records of encouraging worker involvement in public activity, or lower-level Party and trade union activists with an eye on their own performance records, pressure the rank-and-file to "volunteer" for unpaid public work of one sort or another, including work with juveniles. Often, the work exists only on paper: in Riga, of one hundred persons sent at one time to act as guardians under the local police, only *one* actually did any work, while in one Moscow district only six of an originally assigned ninety-five Komsomol members fulfilled their duties.[23] Professional police personnel are often wary of depending on "amateurs," even those who volunteer willingly, because of their lack of training and competence. One Soviet observer sums it up with the statement that "if you can't do anything, then you are sent to this sort of work." [24] Delinquency specialists often recognize that such "organized volunteering" is pointless.

Above all it is necessary to give up the now existing practice of bringing into this responsible upbringing work all indiscriminately: the willing as well as those [who are] unwilling, but have been made to agree only under pressure of public organizations.[25]

The criteria for participation in work with youth should include both sincere desire to do such work and actual ability: only those who "actually wish to and can work" with youth, with "full contribution of their knowledge" should be involved.[26]

Although the 1967 statute on public guardians went some distance toward formalizing their roles, it did little to "professionalize" the function.[27] Suggestions offered that a system of *paid* guardians (as exists in Poland) be developed, in order to give the occupation more status and make it more attractive to those with pedagogical qualifications,[28] went largely by the board. While rewards for the "best" guardians, in the form of extra paid vacation days from their regular jobs, are recommended by the statute, the positions remain unpaid;

and the low status some guardians seem to suffer in the eyes of their charges [29] is likely to persist.

Shortcomings are not the exclusive property of the public agencies. The day-to-day activities of the courts, investigative agencies, and police leave much to be desired. One of the most common complaints centers on the failure of courts and investigators to establish data on the living conditions of delinquents and on the "causes and conditions" which provoked their offenses.[30] A survey of cases in Sverdlovsk where the accused had used tools or weapons in the commission of their offenses showed that the courts had failed, in over one-third of the cases studied, to establish where the tools or weapons had been obtained.[31] One court in the Moldavian Republic left the living and upbringing conditions of offenders unexamined in more than one-fourth of its cases over a period of time.[32] In general, many judges, even in juvenile cases, content themselves with establishing the fact of an offense and determining punishment.

Court proceedings themselves are supposed to have an "educative" effect on the defendant and on other juveniles in the courtroom (as are pretrial proceedings in which the offender is confronted with his act). In this connection, much is made of having persons whose occupations qualify them especially for work with youth—teachers, psychologists, doctors, and others—serve in the capacity of "people's assessors" (lay judges, two of whom preside, along with the regular judge, in court). In many areas, however, such qualified assessors are in short supply. In two districts of Sverdlovsk, out of a total of 545 people's assessors only one was a teacher, and one of the districts had only two doctors on its roster.[33]

This picture of a gap between the ideal of a smoothly functioning set of delinquency-prevention mechanisms, manned cooperatively by professionals in law enforcement and by public volunteers, and the real situation with its flaws is not, or should not be, particularly striking. Soviet society is not unique in this regard. Other nations' experience provides convincing proof that gaps between theory and practice are constant, and never completely closed. What *is* striking about the Soviet system is the attempt, with whatever degree of success, to involve the public, through the forms described here as well as others such as the comrades' courts. While these mechanisms have been somewhat de-emphasized since the fall of Khrushchev, they still are the focus of a great deal of attention. Two reasons seem to account for this.

First, through the "mobilization" of the public, whether by persuasion or coercive pressure, the regime is providing a service to the society without having to allocate funds and other resources for the training and support of social workers, child psychologists, and juvenile parole officers. Reduced to economic terms, "public participation" means unpaid work, largely by nonprofessionals. Although public volunteers, in general, have the formal status of "auxiliaries," in fact they are much closer to functional substitutes for the large number of trained and salaried social-service professionals in Western welfare states. The Soviet service sector as a whole, while undergoing gradual improvement, remains a weak competitor for limited resources at the national level, and this is true as well of that subsector which includes delinquency prevention. The use of untrained and unpaid volunteers reduces the quality of the service they are supposed to render, and investment priorities will have to undergo some change before the situation is altered. For a socialist society given to social and economic planning, the USSR puts relatively little into this type of social work.

Second, it would be surprising if at least some members of the Soviet hierarchy did not see in public participation not only a *manifestation* of a civic, volunteering spirit (on the part of some participants, at least), but also a means of *mobilizing* such a spirit—a mechanism for organizing moral sentiments and energies. If some persons, pressured into volunteering, do little in their jobs, others may find them interesting and rewarding and communicate this spirit to the onlooking public. The rank-and-file Soviet citizen who perceives that many of his fellows are "volunteering" in the struggle to prevent delinquency (or crime, or other modes of deviance) may feel his own moral sentiments quicken. In other words, part of the significance of public participation may lie in its relation to the attempt to form and solidify attitudes the regime wishes to create: to build, Soviet style, a "collective conscience." Whether in fact this is happening is another question. It is difficult to square some of the complaints about public bodies and their lack of enthusiasm with any such result. As a whole, the Soviet public may be relatively short of willing volunteers, given the competition of other private and more pressing concerns. But for the present, public involvement costs little, and, aside from inefficiency, does no damage in the regime's eyes. Thus, the regime will probably be willing to await further developments, hoping they will go in the direction outlined above.

PATTERNS OF DISPOSITION

For the adolescent who eludes the processes of prevention, commits an offense, and is called to account for it, a career begins, whether of short or relatively long duration, within the system of juvenile justice. His career may involve investigation and processing of his case by the People's Court, dependent upon his age and the seriousness of his offense, and an eventual term in a juvenile correctional institution. On the other hand, his case may remain completely within the jurisdiction of a Commission on Juvenile Affairs and its disposition bounded by the measures the commission is empowered to impose.

Any lawbreaker under the age of 14, as well as anyone between 14 and 16 whose violation is not among those which involve "criminal responsibility," falls under the primary jurisdiction of the commissions. With the age of 16, a juvenile becomes "responsible" in criminal law for all his acts, and thus falls under the regular jurisdiction of the courts. The Russian Republic's Criminal Code (and corresponding union republic codes) also enumerate offenses for which criminal responsibility begins with age 14.° In determining which offenses fall into this category, "the legislator selects from the whole

---

° The Soviet position here thus resembles similar resolutions of the problem of distinguishing "delinquents" from criminals in some American jurisdictions and in other countries. Rather than making age the *exclusive* determinant of whether a minor is subject to criminal responsibility, the criminal code takes into account the differential "social danger" of illegal acts and prescribes criminal responsibility at an earlier age for the more dangerous acts, with the possibility of sterner consequences. This does not, however, mean that such juveniles are treated as would be adults guilty of similar offenses; restrictions on the punishments applicable to *any* offender under 18 remain in force.

mass of crimes those whose social significance and prohibition is, as a rule, obvious and understood by minors of this age." [34] Such crimes are described as "exceptions" but in fact encompass a large range of acts: homicide, "intentional infliction of bodily injuries causing an impairment of health," rape, assault with intent to rob, theft, robbery, "malicious hooliganism," intentional destruction or damage, with grave consequences, of state or social property or personal property of citizens, and "intentional commission of actions that can cause a train wreck." [35]

The main linkage between the courts and the commissions is provided for in the criminal and criminal-procedural legislation of the RSFSR and the union republics, in the form of provisions permitting the courts to transfer certain cases to the commissions. Thus, if the court finds that an offending minor "has committed a crime not representing a great social danger" and concludes that he can be reformed without criminal punishment, "the minor may be relieved of criminal responsibility and punishment and sent to a [commission on juvenile affairs] for consideration of the question of applying to him compulsory measures of an educational character." [36] Though conditions vary with individual judges and by area, this provision seems to be employed rather frequently. Under the same conditions the criminal procedure code allows the termination of a criminal case against a juvenile by a *prokuror*, or by an investigator with the *prokuror's* consent, and its transfer to a commission,[37] as well as the transfer of materials without the initiation of a criminal case by *prokuror*, investigator, or court, if this seems warranted.[38]

How do the alternative possibilities of disposition work out in practice? Lacking nationwide percentages on the application of different educational or punishment measures to juveniles, we can nonetheless construct from scattered statistics and statements a general picture of the distribution of delinquents among the various measures.

Soviet sources generally agree that approximately one-half of detected cases of delinquency are disposed of without reaching court trials.[39] Whether this reflects the age limits imposed by criminal legislation (which make it impossible, in any event, for a court to consider the case of one under 14) or a tendency on the part of courts to exercise their remand discretion broadly and transfer many cases to the commissions is not entirely clear. Both should play some role, but their relative weights may differ greatly by jurisdiction. Thus, in 1963, 55.1 percent of the cases considered by the commission in Krasnopresnensk district (Moscow) involved persons 16 or 17 years old—many of these, presumably, on remand from the courts—while in the Tadzhik Republic's capital of Dushanbe, the same age group made up only 3.2 percent of the commission's clientele.[40] The language Soviet writers employ seems to indicate that they are referring to cases which *could* be handled by a court ("terminated at pretrial stages") but are not. If courts in large urban areas like Moscow tend, as the Krasnopresnensk figures hint, to terminate many cases of older juveniles, a nationwide average of around 50 percent of triable cases remanded to the commissions might not be out of line.[41] The question is a complicated one, and the lack of clarity in the data (as well as the complications imposed by differentiating the age of criminal responsibility—14 or 16—according to the crime) make it impossible to give a firm answer.°

When inquiry is confined to the courts, more explicit statements can be found about dispositions of offenders. Most of the courts' business is conducted with offenders 16 or 17 years of age (only 13 to 15 percent of those "brought to criminal responsibility," according to Soviet sources, are below 16 [42]).

It is also within the court's competence to impose virtually the same range of "measures of influence" that the commissions possess, if criminal punishment does not seem warranted. In the sphere of criminal punishment, it has available, with certain exceptions, the range of possibilities the criminal code provides,[43] but the typical life situation of a juvenile renders some of these (such as "deprivation of the right to occupy certain offices") irrelevant. Measures such as exile or banishment are among those which cannot be applied to juveniles. In practice this leaves the court with the possibility of sentencing the juvenile to (1) deprivation of freedom, (2) deprivation of freedom "con-

---

° Of course, an even larger problem pertinent to the whole question of disposition is the possibility that Soviet policemen, like their American counterparts, may occasionally handle a case on the spot by way of a warning to the young offender and not report it at all. Such cases, as well as those which remain undetected, do not enter the formal system of processing. Soviet sources make no estimates of their number, so the figure remains dark.

ditionally" (i.e., a suspended sentence), (3) corrective works without deprivation of freedom, and (4) other measures, such as fine or "social censure."

Among these possibilities, the courts seem to favor deprivation of freedom rather markedly. One source states that among court-convicted delinquents, 60 to 70 percent on the average are sentenced to a term in a labor colony (higher than a reported adult rate of 40 to 50 percent).[44] The basically older population the courts deal with and the more serious offenses involved explain this to some degree. The older the offender, the more likely deprivation of freedom may be. (A sample study of 226 cases from different jurisdictions where the offender received such a sentence showed that 3.6 percent were 14 years of age, 13.7 percent, 15, 26.5 percent, 16, and 56.2 percent, 17 years of age.[45])

Average length of sentence varies both with the juvenile's age and with the nature of his offense. About three-quarters of all sentences to deprivation of freedom are under three years, but for more serious crimes such as intentional homicide and rape, the average sentence is higher.[46] Rarely does a sentence for a minor reach the upper limit of ten years,[47] however.

A large number of offenders receive a suspended sentence to deprivation of freedom and are put on probation. The employment of "corrective works" or fines as a juvenile punishment is, however, relatively rare. Corrective works, which involves compulsory work at one's regular job or at another job for a fixed period with the deduction of up to 20 percent of one's earnings, generally does not fit the juvenile offender, whose income may be low or who may lack a job entirely; and management is understandably reluctant to take on such cases. Data from a study of the distribution of measures of punishment in the Kazakh Republic (table 8) bear out this general picture.

For that group of juveniles sentenced to deprivation of freedom, the question arises of average *factual* length of confinement in a labor colony. Two factors influence this (aside from the original length of sentence): the criminal code provision that permits early release or conditional early release of a minor after one-third of his sentence has been served, if his attitudes and behavior warrant it;[48] and the time the juvenile spends in "investigative isolation" before the trial and while awaiting transport to the colony. Soviet sources generally agree that this waiting period, variously estimated at three and one-half months to four or five months,[49] is too long, considering that here the delinquent is frequently confined with hardened criminals, making the task of eventual rehabilitation all the harder.[50] Time spent in investigative isolation is credited to the sentence. The early-release provision is applied, from all indications, quite frequently. Of a group of 100 juveniles released from labor colonies in Latvia, 80 were released early, the remainder serving the full sentence.[51] An authoritative study of court practice in the RSFSR by researchers at a Moscow

TABLE 8   FORMS OF PUNISHMENT APPLIED TO JUVENILE OFFENDERS, 1962–1965 (KAZAKH SSR DATA)

	Form of Punishment			
Year	Deprivation of Freedom	Suspended Sentence	Other Forms °	Total
1962	70.5%	22.4%	5.3%	98.2%
1963	67.6	26.6	2.8	97.0
1964	70.9	21.9	2.6	95.4
1965	71.4	23.0	1.3	95.7

° Includes: corrective works, fine, social censure, etc.

Source: adapted from V. Fursov, "Nekotorye voprosy sostoianiia i struktury prestupnosti nesovershennoletnikh v Kazakhskoi SSR," in Voprosy bor'by s prestupnost'iu nesovershennoletnikh (Alma-Ata, "Nauka" Kazakhskoi SSR, 1968), p. 17.

police institute showed that, while the "average sentence" in the early 1960s had been three years deprivation of freedom, the factual stay in a juvenile labor colony averaged nine months: three and a half months in investigative isolation plus nine months in the colony equalled the year required before early release could be granted.[52]

Not all, however, leave the labor colony for freedom. Of those leaving juvenile colonies in the RSFSR in 1961–1966, the averages were: early release, 33.3 percent; release upon completion of sentence or for "other reasons" (medical, etc.), 12.5 percent; transfer to another juvenile colony, 7.0 percent, and transfer, upon reaching 18 years of age, to a corrective-labor colony for adults, 47.6 percent.[53]

The dynamics of the system itself explain, in large measure, why so many convicted as juveniles and sentenced to deprivation of freedom end up in colonies for adults. The typical offender sentenced to deprivation of freedom is already seventeen years old. His sentence is unlikely to be less than three years, and, given judicial propensities to deal more sharply with older juveniles, it may be higher. Thus he is unlikely to serve even one-third of the sentence before reaching his majority and, according to standard practice, being transferred. Soviet sources say little explicitly about how many transfers are released early from the adult corrective-labor colonies when their one-third term has been served. For the smaller but not insignificant numbers who are sentenced at age 15 or 16, the likelihood of early release is greater [54] and the probability of transfer to an adult colony correspondingly less.

All in all, the possible modes of disposition of delinquent offenders in the USSR show little in the way of notable innovations. The range of possibilities, from institutionalization to probation, is no broader than in many other societies, and the tendency to reserve the harsher measures for older delinquents is a familiar one. While the description of disposition alternatives and their relative frequency here is unavoidably incomplete, it does point to one notable fact: deprivation of freedom, or its threat through a suspended sentence, is a basic (and for older offenders, perhaps *the* basic) means of punishment. It is important, then, to look as searchingly as possible at the institutions in which such sentences are served.

LABOR COLONIES FOR JUVENILES

The labor colony for juveniles (*trudovaia koloniia dlia nesovershennoletnikh*, or TKN) is organized to contain juveniles sentenced by courts to deprivation of freedom.* Institutions bearing this name or

---

* It is not, however, the only closed or semiclosed institution for problem youth. There are "special schools" and "special professional-technical schools" to which the commissions or the courts can dispatch lesser offenders, the former for those

similar names have existed in the USSR since 1935, although their functions have expanded and contracted with changes in legal policies toward delinquent offenders.[55] Regulation of the types, clientele, and structure of the colonies was, until 1968, largely a matter of internal MVD (Ministry of Internal Affairs) statutes, which were not published.[56] In June 1968, a new Statute on Labor Colonies for Minors was ratified by the USSR Supreme Soviet, and it is this document[57] which defines the types of colonies and their characteristics as they exist today.

The 1968 statute decrees three basic types of colony and allows for the organization of a fourth.[58] Male minors sentenced to deprivation of freedom are held in "standard (*obshchii*)-regime colonies." All female minors sentenced to imprisonment are held in standard-regime colonies for females. Male minors who have previously served a term in a colony, or who commit certain "serious" offenses enumerated in the statute, are sent to "intensified (*usilennyi*)-regime" TKN's. In addition, the MVD is empowered to create special intensified-regime colonies for juveniles who commit crimes while serving their sentences or who "systematically and maliciously" violate the rules in a TKN.[59]

Like the adult colonies to be discussed in a later chapter, the TKN is a corrective-labor institution, to which convicted offenders are sent as a form of criminal punishment. Its legal character differs from the "special educational institutions" to which juveniles may be committed, without a court trial, by the Commissions on Juvenile Affairs. In theory, at least, it is distinguished from adult institutions. While it has punitive elements, it possesses a more clearly expressed "educational (*vospitatel'nyi*) character" than the adult institutions.[60] The TKN is charged with

ensuring that convicted minors serve out the terms of their deprivation of freedom in accordance with the court sentences; correcting and reforming convicted persons in a spirit of honest attitudes toward labor, precise execution of laws and respect for the rules of the socialist community; and preventing the inmates from committing new crimes.[61]

11–13, the latter for those 14–17. Placement in these institutions (until 1964 called "educational colonies for juveniles," or *vospitatel'nye kolonii dlia nesovershennoletnikh*) does not constitute "criminal punishment."

In pursuit of these goals, the labor colony is to rely upon the "basic means" specified in the statute: the "regime" itself (the rules and restrictions which define the internal order of the TKN), socially useful labor, general and vocational schooling, and "political-upbringing work." [62]

Regime. TKN inmates live in a world fenced off from the outside, hedged by "forbidden zones" near the boundaries, and under the surveillance of armed guards in watch towers.[63] They are, or are supposed to be,[64] housed in barracks of the sort that young workers generally live in, without barred windows or other jail-like attributes.[65] The order of daily activities is to be planned by the colony commander and his staff in such a way that each inmate is occupied constantly with "useful" activity.

Inmates of standard-regime colonies are permitted one four-hour visit from "close relatives" every two months, and those in intensified-regime colonies are allowed such a visit every three months. Apparently new in the 1968 statute is a limitation on the inmate's right to receive packages and parcels. Due to claimed parental abuse of the previous lack of limitation, inmates may now only receive one package, no larger than five kilograms, every two (standard-regime) or four (intensified-regime) months.[66] Correspondence with parents is unlimited but may be censored (and presumably is). For those who behave well in the TKN, these privileges may be broadened.[67] In the special colonies for violators of TKN rules, the rights to correspondence, visits, and packages are somewhat curtailed. Inmates are denied free movement within the colony limits and are marched under guard from barrack to school, to work, and to their work place.[68]

Socially useful labor. While the TKN statute specifies that work by inmates is "subordinated to the basic task "of inmate reform," [69] it does consume a good deal of the individual's time. The early post-Stalin years saw moves toward establishing a production base in every TKN, in which inmates could learn and work at trades, making what might well be their first contribution to the economy. As in adult colonies, the TKN's projected output is defined in a regional economic plan: work in the colony should be what Anton Makarenko called "real production." [70] (Makarenko's experiences in organizing colonies for homeless and delinquent youth in the 1920s and 1930s, together with his subsequent writings, are seen as having laid down the basic principles of the Soviet approach to reforming delinquents.)

Metalworking, woodworking, and construction are the basic work profiles of the TKN; metal utensils and furniture are among its products. Inmates 14 and 15 years old, if they are simultaneously going to school, work four hours a day, and those 16 to 18 work five hours.

Pay is calculated according to output on a piece-work basis. (The pay scales themselves are not specified in the statute.) Of one's earnings, 64 percent is deducted for the state, to defray the cost of operating the TKN's; 33 percent goes into the inmate's personal account; and 3 percent goes into the colony commandant's fund, to be used for prizes to outstanding inmates and to provide released inmates, if necessary, with small sums of money.[71] Inmates, during the period of training in which they acquire a "specialty," are paid only for their actual output.

General and vocational education. Each colony is obliged to provide an eight-year school, so that inmates who enter without the compulsory eight-year minimum education can continue studies there. The TKN is also supposed to offer the option of eleven-year ("complete secondary") education, if a sufficient number of inmates want it.[72] As the statistics on educational levels show, the average inmate is usually behind his age group in educational level. Frequently, lack of documents and other information creates problems for colony personnel in assigning an inmate to the proper grade. The problem is compounded by the tendency of the juveniles to understate their number of school years completed in hopes of assignment to a lower grade, "in order not to burden themselves, to achieve 'good marks.' "[73]

Vocational training is organized in the direction of "qualifying" the inmate in a particular skill, which depends upon the occupational specialties of the training personnel. According to the general Soviet specifications of minimal and higher grades of competence in a specialty, training programs are organized to provide a specialty—for example, a lathe operator—competent at the "first level" within about six and one-half months and at a "second level" rating after thirteen months.[74]

Political-upbringing work. This rather general designation covers a variety of measures whose basic purpose is moral and intellectual uplift: overcoming apolitical attitudes and alienation from the fundamental concerns of Soviet life, and generating the taste and the need for a new, more "cultured" way of life among the inmates. The cornerstone of political-upbringing work is the system of regularly scheduled "political sessions": meetings held on particular topics of a "socio-political, moral or legal" nature, in accordance with a schedule worked out in cooperation with the Komsomol.[75] These sessions are supplemented, from time to time, by "lectures, addresses, political information sessions, question-and-answer evenings," and other occasions when party, Komsomol, or state officials, distinguished workers, and other notables from outside the colony may talk to the inmates. The schedule also includes eight movies per month—four "art films," presumably of an "elevating" nature, and four documentaries. Competitions in sports, in productivity, in maintaining clean disciplinary records are seen as an indispensable part of the upbringing process. Ideally, just as on the outside adult workers in their factories compete for the honor of being in a "Brigade of Communist Labor," within the TKN groups of inmates compete to gain the title, "Division of Excellent Work and Exemplary Behavior." [76]

INTERNAL ORGANIZATION AND PROBLEMS

Operating regulations developed over the years prescribe a particular organizational framework for the inmate population: a framework which, in theory at least, is supposed to integrate every aspect of inmate life with the operation of the basic means of correction just described. More importantly, the whole idea of planning a pattern of inmate social organization is aimed at using inmates as *active* participants in the process of reform, at co-opting them for the TKN's mission,

. . . to bring to the business of reeducation the convicted themselves, to create an *aktiv* from among the best inmates, to take advantage of and develop the socially useful tendencies lying deep in each of them, to mobilize the public opinion of the members of the colony toward the process of reeducation. With such an organization of the *kollektiv*, as A.S. Makarenko noted, the individual (inmate) enters into a new position—he is not simply the object of upbringing influence, but its bearer—the subject, but he becomes a subject only as he expresses the interests of the *kollektiv*.[77]

The concept of organizing the inmate population in such a way that the goal of correction is not "subverted" by the development of *informal* inmate organizations and subcultures supporting antireform attitudes is an interesting one.[78] For the present, we can defer the question of how well this and the other "basic means" work in practice and take some note of the organizational forms themselves.[79]

At the lowest level, the inmates are organized into a division (*otdelenie*) consisting of 25 to 30 inmates. Divisions are formed on some basis of commonality—trainees in the same professional-technical instruction group or students from the same general-education class. They are housed together in one dormitory and are under the direction of one "guardian" (*vospitatel'*) from the colony staff, who bears direct responsibility for observing their behavior and influencing it in the right directions.[80] Between three and five divisions [81] make up a "detachment" (*otriad*), under a detachment leader (*nachal'nik otriada*). Finally, made up of an unspecified number of detachments (which would, if specified, allow one to estimate the average size of a TKN) is the "collective of inmates"—the total population of the colony.[82]

At each level, administrative organs are formed. The divisions at their general meetings elect seven to nine inmates to serve as the "division council." From among the members of the division councils and the "best inmates" in each division are selected the members of the "detachment council," ranging between 15 and 17 members. At the top of the hierarchy, the council of colony inmates is composed of representatives of the detachment councils, the editors of the colony wall newspaper, and the chairmen of the various inmate commissions, as well as three or four of the "best inmates."[83] Officers are elected for a period of six months, and then new elections are held. The election process, although not clearly detailed in Soviet sources, seems to resemble other Soviet elections: one gets the impression that the "likely" candidates are selected by the colony staff for presentation as a single slate at the general meetings. In any case, there is no possibility of the election of an opposition slate, since the decisions of the general meetings only "assume force after their confirmation by the colony administration." [84]

If the membership of the councils represents that segment of the inmate population the administration regards as potentially helpful as examples of reform-oriented involvement to their fellow inmates, the commissions provide the context within which the rank and file are to involve themselves in useful activity. The number and variety of commissions, at least in general descriptions of what a colony *should* be like, seem sufficient to guarantee that each inmate can find something to do. Separate commissions are concerned with school, professional training, labor competition, the colony "economy" (presumably maintenance and repair work), mass-cultural work, sports, library, and maintenance of discipline.[85]

The reader may, at this point, be concerned that the foregoing treatment of the labor colonies has emphasized the ideal, the way things "should" be, while little has been said about the manner in which the colonies function on a day-to-day basis—their problems and the points at which they deviate from the ideal. Rare indeed is the correctional institution without problems, without failures, without results which contradict the presumed purposes of its activity; and the TKN is no exception.

Chronologically, the first major problem TKN personnel encounter is integrating the newly arrived offender into the inmate population —a problem complicated by the effects of an average stay of several months, under prison conditions, in investigative isolation. Soviet writers are virtually unanimous in criticizing the lack of administrative coordination which leads to accused and/or convicted juveniles spending such a long period in an environment aimed primarily at containment, rather than rehabilitation, wherein the juvenile may come into contact with experienced adult criminals and be further "corrupted." [86] Usually, little is made specific about what actually goes on in the "isolator." An exception was a 1968 article referring to problems of "previous years" by the deputy head of an investigative isolator in Leningrad. With four or five juveniles in each cell, a pattern seemed to develop wherein one aggressive and physically strong juvenile would become cell "boss" (*vozhak*), and recruit one or two cellmates to his "staff," leaving the rest in the cell but outside the group and at its mercy. Such situations grew into attempts to destroy the dignity of the outsiders.

This process was carried out by diverse barbaric forms and methods. At the beginning, let us assume, the boss asks to be brought water or for something else to be done. If it is not, a peculiar "game" is put into operation . . . wherein the outsider must lose. After this begin humiliation, jeering, violence toward the person of the outsider. Such situations sometimes culminate in crimes, most often of a sexual nature.[87]

To readers familiar with the problems of inmate violence and sexual exploitation in penal institutions in other countries, this rather unsensational account must suggest the presence of similar problems in the USSR. The traumatic effect of such incidents, especially on relatively petty offenders, is hard to overestimate.

Upon arrival in the colony the newcomer is in "quarantine" for a period of up to 21 days.[88] During this time, while his documents and records are being checked and his level of education and job skill determined, he is effectively sealed off from the inmate population at large. The quarantine period ended, he is received into his division in a seemingly rather loosely regulated ceremony in which the "demands" to be made upon him as an inmate are announced by fellow inmates. This procedure brings in, once again, the idea of involving inmates actively in the correctional process, of making the new inmate feel that he is part of a community organized for the purpose of correction, so that he understands that "the demands announced to him come not only from the administration and pedagogical staff of the colony, but also from the inmates themselves, from the *kollektiv.*"[89] However, such procedures apparently provide an opportunity for some experienced inmates to vent hostilities toward newcomers or (although the two may not be mutually exclusive) to score points with colony staff by a tough attitude toward the young lawbreaker entering the TKN. Without careful guidance of the reception process by experienced staff members, it becomes overcomplicated, with "unnecessary fault-finding and demands . . . unwarranted zeal in revealing his past, criminal connections, etc."[90]

Once through the *rites de passage*, the newcomer is a member of the inmate *kollektiv* and begins to undergo the processes of schooling, skill instruction, and work that form a large part of the colony's program. Here some critical problems become evident. Because the intake of new inmates is continuous, school instruction organized around the normal academic year beginning in September proves ineffective. There is no well-defined way for late entrants into a TKN school to catch up with those who began a class in September. Given the generally poor academic records of delinquents, it is no surprise that many (if not most) TKN inmates have little success in making up educational deficiencies while in the colony.

Wide application of the early release or transfer to adult institutions of inmates attaining their majority contributes to the problems of the TKN schools by guaranteeing an extreme fluidity of the student body in the course of any year. A study of colonies in the RSFSR in the 1965–1966 school year revealed that the number of students in the fourth through seventh grade classes grew by one and a half to two times during the course of the year while enrollment in the ninth and tenth grades (which was probably small, since these grades represent the "correct" level of education few delinquents achieve) decreased by a similar proportion, presumably due largely to transfers to adult colonies.[91] In some colonies the combination of new admissions and releases or transfers produces an almost complete turnover in the student population within a single year.[92]

For those transferred to an adult colony at age 18 who may be close to or have completed eighth grade, the problem of continuing education is compounded. Adult institutions generally are not equipped to teach beyond the eighth grade level. While some of the more recalcitrant juveniles look forward to the adult colony as a place where they will not be compelled to study,[93] for others transfer can represent closure of their last opportunity to complete secondary education.

High rates of mobility in and out of TKN classes also subvert the principle that the membership of a "division" should be relatively stable, and thus capable of being formed by the *vospitatel'* into a functioning, tightly knit group. Since divisions are frequently formed on the basis of a common school grade among members, enrollment instability has a direct effect on, and complicates, the work of the *vospitatel'*.

In the area of job training flaws exist similar to those in trade schools on the outside. Soviet sources cite difficulties in recruiting persons equipped and willing to train inmates in skilled trades.[94] Outside of particular occupational skills, few of the instructors have any pedagogical training. Problems of personnel quality contribute to the basic, endemic difficulty with job training in the TKN—the incongruence between the prescribed training program's duration and the average factual time an inmate spends in the colony. Most training programs are planned to cover a thirteen to fourteen month period, to enable an inmate to master a specialty at the "grade 2" level. Yet such a period exceeds by approximately five months the average inmate's time in the TKN [95] and has generally meant that many inmates graduate without a marketable specialty. (It is apparently in response to this situation that shorter programs leading to "grade 1" certification have been established, although they by no means provide a complete solution to the problem.[96])

Given the different production profiles of colonies, not every inmate can receive training in the skill he might most like to acquire. In some colonies, what appear to be statistically popular specialties, like metal working, also are the focus of large-scale dissatisfaction among trainees. Such work was characterized by inmates in one Latvian TKN as "dirty and difficult" and lacking the attraction that more skill-demanding, mechanized jobs offer.[97] To make matters worse, 18-year-old transfers to adult colonies are, whatever their training, frequently used at unskilled work.[98]

In the rehabilitative process, broadly conceived, that segment of the colony staff in most constant contact with the inmates—the general-school teachers and the *vospitately*—is called upon to strike an effective and delicate balance between coercion and persuasion. For a person with psychological and pedagogical training of a high order, this is a difficult enough task; but as of July, 1965, as *Pravda* noted, there was no single school in the USSR devoted to the preparation of personnel for work in juvenile labor colonies.[99] Presumably, some training is available in the MVD's schools for its own workers, especially in Moscow, where pedagogically and psychologically trained staffs are present, but this training is directed toward more general preparation for a variety of functions in corrective-labor institutions in general. Soviet teacher-training institutions have devoted little if any attention to the preparation of TKN personnel, possibly because their preparation, such as it is, takes place within the MVD's own institutions. The lack of trained workers is reflected in complaints about the "tactlessness" and "coarseness" frequently seen in the staff's dealing with inmates.[100] Even after the adoption of the new TKN statute in 1968, "many shortcomings" remained in the area of establishing specialized training for staff workers.[101]

Perhaps these personnel insufficiencies, as well as the general commitment to mobilizing the energies of the public in corrective and preventive work, explain the emphasis on public involvement in TKN operations. Whole factories in proximity to a colony may "adopt" it, sending workers to it from time to time to help with job instruction as well as giving lectures and moral support. On the individual level, volunteer *vospitately*, drawn most often from the ranks of pensioners, may offer their services to support the efforts of colony staff, with the blessing of the local soviets.[102] At least on paper, public involvement is periodically formalized in monthly assemblies of inmates to meet with representatives of sponsoring factories, and in annual reviews of the TKN's accomplishments in which members of the local Commission on Juvenile Affairs, public councils (composed of volunteers), factory representatives, and delegates of local party, government, and Komsomol organizations take part, along with the parents of the inmates.[103]

To some Soviet writers, the structure of the colonies themselves is a source of problems. The 1968 statute's introduction of two regimes— standard and intensified—was in part a response to complaints that the earlier colonies guaranteed little in the way of separation of serious from relatively petty offenders, or of first offenders from repeaters;[104] nor did they always separate those who committed crimes while *in* the colony from other inmates. The last point is especially striking. The official corrective-labor textbook for law schools, published in 1966, mentioned "labor colonies with a strict regime" in which such offenders are contained.[105] Yet, according to a 1967 treatise,

juveniles, who are convicted for crimes committed in a labor colony, after the passing of sentence are sent to serve their punishment in the very same colony. These people have a pernicious influence on the inmates, and attempt to form their own groups.[106]

A 1968 article reviewing the changes wrought by the new statute also refers to a previous single-regime system and makes no mention of "strict-regime" colonies.[107]

Perhaps the new system will greatly reduce the possibility of contamination of petty first offenders by experienced and dangerous juvenile recidivists by placing the latter in separate intensified-regime TKN's. Such separation seems to be at least a move in the right direction. But two problems, both somewhat paradoxical, remain in the present system, even excluding the perennial one of the fate of 18-year-olds graduating to the company of older felons in adult institutions. First, the case load of a *vospitatel'* amounts to 25 to 30 inmates. While this staff-inmate ratio is better than in many other nations' juvenile institutions, it falls far short of some institutions, including some other types in the Soviet Union—the special schools and special professional-technical schools. In these latter, where less serious offenders not deemed to need the strictures of the TKN are sent, the ratio is one *vospitatel'* to ten inmates. Yet, as one writer notes, it is the tougher TKN inmates who need the increased attention a lower ratio would afford.

Second, the present mode of coping with those who commit crimes in a TKN or who habitually violate its rules involves the creation of "special" intensified-regime colonies, quite different from the others both in inmate privileges and in internal organization. The whole panoply of organized councils and commissions is absent in these institutions, nor is there any talk of inmate participation. Through the explanation for this—that such hardened deviants would abuse and violate the principles underlying the concept of organization [108]—one gets the impression that such colonies may be dumping grounds for juveniles of whose reform few have any hope and who are expected to provide trouble as adults in the future. But, as one observer notes, these are the juveniles who most dislike and resist the *kollektiv* and its organizations. Sent to a special colony as a punishment, they find an atmosphere they prefer to the one they left—"the result is absurd." [109] Such absurdity is also evident in the fact that the special colony, through its lack of internal organization, leaves the field open for the growth and solidification of antireform sentiment in an organizationally developed (albeit informal) subculture.

[Such an approach] overlooks the peculiarities and subtleties of the internal relationships of this category of convicts. Among [these convicts], as a rule, there are always found their own "authorities," "bosses," who openly or secretly lord it over the rest. If they, in a majority of cases, turn out to be recidivists, then one can understand what bad influence they will have on other convicts.[110]

RECIDIVISM: THE MIRROR
OF SHORTCOMINGS

The failures (and the successes) in the work of the courts and the colonies are reflected in the conduct of those they have processed, whether with a remand to a commission on juvenile affairs, with a conditional sentence, or with an actual term in a TKN. Recidivism, the commission of another offense or offenses, is an imperfect measure of success or failure. In most cases, the new offense cannot clearly be imputed to ineffectiveness of previous measures of punishment and correction: it may just as well be the product of factors coming into play only after the offender's release. Distinguishing between these two possible causes of a repeat offense is awkward. Can one set a period after release beyond the end of which any new offense is imputable not to correctional failure but to new factors? No answer comes easily to hand. Nonetheless, recidivism is a handy measuring device. It involves clear criteria: a new appearance in court and a new conviction. While Soviet authorities recognize its imperfections, it remains their basic means of assessing the performance of the juvenile correction system.

The statistics on recidivism are fragmentary and in many cases somewhat contradictory, but they illustrate some of the persistent problems of the system in dealing with juvenile offenders. One author, on the basis of "data available," observes that of all juvenile convictions, 6 to 8 percent are handed down against persons already convicted one or more times before. Of those convictions involving a

sentence to deprivation of freedom, 12 to 13 percent of the convicted
have one or more previous convictions on their records.[111] Were we
to accept such figures as roughly characteristic of the nationwide situation (which we cannot do with any degree of firmness), we could assume that the juvenile justice system is not overloaded with repeaters.

Even though juvenile offenders, as a category, are considered to be
a less serious problem than adult criminals, Soviet sources give evidence that a relatively high rate of recidivism is to be expected and
frequently occurs. Over the years 1962–1966, according to a source
which should be authoritative, the crime rate *in* TKN's in the RSFSR
was 2.7 times higher than that in the colonies for adults.[112] Given this
comparatively high incidence of intrainstitutional turbulence, continuing problems after release can be expected. Scattered studies give
varying figures on the percentage of colony releasees who commit
new offenses. Of one group of juveniles on whom data were obtained
two years after release, 30 percent had committed another crime.
After three years, the recidivist total had risen to 35 percent.[113] A
study of a similar group in Latvia in 1962, where returnees were
grouped by destination, revealed that 45.9 percent of those who had
returned to the capital, Riga, committed new offenses; 29 percent of
those who returned to other cities and 18.9 percent of returnees to
rural areas also became recidivists.[114] (The urban-rural difference
may reflect the fact that stability of "delinquent contacts" is more easily maintained in large cities with large, concentrated juvenile populations.) A further Latvian study of juveniles convicted in 1959–1960
(whose small sample—$N = 100$—limits its utility) examined the records, as of 1965, of the 44 juveniles in the sample sent to colonies. Of
this group, 27, or 61 percent, had committed further offenses; 12, one
new offense; 9, two offenses; and 6, three new offenses.[115] Finally, a
survey was made of a "large group" of recidivist offenders in an un-
named republic in the four years 1962–1965; of those released from
the TKN's during those years, 16.7 percent were convicted anew and
returned (compared to 7.2 percent for adult colonies).[116]

Releasees from the TKN's continue to vex law enforcement organs
even when they leave the colonies not for liberty but for an adult colony. A survey of the records of three adult colonies showed regime violations proportionally greater by 2.8 times among TKN transfers

than among other inmates and crimes among this group even more in excess of the rate of the basic colony population. The recidivism rate of those released from an adult colony who entered it on transfer from a TKN is cited as 2.3 times greater than that among other adult releasees.[117]

If the TKN's produce flawed graduates in a significant number of cases, what of the alternative mode of disposition available to the court, the suspended sentence? Such disposition may save juveniles from some of the negative impact of the colony, but it frequently turns out to be only a deferral. Of a group of second offenders studied in the Ukrainian industrial city of Kharkov, 87 percent had received suspended sentences for their first offense.[118] Of second offenders in a Latvian study, 58.8 percent had been initially sentenced "conditionally."[119] The studies cited do not tackle the question of what percentage of those who receive a conditional sentence commit new offenses. A 1967 study does this for a group given suspended sentences two years previously. Forty-seven percent committed a new offense within the period, 35 percent before their probation periods were over.[120]

The evident failure of a stretch in a TKN (though these, as we have seen, are usually short) or a suspended sentence to turn many juveniles away from delinquency requires explanation. Soviet writers cite, among the main factors, inadequate probationary or post-release supervision and a lack of attention to the work of reestablishing a juvenile in society after conviction and imprisonment.

Much is made of the beneficial influence of putting a juvenile given a suspended sentence "in custody" (na poruke) of his fellow workers or students, with the expectation that they will oversee his behavior. Ideally, the members of the worker or student kollektiv or public organization should petition the court for the offender's release in custody,[121] although the court is allowed to "impose," with the kollektiv's consent, the duty of looking after a released offender. Yet court practice frequently ignores this possibility, in many cases, courts simply pass sentence conditionally, and the juvenile is returned to the street. Of one group of conditionally sentenced juveniles, only 30 percent were released "in custody."[122] A study of a group of juveniles who committed new offenses after conditional sentencing found that 85 percent were similarly abandoned: neither court, *kollektiv,* nor public organization had concerned themselves with the probation period behavior of these offenders.[123] As one student of conditional sentencing wrote, court practice shows that "in the absence of upbringing work with the conditionally sentenced, they interpret the conditional sentence as lack of punishment." [124]

Those released from the TKN also find that in many cases the procedures whose purpose is to observe their behavior and to render aid in reestablishing them in jobs or schools either do not work or are completely absent.[125] In the background data on recidivists, one frequently finds evidence of abandonment of an ex-inmate by the colony and the public organizations alike: no help in getting him a job, no aid in securing his admission to school, and little attempt to insure that the ex-inmate does not renew his delinquent contacts.[126]

One root of the problem of inadequate supervision lies in the structure of post-release supervision itself. The Commissions on Juvenile Affairs are responsible for surveillance of the behavior of juveniles released from TKN's.[127] However, given the average age composition of inmate populations, few returnees from the colonies are minors any longer, and the commissions' responsibilities are bounded by age. "From a labor colony for juveniles, as a rule, leave persons already adult, and not juveniles. Who looks out for them? Today, essentially, no one." [128]

Few helpful generalizations can be made about strategies of delinquency prevention in the USSR. It is, after all, of the essence of prevention that, except in rare cases where some sort of controlled experiment is possible, one cannot determine how well it works. In a relatively tranquil, law-abiding society, a prevention system may be weak—but such a society can afford the weakness. In a contrasting situation, where great numbers of young citizens seem delinquency-prone, one may conclude that the strategies of prevention, whatever they may be, are ineffective. Yet, in a sense, such a conclusion is unsupportable, for one cannot be certain that in the absence of apparently ineffective measures, the incidence of delinquency might not be even higher and more alarming.

We cannot then say that the upbringing work required of the school, youth organization, and factory, when it is performed, has no effect. Nor can we be sure that volunteer work performed by truly interested members of the public as auxiliaries to the police children's rooms or to the Commissions on Juvenile Affairs does not have a real preventive effect on some youths characterized as unstable. On the other hand, from evidence provided by Soviet observers themselves we can conclude that at many points the system of preventive measures is subverted by disinterest and incompetence. Against such subversion, the Soviet system evidently has no more immunity than others.

If flaws persist in the preventive process, they are no less present in the practice of the courts and in the operation of juvenile institutions. While many of the *vospitately* who work with the inmates are probably dedicated to their tasks and effective in their performance, for others such a job may be only a temporary post on the way to another MVD job. The average length of inmate exposure to the colony's rehabilitative resources is short. Why massive early release is such standard practice is unclear (although one might hypothesize that the TKN's are crowded, and the need to accommodate new inmates is pressing), but the vast majority of Soviet writers on delinquency, whether or not they favor the application of deprivation of freedom to juveniles in general, are convinced that the short stay in the colony does little good—not nearly enough good, in many cases, to counterbalance the effects of the time spent in investigative isolation. The TKN is not a pleasant place to spend time; whatever its rehabilitative character, the inmate cannot help but notice that he is "guarded by armed soldiers in little turrets around the outer wall." [129]

Within limits, the TKN is a place where the juvenile continues his general education and learns occupational skills. But the time spent in preliminary isolation and the short average term in the colony, perhaps beginning midway through the academic year, may result in no real advancement in his education, but rather a further gap between him and his peers. The 13- to 14-month period of occupational training necessary to achieve grade 2 rating in a specialty exceeds the average duration of a colony stay; and grade 2, in the Soviet six-level rating system, is still "low qualification." (Interestingly enough, adult drunkards and petty criminals frequently are drawn from the population of "workers of low qualification.")

For many inmates the TKN is a way station on the road to an adult colony. Despite many writers' complaints about the negative consequences of the practice of transfers, the 1968 statute leaves the situation relatively unchanged; "exceptional cases" can remain in the TKN until reaching nineteen. The complaints, given three principles of corrective-labor philosophy, are well founded. Transfers violate the principle that one's time should be served in the same colony, in a stable *kollektiv*. In sending persons convicted as juveniles into a society of adult offenders, they violate the rule that decrees separate containment of different classes of offenders. Third, the transfer process controvenes justice: the transfer, upon arriving in the adult colony with its stricter regime and more punitive conditions, is subjected to a punishment the court did not decree.[130]

A suspended sentence combined with thoughtful probationary practice, or a stay in a colony involving contact with experienced and dedicated *vospitately*, might have the effect we must assume the Soviet regime desires. Often enough, however, none of these conditions is present. Until they can be guaranteed, the Soviet system of delinquent rehabilitation will include many failures as well as successes among those it processes.

8

CRIME AND THE
CRIMINAL OFFENDER

ORDERING A SET OF social problems according to their relative seriousness, as perceived either by some broadly defined "public" or by those representatives of society charged with special responsibilities for their control or eradication, is a difficult business, doubly difficult when the society under investigation is as wary of releasing information as is the Soviet Union. But we are probably justified in regarding the third of our problems—crime—as the most serious of the three.

The absolute incidence of alcoholism and drunkenness may be greater than the incidence of criminal offenses. Quantitatively, then, alcohol problems may be more serious. But, with the exception of crimes committed "under the influence," alcohol-connected deviance is only derivatively antisocial. The drunkard or alcoholic, no doubt, frequently harms himself—his deviant behavior may or may not have ramifying consequences for other persons and for property. The drunkard or alcoholic may be impaired in the degree to which he can contribute to societal goals, and in this sense harm society—but he has not necessarily set himself against society.

The juvenile delinquent, whose special legal status is based on age, rather than on any difference between his offenses and those of adult criminals, may or may not have set himself against society. The available statistics indicate, in any case, that juvenile offenses tend strongly toward the petty, the less serious. Of all offenders of whatever age processed through the Peoples' Courts, juveniles make up a very small proportion. They are seen as less fully formed, in attitude and in behavior patterns, than adults and, due to their greater malleability, as more promising prospects for rehabilitation. Delinquency is certainly *a* problem, but it is unlikely that Soviet officials concerned with different forms of defiance would regard it as *the* problem.

Different is the case of the adult criminal. His acts are seen as directly antisocial, and his age does not permit talk of immaturity or diminished responsibility. The crimes of adults are more serious than those of juveniles, and presumably flow frequently from more deeply rooted antisocial attitudes. As an adult, after all, he has been through the major formative processes of Soviet life—family, school, youth organizations, work (usually)—and emerged a seriously flawed product. Though he is seen as redeemable, his resocialization is a matter of more complexity than it would be if he were a juvenile.

Assembling data on crime as a whole, and attempting to explain its causes in a mature Soviet society, has kept criminologists occupied since the late 1950s. The study of delinquency as a special case has been largely an offshoot of this more general concern with law-violating behavior. If what follows in this chapter cannot fully explicate the complex issues surrounding crime in the USSR, it may at least provide the reader with a more detailed appreciation of those issues.

CRIMINALS AND THEIR CRIMES: SOVIET STATISTICS

The criminal codes of the various Soviet republics specify the diverse types of actions which are defined as crimes. Many are of the sort familiar to many legal systems—offenses against the person (homicide, assault, etc.), offenses against property, both of private citizens and of the state, offenses of a variety termed "disorderly conduct" in the

United States and falling under the rubric of "hooliganism" in the USSR. The Soviet codes also present some category headings less familiar, perhaps, to the reader: [1] "economic crimes," such as speculation, illegal production of or trade in certain goods, etc.; "official crimes" (dolzhnostnye prestupleniia)—malfeasance, nonfeasance, and other abuses of office by state functionaries; crimes against the system of justice and against the system of administration—ranging from bribing a judge to resisting a police officer; and "state crimes" (gosudarstvennye prestupleniia)—the whole range of political offenses.

While the codes are clear, the actual predominance of one or another type of offense among crimes committed is not. While one now and then encounters in Soviet writings a statement that "such-and-such" a type of crime makes up "about such-and-such a percent" of all crimes, any attempt at providing a general picture is rare. One such attempt, however, provided the data in table 9,* collected, most probably, over the years 1966–1967.

By and large, the table must speak for itself. No further systematic breakdowns within category of offense or by region are available. One observes that "state crimes" no longer seem to be a problem of large dimensions, as they were in the first years of the Soviet state (see chapter 3). Their incidence, notes the official criminology textbook, is "extremely low." [2] On the other hand, one can conclude from the figures that property crimes and economic crimes, taken together, are major components of the problem facing law enforcement officials, and that hooliganism, the blanket rubric for a number of public order violations, must also keep police busy.

---

* This table itself presents an instructive example of the difficulties of working with Soviet data. While Ostroumov cites Kriminologiia for his information, no such information appears on the pages indicated, or anywhere else, in the cited work. In the Kriminologiia pages cited, there are references running in the text to percentage distributions of convicted offenders by type of offense, identified generally as relating to "recent years" or 1967. Ostroumov's figures, however, relate to percentage distributions of offenses, rather than offenders. Kriminologiia's distributions by offenders, interpreted broadly, total 93.7 percent, and Ostroumov's 100 percent. The percentage differences between Kriminologiia's offenders and Ostroumov's offense types are not large, which indicates that his figures are probably taken from the same set of data (assembled by the Institute of Criminology in Moscow) from which Kriminologiia's figures are drawn. But the "inaccuracy" of the citation is interesting—in any case, Ostroumov's book is (to this author's knowledge) the first published source including the figures in table 9.

TABLE 9 CRIME IN THE USSR, BY CATEGORY OF OFFENSE
(CIRCA 1967)

Theft of state and	
public property	17.0%
Hooliganism	24.0
Crimes against citizens'	
personal property	16.0
Crimes against the person	17.0
Economic crimes	5.0
Official crimes	4.0
Vehicular crimes	5.0
Crimes against the system	
of justice	1.5
Crimes against the system	
of administration	4.0
Other crimes	6.5
Total	100.0%

Source: S.S. Ostroumov, *Sovetskaia sudebnaia statistika* (Moscow, Izdatel'stvo Moskovskogo universiteta, 1970), p. 248, citing *Kriminologiia* (Moscow, "Iuridicheskaia literatura," 1968), pp. 118–19.

These observations are supported as well by the relative distribution of articles on criminal topics in Soviet legal journals. Various types of property offense and hooliganism seem to be the major foci of attention, while violent and nonviolent crimes directed at the person (and of a nature not to be qualified under the lesser rubric of public order crime) are assessed, despite their seriousness, as a smaller component of the total crime problem.

Beyond these general figures, Soviet sources are extremely uninformative. Distributions for a particular area occasionally show divergences from the pattern laid out here. In relatively rural areas, for example, offenses connected with the illegal manufacture of alcohol tend to bulk large.[3] Auto theft may appear as a specific category in reports from some urban areas, but the relative rarity of such vehicles in the countryside makes the incidence of such offenses there minimal.[4]

A larger question is that of the over- or underrepresentation of certain of the broad categories of offense listed above. If one cannot be precise here, patterns observed in other societies, as well as some general impressions of the relative public tolerance accorded one or another type of offense in the USSR, may nonetheless be of some aid in offering tentative observations. Reports of sex crimes, specifically rape, are probably much below their actual incidence; and the number of persons convicted of such offenses is probably an even smaller proportion of their perpetrators. The same constraints of embarrassment and emotional stress that inhibit US victims of such offenses would seem to apply to some degree in the Soviet Union, reducing the likelihood that *all* complainants appear before the police. In another area: violent anti-person crimes resulting in death or serious bodily injury, being relatively difficult to conceal and usually entailing considerable investment of police energy in attempts to capture the offender, seem less likely to be strong candidates for underrepresentation in the fragmentary Soviet figures available. While homicide and serious types of assault generally form only a small percentage of the total number of crimes in most societies (the United States included), the extremely restricted availability of firearms in the USSR probably tends to limit the success rate of would-be perpetrators of homicides. However, there are rather large regional variations in firearms use. A study of homicides in Moscow conducted by A.A. Gertsenzon showed that only 4 percent of those in his sample were accomplished with firearms, while data from two mixed "urban-rural" areas (Briansk, Vladimir, and Kalinin *oblasti* in one study, Rostov *oblast'* in the other) showed a significantly higher percentage of firearms use: 32.4 percent for Briansk, Vladimir, and Kalinin, and 20.8 percent for Rostov.[5]

It is in the area of property offenses, particularly those of a relatively petty variety, that Soviet statistics are probably furthest behind the "real" situation—though we cannot state unequivocally what that situation is. From legal journals and the popular press, which frequently publish complaints about inefficiency in accounting and property control in large enterprises, one receives the very strong impression of a massive incidence of individually small, but *en masse* damaging, thefts by employees. Many such thefts are detected (and among these the *most* petty, handled through the imposition of 10-ruble fines by a comrades' court, do not appear in criminal statistics); many more, apparently, go undetected. Theft of state goods from a large factory where one works is often an easily-rationalized matter, both for the thief and those coworkers aware of his activities and frequently enough engaged in their own petty misappropriations. The rank and file is indifferent, the management, often enough, in no position to search each person as he leaves work. The following words are from a study of public opinion on the topic in one factory where thefts were frequent:

"It is hard to struggle with thefts," wrote one of the factory's workers, "since even those people who are honest in other matters, seeing that a theft from the enterprise is being committed, sometimes don't think it necessary to stop it: it is, they say, not our business." [6]

To many, what belongs to all, as "socialist" property, belongs to no one. A combination of this attitude, fostered partly no doubt by the shortages with which the Soviet citizen contends in so many areas of his life, and the apathy of onlookers creates fertile ground for large numbers of unreported thefts when the factory's detection and prevention capacities are so limited. We are probably justified in assuming that a great deal of the losses Soviet managers must write off to inventory "shrinkage" can be attributed to unregistered thefts.

In many of his characteristics, the Soviet criminal resembles his juvenile variant.* The masculine gender is used advisedly here, since the vast majority of convicted felons are men. A study of a sample of cases from the Central Black Earth economic region of the Russian Republic in 1963 showed men making up 88 percent of the total, a figure which is probably valid for the nation as a whole.[7] The remainder, committed by women, were generally nonviolent crimes, predominant among which was trading illegally in scarce items (speculation), which accounted for 80 percent of the total. The only violent crime category in which women predominate is that of infant murder. Studies are cited as showing that 87 percent of such offenses are connected with unwed motherhood, and that 92 percent are committed during the birth process itself.[8] Crimes of this type, in any case, are said to be on the decline.

Data on criminals' ages vary greatly, especially when they come

* This observation applies, at least, to the common criminal. The perpetrators of large-scale economic crimes, the Soviet versions of white-collar criminals, diverge from other offenders in occupation, education, and other characteristics.

from studies done in only one area. As high as 81 percent of the criminal population has been assigned to the 30-and-under age group,[9] while the above-mentioned study in the Central Black Earth region yielded a figure below 60 percent, as table 10 shows.

In general, the USSR seems to follow the pattern of other societies: most varieties of crime, especially those involving violence, are young men's games. Data from Moscow's Institute of Criminology indicate that 25 percent of intentional homicides are committed by those under 25, while the 25–40 age group accounts for 50 percent of such offenses.[10] Fully 57 percent of hooliganism is attributed to those be-

TABLE 10   PERCENTAGES OF ALL CRIMES COMMITTED BY AGES OF OFFENDERS, CENTRAL BLACK EARTH REGION, RSFSR

Age Group	Percentage
Under 18 years	7.0
18–25 years	31.0
26–30 years	20.6
31–40 years	30.0
41–50 years	7.0
51–60 years	2.6
Over 60 years	1.8
Total	100.0

Source: Adapted from S.S. Ostroumov and V.E. Chugunov, "Izuchenie lichnosti prestupnika po materialam kriminologicheskikh issledovanii," Sovetskoe gosudarstvo i pravo, No. 9 (1965), p. 96.

tween 18 and 29, with a substantial additional percentage of such offenses committed by minors under 18.[11] Age-specific specialization is especially notable in the area of property crimes. Persons under 25 account for only 38 percent of convictions for concealed theft (krazha), but make up 80 percent of those convicted for assault with intent to rob (razboi). These statistics, reflecting convictions, are, of course, very rough and would not include, for example, cases of juveniles committing thefts or other property offenses who are handled by the Commissions on Juvenile Affairs. Nonetheless, among court convictions, juveniles appear more frequently when only open stealing and assault are considered ("over 30 percent" of the total), than when concealed theft (a more common offense overall) is added and the

TABLE 11 EDUCATIONAL ATTAINMENT OF CRIMINALS (TWO SOVIET STUDIES)

Educational level	Gal'perin, 1968	Ostroumov and Chugunov, 1965
Illiterate	2.0%	2.6%
Up to 4 years (primary)	38.0	45.6
5 to 7 years (incomplete secondary)	42.4	37.7
8 to 10 years (up to complete secondary)	15.6	8.2
Higher, incomplete higher	2.0	0.9
Total	100.0%	95.0%

Sources: Col. 1, I.M. Gal'perin, "Ob ugolovnoi otvetstvennosti retsidivistov v svete nekotorykh kriminologicheskikh pokazatelei effektivnosti bor'by s retsidivnoi prestupnost'iu," in B.S. Nikiforov, ed., *Effektivnost' ugolovnopravovykh mer bor'by s prestupnost'iu* (Moscow, "Iuridicheskaia literatura," 1968), p. 244; col. 2, S.S. Ostroumov and V.E. Chugunov, "Izuchenie lichnosti prestupnika po materialam kriminologicheskikh issledovanii," *SGIP*, No. 9 (1965), p. 98 (a study of offenders in the Central Black Earth Region).

three are taken together: then, the share of juveniles drops to 15 percent.[12]

Crimes such as large-scale embezzlement, which usually demand for their perpetration a job with access to funds and with some responsibility, tend to occur among an older contingent. Embezzlement "in especially large quantities" involves persons under 30 only in about 15 percent of cases, while 20 percent is accounted for by those over 50, according to the criminology textbook.[13]

Much is made in Soviet writings of the generally low educational and "cultural" levels of criminals, and among the most frequently collected statistics are ones dealing with educational accomplishment. Interpretation of these figures is difficult, since frequently the comparison is to the educational level the criminal *should* have attained according to legal standards, rather than to the *actual* average levels of comparable noncriminal populations. Nonetheless, such data are in themselves interesting, illustrating as they do the fact that many slip through the Soviet Union's universal educational system with only minimal levels of attainment. Table 11 presents the results of two different studies of educational level. Other studies have varied in the

TABLE 12   EDUCATIONAL ATTAINMENTS OF CRIMINAL PRISONERS AND
GENERAL POPULATION, SVERDLOVSK OBLAST'

Level	Criminals	Control
Elementary (4 years)	21.0%	19.1%
5–7 years	50.0	21.9
8–10 years	28.0	56.6
Complete or incomplete higher	1.0	2.4
Totals	100.0%	100.0%

Source: M.I. Kovalev, "Issledovanie obrazovatel'nogo urovnia prestupnikov,"
SGIP, No. 2 (1968), p. 90.

breaking points chosen by their authors to mark categories and are
not directly comparable. (One 1960 study reported 8 percent of the
criminals to be illiterate; in later studies, this figure tends to be
lower.[14]) It is interesting to note that the select group of "especially
dangerous recidivists" who make up column 1 in the above table have
a generally higher educational level than does the more mixed population of column 2. This runs somewhat contrary to expectations and
might be explained by column 1's sample having been drawn from a
more urban, developed area, where general educational attainment is
higher. Whether this was in fact the case cannot be ascertained.

Of greater interest is a study by the Sverdlovsk criminologist
M.I. Kovalev, which compares the educational attainments of persons
imprisoned in Sverdlovsk province for criminal acts with the attainments of the population of the province as a whole, thus supplying a
rough control group. Table 12 presents Kovalev's results. (Time of the
study was apparently 1966 or 1967.) The gap between the criminal
and control groups is demonstrated rather clearly here. While 41
percent of the province population (including the large industrial city
of Sverdlovsk, some smaller cities, and countryside) lacks eight years
of education, a much higher percentage (71 percent) among the criminals has a similarly low level. In his sample of especially dangerous
recidivists, I.M. Gal'perin found that only 8.9 percent had 10 or more
years of education (i.e., complete secondary or better), while 32 percent of the USSR's population (1964) had achieved such a level.[15]

Low educational levels are not, of course, characteristic of all criminals. As Kovalev notes, large-scale embezzlers who achieve their

criminal results through abuse of office tend to much higher educational levels.[16] Thus, while low educational levels are seen as a predisposing factor, they cannot be relied upon to provide a total explanation. Kovalev views antisocial attitudes and behaviors on the one hand, and low educational and cultural levels on the other, as being frequently in a relationship of mutual reinforcement: persons with low educational-cultural levels may be more likely to develop antisocial attitudes and to act upon them in situations of stress and temptation. But such antisocial views themselves, when imbibed early in life in familial and peer-group settings, make one less likely to aspire toward and achieve education and culture of a high level.

We have reached a point where it would be logical to next consider the relationship between social class membership and criminality—logical indeed, were there any Soviet data that speak directly to this issue. But here we lack even the sort of data that were available in fragmentary form in various studies of juvenile delinquents and must confine ourselves to indirect inference. First, it need be said that attempts to relate income (as an indirect measure of class) to crime, in any linear fashion, are doomed to failure. Those with the lowest incomes in the USSR—the workers on collective farms—are, of course, located in rural areas. Yet, for its size, this most economically depressed category of the population yields less convicted criminals by far than do the generally more affluent residents of the cities. Soviet statistics on criminals' incomes are extremely spotty [17] and are not sufficient to give any strong hints as to the total picture. The claim is generally advanced that criminals, on the whole, have average income and living standards. Lacking any precise occupational data, or even a breakdown of criminals into peasant, worker, and employee, we are not in a position to confirm or deny such claims unequivocally. To the degree that relatively high levels of education may be indicators of relatively elevated status (in occupational prestige, if not always in monetary terms), the data on education just presented are of some interest. *Very* few criminals have complete or incomplete higher education, as the tables show. This, however, is not crucial. As the Sverdlovsk province data show (and if not strictly representative, they are nonetheless not atypical), the proportion of higher-educated in the general population is also quite small. The Sverdlovsk data also show a near-inversion of the two middle levels. With roughly similar percentages of the criminal and control groups limited to primary education, more than twice as many criminals fit into the 5–7 year bracket as do members of the general population, while at the 8–10 year level the proportions are reversed—proportionally less than half as many of the criminal as of the control group have achieved this level.* It may then be suggested tentatively (to the degree that the Sverdlovsk figures are *not* atypical) that, while there is some overlap in the educational profiles of criminal and control populations, the differences are no less impressive. The low educational level of the average criminal is probably a symptom of a larger complex of problems, the product in many cases of unfavorable circumstances earlier in life; but Soviet criminologists' preoccupation with it and its implications seem justified by the available figures.

Beyond these general matters, Soviet statistics do not tell us or even suggest very much about crime as a whole. There is ample evidence to connect drunkenness with crime, as the chapter on alcohol problems showed; but this is not so much the location of a cause of crimes (though it is frequently taken as such) as a demonstration of the presence of *two* forms of deviance in certain persons. For some with antisocial attitudes, drunkenness releases inhibitions and lowers the ability to reckon with consequences of a criminal act, but it scarcely can be cited as a basic cause. We learn from Ostroumov and Chugunov's study of criminals in the Central Black Earth region that of those lawbreakers surveyed, 95 percent had never participated in civic activity of any kind, 55 percent had not read creative literature, 41 percent had not read papers or magazines, 79.5 percent had not gone to the theater, 15.6 percent had not even attended movies, 24.5 percent had not engaged in sports, and 4.9 percent had not pursued mechanical hobbies.[18]

In the absence of similar data for the noncriminal population, we

---

* The relationship may in fact be even stronger. Kovalev notes that 71.0 percent of the adult criminals lack an 8-year education (which the figures show) and that only 35.7 percent of the *adult population* of the province have similar deficiencies (less than the 41 percent in the table). This suggests that the table figures for the control group refer to the province population as a whole, not only to adults—the more comparable control group to use as against imprisoned criminals.

cannot ascertain the degree to which these figures bespeak extraordinary "cultural deprivation." But they do indicate how wide is the gap between the official model of the Soviet citizen—an enthusiastic participant in volunteer work, a heavy consumer of both informational and cultural media—and the reality of some citizens' unconcern and alienation.

As a criminal type, the Soviet murderer, for one, is not all that different from his counterparts in many other societies. Homicides arise from strong emotions, intense quarrels, in the context of hooliganism or other crimes. Over three-quarters of such crimes are not the subjects of long premeditation but are acts of impulse. Almost 80 percent of the victims, according to one report, are well-known to the murderer. Every third victim is a relative, nearly every fifth victim the legal or common-law spouse of the offender.[19]

There are indications as well that the Soviet criminal, in committing the act that may bring him into the dock, thinks little or not at all about the possible consequences to himself. To the question, "Did you think, before your crime, about punishment, and if so, why didn't it keep you from committing the crime?" 64 percent of a group of 245 inmates in a penal institution replied that they had not thought at all about punishment.[20] For those who see the threat of punishment as effective *mainly* against those of low educational-cultural level, another finding is equally damaging to the idea of deterrence: of that 64 percent into whose heads punishment, by their own testimony, never entered, only 14.7 percent had seven or more years of education.[21]

If several aspects of Soviet crime and Soviet criminals seem familiar to those interested in such matters in the West, another element is bound to be less so: the frequent assertions that crime is, on the whole, on the decline in the USSR. While specific deviations from this pattern in various areas and types of crime are acknowledged, the general picture is presented as one justifying optimism. The total absence of raw figures, however, gives the reader little reason, beyond faith in those who make the assertions, to believe them. R.A. Rudenko, Procurator-General of the USSR, set the pattern for such assertions at a conference in 1957, when he declared that if the number of convicted persons in the USSR in 1928 were to be represented by the number 100, then for 1955 the corresponding number of convictions could be represented by the number 63.[22] Of course, patterns of disposition of criminals are not unchanging, and these numbers generally refer to court cases, not to the total incidence of offenses of all types, some of which are unknown to the police, others of which are handled without criminal sanctions. But over 10 years later, the same pattern prevails. In 1968, basing his assertions on data assembled by the Institute of Criminology in Moscow, its director informs readers that "taking into account the growth of the population, the number of persons detected who have committed crimes was lower in 1967 in comparison with 1946, on a per 100 thousand basis, by more than 2 times."[23] Crime as a whole may or may not be declining in the USSR. We cannot really tell. It is interesting to observe, however, that the only attempt to present chronological data on convictions over a relatively long period which has yet appeared in the criminological literature indicates the opposite. Table 13 presents such data —for a small, relatively rural area, to be sure. We cannot generalize from these figures, yet they should not be disregarded. Crime grew in Lida *raion* in the ten years after Stalin's death, and the growth was not "mechanical"—it could not be accounted for by growth of the population itself. In the years covered, the population increased by approximately two-thirds, but the number of registered crimes at the end of the period was more than two and a half times greater. Is Lida *raion* a "deviant" case? We cannot tell—but such internal evidence may encourage skepticism about claims that would paint a different picture of the country as a whole.

Not even those in the USSR with access to classified materials on crime can really know the extent of the phenomenon as a whole. They rely on local police jurisdictions for initial collection of much information, and there is evidence that Soviet police sometimes succumb to the temptation of minimizing crime in their areas to convey the impression of effective law enforcement.[24] Thus any estimates one makes from afar would be very general indeed.[25] Whatever the size of the criminal population, whatever the real incidence of offenses, crime presents a problem whose existence Soviet criminologists are called upon to account for. This they have been attempting to do since the late 1950s, in an atmosphere of basic agreement on many aspects of theoretical presupposition and framework but with some no-

TABLE 13 CRIME RATE INDICES, 1953–1963, LIDA RAION, GRODNO OBLAST', BELORUSSIAN SSR (1953=100)

	1953	1954	1955	1956	1957	1958	1959†	1960†	1961	1962	1963
Registered crimes											
All	100	78	134	164	194	251	171	126	180	233	259
Per 1000 population	100	77	109	126	149	206	143	103	149	186	160
Number of persons whose cases were sent to court											
All	100	80	104	125	134	194	106	75	100	130	134
Per 1000 population °	100	80	88	100	110	166	94	66	84	108	106

° Data on age structure of population was not available. Consequently, a more correct calculation, on the basis of that portion of the population which had reached the age of criminal responsibility, was not possible (pp. 38–39).

† The drop in the crime rate in 1959 and 1960 reflects "significant errors" in the recording process in those years, which were marked by large-scale transfers of cases to comrades' courts, "the public" and other "social" measures. Therefore the data for these years " . . . cannot be regarded as complete" (p. 39).

Source: N.N. Kondrashkov, "Analiz raionnoi statistiki prestupnosti," *Voprosy preduprezhdeniia prestupnosti*, No. 4 (1966), p. 39.

table disagreements. It is difficult to do justice to the "criminological enterprise" in a limited number of pages, but it is to be hoped that something of the sort emerges from the section which follows.

THE STUDY OF CRIME
CAUSATION

The statistical data presented in the preceding section, such as they are, may already have given the reader some hints concerning the dominant emphasis or assumptions in the Soviet attempt to account for criminal behavior. The data focus on *properties* of the phenomenon of crime itself, notably the relative weights of different types of offenses, and on the linkages between criminal offenders and various contexts of socialization and control. With regard to the latter, it seems that the main thrust of research is to establish the majority of offenders as "flawed products" of certain institutions: the family (incompleteness or ineffectiveness in socialization), the school (wherein the criminal was unsuccessful and perhaps dropped out at an early age or was never reached by educators at all), the factory (where insufficient attention was given to the criminal's behavior off the job, and insufficient encouragement to "raise his qualifications"), and others.

The dominant emphasis, then, is on social factors which produce a person who leans toward criminal behavior. Soviet criminology moved toward its demise in the early 1930s after relatively open debate over the nature of crime and its causes was terminated in favor of a single, "social" approach. This conversion to the orthodoxy of one interpretation of Marxism saved neither criminology nor other social sciences from a long period of virtual extinction. There was a need to present criminological research during its revival in the late 1950s as an injustifiably repressed "orthodox" social science with real potential for providing information on which criminal-law policy decisions might be made. These facts go some way toward explaining the dominant emphasis on strictly social factors, initially external to the individual, pushing him toward crime (though not "determining" his criminal behavior).

To say, however, that this generally sociological approach, emphasizing the collection and interpretation of background data on offenders, is the dominant one in Soviet criminology today is not to present it as the only one. If one cannot talk of competing schools in Soviet criminology, one can readily detail serious differences in emphasis among criminologists themselves—differences which have become foci of controversy. It is perhaps best to think of the three approaches we are about to examine as "trends," as "orientations," rather than positions competing for recognition of their exclusive validity. The first, social approach is clearly the one with the best claim on ideological validity, and to some degree its protagonists do argue that it is exclusively so. The importance of this ideological dimension becomes clear in the attempts of those who back the other trends—the social-psychological and semibiological—to validate them not as competing theories but as contributions to an ideologically sound *general* theoretical framework, the social approach.

THE SOCIAL APPROACH

This orientation, of the three, makes the most explicit use of the concept of survivals as a base point for further specification of the sources of criminality. Its importance goes beyond its relatively tight fit with Soviet Marxism-Leninism. Organizationally, it seems accurate to say that it is the generally dominant approach at the Institute of Criminology in Moscow, the center of the discipline. It is, by and large, the approach which pervades the official criminology textbook (published under the Institute's auspices, with the authors' *kollektiv* dominated by the Institute's members).

The "social" approach involves the identification and description of various factors which account for the existence of crime as a social phenomenon and the criminal acts of individuals (though the latter issue, posed most sharply in the question of why, when two individuals are placed in similar social circumstances with criminogenic po-

tential, one commits a crime and the other does not, is the more difficult to resolve to the satisfaction of the theorists themselves). The
factors themselves are not all of the same order; some are seen as
having more impact than others. In exploring the theoretical content
of this approach, we may be well advised to rely on an authoritative
formulation—that of I.I. Karpets, director of the Institute of Criminology. While different authors use somewhat varied terminology, his
is sufficiently representative of this trend in criminological thought to
provide an adequate summary of its main points.

Karpets presents three "main general causes of the first order" that
are seen to account for the existence of crime as a "social phenomenon" in the USSR: "the historically conditioned quality of social phenomena," the "operation of the objective law of the lag of consciousness behind social life," and the "presence and influence of antagonistic socioeconomic formations along with socialism." [26] These
three causes all locate crime, in one way or another, within the
sphere of social evils generated by past or present capitalism. The
first, in the criminological context, signifies simply that the construction of the new socialist state could not but take place on the social
base inherited from Tsarist (capitalist) society. This base included a
large population of criminals, whose continued activity amounted to
an inherited crime problem. The "lag of consciousness behind life," as
an "objective law" dictates that attitudes and behavior patterns characteristic of one socioeconomic formation (capitalism) will in some
measure survive into another (socialism). Consciousness, at any given
point, will reflect life only imperfectly; "only in the final analysis is it
[consciousness] determined by the economic base." [27] Deviant and
criminal attitudes to which socialism itself has not given, and, it is
stated, *cannot* give birth survive and are propagated among persons
who never themselves experienced the capitalism that was the presumed source of those attitudes.

The simultaneous existence of capitalist and socialist "camps," of
"antagonistic socioeconomic formations," has both direct and indirect
"causal" effects on crime. Obviously, in the area of political or "especially dangerous state crimes," *direct* subversion by capitalist powers
can be brought into the dock and identified as the cause. But in a less
direct way, the capitalist world is seen in the role of an "attractive

nuisance," pregnant with danger for the attitudes and behavior of Soviet citizens. While capitalist society and ideology are "corrupt and crudely individualistic," Karpets is forced to conclude that

at the same time, with the high level of production in the leading capitalist countries and the rather high, though for a minority of people, standard of living, [capitalism] exerts a demoralizing influence on the minds and moods of insufficiently mature members of socialist society.

Such an influence is not always directly linked with crime. This link is far more subtle. Initially one may encounter incorrect views and a striving to imitate "Western style," way of life, striving for the "beautiful" life . . .[28]

Western radio, magazines, films, and tourists are all cited as sources of these "incorrect views," to which are laid such offenses as speculation in Western currencies, theft of "luxury" consumer goods, and the like.

Karpets is careful, however, not to project the blame for crime on capitalism as a single, decisive factor (the rhetoric of "capitalist encirclement," as Soviet criminologists admit, was overused as an explanation for crime in the past). Rather, capitalist influence is viewed as a "brake," an obstacle in the general tendency toward a reduction of crime, a factor injecting life into undesirable attitudes otherwise to be characterized as survivals.[29]

These, then, are the "causes of the first order." Secondary to and derived from them are other causes, themselves still on a rather high level of generality: "nonantagonistic contradictions" in socialist society. These contradictions, which flow from the historically conditioned quality of social life, might be regarded, in other words, as the growing pains Soviet society cannot escape. One variety encompasses contradictions in economic life: specifically, the gaps between urban and rural life and living standards, the differences, in levels of remuneration and job satisfaction, between mental and physical work, and lastly, the gap between the economic demands of the Soviet population and the ability of the socialist economy, at its present level of productivity, to satisfy them. These contradictions are seen as sources of dissatisfaction in persons who view their lot as less than they deserve, facilitating, *inter alia,* such attitudinal survivals as greed, selfishness, and others potentially related to crime. They are by definition problems of the *socialist* phase of the development of communism—the phase in which each contributes according to his abilities, but is rewarded according to his "work," rather than to his "needs" as in the ideal solution of "full communism." Reward according to the significance of one's type of work is seen as "socially just" in the socialist phase, but that phase itself is imperfect. The connection of these nonantagonistic economic contradictions to crime is occasionally challenged on the grounds that it is not the inequality-creating principle of reward according to work that fosters crime, but *violations* of the principle; [30] generally, however, the affirmation of their role remains a part of the theoretical underpinnings of the social approach to explaining crime causation.

There are nonantagonistic contradictions of an ideological variety as well, which return us to the notion of survivals: first, contradictions or gaps between individual and social consciousness, the "lagging" of those whose attitudes are infected by survivals behind the consciousness of the population as a whole. Second, *within* the individual himself, one element of consciousness may lag behind another, making for a person whose views on some dimensions are "progressive" but on others amount to survivals. The dimensions upon which the impact of socialism has been least remarkable are often those closest to individual day-to-day behavior. As Karpets notes, each form of consciousness is differentially responsive to progressive influence.

For example, the political views of Soviet people have progressed very rapidly. However, legal and moral-ethical views are much more tightly linked to national and cultural traditions of the past, to the sphere of everyday attitudes, social and individual psychology. Thus, they are more stable, and at times even inert.[31]

Politically loyal Soviet citizens whose general attitudes are progressive nonetheless can show certain blind spots. Petty pilfering and other forms of disrespect for socialist property and drunkenness are among the most frequently cited examples.

The reader may find the foregoing summary somewhat schematic and unsatisfying. If these "basic causes" are seen as underlying the social *phenomenon* of crime, how do they fit into an explanation of individual criminal behavior? This question is not easily answered by Soviet theorists themselves, and is even more difficult for an outsider. Throughout the 1960s, Soviet criminologists grappled with terminological and more substantive issues in an attempt to develop coherent schemes that would relate the class of factors Karpets refers to as the "first order" causes to the commission of particular crimes by particular citizens. These efforts have taken different directions and provoked moderate debates between partisans of one causal scheme or another, but most have involved the addition, in one form or another, of two lower-order factors, "conditions" (*usloviia*) and "circumstances" (*obstoiatel'stva*), to the "causes" (*prichiny*) themselves.

An example is the scheme published by V.N. Kudriavtsev, vice-director of the Institute of Criminology, in 1964.[32] Kudriavtsev labeled all three classes of factors as "circumstances," but the distinct nature of each is evident:

> 1. Circumstances which amount to elements of the "moral formation of the personality": the impact of family, school, peer-groups, labor collectives, and other elements of the immediate environment on the criminal's attitudes and values. These circumstances, taken as a whole, account for the infection of consciousness with survivals and thus come closest to being "causes" of crime.

> 2. Circumstances "impelling the person to the commission of a given crime": situational factors which are operative "only within the limits of a comparatively short time before the commission of the crime, and in the majority of cases directly and immediately precede it." These are, roughly, motivational elements within a particular situation, which push the actor toward the crime: e.g., a quarrel which motivates the actor to a physical assault. Some other Soviet writers would label these as "conditions."

> 3. Circumstances "making possible the achievement of a criminal result": factors of which the actor may or may not be aware that facilitate success in committing the crime. Examples of these (which *are* generally called "circumstances") might be faulty accounting procedures which make embezzlers' activity easier, or inadequate police patrolling which reduces the possibility of intervention before the fact in "street crimes."

The distinctions between the three classes are not airtight: a type 3 circumstance, perceived by a person prone to criminal acts, might well act as a type 2 condition sufficient to impel him to commit a crime, since he lacks moral restraints; whereas for a morally stable person, the presence or absence of type 3 circumstances will have no effect on behavior. But it is clear that Kudriavtsev attempts to isolate three different types of phenomena: first, the socialization processes which contribute to the development of deviant, antisocial attitudes; and their "result," the "moral deformation" of the actor—a relatively stable, enduring element. Second are the situational stimuli which push a morally unstable person toward crime but which are resisted by persons who have been adequately socialized. Finally, he takes into consideration aspects of the situation which reduce or increase the actor's chances of committing the crime successfully.

But there are differences in Soviet interpretations of the exact content of "conditions" and "circumstances." For S.S. Ostroumov of Moscow State University, as his scheme below shows, "conditions" themselves may be relatively enduring, and "circumstances" may be partly the product of the acts of the criminal himself.[33]

Causes: survivals of the past in consciousness and behavior of persons.	Conditions favoring the actualization of these causes.	Occasions or circumstances making possible the commission of a crime.
EXAMPLES	EXAMPLES	EXAMPLES
Profit motivation: greediness, unconscientious attitudes toward socialist property.	Work in a store where accounting and control are poorly organized; shortage of scarce goods; "approachable" friends, ready to take part in embezzlement and speculation.	Delivery of lot of scarce goods and possibility in connection with sickness of store manager to make out a false document for illegally obtaining these goods.
Disrespect for rules of socialist communal life.	Abuse of liquor, constant drinking bouts with companions in communal apartment or dormitory.	Fight in response to complaint of neighbor about violation of rules of socialist communal life, which leads to homicide or bodily injury.

Clearly there is some common ground here between Kudriavtsev and Ostroumov but no one-to-one correspondence between their concepts and the content of those concepts. Ostroumov's "causes" are themselves *effects* of socialization processes that lead to moral deformation, while Kudriavtsev's type 1 circumstances, viewed as processes rather than outcomes, could be the causes of Ostroumov's causes. Other Soviet criminologists have presented other schemes and reorderings of factors across the categories of condition and circumstance but, in common with Karpets, Kudriavtsev, and Ostroumov, generally work from a base which identifies crime as a survival, one of socialism's unwanted but inescapable inheritances.[34]

There are many conceptual difficulties on the general and the individual levels with these Soviet characterizations of the mechanics of crime causation. The identification of crime and other undesirable social phenomena as survivals may indeed flow logically from Marxist-Leninist "social science"; but no Soviet criminologist is in a position to question whether Marxism-Leninism *is* scientific, whether it provides an adequate base for explaining social phenomena. The clear point the survivals formula makes is an ideological one: "socialism" is in no way to blame for crime. Karpets, for example, recognizes that survivals are a general formula only—and that criminology requires that one inquire into the varied content of the formula. Survivals are the starting point, not the total explanation for why people commit crimes, nor does the identification of crime as a survival justify nonintervention born of a confidence that crime will eventually wither away. Intervention is not only the task of police and courts but also of criminologists, whose research must clarify and amplify the content of general formulae and provide a base for scientific crime prevention. But their research will not change the survivals formula—it is, and barring thoroughgoing ideological changes, will remain "nondisconfirmable." The formula itself is correct as the point of departure in explaining the presence of crime under socialism, because, as Karpets notes, it and it alone *"explains the historically non-immanent character of crime and helps to reveal the fact that socialism does not give birth to crime, that the regularities (zakonomernosti) immanent in socialism, do not give birth to crime."* [35] (Italics in original.)

The validity and utility of the survivals formula is not the only problem Soviet theoretical formulations present. Typical "catalogs" of second-order causes, or conditions, seem to lump together, in a confusing fashion, elements on very different levels. Ostroumov (in above diagram) sees the bare fact of a person's working in a store where accounting is poor as a condition favoring the actualization of survivals in attitude in the form of crime, and he regards abuse of liquor—which in itself is already a "deviant" act—as a condition on the same level. In both cases, there is "deviance": but in the first, it is the poor work of the accountant, not any act of the criminal, while in the latter case, the "condition" is the criminal's alcoholic deviance. Similar examples in the work of other Soviet criminologists are not lacking.[36]

For all the differences in these theoretical formulations, however, the research efforts of criminologists reflect rather striking similarities. They "operationalize" the survivals formula in the only way that seems possible: by focusing on those elements of the criminal's background where evidence of faulty socialization and control, of the passing on of attitudinal survivals (or "deviant orientations"), may be sought. As noted at the beginning of this section, the criminal is a "flawed product" of Soviet society, whose flaws are imputed to malfunctioning institutions, such as family, school, youth organizations, factory, local propaganda and cultural organizations, and also attributed to negative aspects of the immediate environment—drunkenness, immorality, venality, and so forth on the part of one's neighbors, work mates, etc.

Yet, even assuming that a connection of these negative inputs in a life history to high risks of criminal behavior on the part of an individual receiving them is a logical one, the question of why *this* person, a bearer of all this negative baggage, commits a crime, while in similar circumstances *that* person, with no lighter a load of disadvantaging inputs, does not, remains unresolved. (It should be noted that Soviet criminology and criminal law both view the offender as acting voluntarily. Being the bearer of survivals may increase one's tendency to criminal behavior, but it will not *determine* that one will commit a crime. While crimes are seen as socially "determined," social in their causes, the determinism is of a sufficiently soft variety to accommodate the view of a crime, in the last analysis, as a "subjective, voluntary act." [37])

This is by no means a problem unique to Soviet criminology. Students of crime in other lands who take a generally sociological approach to crime causation have also found that while predictive indices of crime-proneness may emerge from the collection of background data on criminals, the establishment of the final links in the causal chain that leads to an individual's committing a crime is the hardest task of all. For Soviet criminology, it is made harder by the relative lack of psychological training among criminologists (a legacy itself to some degree of the proscription of psychological criminology over forty years ago) and the absence of any useful model of the individual criminal actor. It is this weak point in social criminology in the USSR that, more than any other, seems to be responsible for the development of the two divergent trends to be discussed later in this chapter. Before moving on to consider them, however, two further aspects of the social approach demand consideration: the roles assigned, in the overall causal analysis, to "material" factors and to the consequences of rapid industrialization and urbanization. Western criminologists have dealt at length with the impact of poverty and low living standards on crime, as well as attempting to specify linkages between the large-scale social transformations that create modern industrial societies and what may be their negative consequences —among others, a weakening of traditional (and, as frequently assumed, more effective) mechanisms of social control, resulting in increases in the incidence of deviant and criminal behavior. Soviet criminology, in its own way, has also been forced to grapple with these questions, though its answers have generally been different from those arrived at in the West. Yet there are some indications (tenuous at best) that the answers themselves are no longer as certain as they once were.

Economic causes of crime, such as unemployment, hunger and poverty, have been eradicated "for all time" in the USSR: [38] whatever the validity of this assertion (and validity depends, greatly if not entirely, on the definition one or another observer attaches to these economic categories), it *is* an article of faith for Soviet writers. Dealing with economic factors in crime becomes a difficult business, since crime cannot be attributed to the same economic conditions that "inescapably" produce it under capitalism. Yet, that there *are* economic factors in crime Soviet criminologists no longer deny.

One cannot be distracted from the fact that the existing nonantagonistic contradiction between the demands of man and the possibilities of their satisfaction exert a certain level of influence on the life of our society. The individual sometimes tries to satisfy these "demands" in a way that is not at all legal.[39]

However, are the demands, the needs, that drive people to theft and other property crimes, legitimate? Are such offenses born of a gap between resources and needs that threatens physical existence, i.e., poverty? Predictably, since the latter has been "eradicated," the answer is no. While the contradiction between demands and their fulfilment remains one of the marks of an imperfect transitional phase of communism,

only an insignificant number of property crimes depend directly on this contradiction. Criminological researches show that the guilty person explains his crime thus: "he didn't have enough money for vodka." This, of course, cannot be taken as a material factor. Practically, such phenomena are testimony to the moral instability, the lack of socialization, the low culture of the individual.[40]

The average property crime, then, is seen as a product not of pressing need but of a lack in moral strength which permits the choice of illegal means in attaining wanted but not needed items. As for those offenses which do involve *real* need (theft of grain from collective farm storehouses by farm workers without sufficient food is cited), their cause is not a quality of the system, not a "contradiction," but rather shortcomings in administration on "some" farms.[41] The concatenation at a given point in time of pressing material needs and the absence of a legal way to fulfill them is seen as "incidental" to the Soviet system as a whole.

Hence, as a general cause of crime, poverty is given less than a small role to play. There is, perhaps, something of a contradiction between the Soviet view that rising living standards represent an element of "general" preventive significance and assertions that "even now" few property crimes, of the large number committed, can be attributed to low living standards.[42] But it is a contradiction that Soviet criminologists manage to live with.

Even this much discussion of material factors, and the admission that *some* Soviet citizens, at *some* times, are in circumstances of real need, represents a departure from earlier denials that economic factors had anything to do with Soviet crime. If the argument disposes, in a way satisfactory to those who make it, of "absolute" deprivation

as a cause of crime, it cannot deal so easily with "relative" deprivation: the stresses to which lower-paid, less advantaged Soviet citizens
may be subject as they perceive the gap between their own situations
and that of the better-paid, who enjoy more of life's benefits. That
there are inequalities flowing from the principle of payment "according to work" is admitted. That there are "still low-paid categories of
working people" [43] (and, by implication, relatively high-paid categories) is also admitted. These inequalities provide a basis for manifestations of "parasitic and mercenary" desires, aimed at increasing one's
share at society's expense, rather than through upgraded productivity.[44]

There is no easy way to fit the concept of relative deprivation into
an analysis of the forces behind Soviet criminal behavior. It is relatively easy for one whose background gives him Western standards of
comparison to conclude, from impressions of Soviet life, that the
spread of material goods between the bottom and top layers of society is not so inequalitarian as in some Western countries. Such impressions are fostered by a relatively general lack of many consumer
durables as well as an absence of variegated "private" housing, both
of which exercise a homogenizing effect on outward appearances. Yet
levels of reward *are* very different, the wage-and-salary range from
bottom to top is a very large one, and the distribution of privileges,
economic and other, is as unequal as in many capitalist countries.
The gradations of privilege and deprivation, difficult for an observer
from a more affluent society to detect, are probably much clearer to
the Soviet citizen with his own more realistic standards of comparison. Until Soviet scholars attempt to discover these standards and relate them to the difficult and sensitive issue of deprivation, the gener-
alities about "material factors" will probably remain the official line
on the linkage of living standards to crime in the USSR. It has been
much easier for Soviet criminologists to recognize the white collar
criminal, who diverts large sums to his own account through manipulation of a responsible job, as a property offender *not* motivated by
need than it has been to come to grips with those whose offenses are
to some degree products of felt needs, whether or not they are
"legitimate."

It has been fashionable in the West to connect rising rates of crime to varieties of social isolation, alienation, and general *malaise* which are putatively the products of urbanization and industrialization. These modernizing processes, entailing the often abrupt rupture of traditional social and locational ties and a consequent weakening of traditional modes of social control, introduce people to new and unfamiliar situations, new problems, and new demands without simultaneously supplying new and effective modes of integrating the individual into the new contexts: hence, higher rates of "deviation" tend to result.

Whatever the merits of this position (stated here in a very general form), Soviet criminologists in the past have been very much of two minds about it. Quite willing to acknowledge the negative consequences of industrialization and urbanization in their nineteenth-century capitalist variants—overcrowding, overwork, exploitation of men in jobs and surroundings new and strange to them, and the production of a new class of urban poor—they have denied any similar effects to modernization under a socialist banner.

Industrialization brings about changes in the lives of people, but in socialist society it is a positive social factor. The possibility of planned regulation of the phenomena accompanying industrialization, such as urbanization and migration of population, makes it possible to neutralize the effect on people's life of possibly negative factors linked with urbanization and migration (changes in the habitual life surroundings, displacement of large masses of the population, over-population, etc.).[45]

Certainly, Soviet industrialization was "planned"—but the rapid migration of peasant recruits to the new industrial centers and their subsequent overcrowding in cities where housing construction was a matter of low priority produced conditions scarcely "neutralized" by planned regulation. The "possibility" was not realized during the period of forced-draft economic development. But, until recently at least, criminologists continued to view "socialist" urbanization and industrialization as progressive processes and refused to acknowledge that such processes, in themselves, had any potential for generating the social disorganization that may give rise to crime.[46] There was no "content" in these processes that remained independent of their socialist or capitalist auspices.

This optimistic position took little account of a stubborn fact: that the crime rate in Soviet cities was much above the rural rate. In this, the USSR mirrored other modern societies. On a crimes-per-10,000-persons basis, the rate in urban areas exceeded that in rural areas by as much as 40 percent.[47] Unless by some process of natural selection crime-prone persons were settling predominantly in cities, the urban-rural crime rate disparity demanded some explanation.

An attempt to meet this demand was made in 1968, when an article on criminological aspects of population migration by a researcher at the Institute of Criminology appeared in *Sovetskoe gosudarstvo i pravo.* Connecting migration with the urbanization-industrialization processes still going on in underdeveloped areas of the USSR, the author, M.M. Babaev, while noting that higher urban crime rates were not, in socialist society, a "fatal" attribute, argued that they were a product of the fact that

in many cases the scale of organizational and upbringing work does not yet correspond to the scale of the phenomenon itself—the tempo and scale of city construction in the USSR. As a result, in the cities there exists a larger quantity of negative factors, promoting the formation of antisocial views, habits . . . than in rural locales.[48]

Babaev does not expand in great detail on the "negative factors." But it is clear that he has in mind the large-scale introduction of young, male workers, predominantly of rural background and either single or at a distance from their wives and children, into cities undergoing rapid development of the industrial base but much less rapid construction of housing and leisure facilities. In this frontier-town environment, a high incidence of violent behavior is perhaps to be expected—but such migrants, male, relatively young, of rural origin, make up much of the mechanical population increase in older Soviet cities as well. With appropriate phraseological modifications, Babaev's observations on the situation of such migrants might have come from a Western social scientist.

Processes of migration may be and often are accompanied by some negative phenomena: with the move to the city, social control over the young man on the part of the family, the immediate everyday environment and the like, which is as a rule more effective in the village than in the city, weakens or is completely lost; the young man, coming from the village, is not always able to understand correctly, and manage to distinguish the real, progressive urban culture and as a result sometimes accepts the worst and most harmful things for the model of urban culture and "city behavior." [49]

Much more could be written about the social approach to the explanation of Soviet crime. Throughout the now more than ten years of reestablished criminology, it has been the basic framework within which most Soviet criminologists have worked. To consider in greater detail the many differences of terminology and nuance that have emerged *within* the approach over this period would be to add many more pages without, perhaps, any comparably greater increment of understanding for the reader. For, in a sense, the social approach is a rough label for a general focus on social factors—a focus which differs in its particulars from one criminologist to the next. The other approaches we are about to discuss may be seen as deviations from this approach, emphasizing those psychological or biological elements which are either proscribed or left relatively unexamined within the social perspective. Yet as a *category* of criminological thought and of research itself, the social approach might also be seen as residual: that category which lacks these other foci, which does not examine these questions. To describe it other than has been done here would be to impose a unity that does not exist. This is all the more true when note is taken of elements of change within the approach itself, most specifically those examples of increased attention and greater readiness to examine the implications of material factors, urbanization, and industrialization, which were once accorded little discussion or dismissed outright as having no relevance to contemporary Soviet crime.

If these elements of change cause few lifted eyebrows among Western readers, they are nonetheless significant in their intimations of an increasing readiness on the part of Soviet criminologists to examine their own assumptions about urban industrial life, socialist-style. Babaev does not argue that relatively high urban crime rates are inescapable under socialism. He only recognizes that they exist, and links them with shortcomings in those aspects of socialist planning and its execution which are supposed to "neutralize" the unsettling consequences of urbanization and industrialization. This in itself amounts to greater frankness in treating the topic than many other writers have manifested.

THE CRIMINAL
PERSONALITY

The clearly social orientation of Soviet criminology in the years of its rebirth is neither surprising nor difficult to explain. To be consistent with Marxism-Leninism, and thus to achieve the status of a "valid" enterprise, it had to be social in its emphasis. In the late 1920s, *any* "psychologizing" of the criminal, whether rooted in biological ideas or not, came to be identified with "error."

However, in the late 1950s, some Soviet scholars came to realize that the reborn discipline of criminology was, in its emphasis on the social, almost completely avoiding consideration of the personality of the criminal—the lawbreaker as an individual. Data might be assembled on the types of crimes individuals committed, on the occupations and educational levels of criminals; but these, however informative, were attributes only and said little about the attitudes, emotions, and other components of the criminal's mental world. Various statements appeared in the legal journals referring to the necessity of studying the personality of the criminal,[50] evoking little active response but at least demonstrating that there was little consensus on what the term itself meant. In a sense "the personality of the criminal" was the label for a residual category, representing a set of issues Soviet criminology had yet to confront.

These issues were confronted in 1961 in what was the most ambitious monograph yet published in the criminological field during the rebirth period, A.B. Sakharov's *On the Personality of the Criminal and the Causes of Crime in the U.S.S.R.*[51] Sakharov focused his attention squarely on the criminal actor, to a large degree but not entirely within the larger, "valid" context of Soviet "social" criminology. Accepting the existence of deviant immediate environments, themselves products of the lag of consciousness behind reality and of the influences of the hostile capitalist world, he viewed such environments as bases for deviant socialization ("moral formation") which produced antisocial attitudes and habits in the individual. Such subjective characteristics rendered the individual crime-prone. Persons with antisocial characteristics in a situation where objective circumstances facilitated committing a crime would be most likely to do so.

Though there was little in this "causation model" to link it with the biologizing and psychologizing of the 1920s, Sakharov perceived that his insistence on a deep study of the "psychic peculiarities" of the criminal might raise objections. The role of such personality characteristics, he noted, had not been studied in the USSR for "over 30 years," since Soviet scholars had rejected explanations of crime employing "biological, psychic or psychophysical, inborn and unchangeable properties of the individual." While such a rejection was ideologically correct, it did not exclude the "allowability and necessity" of studying, in the proper way, the role and significance of personality characteristics in the causation of criminal behavior.[52] As Sakharov noted, Gertsenzon himself had said that external causes did not work on the individual "mechanically," but through his "psyche, temperament and character." But nowhere had Gertsenzon *explained* the role these psychological elements played.[53]

These disclaimers, however, were not enough to protect Sakharov from criticism, as he developed his conceptions of temperament and character as elements of the personality. He began his examination of the criminal's personality from a Pavlovian standpoint, focusing on qualities such as "force," "balance," and "liveliness," variations in which make for different types of "higher nervous activity."

The force, balance and [degree of] liveliness of nervous activity, which themselves characterize the types of higher nervous activity of persons, are the physiological basis of their temperament, and temperament is also the manifestation of the type of higher nervous activity in the behavior, in the actions of a person.[54]

Four types of "temperament," corresponding to the predominance of particular types of higher nervous activity, provide the bases for four types of personality. The sanguine person (*sangvinik*) is lively and responsive, with impulsive feelings which may override his thought and will. His feelings are, however, of relatively short duration. His joys and sorrows alike pass rapidly. The choleric (*kholerik*) person is resolute and decisive, quick to respond to insult, and his feelings are deep-rooted and enduring. The phlegmatic (*flegmatik*) shares deep-rootedness of feelings with the choleric but is lower in "impressionability." He responds slowly and with a greater degree of deliberation. The melancholic (*melankholik*) is marked by indecision and wavering, leans toward passivity, and has a pathological capacity for psychological suffering from "even insignificant" causes.[55] Sakharov observed that these are, in a sense, "pure types." They are not full descriptions of concrete individuals, but rather indicate relatively commonly encountered ensembles of temperament traits.

If temperament is an important component of the personality, and varies in type, it is not the sole determinant of behavior nor of variations in behavior. "Character" plays a large role also. It is built of such elements as "level of intellectual development, world-views, moral tendencies, the character of the individual's interests and demands, the qualities of his will, etc." [56] Character influences the objectives one chooses, how one proceeds in their pursuit, and how one relates to oneself and to others. People's characters differ—some are highly principled, others "unprincipled"; some are optimistic, some pessimistic.[57] Characters, it seems, can be relatively good or bad, and variations along this moral dimension have great import.

In the individual, character and temperament form an "indissoluble unity." The important questions are the kind of character and temperament traits that have been combined in the unity and the implications of particular temperament traits when linked with certain characterological elements.

Depending on the tendency of the personality, the level and breadth of its demands and interests, the moral qualities, properties of the will and the other social qualities of the individual, the marks of temperament assume a positive or negative significance, insofar as they strengthen or weaken the characteristics referred to, [and] determine how these characteristics will be manifested in the individual's behavior, in his acts.[58]

Sakharov discussed the sorts of possibilities arising from various combinations of temperament and character traits. A sanguine person with positive qualities of character, with a high level of intellectual development, and with correct social views will be an optimistic, enthusiastic, and effective citizen at work and in private life. Conversely, if the *sangvinik* lacks serious interests and firm moral views (if, in other words, his character is flawed), his temperament renders him susceptible to negative influences from other persons, and his impressionability increases the likelihood of his committing deviant acts at the instigation of others. The combination of choleric temperament and "good" character traits Sakharov sees as producing a personality marked by sincerity, love of work, independence, purposefulness, and manliness. A deformed character added to a choleric temperament may produce individualism, egoism, and other antisocial characteristics. In view of the *kholerik*'s decisiveness and quickness to act, these characteristics may well be translated into antisocial behavior.[59] Such an outcome seems more likely here, for instance, than in the case of a person with a phlegmatic temperament. Sakharov also detected a tendency toward oversimplification among those criminologists who conceived of criminals as weak-willed persons. The Soviet definition of will as the "capacity to subordinate one's own actions to the demands of objective necessity and above all to ends having social significance, to social duty," he felt, obscured the significance of certain combinations of character traits, especially combinations of certain moral qualities with differing strengths of will (here taking "will" in the more general sense of resolve). Negative circumstances may evoke antisocial acts in weak-willed persons when they are not basically "morally corrupt." Much greater, however, is the danger presented by the strong-willed person whose antisocial attitudes point him toward antisocial acts.[60]

Despite the rather vague character of his concepts, Sakharov had gone further in discussing the makeup of the criminal's personality than any other Soviet writer. The most important question his monograph (which received generally favorable reviews) raised for other criminologists was the "validity" of concentrating research effort on the personality characteristics of individual criminals, when it was already an item of dogma that crime was a socially caused phenomenon. Was Sakharov leaning toward the biologizing of the 1920s?

According to Sakharov himself, the answer was no. Though he

went so far as to say that temperament was "originally" (*pervona-chal'no*) conditioned by heredity, he observed that it was further developed and transformed during the life of the individual.[61] Thus, neither temperament, nor even less character, are preordained, inborn, and unchangeable, but depend in the end on the conditions of social existence of the person, on the influences of the surrounding environment to which the individual is unceasingly subjected in the whole course of his life.[62]

No type of temperament, in combination with a set of character traits, determined that a person would become a criminal. But Sakharov had introduced a seemingly morally neutral element, temperament, which had some roots, however shallow, in heredity as a relevant consideration in accounting for criminal behavior. Some reviewers seemed to misunderstand Sakharov, seeing in his views a notion of the existence of the "criminal personality" as a particular *type*. N.S. Leikina, in commenting on the book, ranked Sakharov with those criminologists who seemed to feel that "all criminals have antisocial orientations"; whereas some crimes, at least, "do not express antisocial orientations but only testify to the absence in sufficient measure in the guilty one of intensive forces sufficient to counteract the negative situation and not go beyond the bounds set by law." [63] Yet this description would seem to fit Sakharov's noncorrupt but weak-willed, impressionable criminal. Sakharov, in any case, was not at the time arguing the relevance of any concept of the *criminal personality* but rather the importance of studying the *personalities of criminals*— a very different idea.

Nonetheless, critics were quick to find unacceptable elements in Sakharov's notions. Those who held to a strictly social view of crime read him as reintroducing irrelevancies. A.A. Gertsenzon, after complimenting him on his capable treatment of the operation of some social causes of crime, complained that, on the same level, "A.B. Sakharov places also 'causes' of a purely individual, biopsychological character." [64] Gertsenzon remains relatively unreconciled to the "innovative" elements in Sakharov's work.[65]

Most reviewers, however, praised the work as a whole. The issue of whether temperament is a biological concept has moved into the background, and other writers have heeded Sakharov's call for more investigation of the qualities of the criminal's personality and how flaws in "moral formation" can be traced to deviant "immediate environments" in which some persons are socialized. In the later 1960s, some Soviet authors were discussing "reference groups" and their significance for the individual, especially when such groups supported informal norms in conflict with the demands of the criminal law. More attention is now being paid to the multiple possibilities of personality formation that arise because of the Soviet citizen's membership in numerous small reference groups over which the "healthy" society of which he is also a member has little direct control.[66]

Sakharov's writings in the late 1960s extended some of the lines laid down in his 1961 work. He continued to argue that "personality" was a social concept, and thus that it and its components were quite valid objects of criminological inquiry. Further, he saw the study of the personalities of criminals as aiming toward the establishment of knowledge about complexes of characteristics more or less typical of lawbreakers as a whole or of diverse types of offenders (thus seeming to leave the door open for the notion of types of criminal personality). Linking such complexes of psychological characteristics and their interrelations with knowledge of external, situational factors would allow criminologists to make "definite prognoses" concerning the behaviors to be expected from different personalities in similar situations, or from the same person in different situations.[67]

In his later writing, Sakharov has ranked himself with those who see crime as generally, but not totally, socially conditioned. While crime in the large is a social phenomenon, those who reject totally all nonsocial factors in the explanation of criminal behavior are, in his opinion, unduly narrowing their perspective.

Let us say right away: crime has no purely biological "roots" whatsoever. . . . This, however, does not mean that psychophysiological and biological symptoms have no significance whatever in the structure of the individual's personality properties and qualities which condition his commission of a crime. The human personality, including the criminal's personality, is a product of definite social influences, linkages and relations. But social influences address themselves to and fall upon definite, often very different, natural bases. To ignore these bases would be incorrect.[68]

In general, Sakharov and those who show his influence remain within the general boundaries of criminological orthodoxy, though at times they seem to tread very close to them. One can credit Sakharov with bringing a social-psychological perspective to a Soviet criminology which completely lacked it. To some, this approach, with its talk of "antisocial personality sets," whatever their source, remains suspect.[69] The lines which mark a boundary between the "strictly social" approach already described and Sakharov's mix of social influence and individual psychology are still visible and justify our description of the two as different "persuasions." But the work of some younger criminologists suggests that the lines are gradually fading.

CRIMINALITY AND BIOLOGY

The opposition manifested during the period of criminology's revival to attempts to psychologize criminal behavior made for the mixed reception accorded Sakharov's work, though in itself it was social-psychological in nature. Opposition to another small school of criminologists was much sharper.

This school, whose main protagonist is I.S. Noi of the Saratov Juridical Institute, emerged in the late 1950s with arguments that seemed to reintroduce the idea of the criminal personality as a thing distinct—arguments its critics were to find too reminiscent of the psychologizing and biologizing of the 1920s. At a conference in Saratov in 1958, Noi and a collaborator, L.G. Krakhmal'nik, argued that among the causes of crime, in addition to survivals in consciousness, were the "bad characters of persons and definite qualities of their temperament." [70] While the authors saw these as the results of poor socialization, such an emphasis on "psychic characteristics" was not fated to go unchallenged.

In 1959 Noi and Krakhmal'nik went further into disputed territory, arguing that some criminals were psychopaths and that they should be viewed as having "reduced responsibility" for their acts.[71] In Soviet psychiatry and psychology, the notion psychopath carries with it the idea of *physical* causation, differentiating it from Western notions of "sociopathic" personalities which do not necessarily include elements of a physical, neurological nature. Noi and Krakhmal'nik had reintroduced biological questions into criminology.

In the following years, Noi and his collaborators expanded their ar-

guments on the large incidence of psychopaths in the criminal population, most frequently in the context of writings referring to the necessity to treat psychopaths in a different way from other prisoners in
penal institutions. (It is probably worth noting that these opinions
generally were not published in articles in the "national" legal journals but in collections of conference papers from provincial cities or
in monographs published in Saratov. Whether Noi failed to seek national outlets or found access to them blocked is an interesting question.)

In a 1961 essay, Krakhmal'nik and Noi asked whether the study of
the crimes of psychopaths had "a right to exist," and, in answering that
it did, remarked that for the "past 30 years" not only had such studies
not been conducted, but the very posing of the question [of psychopaths as a component of the criminal population] had been "mistakenly held to be methodologically fallacious." [72] Most interesting were
the sources they used to justify their position: N.P. Brukhanskii's
1928 textbook in forensic psychiatry, where the author states that "a
good half of the criminal world is recruited from the ranks of
psychopaths"; [73] another 1928 text in which the authors refer to the
high "specific weight" of psychopaths among criminals; [74] and a 1958
paper by a relatively young Moscow criminologist who argued that
especially dangerous recidivists were "often characterized by psychopathic characteristics." [75] Even Khrushchev's support was enlisted,
though a statement the then Soviet leader made to a May 1959 writers' congress: "crime—it is a deviation from the generally accepted
norms of behavior in a society, not infrequently called forth by disturbances in the psyche of a person." [76]

The return to sources from the 1920s to defend a point was somewhat striking. Writing alone in a 1962 monograph, Noi presented virtually the same sources in defense of his argument. [77] It is certainly
possible that at this early stage of the criminological revival, the
1920s had not yet been reconsidered in full from an ideological standpoint, and it may have been unclear which writers and opinions of
that time would remain unfashionable. In 1968, a critic was to re-
mark:

As we see, I.S. Noi leans on the statements of those authors who in 1929
were already subjected to just criticism because they had attempted to

bring the methods of narrowly specialized natural sciences into the area of social phenomena, and whose data do not withstand examination.[78]

In a conference paper published in summary in 1965, Noi and two other colleagues, V.A. Shabalin and Iu. A. Demidov, went further toward a confrontation, stating that "until recently an oversimplified, at times vulgar-sociological approach to the explanation of the causes of antisocial tendencies in the behavior of lawbreakers has dominated in Soviet legal science." [79] Noi and his coauthors write of "innate programs of the individual's behavior," which were "coded" into the consciousness at the instinctual level.[80] Having raised the specter of instinct, they noted that their position had "nothing in common with antiscientific reactionary bourgeois biocriminological and sociological theories." [81] But this qualification was not enough.

I.I. Karpets led off the accusations in 1966.

Distorting the real essence of the phenomena, he [Noi] has attempted to explain the committing of crimes in terms of biological features of the human organism. . . . However, if social instincts in general have been "coded" from birth and therefore criminal instincts are also "coded," . . . criminal law becomes senseless, as does the punishment of the criminals. . . . It must be emphasized, to begin with, that in seeking to validate their pseudo-scientific theory, the authors offer a false interpretation of the postulates of prominent physiologists, and clearly mold those statements to fit their concept.[82]

V.N. Kudriavtsev, who had criticized Noi's ideas back in 1960,[83] wrote in 1967 that "the acceptance or denial of hereditary factors in crime" was one of the most crucial questions for criminology. Just as Karpets had, he saw Noi and his colleagues as arguing for their acceptance. In refutation, Kudriavtsev cited the example of so-called "feral" children to show the preponderant influence of social environment in developing patterns of behavior. The radical variation of such children from the norm made it impossible, in his view, to speak of "innate behavior programs" coded into the individual.[84]

During the same period others who shared, or seemed to share, the views of Noi and his colleagues also met with criticism. During a 1964 conference at the Institute of Criminology, one I.L. Petrukhin suggested that the Institute concern itself with the causes of socially dangerous acts committed by the mentally ill, using the resources of "biological as well as legal science." A.A. Gertsenzon, who had been critical of Sakharov's much milder thoughts on the personality, replied that there was "no place" for biology in the study of crime's causes.[85] Support for the idea of inborn predispositions to criminality, even when it came from nonlegal scholars in out-of-the-way sources, was criticized. Both Gertsenzon and Karpets entered the pages of *Izvestiia* to deal with a young geneticist from the Academy of Sciences who had argued (in a journal devoted to radio and television) that studies of the parallel development of twins showed an element of heredity in such phenomena as crime and alcoholism.[86] Criticisms continued to be aimed at those who claimed their research showed that many crimes were conditioned by psychopathy.[87]

Support for the idea that certain biologically conditioned psychological characteristics play some role in increasing some individuals' propensities for antisocial behavior was not, however, lacking. Generally, it came from scholars with legal or psychological training, who specialized in "corrective-labor science" (penology). One of this number, N.A. Struchkov, argued that in his 1966 criticism of Noi, Shabalin, and Demidov, Karpets had misunderstood their point, which Struchkov took to be only that "the qualities of the criminal's personality" should "also" be taken into account in explaining the mechanism of crime causation.[88] In complaining of the dominance of a "vulgar-sociological" approach, Noi was not seeking to answer all criminology's questions with biology but only to call attention to the role and significance of those "internal factors" left unexamined so long. That the "internal factors," the traits of the criminal's nervous system, were to some degree biologically conditioned, Struchkov did not deny, nor did he deny that they might be inherited. But they operated only in conjunction with external factors, results of socialization and situational elements, to cause crime. There were no Lombrosian "born" criminals, nor, according to Struchkov, had Noi and his colleagues claimed that there were. Together with the doyen of Soviet corrective-labor law specialists, B.S. Utevskii, Struchkov defended the same points in 1967 in an article in *Literaturnaia gazeta* entitled, "It Is Not So Simple." [89] The debate continued with a rejoinder from Karpets, Kudriavtsev, and others in *Izvestiia* in 1968.[90]

Karpets' summary position on Noi, his ideas and defenders appeared in his 1969 monograph, *The Problem of Crime:*

Ignoring the circumstance that man is an essence above all social, and those conditions that influence him are themselves the result of social processes in the life of society, some scholars have begun to seek an explanation of the causes of crime in biological factors.[91]

Among "some scholars" he numbered Noi and his various collaborators. Nor, as Struchkov suggested, had he "misunderstood" Noi. In attempting to "broaden the scientific base" for studying the personality of the criminal, a necessary task, Noi had gone too far. A "broadened base," according to Karpets, could not include biologically "innate" (and hence, in some cases, nonmanipulable) properties. In answer to Utevskii and Struchkov, Karpets said the following:

Stating that they are opponents of Lombrosianism, the authors further affirm that the individual is born with socially useful or socially harmful instincts in him, that the individual happens from nature [to be] brutal and so on. At the same time they argue that "in general" V.N. Kudriavtsev has shown results of research on the personalities of lawbreakers refuting the biological character of crime.

The arguments of B.S. Utevskii and N.A. Struchkov about "predispositions" and so on are reminiscent of the fruitless discussions of the 1920's on the very same theme.[92]

In the same year (1969), Noi restated his own position once again, criticizing criminology for a treatment of the interrelation of the biological and social in man that was "still far from adequate." He again confronted the positions represented by Karpets, Gertsenzon, et al.

A vulgar-sociological approach to studies of the criminal, linked with an underestimation and even denial of the psychic peculiarities of the individual in the genesis of his behavior, has caused serious harm to Soviet criminological science.[93]

Not only the theoretical approach, but the research methods as well, were seen as hampering criminology's development.

The struggle of certain representatives of the social sciences against the penetration of natural-science methods into social research is becoming a serious obstacle on the path to the furthest development of Marxist sociology and especially Soviet criminology.[94]

Noi made clear in further statements the gap existing between himself and his opponents. Criticizing the first edition of the criminology textbook for ignoring biological elements in explaining criminal behavior, he identified such a position with a "vulgarization" of Marx and Engels, citing Engels' admission that, in their attempt to dispose of Feuerbach's view of man as a totally biological essence, he and Marx purposely overstated their position on social relations as the prime determinant in personality formation.[95] Finally, in a move scarcely calculated to convince his critics that the "broadening" he proposes is one that Soviet criminology can accommodate, he notes that the science of genetics ° might play a major role in opening new and unexplored areas in criminology.[96]

Noi's position and, to varying degrees, those of his supporters and defenders present a number of problems which Soviet criminology has yet to resolve. As a statement on the mechanics of crime causation, it introduces an element that had been alien to Soviet criminology since 1929—biologically conditioned properties of the nervous system and the "psyche" of the offender, regarded as relevant to his conduct. His is scarcely full-blown Lombrosianism, although it may appear such to his critics who reject "biology" out of hand.

The problem Noi's position presents is both scientific and ideological—but the two are to some degree intermingled. Without attempting here to judge the scientific merits of the position, one can state that Western criminology (with some exceptions) has generally not only rejected Lombrosianism, but refused to grant any important role to biological factors as elements in crime causation.[97] Nor have Karpets and others among Noi's critics hesitated, in attacking his ideas, to note that many "bourgeois criminologists" have likewise rejected biological notions of inherited criminality and crime causation.[98] Many of the arguments made against any biologizing tenden-

---

° However, it is worth noting that Noi, at least in those writings available to the author, says nothing directly about *heredity* and crime. Nowhere is the argument made that criminal fathers breed criminal sons through any biological mechanism. But it is not *denied* that the biologically based characteristics to which he attributes "relevance" can be passed on in this manner. The matter remains rather unclear.

cies by Soviet scholars are based on the same principles that their
Western counterparts use. At a 1970 symposium, Kudriavtsev argued
that the variety of norms given expression in Soviet criminal law was
so great and that many of the norms were so formal that one could
not talk reasonably of genetically inherited biological propensities to
transgress them. How, he asked, could one argue that genetic properties would account for a violation of the law against "negligent cutting of a marine telegraph cable"? [99] Kudriavtsev was attempting a
reductio ad absurdum (though his selection of a crime of negligence
for the purpose was a poor one) which, successful or not, in a way resembles the American criminologist Donald Cressey's statement that
one "cannot inherit a biological predisposition to behave in a manner
that is criminalistic only because it has arbitrarily been so labeled by
a social group." [100] Neither Kudriavtsev nor other critics of Noi, however, have confronted squarely the implications of his ideas for violent crimes against property and the person, which lie closer to the
main concerns of criminal law than do offenses of negligence.

The main response to Noi's position on the psychological abnormality of many criminals has been to argue their minimal relevance in
criminology and criminal law. On the one hand, some of his critics,
recognizing that "psychopaths" do exist, claim that they make up only
an infinitesimal percentage of all criminals.[101] It is also argued that
the fact of psychopathy does not justify the conclusion that it, in itself, *caused* the criminal act: by and large, the "psychopath" can be
considered responsible for his acts,[102] just as is the "normal" criminal.
Results of forensic-psychiatric investigations are cited to support this
point [103]—although Soviet forensic psychiatry is not a permissive science in the scope it gives for claims of non-responsibility.[104]

On the other hand, those persons whose mental illnesses are serious
and who are found to be non-responsible for their acts are not "criminals" at all, nor are they the concern of criminologists.

Research on psychopathology, even [that] connected with the commission
of socially dangerous acts, is the province of psychiatrists, not of criminologists; nor are pathological conditions and psychic deviations the causes of
crime, for these very same [socially dangerous] acts, when committed by
those not responsible, are not crimes.[105]

Thus, the "average" psychopathic criminal is responsible. His psychopathy, not being the *cause,* cannot serve as an excuse for his criminal acts. The psychopath or other ill person whose illness renders him irresponsible is not a criminal at all. The problem is defined away.

Ideological problems, however, remain. Karpets, though he may have concluded more from Noi than the latter wished to say, was not far off the mark in noting that, if some "instincts" (orientations, "tendencies") are coded from birth, "criminal law becomes senseless, as does the punishment of criminals."

Certainly, if Noi were correct, Soviet criminal law, as well as the relatively voluntaristic, "free will" image of man which Soviet social science has held since the 1930s and still defends, would be in need of revision. Man is seen as generally plastic, "malleable," and susceptible to change by way of environmental influence, though not completely determined by it. Certain socioenvironmental elements of a negative sort condition the formation of deviant personality traits. He who commits a crime will have such traits, but he will not have been born with them, and they will not excuse his acts. Consequently, "correction and reeducation" in a penal institution are seen as logical ways to "re-form" that personality, to substitute new, positive traits for the old, negative ones. Noi's ideas, at least in a limited way, hint at limits to this *tabula rasa* image of man. Given the years that it has prevailed as the "orthodox" model, and given the apparent adherence of most Soviet criminologists to it, it is not surprising that Noi's attempts to modify it have met with such criticism.

9

CRIME PREVENTION AND CRIMINAL CORRECTION

PREVENTIVE MEASURES

SOVIET THEORISTS VIEW crime prevention as a function not only of specific preventive measures but also of "progressive" social and economic changes since World War II. Rises in average living standards, gradual efforts at coping with chronic housing shortages, and increases in the average levels of educational attainment are all seen as rendering less likely the persistence of survivals arising from shortcomings in the environment of Soviet citizens.

General measures of prevention of crimes are general socioeconomic, cultural, and upbringing measures, aimed at the resolution of the tasks of communist construction, which moreover eliminate the causes of crime, [and] eradicate survivals of the past in the consciousness and behavior of the people . . .[1]

This amounts to an endorsement of environmental improvement as a process tending toward the reduction of levels of crime and other deviation. As such, it is not peculiarly Soviet. It would be difficult indeed to find a society in which persons addressing themselves to the problem of crime had *not* seen at least a great part of the solution in the abolition of poverty, discrimination, and other general evils, as well as in increasing literacy and the cultural-educational level of the population as a whole. What *is* interesting is that there is, as yet, little sign that Soviet criminologists are bothered by the more subtle potential problems of affluence. Concern about this would certainly be somewhat premature—while the Soviet living standard shows fairly steady improvement, one can scarcely speak of the USSR as an "affluent" society by American or West European standards. But high living standards in the United States have not been accompanied by a decline in crime and violence. With reference to deprived segments of the American population, improved living conditions may be a desirable end in themselves; but crime is hardly restricted to the deprived, and affluence is hardly a panacea. The phenomenon of crime is an exceedingly complex one. While the seemingly higher incidence of criminal acts among the less educated, less skilled, and lower-paid segments of the Soviet population make it as "logical" to seek solutions of a broadly economic nature in the USSR as in the United States, Soviet criminologists may in the future find that such logic does not take them far enough.

But, in any case, "general measures" to bring about results gradually are not the only ones relied upon. More important, and more relevant to our concerns here, are "special measures" carried out by Party organizations and governmental bodies, the police and the courts, and bodies made up of public representatives—the volunteer police auxiliaries (*druzhiny*), the comrades' courts, and others. Limitations of space make it impossible to discuss in full all the "special" preventive measures as they are classified in Soviet texts,[2] but they may be summarized as follows.

Measures applied in connection with a crime already committed, directed at the guilty person:

    1. criminal punishments which, in addition to rendering difficult or impossible the commission of particular crimes by isolating the offender from society, removing him from a position he has abused in a criminal manner (e.g., by way of embezzlement), etc., are viewed as having a reha-

bilitative effect on the offender and as a deterrent to further commission of crimes, both by himself and by "other morally unstable members of society, who are capable of committing crimes";

    2. compulsory measures of a "medical character," applied to alcoholics and drug addicts;

    3. measures of "social pressure" taken when the court decides not to impose criminal punishment on the offender —primarily, transferring his case to a comrades' court or releasing him in the custody of his *kollektiv*.

To these measures may be added "compulsory measures of educational character," which the courts (and Commissions on Juvenile Affairs) can apply to young offenders,[3] and the "administrative and disciplinary" (i.e., noncriminal) sanctions applicable to some petty offenders and abusers of office.[4]

Measures of "averting" (*predotvrashchenie*) a particular crime:

    4. police investigate work in order to discover "criminal groups" or individuals preparing to commit crimes and to discover individuals in situations where criminal intent may develop (e.g., juveniles who frequently gamble or engage in drinking bouts);

    5. halting crimes in process, by the intervention of the police, people's volunteer police auxiliaries, etc. (Here also fit investigations to discover long-term criminal activity, such as embezzlement, regular theft of goods from inventories, and similar serious property offenses.)

Measures for "eradicating the causes and conditions" which facilitate the commission of crimes. This category is itself a broad one, spanning measures taken in the context of an individual case by the investigative agencies, prosecutor, and court to deal with the *particular* causes of the offense, and also including measures more general in application. It can be broken down into the following types of measures:

    6. "organizational"—aimed at overhauling practices in government organs and economic organizations which may hamper the "struggle" against crime and at improving the performance of law-enforcement agencies;

7. "economic"—limiting the trade in goods connected with crime, such as alcohol, and promoting capital investment in custodial and "rehabilitative" facilities;

8. "technical"—introduction of sophisticated and embezzlement-proof automated calculating machines, technical means of guarding against forgery, etc.;

9. "legal"—reworking and improving criminal and criminal-procedural law toward the end of more "efficiency" in its administration; providing for deprivation of parental rights over minors from those who abuse them; legally obliging the courts and investigative agencies to "respond" to evidence of amoral behavior and noncriminal violations, so that crimes do not result;

10. "ideological"—generally, raising the level of political (and hence, moral) consciousness of the population: more specifically, extirpating "false views" from the "immediate environment" surrounding a person—e.g., dishonesty and indifference toward the public interest from a production *kollektiv*.

Even in summary form, this is a lengthy catalog. The diverse types of special measures are generally concentrated around two central ideas about the dynamics of crime prevention. First, measures applied to individuals, whether "punitive" or not, *do* have deterrent and rehabilitative effect; and punitive measures, especially, deter "morally unstable" noncriminals from criminal acts. For all its conventionality, this idea is of great importance. It has constrained experimentation with "radical" alternatives to criminal punishment and helped produce a system of criminal justice similar in its broad outlines to that of many other nations. Second, much of "special prevention" revolves around the improvement of institutional performance, the eradication of the institutional malfunctioning blamed for creating conditions favorable to crime. It is through the institutions that socialize, educate, and control that the basic solution to the problem of crime is sought.

The day-to-day tasks of crime control fall mainly within the scope of the regular police ("militia") under the Ministries of Internal Affairs. Three functional subdivisions perform what would be regarded in most societies as routine "police work." First is the Patrol Service, whose main task is the preservation of order in public places—the Soviet blue-coated equivalent of the policeman "on the beat." Responsibility for policing and preventing property offenses, swindling in state stores, and the like belongs to the OBKhSS—the Department for Combatting Theft of Socialist Property. Finally, the Criminal Investigation Department performs the investigatory, detective, and apprehending functions its title implies.[5] Beyond the normal police activity, the militia since 1966 has possessed rather broad summary powers in the disposition of certain minor offenses. A local police chief may impose a fine, without trial, on a petty hooligan or may hand him over to a court or to the representatives of the public. Fines may also be imposed directly by the militia on persons who appear in public intoxicated.[6] Speedy "justice" meted out to petty offenders is viewed as preventive with reference to possibly more serious offenses in the future.

A much less routine element in Soviet crime prevention has been its "popularization" through the establishment of institutions outside the formal justice and law-enforcement system. Most important here are the squads of people's volunteers (*druzhiny*), the comrades' courts, and the application through the first half of the 1960s of the controversial "antiparasite" laws. The *druzhinniki* are not the first representatives of the public to aid the police. Under various titles, and with varying degrees of direct connection and subordination to the professionals, such organizations have existed since 1930.[7] The present variant began with the organization of volunteer squads in various Leningrad factories in 1958. The experiment was "regularized" on a national basis by decree in March 1959.

Nominally subordinate to the local government, the *druzhiny* "cooperate" with the police, and are apparently more under the control of Party organizations than of government organs.[8] Members are supposedly volunteers, and their numbers, on paper at least, have been impressively large—in 1965, more than 5.5 million persons, organized into 130,000 squads.[9] But evidence is not lacking that the participation of many is confined to paper and that, as in the case with other varieties of public activity, many have been pressured to volunteer.[10] The main functions of the *druzhinniki* are patrolling the streets on the lookout for drunkards and hooligans, helping the regular police in crowd control, and generally maintaining a watchful eye in public places.[11] Without arms or powers of arrest, they may nonetheless "escort" offenders to their own headquarters or to the police.

The preventive effectiveness of the *druzhiny* is difficult to gauge: the occasional recruitment of "vigilante" types leads to transgressions of their legal powers and scarcely contributes to crime control. There is evidence, in complaints about the indifference of some *druzhinnki* to offenses taking place within their purview, that as direct agents of crime prevention they leave a great deal to be desired.[12]

Like the *druzhiny*, the comrades' courts emerged in roughly their contemporary shape between 1959 and 1961. And, again like the people's squads, they had predecessors in earlier Soviet history, first in the period of "War Communism" immediately after the revolution and then during a second period of growth in the years 1928–1933. They fell victim, as did so many innovations, to the later Stalin years.[13]

The courts are set up as arms of various *kollektivs*—factories, organizations, collective farms, apartment blocks—and have experienced in their recent history successive broadening of their powers. In 1961, they were given jurisdiction over small property suits, violations of labor discipline, "antisocial behavior" not carrying criminal liability, and remand jurisdiction over "minor offenses" referred to them by courts, prosecutors, or the police. In 1963,[14] they received jurisdiction over first-time offenders guilty of petty hooliganism, petty speculation, petty theft, and petty embezzlement of state property, as well as minor assaults and other "criminal actions" where great social danger was not involved. Penalties at the disposal of the courts originally ran from meting out "condemnations" and "reprimands" to initiating discussions on "disciplinary action" with management at the offender's work place, as well as recommending eviction from housing. The imposition of fines up to 10 rubles was also allowed. In 1965, the penalties were expanded: for petty embezzlement, in addition to restoration of loss, fines of up to 30 rubles for a first offense and 50 rubles for a second could be imposed.

The fining power, clearly, is not a "measure of social pressure" in the same sense as a "reprimand." The difference between a fine imposed as part of proceedings in a people's court and a fine imposed in the noncriminal comrades' court is academic. The lack of standards of proof, and of defense counsel in the latter, is not so academic a matter. Clearly, and without the procedural restraints imposed on the regular courts, the comrades' courts are meting out what are, in effect, criminal punishments. Yet, they continue to be seen as primarily "preventive" bodies that also reduce demands on court energies by handling minor cases in an "informal" manner. Their "preventive" aspect is double-edged. Being subjected to accusation and attack from others at the "trial," the offender may be dissuaded from similar or more serious offenses in the future. But the session is "educative" (*vospitatel'nyi*) for the spectators, too. "Evil" has been identified and dealt with in a ritual in which they have partaken; and those who might have committed similar acts, witnessing the fate of the accused, may be deterred. Indeed, the main target of the comrades' court may well be the audience—this would help explain the position that the maximum number of members of the involved *kollektiv* be present at the "trial." [15] Whether such confidence in the comrades' courts' preventive effectiveness (as opposed to their role as an alternative for disposal of certain types of cases) is justified is questionable. Complaints are aired, on the one hand, that some criminal offenders were not deterred by earlier appearances before their "comrades"; on the other, that intervention of the comrades' court was conspicuously absent in many cases where before committing his crime the offender perpetrated "petty" offenses or showed other antisocial tendencies.

The "antiparasite" laws emerged, somewhat earlier than the *druzhiny* and comrades' courts, in draft versions in various republic newspapers in 1957. They were aimed at "able bodied citizens leading an antisocial, parasitic way of life, deliberately avoiding socially useful labor, and likewise those living on unearned income." The forum was simple: not a People's Court, nor even a comrades' court, but only a "public meeting" of fellow residents convoked by a street or apartment complex committee in the cities or by the village soviet in the countryside. Sentence was by majority vote of those attending, who had to constitute a simple majority of the adults in the given dwelling area. The main antiparasite "measure" (since it was not defined as criminal punishment) was two to five years exile with compulsory labor.[16]

Whether the antiparasite laws fit the description of "crime prevention measures" is debatable: certainly, as one student of the laws has noted, they were aimed at some typical high-risk types—"the violent drunkard, the wife-beater, the man who has never made it."[17] But they also were used against young "loafers" living off their parents and the young *stiliagi* who aped Western clothing and mannerisms—"deviants," to be sure, according to Soviet definitions, but not necessarily pre-criminal types.

The vagueness of the offenses specified and the lack of procedural safeguards (the "sentence" of the meeting was not subject to judicial review, but only to confirmation by the executive committee of the local soviet) provoked some opposition, notably from lawyers and legal scholars, in the 1957–1958 atmosphere of emphasis on "strengthening socialist legality." Still, between 1957 and 1960, nine republics enacted such legislation. Stronger opposition in the Russian Republic appears to have delayed adoption of antiparasite legislation there until May 1961, after a general intensification of "hard-line" anticrime campaigning in the press. But the Russian Republic law (to which other republics' laws were later made conformable) changed the situation by giving the People's Courts exclusive jurisdiction over nonworking parasites and alternate jurisdiction, with the public meetings, over those with "sham jobs." For the latter, administrative confirmation of the meeting's decision remained the only "qualification," while court decisions on nonworking parasites, though not subject to ordinary appeal, could be "protested" by the *prokuror* in his role as overseer of legality. Under the 1961 decree, the "parasite" had to be warned and to disregard the warning before proceedings could be instituted.

For the next four and a half years, the antiparasite laws presented problems in both enforcement and the results of that enforcement. Persons with disabilities that prevented work were sometimes exiled. The required warning and the post-warning period during which the parasite was supposed to find work were sometimes ignored.[18] Even in the cases handled by the People's Courts, procedures were "oversimplified," and cursory or even nonexistent investigations of the facts were tolerated.[19] In short, many of the wrong persons were being sentenced.

Even when real parasites were sentenced, the results often ran counter to the announced intent of the laws. Parasites, mainly urban, were sent to relatively rural areas and generally grouped together in such places. Managers were reluctant to hire them.[20] In relatively large numbers, they frequently became a liability to the receiving area, further corrupting each other through mutual influence. Under such circumstances, reform was often a rare commodity.

A 1965 decree of the Russian Republic Supreme Soviet responded in some measure to the problems of capriciousness the public meetings presented.[21] The executive committees of the local soviets (and in Moscow and Leningrad the People's Courts) replaced the meetings as the forum for "trial." While the proceedings remained noncriminal and thus without right to defense or appeal, the changes represented a procedural tightening, a depopularization of the whole antiparasite campaign. In fact, relatively little has been heard about the antiparasite laws since 1965, although at the time of writing they still remain on the books. Whether, as some have predicted, the 1965 decree was the "first move" toward eventual abolition [22] is still questionable, but such laws apparently no longer represent one of the major thrusts in crime prevention.

Soviet preventive measures have been, and are, a combination of efforts by official bodies—the courts, police, *Prokuratura,* and others —to identify and cope with the crime-prone and with situations that cause crime-proneness, and, as the latter part of this discussion has shown, various modes of involving unpaid "volunteers" in processes related to maintaining public order and dealing with more petty types of offender. The measures are not, obviously, always effective. We turn, then, to the processes and institutions which follow failures at prevention—those which have the detected criminal offender as their target.

PATTERNS
OF DISPOSITION

A number of possibilities arise regarding the immediate fate of an apprehended criminal. Though there is no adult equivalent of the Commissions on Juvenile Affairs to add a second, nonjudicial track to the adult justice system, mechanisms do exist whereby the criminal may be filtered out of the system, escaping criminal responsibility and a conviction.

When the crime is "insignificant" or does not represent great "social danger," the court or procurator, or investigate agencies with the latter's consent, can forego the initiation of a criminal case and release the offender to a comrades' court or "on surety" to a workers' *kollektiv* or public organization, if convinced that the "measures of social pressure" to be applied will suffice for the offender's correction.[23]

Under roughly the same circumstances, a criminal case already in process may be terminated and the offender relieved of criminal responsibility through a transfer of his case to a comrades' court [24] or his release on surety to a *kollektiv* or organization which assumes responsibility for his reeducation and correction.[25] Such "releases" from further involvement with the courts apply only to offenders who admit their guilt, and by and large, only in connection with first offenders.

For those who are not filtered out of the system at these early stages, the Criminal Code of the RSFSR and corresponding codes in the republics establish a wide range of punishments: (1) deprivation of freedom; (2) exile; (3) banishment; * (4) corrective works without deprivation of freedom; (5) deprivation of the right to occupy certain offices or engage in certain activities; (6) fine; (7) dismissal from office; (8) imposition of the duty to make amends for harm caused; (9) social censure; (10) confiscation of property; and (11) deprivation of military or special rank.[26] The death penalty (by shooting) is available to the courts as an "exceptional measure of punishment" for certain offenses.[27]

The courts have a good deal of maneuvering room in assigning punishments, despite the specification of a range of penalties for each offense and an upper and lower limit for terms of deprivation of freedom. In sentencing to corrective works or deprivation of freedom, the

---

* Exile is the removal of the offender from his place of residence with obligatory settlement in another designated place. The banished offender is also removed from his place of residence but is merely prohibited from living in certain areas, generally larger cities.

court may convict "conditionally"—that is, suspend the sentence and set a probation period of one to five years.[28] The courts are also empowered to nullify certain punishment provisions and "assign a punishment lower than the lowest limit provided by law for the given crime or resort to another milder kind of punishment" when circumstances warrant.[29] The punishment a particular criminal receives will, of course, depend to a large degree upon the crime of which he is convicted and the court's estimate of his degree of "corruption"—how deeply imbedded are his criminal attitudes, and how much correction will be needed to change them? But, looking at the criminal justice system as a whole, it becomes clear that it operates according to certain patterns, selecting for the most part a small range of punishments from the lengthy list above. Different Soviet sources present rather consistent pictures of the distribution of criminal offenders across the various possibilities of disposition.

About 20–25 percent of adult offenders—the vast majority of these, to be sure, petty offenders—escape criminal responsibility through decisions not to initiate formal prosecution or through termination of a case in process.[30] For these offenders, there is no sentence and no convic on, conditional or otherwise. Although guides for court practice inuicate the desirability of discharging such offenders "on surety" to an organization or to their coworkers, frequently the court simply washes its hands of them.

Loss of this 20 percent to one-quarter of the detected criminals leaves the other three-quarters to be dealt with by sentencing to various forms of punishment. Here the preferences of the courts become clear: corrective works and deprivation of freedom are by far the most frequently imposed punishments. As a basic measure of punishment, fines are imposed in "only three to four percent" of all cases.[31] Exile, banishment, and the other punishments enumerated earlier are also relatively rarely encountered.

Between all the other punishments and deprivation of freedom there exists, of course, a great gap—the latter implies isolation from society, under guard, in a special institution. Soviet correctional theorists see an emphasis on in-society rehabilitation as "progressive" and therefore are interested in the relative propensities of judges to assign one or another type of punishment. In the absence of comprehensive statistics, one can only compare claims that "about two-thirds" of all criminals are rehabilitated without isolation from society [32] with available statistics on the practices of some courts. Such a claim, by the editor of the journal *Sotsialisticheskaia zakonnost'*, may be somewhat inflated, and even more so a claim that of all *convicted* adults, the percentage sentenced to deprivation of freedom does not, "as a rule," exceed 40–50 percent. [33]

Assuming that the first claim includes in the two-thirds figure cited the one-quarter of all apprehended criminals who are released from responsibility, it means that courts, in assigning sentences to the remaining three-quarters, would have to limit themselves to deprivation of freedom in only about half the cases carried through to conviction. The few statistics available on court practice show that this is not the case—judges, it seems, over-elect deprivation of freedom. A study of two groups of courts presents the percentage distributions for the year 1964: in the first group (25 courts), 67.7 percent of the convicted were sentenced to deprivation of freedom, 25.2 percent to corrective works, and 7.1 percent to "other measures" (fine, etc.). In the second group (33 courts), 63.8 percent of the convictions involved imprisonment, 23.9 percent were to corrective works, and 12.3 percent to other punishments. [34] Even assuming that these courts had dismissed about one-quarter of their cases and liberated the offenders from criminal responsibility, their selection of deprivation of freedom in roughly two-thirds of all completed cases would involve sentences of imprisonment for about one-half, rather than one-third, of the total criminal population with which they had any contact.

This broad estimate is generally supported by other Soviet sources, frequently estimating the share of "corrective works" among all criminal sentences at around 25 percent. [35] No estimates place the share of "other" non-imprisonment penalties this high, as they would have to be to yield an imprisonment rate, among all convictions, as low as 50 percent. Yet a rate of below 50 percent is also cited by the director of the All-Union crime study institute. [36] One possible solution to the question may lie in an apparently high rate, in some areas, of higher court changes of original sentences to short-term (up to one year) imprisonment, substituting "corrective works." (In one autonomous republic it is reported that 35 percent of sentences to short-term deprivation of freedom were changed by higher courts to less severe sentences.) Thus, if the claims reflect "corrected" sentences rather than those handed down by the People's Courts, which possess initial jurisdiction, it is possible that the "final" figure may fall below 50 percent.[37] It is also possible, since the Soviet sources just cited do not distinguish between suspended and "real" sentences, that the former are being counted in making the claims noted above, though suspended sentences do not appear as a separate category in the study of two groups of courts. If some substantial segment of the sentences to deprivation of freedom are suspended sentences, then of course the percentage of those "rehabilitated without isolation from society" rises. Some support for this possibility is provided by a source from the USSR Supreme Court, which states that 13.2 percent of those convicted (apparently, nationwide) in 1965 received suspended sentences.[38] Another source gives parallel figures for 1960 (17.0 percent) and 1966 (9.0 percent).[39] In light of the other figures presented, these percentages for suspended sentences, if the "typical" suspended sentence was one to deprivation of freedom, *would* indicate a total real imprisonment rate in the 40 percent range. Beyond estimates such as this, we can only speculate.

Corrective works and deprivation of freedom are, however, clearly the dominant forms of punishment, and it is with these that we must concern ourselves. "Corrective works without deprivation of freedom" is a punishment with a long history in Soviet criminal law.[40] Current legislation provides for two forms of corrective works; one in which the sentence is to be served by working at one's regular job, the second involving work, not necessarily in one's specialty, in some other place within the offender's district of residence.[41] The second type is applied relatively rarely; a recent large-scale study of sentencing found it applied in only about 8 percent of all corrective-works sentences.[42] The court is limited to a minimum of one month and a maximum of one year in length of sentence and to a range of 5 to 20 percent monthly wage deduction during the sentence period. A study of the practice of 88 courts in different republics in 1964 showed a tendency to approach the upper limits in imposing corrective works as a penalty. Of such sentences 77.8 percent were the one-year maximum, 16.9 percent between six months and one year, 4.9 percent between three and six months, and only 0.4 percent less than three months. Over half the sentences (54.6 percent) involved the 20 percent wage deduction, 36.2 percent fell between 10 and 20 percent, and in only 9.2 percent of the cases did the deduction go below 10 percent.[43]

For what sorts of offense is corrective works a typical punishment? Data from the USSR's main criminological research institute in Moscow for the years 1961–1964 indicate that about one-third of such sentences (33.6 percent over the four years, on the average) were meted out for relatively minor property crimes—small thefts of state and private property, petty embezzlement and misappropriation. Over the same period, of *all* sentences for these offenses, corrective works amounted to an average of 22.9 percent of the total.[44]

Other offenses supplying a basis for imposition of corrective works were public order offenses (hooliganism, resistance to police or public auxiliaries), 13.7 percent of the total of such sentences; and minor crimes against the person ("infliction of light bodily injury," insult, defamation), 14.1 percent of the total. Abuse of office, whether malfeasance of nonfeasance, was the category of offense most frequently handled by this penalty rather than others, 48.9 percent of such violations leading to a corrective works sentence over 1961–1964.[45]

When in-society rehabilitation does not seem sufficient, the court's only alternative involves deprivation of freedom. The court is given minimum and maximum ranges for each offense, the broad limit imposed by the general provision of the criminal code being three months to ten years. For specified "especially grave crimes" and "especially dangerous recidivists," the upper limit is raised to fifteen years.[46] How the courts use the relatively wide discretion permitted by the law in fixing length of sentence is difficult to estimate, although the preoccupation of corrections specialists with the impact of "short-term" (up to one year) deprivation of freedom gives us some general indications. Sample data on sentences collected and analyzed by researchers at a Moscow institute showed that, of all sentences to imprisonment, short-term sentences made up 19.9 percent in 1960, climbed to 20.2 percent in 1961, had fallen to 17.2 percent by 1964, and further declined to 14.6 percent of the total in 1965.[47] The decline in popularity of such sentences followed closely upon complaints that courts were exhibiting some unjustified leniency on the basis of the reformed criminal and criminal procedure codes adopted in 1960. A resolution of the USSR Supreme Court against this alleged leniency in July 1962 seemed to have its desired effect, in that the relative incidence of sentences to short-term imprisonment was reduced. (As a percentage of all sentences, of course, its share is even lower. The study of two groups of courts in 1964, noted above, found that in one group—25 courts—short-term sentences equalled only 7.1 percent of the total; in the other—33 courts—short-term sentences were 6.5 percent.[48]) Hooliganism and relatively minor offenses against state or personal property provide the main occasion for imposition of short-term deprivation of freedom.[49]

Given the variations in sentencing limits for various crimes in the RSFSR Criminal Code, and the differences in limits for the same offense among some republican codes, it is beyond our capacity to estimate the "average" length of a (non–short-term) sentence with any degree of confidence. For "less serious" crimes, given code provisions, sentences may average around 4–5 years: for more serious but less frequently committed offenses, rather more. While conditional early release is fairly widely applied, as we shall see, Soviet sources are rather puzzlingly silent on the percentage of conditional sentences passed by the courts.

PUNISHMENT IN OPERATION

CORRECTIVE WORKS

A sentence to corrective works without deprivation of freedom is supposed to amount to more than a fine paid by installment. Even if the work is to be performed at his regular job in his own factory, the offender is subject to checks on his behavior by the *inspektsiia* (the organ charged with surveillance over convicts so sentenced) and, in theory at least, to the stern eye of his fellow-workers, who are supposed to carry on "educative" work with him.[50] The time he works under sentence is not, as a rule, included in his labor record for purposes of seniority, pension, and other social insurance provisions; but a notation that he has served such a sentence is made.

For the convict sentenced to corrective works at another location the consequences are more severe: he may lose his original job, he may be forced to work at a specialty for which he has no training, and, placed in the position of job-changer, he loses access to many social insurance benefits he might have retained had he been allowed to remain at his regular work.[51] This second variety of corrective works is assigned predominantly to more serious offenders, to those who attempt to evade performance of the milder variety, to persons who have no permanent job, or when the return of the offender to his normal occupation makes no sense, given the nature of the offense.[52] (An obvious example of the latter, provided by a criminal law textbook, is that of a trade worker with access to cash convicted of fraud or misappropriation.[53])

Corrective works appears, then, to be a relatively simple form of punishment. There is little administrative overhead to increase its cost of administration per offender, and its application conforms to the preference many specialists express for in-society rehabilitative strategies. Yet there are many problems which complicate its administration. Sometimes, managerial indifference to the factory's social-welfare tasks combines with poor communications between court, *inspektsiia*, and factory administration to create a situation in which coworkers do not even realize that one of their number is serving such a sentence. Here, there can be no talk of a stern collective eye focused on the offender and alert for signs of backsliding.[54] The harsher form of sentence, as some corrections specialists have complained, tends to vitiate the whole concept of rehabilitation by one's peers—the offender is transferred to an unfamiliar work environment among people who are essentially strangers and are hardly likely to be concerned with his reclamation.[55] Nor are managers enthusiastic about taking on new workers whose availability is the result of a court conviction. Their understandable reluctance causes difficulties in the placement of this category of convicts.[56]

Compared to other forms of punishment, corrective works is rather soft, and instances of evasion or attempted evasion are frequent. Studies in two areas showed evasions amounting to 25–30 percent of all so sentenced, resulting in a longer eventual factual service than originally decreed in the sentence, to make up the lost time.[57] To a degree, such problems may be complicated by the tendency of some managers to fire workers so sentenced [58] (an alternative response to simply ignoring the fact of the conviction, also encountered).

To a considerable extent, carrying out the sentence provisions becomes the responsibility of managers, trade union officials, and bookkeepers at the factory level, rather than of professional law enforcers. Here more problems crop up: bookkeepers and personnel officials are generally not familiar with all the restrictions on vacations, time off, fringe benefits, and the structure of wage deductions for those sentenced to corrective works and often fail to enforce them. Nor does the *inspektsiia* always check carefully to see that each such a sentence is being carried out in full. A study of 126 such convicts in one province in 1962–1963 revealed that, due to lack of attention to deductions, the sum of 13,760 rubles had been overpaid to them in the two-year period: [59] not a greal deal per convict when divided among so many, but enough to illustrate the problem.

Court practice in sentencing increases the problems. Some judges, ill-informed as to the limits on their discretion, exceed the 20 percent wage deduction ceiling.[60] Others tend to apply the penalty itself too widely and to the wrong type of offender. In using their discretion to fix punishments "below the lower limit" for any particular offense, courts sometimes pass such sentences on first offenders guilty of serious offenses.[61] The recidivism rate (to be discussed in greater detail later) among those sentenced to corrective works is increased greatly by the application of such sentences (again, within the court's discretion) to second offenders, and even to persons who have previously served long terms of imprisonment.[62]

DEPRIVATION OF FREEDOM

One cannot begin a discussion of Soviet penal institutions without giving some attention to factors that place a strain on the ability to maintain scholarly objectivity, and that may limit, to some degree, the accuracy of one's perceptions.

Few societies are proud of their penal institutions; fewer have any reason to be. For those who care to read it, the record of the Soviet Union in this regard must be especially appalling. While the labor camps of the Stalin era were probably overmatched in their inhuman aspects by the concentration camps of Nazi Germany, there is little honor in finishing second in such a race. From the mid-1930s up to the mid-1950s, millions of Soviet citizens lived a life of hard labor, with semi-starvation ration and other severe deprivations, behind the barbed wire of the camps. It is true, of course, that the majority were "politicals"—not at all criminals in the sense employed in this book. Mixed in with the political prisoners were the real criminals— the thieves and murderers and other offenders—who were a relatively privileged stratum in the camp population, victimizing the politicals with the tacit or open agreement of the guards and commandants.[63] In such circumstances, one can scarcely speak of the "correction" of criminal offenders.

According to official Soviet sources, these "excesses" of the Stalin era have now been corrected. In some cases, this statement is accurate. It is unlikely that one can number political prisoners in the USSR in the millions. But they still exist, and the conditions in which they are confined in many cases seem not so different from those experienced by an earlier generation of politicals.[64]

The criminal offenders who concern us here are for the most part separated from the politicals. In general, the conditions of their confinement are probably better than they were before Stalin's death. With the reform of the Soviet legal system in the late 1950s, their sentences grew shorter, their chances for release on parole immeasurably greater. This, at least, is a clear improvement in the direction of a more humane system of criminal justice, for *criminals*, and it must be borne in mind.

On the other hand, the extreme reticence of Soviet authorities to release any information to the general public about gaps between the ideals of correctional policy and their everyday execution cannot but be disturbing to one who attempts to compile a clear and fair picture of the correctional system. Not until 1969, after the promulgation of "secret" unpublished statutes governing the penal institutions over the years to supplement the moribund corrective labor codes of the republics which had been drawn up in the late 1920s and early 1930s, were new All-Union Principles of Corrective-Labor Legislation finally published.[65] The legal journals available to the public have relatively little material to give the reader a feel for what goes on within the institutions. For such information, one must turn to the "closed" journal, *Toward a New Life* (*K novoi zhizhni*), published by the MVD administration responsible for operating penal institutions. It is not available to the Soviet public at large, few of whom probably know of its existence. It is published primarily for the administration and staff of penal institutions, but it is available to other professional users— judges, court officials, legal scholars, and law students.

It is with all this in mind that the reader should approach the pages to follow. The grim history of Soviet penal practice and the continuing, if somewhat abated, bias toward secrecy in matters concerning penal institutions cannot be dismissed as unimportant, but it is to be hoped that they do not lead to a premature judgment of the corrections system as it exists today, many of whose problems are not unique to the USSR.

TYPES OF INSTITUTION

Since 1961,[66] the institutional side of the corrections system has been divided into corrective-labor colonies (*ispravitel'no-trudovye kolonii*, or ITK) and prisons (*tiurmy*), the latter containing a relatively small percentage of all prisoners. The colonies are of four varieties, differentiated by the strictness of their internal organization and the rules governing prisoner privileges and liabilities (regime):

standard-regime colonies—for first offenders convicted of crimes that are "not grave";

intensified-regime colonies—for first offenders convicted of grave crimes;

strict-regime colonies—for those who have committed "especially dangerous state crimes" or have previously served a term of deprivation of freedom;

special-regime colonies—for those adjudged "especially dangerous recidivists" and those with commuted death sentences.[67]

Prisons are of two types, standard- and strict-regime. At the court's discretion, especially dangerous recidivists and persons convicted of grave crimes may be sent to prisons instead of ITK's. Another main function of prisons has been the containment of regime violators and of those who commit crimes in the ITK, as a further punitive measure.[68] Women convicted of crimes are confined in separate standard- and strict-regime colonies.

One other type of institution, in existence since 1963, deserves mention—the "colony-settlement" (*koloniia-poselenie*). This is a minimum-security institution, frequently organized around lumbering or agriculture, where inmates transferred from ITK's and firmly on the "path to reform" may live with their families, wear their own clothes, enjoy free movement within the colony grounds, and have certain other advantages. There is relatively little information on these institutions, and it seems unlikely that any large proportion of prisoners spends time in them.[69]

It is difficult to convey the feel of the regime, what it means in the everyday life of the inmate, especially since so much of the quality of life in any penal institution will depend on the manner in which staff and administration implement the rules. But the general description given in the 1969 Principles is illuminating, to a degree:

All inmates wear the same type of clothing, and they may be searched. Inmates' correspondence is subject to censorship, and the parcels and packages they receive are subject to inspection.

Inmates serving their sentences in special-regime corrective-labor colonies are confined in cells and wear special clothing.

A strictly regulated internal order is established at corrective-labor institutions. Inmates are not permitted to keep with them money and valuables or objects the use of which is forbidden in corrective-labor institutions. Money and valuables discovered in the possession of inmates are confiscated and, as a rule, become state revenue at the decision of the director of the corrective-labor institution, which must cite reasons and be sanctioned by the prosecutor.

Under the procedure established by these Principles and the Union-republic corrective-labor codes, inmates are allowed to obtain foodstuffs and other necessities by written order, to have visitors, to receive parcels and packages, to send and receive money orders and to carry on correspondence.[70]

The generality of the description does not convey the differences between regimes. (See Appendix 1.) Stricter regimes impose greater limits on the number of visits an inmate may receive, his rights to receive packages and mail letters, and his freedom of movement within the ITK.[71] In prisons and special-regime colonies, confinement in cells is the rule. Prisoners in other colonies are housed in dormitories, which, while they are preferable to cells, appear to be extremely crowded.[72]

To persons confined in institutions, food is a matter of perhaps greater concern than to those on the outside. The 1969 Principles cover the subject in the following manner.

Inmates receive food that ensures normal bodily activity. Dietary norms are varied according to the climatic conditions of the area in which the corrective-labor institution is located, the nature of the work performed by the inmates and their attitude toward labor. Individuals confined in punitive or disciplinary cell blocks, in punitive dungeon cells, in cells or in solitary confinement in special-regime colonies receive food on the basis of reduced norms.[73]

How much food "ensures normal bodily activity?" How reduced are the norms for those undergoing disciplinary confinement? The Principles themselves are silent on this, but some indication may be drawn from the appendix on daily caloric norms which accompanied the unpublished 1961 corrective labor statute (see Appendix 2). In 1961 rations ranged from a "high" of 2828 calories a day for colony inmates engaged in especially strenuous work to 1324 calories for inmates "maliciously refusing" to work or underfulfilling their work norms. For those serving sentences in prisons, the maximum was 1937 calories per day, the minimum (for those in punishment cells) 1324 calories; but for these, "hot" food was only to be served every other day. In the intervening periods, only bread, hot water, and salt were distributed.

As in other penal institutions, the ITK inmate's career depends on how he "does his time": how many violations of rules are marked against him and how many "exemplary" acts or performances are credited to him. For model prisoners, the Principles provide increases in privileges, awards of honorary titles, and in some cases, transfers to softer regimes [74] (in addition to conditional early release). For the troublesome prisoner, rights to visits, packages, and other privileges are subject to revocation, and some violators may be confined for a period in punitive cell blocks in the ITK or punitive dungeon cells in prisons.[75]

INSTITUTIONS: ORGANIZATION AND
MEANS OF CORRECTION

The organizational principles of the ITK bear a notable resemblance to those of the labor colonies for juveniles, especially in their focus on the creation of stable *kollektivs* of inmates and on the involvement of inmates in various types of "healthy" activity.

The basic inmate grouping is the "detachment" (*otriad*), organized from persons living in the same dormitory and placed under the general supervision of one colony staff member. Detachments vary in average size, depending on regime, from 50 in the stricter ITK's to 110 in general-regime colonies.[76] The colony *kollektiv* is made up of detachments. As in the juvenile colonies, there are "councils" at each level. The detachment council will be made up of five to seven members, depending on the detachment size, while the colony council will, dependent on size, range between seven and twenty-five members.[77] Members are elected for a one-year term, but as a corrective labor law textbook makes clear, all is within the hands of the administration.

The administration of the colony, in the person of the commandant, confirms the membership of the *kollektiv* councils, removes from membership those who do not justify the confidence shown them, or even dismisses the whole membership of the *kollektiv* council and arranges new elections.[78]

Subordinated to the colony-wide councils are various specialized "sections" performing different functions. In these sections, the inmate rank and file are supposed to participate, and the membership is generally unlimited. Typical section specializations are: "mass-productive work and labor competition," "professional-technical and general educational instruction," internal order, mass-cultural work, physical culture and sport, and sanitary maintenance.[79]

All this, in theory at least, is independent inmate activity. As such, it is supposed to mesh with the main aspects of colony life, as expressed in the "basic means" of correction and reeducation: "the regime according to which sentences are served, socially useful labor, political-upbringing work, and general-educational and vocational-technical instruction." [80] We have said enough, for now, about the regime. It remains for us to examine the other means.

Work by convicts, if not seen as a panacea for all the problems they present, is nonetheless viewed as a process with impact on many aspects of the convict's personality. Lawbreakers are frequently those with no steady job, with work histories punctuated by firings, short periods at any single job, and long stretches between jobs. For these the obligation to work, every day, during definite hours at a particular job introduces a regulating element into their lives. Working and receiving some reward for it are seen (through a Pavlovian conditioning perspective) as bringing about a long-range change in the convict's personality. From an obligation, work transforms itself into a need for a personality previously distorted.[81]

Criminal offenders may also be loners, isolates from healthy associations. Work, day in and day out in one's brigade, is seen as fostering a spirit of collectivism, a feeling of interest and involvement not only in oneself, but also in the performance and welfare of others. Work itself is healthy; it is described as man's "material and moral necessity" in a socialist society. Thus it is a general civic obligation, incumbent on the inmate as on all Soviet citizens. It is not regarded as a punitive element of the colony routine.[82] Productivity, though important (since ITK output is "planned" and geared into more general economic targets °), is to be subordinated to the colony's rehabilitative mission. Ideally, work should be mechanized, of a respectable skill level, and socially useful so that the convict can perceive his contribution to the general welfare.[83]

To the convict himself, according to present legislation, work will mean an eight-hour day and a six-day work week in any of a number of jobs.[84] Some ITK's are organized on an industrial base, some

---

° The USSR and other socialist countries would seem to have some advantage here over countries in which pressures from private enterprise limit the kinds of production inmates can engage in. With no private industrial sector and no complaints of unfair competition to contend with, Soviet authorities need not confine prisoners to production of goods only for use of the state or of items not produced at all in private sectors (e.g., license plates in many American states). Hence, to some degree at least, "makework" activities should be easier to avoid, and (though this is far from always the case) skills gained in a "prison trade" should be marketable in the same trade in the outside economy.

mainly concerned with agriculture, and a number specialized as lumbering operations. Metal working, wood working, cultivation, logging, and a whole variety of skilled and unskilled jobs may await a convict, depending upon the "production profile" of his colony.

Work performed by convicts in the ITK's is not entered into their labor records, nor is it paid at the going rate for similar work outside. Until 1969 base pay was 50 percent (in lumbering operations, 60 percent) of the rate set for a given job in the economy as a whole. From this base, deductions were made for food and clothing issued by the colony. After these deductions, further ones could be made, if necessary, toward payment of alimony or outstanding civil suits.[85] The remainder was placed in the prisoner's account, and, depending on the regime, a certain amount of this might be spent in the colony store. For reasons we shall examine later, the 1969 Principles changed this procedure, providing for assignment to the prisoner of 10 percent of his total monthly earnings before any deductions are made.[86]

Overtime work of up to two hours per day may be imposed on inmates and is to be compensated either by pay or through corresponding time off. Though productivity is "subordinate" to rehabilitation, it receives a great deal of emphasis as an indicator of rehabilitation, and overtime work may be a relatively frequent phenomenon. "Labor competitions" between brigades or individuals, or in some cases between colonies, are among the vehicles the administration may use to increase production.[87]

Vocational-technical instruction is obligatory for inmates who do not have job specialties. Sources are relatively vague about how instruction takes place. Apparently, it can be organized on a brigade or an individual basis and is confined generally to off-work hours. (Those without specialties do unskilled or service work pending acquisition of a skill.) For younger prisoners (under 25 years of age) training may take place in a more organized fashion, with some released time from work, where "theoretical" study is necessary.[88]

Each colony is required to provide facilities for eight-year schooling, in order to raise convicts to the level required as a national minimum. Inmates in good health and under 40 years of age are required to participate; for others study is optional.[89] (Before 1969, the upper age limit was 50. The reduction can probably be attributed to the lack of interest and high rate of failures among older inmates brought to school against their will.)

Political-upbringing work as described in Soviet sources is varied in its forms. Amidst all the other demands on inmate time, fifty minutes a week are set apart for "political activity." This usually consists of lectures and discussions run according to a "program" established by the MVD administration in charge of the colonies.[90] Visits and lectures by prominent outsiders (party officials, war heroes, workers who have won awards for over-production), presentation of "uplifting" films (at the rate of three to four a month in standard- and intensified-regime colonies), inmate participation in various "cultural" circles and in editing the colony newspaper—these represent, but do not exhaust, the "ideal" scope of political-upbringing work. The very fact of a convict's taking part in the work of one or more of the sections under the colony council is also seen as a major part of political upbringing. Here, once again, the idea emerges of active participation in one's own rehabilitation through investing energy in "worthwhile" activity. It is also good tactics for the wise con: the "participation of inmates in political-upbringing measures," read the 1969 Principles, "is encouraged and is taken into consideration in determining the extent of their correction and re-education." [91]

Support for political-upbringing work and the rest of the colony's functions is sought from the public just as it is in juvenile institutions.[92] Nearby factories may become the "sponsors" of ITK's, rendering aid in the form of pep talks, instruction in job skills, and maintenance of the colony's physical plant. Relatives of inmates and ex-inmates who have "gone straight" may also be called upon to contribute their efforts in an attempt to increase the impact of the colony's rehabilitation program.[93]

The most organized form of public participation, however, is as official as it is public. This is the institution of "observation commissions" under the executive committees of the local soviets. Numbering seven or more workers (drawn from the volunteer ranks of the soviet itself, the trade unions, Komsomol, or other organizations), the commissions have tasks ranging from enlisting the broader public in auxiliary work to participating in the hearings at which convicts are presented as candidates for early release and aiding inmates in securing work after release.[94] The commissions have functioned under various republic statutes since 1957, dating back to the early post-Stalin years when calls for strict observance of "socialist legality" were loudest. Along with the courts and the *Prokuratura*, they share a responsibility to see that colony administration and staff operate within the bounds of legality.[95]

This, then, is the general outline of how and with what means the corrective-labor colonies [96] are supposed to carry out their tasks of correction. To determine how the mix of compulsion and persuasion, of punitive and rehabilitative measures works in practice, we must turn our attention to the evidence available on the problems, successes, and failures of the correctional system.

LIFE IN THE COLONIES

Work. Since it absorbs eight hours per day of the convict's time, "socially useful labor" is a critical element of everyday life for the inmate population. If, in practice, work approximated the ideal—if it were skilled, mechanized work, related to real economic goals (not pointless, punitive, "made" work), if it were paid, and if, on the whole, productivity at work did *not* replace rehabilitation as the major purpose of the institution—then one could argue that it was indeed "corrective." But approximating these ideals is a difficult matter, and many factors militate against it.

Most important is the stubborn fact that decreeing the subordination of productivity considerations to those of rehabilitation in no way guarantees this subordination. The commandant of an ITK is faced with demands from two sources: those whose concern is economic; and those who are more concerned with correction, for whom the main task is the graduation of reformed convicts who will not trouble law-enforcement agencies after release. Commandants, presumably, seek to fulfill both demands; but there is much evidence to indicate that economic demands receive the greater amount of attention. This is not surprising, or should not be. As an indicator of success in administering an ITK, production is more quantifiable, more

easily measurable, than the comparatively elusive target of rehabilitation. In addition, it is a simpler goal to pursue. Some colonies may
have deplorably inefficient correctional staffs, while others may be
better-equipped in this regard—but *all* have a production base. It is
simpler to insure that a convict works than it is to insure that he re-
forms.

The practical subordination of rehabilitative goals to production
goals in many ITK's has produced various combinations of the "carrot
and stick" approach to convicts. In maximizing economic concerns,
some administrators have granted illegal privileges (access to alcoholic beverages, "furloughs" from the colony) to those who over-pro-
duce.[97] Others have used the stick, imposing noncompensated overtime above the maximum to meet monthly production targets.

How skilled, how mechanized, is the work convicts typically
perform? Complaints indicate that it is often neither. While metalworking and woodworking may require a modicum of skill, many inmates are employed at such jobs as making work gloves, overalls, and
mesh shopping bags. The level of skill necessary here is minimal, and,
since such jobs in the outside economy are generally held by women,
experience gained in the ITK has little effect on the convict's chances
of being hired for such a job after release.[98] Work in the ITK's whose
production profile is agricultural is even less likely to provide a marketable skill to convicts who, for the most part, come from and return
to urban areas. Finally, a not inconsiderable number of inmates are
employed in maintenance and clean-up work in the ITK, rather than
in its production units. For these there is no possibility of acquiring a
skill.[99]

The granting of a role to material as well as moral stimuli in encouraging a positive attitude toward work brings up the question of
pay. It was noted earlier that the 1969 Principles changed previous
practice in this regard, "guaranteeing" 10 percent of his pay to the
prisoner before any deductions were made. The reason is clear: under
the old system, the deductions often exceeded the total pay, completely negating the material stimulus. Prisoners, it will be recalled,
start with a base pay for a job half of that in the economy as a whole.
Deducted from this are costs of food, clothing, housing, income tax,
and, where applicable, payments on civil fines or alimony. What fre-

quently results was shown in a study of inmates in standard-regime ITK's in Perm and Kirov provinces in 1966. The average monthly pay equalled 23 rubles, 10 kopeks. Deductions for food *alone* averaged 16–18 rubles per month. With other deductions, the situation for the convicts worsened to the point where 28 percent of them received no pay after deductions.[100] The new Principles aim at correcting this. Whether they bring about any major increase in the inmate's real income remains to be seen.

Certainly, most convicts do not enjoy the work they perform and find the compensations inadequate. Frequent attempts are made to simulate illness and receive permission to remain off work for a few days.[101] With the experience gained through several "stretches," it often happens that hardened criminals monopolize the softer jobs in the ITK, while newer and lesser offenders are concentrated, disproportionately, in a range of more strenuous jobs.[102]

Presumably, many first offenders, especially those housed in ITK's with relatively complex production facilities, *do* acquire some sort of skill and do find it marketable after release. But for those in less-favored institutions and for repeated offenders the impact of work on post-release prospects is far less impressive.

Education. The reclamation of what is, for the most part, a poorly-educated population of adult convicts demands the provision of educational facilities. However, given the eight-hour work day and the lack of interest in education on the part of many inmates, the facilities for eight-year education the ITK must provide are certainly under-utilized. Those sentenced to short terms and arriving in the ITK after a few months in isolation will remain there for a considerably shorter period of time than it takes to upgrade their educational levels by even one year. If they arrive late for the start of the academic year, they cannot begin study; if they begin on time, they will be released prior to completion of the year.[103] Study is "optional" for those over 40 years of age, and it seems more than likely that few persons of such age (who make up a significant percentage of the ITK population) will wish to, or see much point in, adding to their burdens through voluntary study. A study of the effectiveness of punishment cells in ITK's as deterrents to further violation of rules found one of the weak points to be the vacation from study a stay in such a cell provided—many preferred it that way.[104]

From all indications, general schooling is very much of a low-priority sideline in the main work of the ITK. Complaints about the low level of staff preparation certainly extend to the general-education staff. Teaching in an ITK is hardly a desirable job, and many of those who fulfill such functions are probably drawn to them not out of a desire to serve, but through lack of better opportunities. Colony administrations seem to have little interest in enforcing the education rules. In one colony, 73.5 percent of a group of 85 regime violators were under the age of 30, yet of the whole group only 10 percent were studying in the school (although 84 percent of the group had educations below the compulsory minimum). Even though "violators" are a special group, the fact that so many relatively young (and hence, "compelled" to study) inmates are not undergoing any addition to their education is instructive.[105] On the whole, the corrective labor institutions do not seem to be enjoying any great degree of success in raising the educational levels of the inmates.

Political-upbringing work. This aspect of the ITK is rarely the subject of any extended discussion in Soviet sources, but when mentioned, it is frequently in the context of shortcomings those responsible for it show. One could, certainly, argue that the allocation of only 50 minutes per week to political activity indicates its rather low priority among the other concerns of the ITK. We may also question the effect of the films regularly shown the inmates as part of political upbringing; these may be viewed as entertainment, a break in the routine, rather than as "uplift." Testimony to such a possibility is provided in complaints about commandants of both ITK's and juvenile colonies who show too many movies, presumably to keep the inmates "happy" and more cooperative.[106]

We cannot tell how frequently the political-upbringing staff makes use of outside lecturers, how "typical" it really is for local party or state officials, "leaders of production," and the like to appear before the inmates. There is evidence that ITK staff may take the path of least resistance and confine themselves to a program imposed from above, generally by reading prepared pieces to the prisoners. (The MVD journal *Toward a New Life* publishes sections entitled "for reading to prisoners," providing set pieces for possible use in the fifty-minute weekly sessions. Considering the low levels of training and qualification complained of in low-echelon staff, it is hardly surprising that they would confine themselves to this type of upbringing work.)

CONVICT CULTURE AND INMATE ORGANIZATION

A major problem for any correctional institution is the challenge posed to both its custodial and its rehabilitative efforts by "unofficial" but persistent forms of social organization, with complexes of shared antireform attitudes, among the inmate population. The inmate subculture, with its unofficial norms enforced through inmate social organization, represents a subversive element in the structure of the ITK. It is specifically troublesome in a number of ways: first, it provides a context within which criminal attitudes may be maintained and strengthened, rather than weakened; second, within the same context, relative beginners in criminal activity may form criminal self-images and find that their consistent manifestation of newly learned criminal attitudes, jargon, etc. confers status on them within the inmate population and renders them more resistant to rehabilitative efforts. In addition, the presence of informal organization patterns in the inmate population frequently leads to "accommodation" between administration and ranking members of the inmate group. Such accommodation, while it may simplify administrative tasks and make for a quiet institution, essentially subverts efforts at rehabilitation. In such cases it is hardly clear who is being "co-opted."

While little Soviet research is available on the structure and dynamics of convict culture, some of its general properties emerge with a great deal of clarity from discussions of administrative problems in the colonies. Important among these is the question of what characteristics and what attitudes are the basis for conferral of high status within the convict population. The answer, a vexing one for those administrative officials interested in rehabilitation, is that lengthy criminal experience, large numbers of convictions, and previous service of sentences seem to be the main enhancers of status. On their basis, a system of stratification develops wherein the hardened, experienced criminal is often both looked up to and feared, as one who has grown "wise" and tough by virtue of time spent in imprisonment. Experienced criminals tend to band together, holding themselves apart from younger offenders with shorter records.[107] Yet, for at least a portion of the younger inmates, those with criminal experience act as socializing agents, passing on the "thieves' traditions" and "romanticism" of criminal life,° as well as information on how to adapt oneself to the institution.

While according to the organizational blueprint of the ITK, convicts are organized into detachments, informal groupings develop as well, often with more impact on their members' lives in the colony than the detachment to which they belong. Frequently, a group of recruits will coalesce around an older, more experienced convict who knows the ropes. In return for the measure of protection his experience may afford, and for the connections he may have with other "professionals" which make easier the smuggling of liquor, narcotics, and other forbidden goods into the colony, the group's "boss" enjoys the perquisites of leadership—giving orders, selecting a bunk, helping himself to some of his followers' rations.

The process of group formation as a whole, however, is more complex than this. Soviet students of colony life distinguish "spontaneous" groups of different types: those with positive, neutral, and negative inclinations. As a general phenomenon, group formation is seen, probably correctly, as a response to the gap left in the individual's life when imprisonment removes him from his regular social networks.[108] "Grouping" is also interpreted as a defensive response to a situation (imprisonment) which creates elements of uncertainty and fear.[109]

Groups with positive inclinations seem to be structured around in-

---

° The use of such terms is especially interesting, considering the extreme reluctance of Soviet writers to admit that there are many "professional criminals" in Soviet society. Yet, judging from the evidence Soviet sources provide, there are many such persons with long histories of involvement in crime and with what appear to be strong criminal self-images, usually confirmed by long periods of confinement and association with other criminals. For them, "Soviet society" may realistically be considered the "society" of the ITK, in which, with intermittent and generally short post-release periods at liberty, they spend much or most of their adult lives.

terest or competence in activities relevant to rehabilitation. They include persons united by a liking for a particular type of work, by study or skill training in the ITK, or by an interest and participation in some variety of "volunteer" work.[110] They tend to be small, and though hierarchical, leadership is exercised in a reasonable way. Other bases characterize the groups whose inclination is indefinite. Common material interests, manifested in sharing colony food or in dividing up parcels from home, are one possibility; another, common problems, most often involving divorce or abandonment by relatives on the outside. In addition, groups develop among relatively elderly prisoners and among the younger prisoners (seemingly, those under 25), although from some comments by a colony worker, the latter groups seem more "negative" than indefinite in their inclinations.

They are linked by a commonality of views on life, characterized by clearly expressed parasitic aspirations, a scornful attitude to labor, to public work, to the section on internal order, to the rules of the regime and the organization of the day. In the majority they have insufficient education, a narrow mental outlook, sometimes base interests. Among them one often observes a loss of perspectives [looking toward] conditional early release, and of faith in their powers. Characteristic also is a striving for "amusements," adopted from the more experienced inmates. They have a strong urge . . . to show defiance: they will not wear the red armband of the brigade monitor (*dezhurnyi*) . . . A feeling of false solidarity characterizes them.[111]

Most troublesome, of course, are the groups regarded as negative. Different writers subdivide this category in different ways, but agree on some commonly encountered types: (1) groups who "hold to robbers' rules and traditions"; (2) groups whose members have a common interest in some violation of the rules, e.g., drinking or malingering; (3) groups of persons who know each other from previous criminal activity or prior confinement.[112] Another variety is composed of those who come from the same areas, and possibly knew each other before conviction. "These are 'fellow-countrymen' from one and the same province, city, or district. They are drawn to one another, hold themselves aloof from other, similar groups; each of these groups considers itself 'better and higher' than the other." [113]

Within all the negative groups, leadership seems to be dictatorial and tough. The winner in what are frequently violent competitions over who will be boss lords it over his followers. But, in any single negative group, leadership is unstable—there is no lack of challengers for top position. There is no equality among members, but neither is there any guarantee of long-term subordination of the group to any boss. Each man is for himself.[114] An ITK worker, observing such groups, remarks that for all groups with negative inclinations

it is also characteristic that there you have a "boss" ("*vozhak*") directing the rest behind him. But relations in these groups are structured on an egotistical principle: "The main thing is my interests, and those of others are not my affair." These groups, as my observations show, always turn out to be unstable and impermanent in their makeup. Just as it was necessary to transfer the convict "boss" U. to another shift, so the whole of his group fell apart.[115]

Yet, when bosses like the above-mentioned U. are removed from one group they are soon, apparently, the centers of others. Colony populations change; the composition of individual groups changes. But the groups themselves are a permanent phenomenon in the colony. The bosses, after all, are mainly experienced "cons" with long records, and their sentences are likely to be longer than the average. Hence, they are always in adequate supply.[116]

What impact, one may ask, do these groups have on the ITK? Obviously, they propagate antireform attitudes, which may penetrate beyond the membership of any one group to other prisoners as well. They also complicate administrative and control tasks—group refusals to work, instigated by the boss for one reason or another, are among the problems administration encounters.[117] More seriously, many crimes and violations of the colony regime are committed by members of negative groups.[118] Even "massive disorders," involving large numbers of inmates, are attributed to the impact such groups may have, at certain critical junctures, on the rest of the inmate population.[119]

Less directly observable but potentially even more important effects flow from the networks of informal groups and the convict culture in the ITK. The rehabilitative strategy involves penetration of inmate groups by the responsible staff member, subsequent identification and co-optation of "promising" inmates to mobilize proreform sentiments among their peers, and finally isolation of the really recalcitrant by means of mobilized "inmate opinion." [120] The organizational expressions of this strategy—including the appointment of a "brigadier" from among the prisoners in a detachment to "responsibility" for his fellows at work and in the barracks—are open to various kinds of subversion. The brigadier may not live up, and have no intention of living up, to his responsibility. Taking advantage of his position, he may employ force and threats against his subordinates and lord it over them like the unofficial bosses. Alternatively, some less aggressive (and simply frightened) brigadiers, terrorized by tough "cons" and fearing reprisal, become the latters' executives, assigning them the best places in the barracks and the softest jobs and manipulating work records to their advantage.[121]

The vitality of the inmate subculture also impedes the process of individual reform. Frequently, convicts who *are* on the road to reform find themselves in a strained situation. The opinion of the prisoner *kollektiv* is not unitary; it flows from the positive and the negative groups, between which there is at least the solidarity borne of being all prisoners. Called upon to demonstrate his changing attitudes by bringing to staff attention any rule violations by other inmates, the convict has to square his behavior both with the administration and with his fellow prisoners' widely shared prohibitions against "squealing." [122] This problem often defies solution. The colonies are well guarded; but the risks of ostracism at best, physical reprisal at worst, are still present for one who breaks important informal rules.

There is probably no such creature as the "average" inmate; yet it may be useful, having discussed subcultural and informal organizational aspects of prisoner life, to give some attention to the content of prisoner experience as personally felt by a large number of inmates. Colony life is surely disagreeable for most persons. One is confined away from family, friends, acquaintances. Work may or may not be physically arduous, but it is likely to be boring and relatively ill-paid. The barracks are crowded, and the food is sparse and sometimes, at least, barely edible. One's rights—to receive packages and letters, to visits from relatives or a conjugal visit from a wife—may be revoked for a number of acts.[123] One may be punished by transfer to prison or to a punishment cell.

Under such circumstances, it is not surprising that some convicts, especially those with long sentences or repeaters with no hope of parole, give up. As one Soviet source frankly puts it, they "lose hope of a better future and abandon themselves to 'fate'—some of these, when in severe periods of depression, attempt escapes under the eyes of the guards, in order to be killed." [124]

Most reactions are not so extreme, but for all prisoners, subjective time passes very slowly.[125] Each inmate, according to two corrections specialists, seems to be counting the days on his own internal calendar.[126] The holding out of the possibility of more privileges, transfer to an easier colony, or eventual early release keeps some from losing hope and sinking into apathy; but for many, boredom, apathy, and frustration are moods of indefinite duration. The convict who tries to reform may find that his attempts are not noticed by the administration, and his feeling of frustration is increased.[127] Those who are not interested in reform avoid or sometimes defy the rules as best they can. There are those who simulate illnesses to escape work and to receive better food for a time. Others, like the "Iu." described below by a colony staffer who worked with him, "do their time" but are uncompromising in the stand they take against the ITK as a whole, even when it means punishment.

In which colonies and brigades hadn't Iu. been! He knew them all, he had tasted them all. He sat in the punitive cell for more than a hundred days, he was left without packages, he received reduced rations . . . It seemed that the [staff] had exhausted all their resources in order to put him on the path to an honorable working life. As Iu. had always been, so he resolved to remain, when he came to me. Unwillingness to work, a craving for liquor, for gambling—that was the simple "credo" of this convict. Among the prisoners he said, slyly laughing, "I came to serve out my time, not to work." [128]

Iu., according to the author of the sketch, *was* eventually reformed.[129] Such, however, is not the case with many. In the USSR as elsewhere, convicts frequently feel themselves to be victims of a vengeful law enforcement system.[130] To them, the work, the study, the restrictions on movement, food, and contact with the outside world that go to make up the regime are evidences of the state's desire not to return them to the paths of righteousness but simply to get back at them for what they have done. Abstract discussions of the "general purposes" of punishment do not impress them.

It often happens that because some convicts cannot correctly relate the general purposes of criminal punishment to the concrete circumstances of their undergoing it, it seems to them at times contrived and unnecessary, like revenge according to the principle of "evil for evil." [131]

Such feelings are by no means remarkable. That they exist only shows that despite the relatively enlightened principles formally embodied in Soviet corrective-labor law, operationalizing these principles in such a way that the corrections system becomes a really effective instrument for "changing" criminals is a goal that has been just as elusive in the USSR as in many other lands.

RELEASE—THE FINAL STEP

An inmate may depart the colony after having served his whole sentence. He may, and frequently does, receive a conditional early release, when half his sentence has been served. This benefit is, theoretically, only to be conferred on those who have shown they merit it. Soviet jurists themselves are in some disagreement over exactly how to apply the criteria of merit, which are only generally formulated in the relevant legislation as "exemplary conduct and an honorable attitude toward labor." [132] The law as such provides no binding guidelines as to what constitutes "exemplary conduct." Need there be enthusiastic cooperation with colony administration or only a lack of citations for rule violation? Are productivity and an "honorable attitude toward labor" the same thing? If not, how does one measure the latter? The difficulty of answering these and similar questions is reflected in frequent complaints about shortcomings in applying conditional early release.

Responsibility for the granting or denial of conditional early release falls upon three bodies: the colony administration, in the persons of members of a special commission on releases; the public inspection commissions mentioned earlier; and the local courts. The first two make a joint proposal concerning release of a given individual to the court, which then may act on the proposal.[133] Inclusion of the observation commissions in the process is supposed to guarantee public participation. The final, formally decisive role of the court takes the ultimate decision out of the hands of colony administration.

In practice, however, the colony's commission on release still seems to play the dominant role, and in a way that does not coincide with ideal operation. The commissions frequently consider *all* inmates who have served the necessary part (usually half) of their sentences, without regard to their behavior and attitudes, resulting in a substantial waste of time as well as some unjustified releases. A study of hearing records revealed that, of a group of recidivists previously granted conditional early release, about 25 percent were released despite regime violations and another 30 percent solely because, while not demonstrating any "exemplary" characteristics, they also had not committed any violations.[134]

The colony commission decides which inmates to present as candidates for early release at a closed meeting of its own. This list is considered at a second meeting which includes the representatives of the public who make up the observation commission. Because of the already defined position of the colony commission and its control over the information available, the inspection commission generally limits itself to rubber-stamping the colony commission's recommendations. As two authors complain, "at the second meeting the question of conditional early release of the convict is, in essence, not considered; [rather] the decision already formulated by the commission at the first meeting is only confirmed." [135] The minimal impact of the observation commission is not hard to explain. They only meet for this purpose, on the average, three to four times a year, and *in one day* may handle anywhere from 40 to over 100 applications.[136] Under such circumstances, it would be futile to expect the commissions to do more than rubber-stamp the recommendations they receive.

In making the ultimate decision, the courts are hardly better off than the commissions. The information before them is limited to what they receive in the joint communication from the commissions, and other demands on judicial time limit the amount devoted to parole proceedings. Judges set aside days in which to hear these petitions and in one all-day session hear a great many—from around 30 per day in some Belorussian areas to an impressive high of 140 per day in Krasnoiarsk province.[137] When once understands that the materials the court receives are recommendations for release, it seems clear that the court's path of least resistance is to agree with the recommendations. Complaints about the unfounded early release of many unreformed convicts bear this out.

Post-release supervision of the parolee also suffers as a result of inadequate judicial attention and the lack of public resources for maintaining a watch over his behavior. "Public organizations and collectives of working people" are, at the court's request, supposed to observe the parolee's behavior and conduct upbringing work with him. But courts frequently do not bother requesting any such observation. A survey of court practice over the years 1961–1965 showed that the percentage of all parolees who were "committed" to any definite organization or persons was low—1.5 percent in 1961, reaching a "high" of 11.2 percent only in 1965 (a low of 0.6 percent was reached in 1962).[138]

Despite all the shortcomings, it can at least be said that the inmate who receives a conditional early release has been judged, on whatever foundation or lack thereof, a relatively good risk for post-release adjustment. At the other end of the spectrum, there are the "especially dangerous recidivists," perpetrators of "grave" crimes, and regime violators, all of whom generally serve out their full sentences. Upon release, "especially dangerous recidivists" automatically, and those sentenced for "grave crimes" upon the decision of the colony and observation commissions, are subject to "administrative supervision" by the police.[139] Until 1969, apparently, such supervision could only be invoked if in his post-release behavior the convict gave reason for alarm and continued to do so in the face of police warnings.[140] At present, it can be invoked immediately upon release when the convict is deemed a bad risk.

How effective post-release supervision is in preventing recidivism cannot be readily determined; that there have been problems in implementation is clear. Under the pre-1969 provisions, police were sometimes overzealous and invoked supervision in the absence of the sort of behavior from the convict that justified it. Some police even failed to inform a convict when procedurally unjustified supervision over him had been terminated.[141] Supervision entails limitations on leaving one's residence at certain hours, on traveling to certain areas, and other measures aimed at manipulating and controlling the convict's environment. In practice, invocation of some limitations or failure to specify them sufficiently produces undesired results. The police forbade one ex-convict to leave his dwelling between 8 P.M. and 7 A.M. to keep him off the streets and out of trouble. Unfortunately, it was in the evening hours that he attended secondary school night courses for workers. On the other hand, another ex-convict was forbidden to leave his home in the evening, and in this case, "home" was specified as the address of his apartment building, wherein his was only one of many apartments. "Within the law" he visited cronies in other apartments, got frequently intoxicated, and engaged in brawls and other disorders—a testimony to the necessity of defining clearly what confinement to one's home means.[142]

If the courts, police, and commissions have problems in administering release procedures and post-release supervision, this is no less true of the ex-con himself. Like their counterparts in the West, Soviet corrections specialists have expressed concern over the effects of a term in a correctional institution on the inmate's ability to acclimate himself to life at liberty, to make new friends, choose new activities, and generally make his own decisions.[143] It is admitted that the released convict often faces "great difficulties" in reestablishing his good name and re-earning society's trust.[144] Some persons argue that the competition to secure early release encourages not rehabilitation so much as shrewdness and "toadying," adding to the overall negative effects of institutionalization:[145] a problem many non-Soviet penal administrators will recognize as well.

The stigma attached to a prison sentence and the frequent failure of the convict to upgrade his education or master a job skill during the sentence complicate the problems he faces in getting a job after release. A 1964 study of Leningrad recidivists showed that 9 percent had never secured a job after their last release—a substantial but not overly alarming proportion.[146] Another study of recidivists found 36.1 percent jobless at the time of their most recent offenses; two-thirds of these had not secured jobs since their last release.[147] These and similar figures on post-release unemployment seem relatively modest, in light of proverbial difficulties of the ex-convict in many other societies, including the United States. But in a system where the state is, by and large, the only employer and takes the official position that the ex-convict should be given work, they reflect the reluctance of managers to hire persons whom they are unwilling to trust or in whose "skills" they have little confidence. Whatever the absolute number of unemployed ex-convicts may be, it is regarded as sufficiently large to demand action.

A base for such action was provided in 1969, when the new corrective-labor principles specified that released convicts "must" be provided with jobs by the executive committees of local soviets within 15 days after a request for placement is made. The soviet's instruction to hire is to be "binding" on the enterprise involved.[148] Whether the local soviets in fact have enough "clout" to make their instructions binding on large enterprises is at least questionable; whether among their many other functions they will devote much energy to providing jobs for ex-convicts is perhaps even more so. There has been little evidence on either question in the relatively short period since 1969.

RECIDIVISM

Recidivist crime is, understandably, a sensitive matter for those who manage correctional systems. While it is an imperfect indicator in itself, the incidence of recidivism is the measure most generally accepted by Soviet corrections specialists in assessing the effectiveness of different forms of punishment.

Like their counterparts in other countries, Soviet researchers face the problem of determining the significance of a recidivist crime in assessing the effectiveness of punishments previously applied to the offender—how long after release must a crime be committed for it to be assigned to new "causes" rather than failures in correctional techniques? They have generally settled on a three- to four-year time frame, as modes of reporting statistics on recidivism will show. The authors of a lengthy study on institutional effectiveness support the three-year period, arguing that by

the expiration of a longer period of time, punishment loses its significance, and already a whole set of new positive and negative factors exert an ever more determinant influence on the conduct of the released convict. Under their influence a new crime may be committed. But in this case it cannot be attributed to a defect in the work of the corrective-labor institution.[149]

Given the choices courts enjoy in assigning either in-society punishment (corrective works, primarily) or imprisonment in an ITK of whatever regime, it has been a matter of interest to Soviet writers to determine differences in recidivism rates according to forms of punishment. We shall follow the same procedure in discussing the available data.

Corrective works. A major study focusing on the effectiveness of corrective works was carried out with a group of unspecified size who served punishment terms during 1962, according to their records as of July 1, 1965.[150] At that time, 9.2 percent of the sample had committed new offenses. This rough average, however, does not reflect the much higher rates of recidivism among some subgroups in the sample. Not surprisingly, these groups included persons to whom corrective works should not be applied, according to the many critics of overexercise of judicial discretion. Of those who had previously been convicted of a crime and for that crime been sentenced to corrective works, the rate of recidivism was 18.4 percent, double the average. For those with more than one previous conviction, it climbed to 21.0 percent. For those who had in the past served over five years of imprisonment, the rate reached 39.0 percent, or more than four times the average.

Corrective works is a relatively mild form of punishment but, as we have seen, is frequently applied by courts, exercising their discretion, as a punishment below the normal limit for an offense. In a Moscow subsample of the study just discussed, 100 of 247 convicts sentenced to corrective works had been "exceptions." Depending upon the occasion for sentencing, the recidivism rates also varied: from 10 percent for those (in the Moscow subsample) for whose offense corrective works was one of the specified penalties to 26 percent for those who had committed a "serious" offense and received corrective works as an exception.[151] For the final category of persons who may serve time at corrective works,[152] those previously imprisoned who, due to good conduct, are permitted to serve out the remaining time in this fashion, the study found the rate of recidivism to be 17 percent.[153]

How long before the effect of corrective works wears off? A good deal seems to depend here on the amount of surveillance and control exercised over the convict's behavior. Subsamples of the study for the Georgian capital, Tbilisi, and Voronezh province show wide divergences. In the former, no more than 4.6 percent of all recidivists committed a new offense while serving the sentence, while in Voronezh a whopping 45.8 percent went astray during this period. Of all recidivists, 19.2 percent in Tbilisi and 35.4 percent in Voronezh committed their new crimes within the first year after completing the sentence, while an additional 27.9 percent (Tbilisi) and 14.6 percent (Voronezh) became recidivists in the second year after release.[154]

It can certainly be argued that an overall recidivism rate of 9.2 percent (or any figure reasonably close to it) does not reflect badly on a particular mode of punishment, even one aimed for the most part at less serious offenders. The problems of corrective works seem to be, above all, the lack of any guarantee that the sentence will be carried out with the needed degree of rehabilitative attention to the offender and the practice of applying it widely as an exception or in unjustified circumstances. The exception has become more of a rule for some courts, whose practice, while it may be motivated by commendable leniency, is, in the words of one Soviet specialist, "hardly justified." [155]

Deprivation of freedom. Few studies have attempted to give anything approaching an overall picture of post-imprisonment recidivism. One author, surveying a "large group" of recidivist crimes in one union republic over the years 1962–1965, reports that 7.5 percent of those released during this period had been returned to deprivation of freedom for a new crime within the period.[156] Such a method of accounting, however, tends to underrepresent recidivism on the part of those released late in the period. Data from a study of recidivism rates by colony presented in table 14 reflect this problem (note the exceedingly low rates for the last year of study, 1965) but do illustrate the expectably higher rate of recidivism from strict and special regime ITK's where more hardened types are sent (as well as the less-expected higher rate from standard- than from intensified-regime colonies).

The recidivism rates in table 14 may look exceedingly low to

American readers accustomed to complaints that large majorities of releasees from American penal institutions return to society only to commit new crimes. The Soviet rates reported *are* indeed lower than those generally found in American studies, but it is worthwhile to note in passing that some findings contradict this generally gloomy picture. Daniel Glaser's large-scale study of the federal prison system, for example, indicates that recidivists made up about one-third of the prison population—not by any means the overwhelming majority.[157]

We cannot, of course, gauge the absolute number of recidivists, but we can get a somewhat clearer image of the recidivist population from further data. While the standard-regime ITK's have a relatively

TABLE 14   RECIDIVISM RATES BY TYPE OF CORRECTIVE-LABOR COLONY, 1963–1965

Type of Colony	Percentage of Recidivists among All Inmates Released in Year		
	1963	1964	1965
Standard regime	7.0%	6.3%	1.9%
Intensified regime	5.7	5.7	1.4
Strict regime	17.0	14.2	5.3
Special regime	20.0	16.0	. . .

Source: adapted from A.P. Safonov, "O retsidive prestuplenii, sovershennykh litsami, otbyvshimi lishenie svobody," *Sovetskoe gosudarstvo i pravo*, No. 3 (1967), p. 108.

low rate of recidivism, more than half the imprisoned population is lodged in such colonies (and over one-third in strict-regime ITK's).[158] The number of veterans of standard-regime ITK's relative to all other recidivists is bound, then, to be rather large. Such a conclusion is supported by findings published in an MVD journal of the same date as the table. Of all recidivists sent to places of confinement in the RSFSR in 1965, 36.1 percent had been last released from standard-regime, 19.1 percent from intensified-regime, and 44.7 percent from strict- or special-regime colonies.[159]

These observations, it should be remembered, are based on what are described as "large" samples and may obscure local variations in rates. A report on two ITK's in Perm province—one general and one intensified regime—cites recidivism rates of 39.0 percent and 24.2 percent, respectively.[160]

The relative incidence of recidivism by colony type is influenced by a number of factors discussed previously: judicial discretion in sending repeated offenders, as "exceptions," to standard or intensified regime ITK's; short-term sentences and the problems connected with them; and varying practice with regard to conditional early release. Though recidivism from standard and intensified regimes is relatively low, it might be lower were not so many repeated offenders lodged as exceptions in such institutions. Studies in one republic showed that, of recidivists with two, three, or more convictions prior to the last one, 38.4 percent were sent, *after* the last conviction, to a standard-regime ITK, and 18.5 percent to an intensified regime ITK.[161] Roughly more than half of the recidivists, then, were out of place.

Short sentences seem to yield more than their share of recidivism. A study of persons released from such sentences in 1961 and 1962, as of July 1, 1965, showed 30.2 percent (1961) and 14.0 percent (1962), to have committed another offense. At the same time, a Moscow sample of persons so sentenced in 1961 and 1962 had produced a 24.2 percent recidivism rate (for 1961) and a 17.6 percent rate for 1962.[162] (The Soviet concern with the potentially negative impact of short sentences as opposed to somewhat longer ones may, however, be misplaced. The few studies conducted in the West which have compared the impacts of longer and shorter sentences to institutions of the same type have generally shown that longer sentences do not produce lower rates of recidivism.[163])

Ideally, conditional early release is supposed to reflect a feeling by colony personnel that the offender has reformed. To what degree is the fact of early release a predictor of nonrecidivism? This question was explored with regard to the short-termers released in 1961 and 1962. For 1961, 33.6 percent of those who had fully served the sentence had committed another offense by the middle of 1965, while only 11.7 percent of those released early had. For 1962, the comparable figures were 17.0 percent and 10.9 percent.[164] These findings fit, generally, the assertion made in another study of release practice—

that, on the whole, the percentage of recidivism among the early-released is 1.5 to 2.0 times lower than among those who serve out their sentences in full.[165]

This impression is altered radically, however, when institutions that practice early release on a massive scale are examined. In one such colony, of short-termers released in 1962, 75.6 percent left early and the remaining 24.4 percent at end of term. The recidivism rate among the early released was 10.2 percent, as opposed to 4.9 percent among those who had served the full time.[166] Conditional early release seems to have been applied rather more widely in the early 1960s than in later years.[167] The decline in its frequency may be traceable to the negative effects of applying it massively. (While many Soviet convicts are released early, it is interesting to note that the practice of early release, or release "on parole," is perhaps even more widespread in the United States. Department of Justice figures for 1964 show that, averaging nationwide, about 65 percent of all those released from state prisons in that year were released on parole. The variation between states is great, however, with some releasing virtually all prisoners on parole, and some releasing less than 20 percent in this manner.[168])

Who are the recidivists? For the most part, they commit property offenses (most frequently theft) and the public order offenses categorized by the label hooliganism.[169] They show some tendency to specialize in the same type of offense, with the seriousness of their offenses increasing and the length of the sentence received tending also to increase.[170] Many, perhaps most, recidivists committed their first offense while still juveniles. If one cannot in these cases talk about full-blown criminal careers, one does see in their backgrounds a history of recurrent and frequent involvement with the law.[171]

In summary, one can say the following about recidivism and its significance in the USSR: some of it, undoubtedly, is attributable to the persistence of antisocial, criminal attitudes on the part of persons whom Soviet correctional methods (as well, probably, as those of any other society) cannot reach. Those confined for long "stretches" in strict- and special-regime colonies and those who are categorized as especially dangerous recidivists seem to live large segments of their lives outside the law in terms of their orientation, and likewise large segments of their lives *inside* penal institutions. Their generally low levels of education and training provide them with few resources to succeed in staying out of trouble when at liberty—and hence such periods tend to be relatively short.

On the other hand, the first offender sentenced to a short term in a corrective-labor colony and later turning again to crime may be truly a "product" of the correctional system. A post-arrest period of three months or thereabouts in investigative isolation, where he mixes with criminals of all types and histories, followed even by a relatively short stay in and early release from a standard-regime ITK, may effectively disrupt many aspects of his life. His job may be lost, his family and friends may become distrustful, the police will be suspicious of him. He *has* been isolated, but his mode of isolation has not guaranteed his rehabilitation, so that he reenters society ill-equipped to deal with the new problems he may face. He may turn once again to crime, and his stay in a correctional institution may have increased the probability of his doing so.

About the first type of recidivist, who may in some cases fit the label "career criminal," Soviet corrections specialists can probably do little. About the second type there is, it seems likely, much more that can be done. Many specialists recognize this. But translating such recognition into policy and policy into action has yet to be accomplished. Until it is, the Soviet corrections system, like many others, will continue to contribute to the problem it is, in theory, designed to alleviate.

10

DEVIANCE AND CONTROL IN SOVIET PERSPECTIVE

CRIME, DELINQUENCY, AND the abuse of alcohol are major social problems in the Soviet Union. The Soviet sources upon which this book is largely based make that fact abundantly clear. Even if, in themselves, they tell us little about the incidence of these problems in strict quantitative terms, the very number of such sources and the volume of discussion the problems provoke point to deep governmental concern.

Of course, to say that they are major problems is not to say or even imply that they are the most critical internal problems the USSR faces, or that the state regards them as such. Even in the United States, a nation which views itself as peculiarly crime- and violence-ridden, national priorities lie elsewhere—in defense, in economic policy, in policies (some, perhaps, with "preventive" potential) aimed at coping with the stresses a legacy of discrimination against racial minorities has created. The Soviet case, surely, is similar. More of the attention of the Soviet leaders goes to the problems created by an increased nationalism within the countries of the socialist bloc, by conflict-laden relations with China, and by the perennial concerns of industrial and agricultural production than to the vexations the criminal, delinquent, and drunkard provide.

But, incomplete as they are, the data on these latter problems assembled here say something very important about Soviet life: that the experience of over fifty years of social change carried out under the banner of Marxist-Leninist ideology by a leadership often as pragmatic as it is ideological, an experience which has produced a society rivaled by few in centralization of power and relative completeness of control over many of the aspects of its members' daily lives, has not brought the extermination of common, nonideological deviance. Nor has it even approximated such a state. Neither the socialist nor the totalitarian ingredients of the recipe have yielded those results. While our data reflect most directly the activity of agencies of detection and control, rather than the acts of the deviants themselves, the multiplication of such data in the last decade, the increased resources devoted to research, and the increased dissemination of information about deviant behavior to professional audiences and public alike all indicate the current concern with deviance and encourage skepticism about any claims that its eradication lies in the forseeable future.

Emerging less directly from the data, but with considerable clarity nonetheless, are indications of striking similarities (along with, to be sure, dissimilarities) between deviant behavior in the Soviet Union and in other societies of the modern type. Our information about crime and delinquency points toward a preponderance of property crimes and public order violations among the different categories of offense. This Soviet pattern is roughly parallel to that of the United States, as well as some other countries. Proportionally, crimes of violence in the two societies represent a rather small proportion of all officially reported offenses.

In a like manner, when dealing with the perpetrators of criminal and delinquent acts and the abusers of alcohol, Soviet data tend to direct our attention, as do American data, to the less-educated, frequently lower-paid, relatively less advantaged strata. The delinquents who appear before the commissions and the courts tend to lag behind their peers in educational level—often enough, they are dropouts. The probability of delinquency tends to increase when the juvenile is already a worker, to decrease if he is still in school, to be lowest of all if he still attends a school in the academic track. The typical delinquent is urban rather than rural: according to figures, the Soviet, like the American, countryside is not so productive of problem youth.

Excluding white-collar criminals, the adult offender (and, to a degree, the habitual drunkard and alcoholic) is found, perhaps predominantly, in the less-advantaged milieux of Soviet society. Writers claim, sometimes citing statistics, that criminals and drunkards tend to be less cultured: their educational attainment is lower than the average, their interest in "higher things" weak or nonexistent. Most seem to be workers of low or intermediate skill; few are among the "leading production workers." Of course, the title "worker" encompasses a great proportion of the adult Soviet population, and it is natural that many criminals and drunkards should also be workers. Still, the miniscule proportion or virtual absence of the intelligentsia in the statistics available suggests that the better-educated, the more advantaged in knowledge, skills, and employment (if not always in income), may not contribute a share to the criminal population proportionate to their share of the total population. In this again, the USSR resembles rather than diverges from other societies.

With varying degrees of sophistication, many students of crime have argued that its main determinant is economic: poverty, relative or absolute, deprives, degrades, frustrates, and ultimately "pushes" many persons to criminal acts. Yet, in both the Soviet Union and the United States, where rural incomes, especially those derived from farming, have generally been lower than the urban average, statistics suggest that crime is less of a problem in the rural areas. Is there something in the slower pace of rural life, in the persistence of tradition there, that insulates dwellers from crime; is there some noneconomic explanation? Many criminologists, Americans among them, have argued that there is; and there are indications that some of their Soviet counterparts may be moving toward similar ideas.[1]

It may be objected that these impressions of similarities are based on data that cannot even roughly sustain them; that the working-class image of the delinquent, for one, is a product of enforcement practices. Perhaps there is a substantial degree of legally defined delinquent activity among the offspring of the intelligentsia, the middle level, and top bureaucrats which goes undetected and/or unrecorded due to the relative privacy with which their parents' positions provide them and, on occasion, parental influence with the police? Perhaps the incidence of white-collar crime is proportionally much higher than it appears to be, but many of its "advantaged" perpetrators manage to escape detection? Perhaps many hidden alcoholics might be found among those who occupy important jobs? In general, perhaps there exists some form of middle-class bias among criminologists, judges, doctors, and other professionals, which results in a projection of a disproportionate amount of the total of deviance onto lower-class Soviet citizens?

One cannot deny that something of the sort is possible. Too many tales of the peccadilloes of Soviet "gilded youth" exist for us to claim that in the USSR conformity to the law always increases with social status. But a systematic bias of this sort, to whatever degree it exists under Soviet conditions, cannot be measured with any accuracy. Even the foreign observer who lives in the USSR for an extended period does not live Soviet life, though he lives close to it. The subtle nuances, the behavioral cues that might help answer the question, are by and large inaccessible.

However, there is another response to the objection: if such a bias does exist and works its effect in the production of data of the sort we have examined, this is but another point of similarity between the Soviet case and that which most of the readers of this book know best, the American. Such an enforcement bias against the less-advantaged, the relatively defenseless, may be a general property of large, stratified societies—a description to which both the United States and the Soviet Union correspond.

Conversely, the reporting of offenses is susceptible to inaccuracies not only from bias, but also from inefficiency, administrative overload, and a number of other problems. While official statistics in the United States underrepresent the number of affluent, middle-class adolescents who commit delinquent acts, giving to some a false impression of immunity conferred upon "good" families, studies of inner-city areas with higher reported delinquency rates have tended to show that, in *those* areas, the amount of hidden delinquency is massive. If an inner-city youth is much more likely to be identified as a delinquent by agencies of law and order than his advantaged suburban counterpart, it is nonetheless also true that the number of offenses for which such disadvantaged youth are prosecuted, or even the number known to the police, is far below the number of offenses actually perpetrated. We are not in a position, in examining the Soviet case, to reject the possibility that lower-class Moscow and Leningrad delinquents, for example, commit many more offenses than those with which they are officially charged.

There are, certainly, differences as well as similarities. One need not compose a lengthy catalog here, since the source of many of the most important differences is obvious. Offenses against state or socialist property have to be an important part of property offenses in the USSR, since so much property answers to this description. Auto theft, an offense of great frequency in the United States, could not approach any such magnitude in the Soviet Union, since the vehicle-population ratio is so much lower there. It seems unquestionable as well that proportionally fewer physical assaults result in the death of the victim in the USSR than in the United States, due to the lesser availability of "private" firearms in the former.

The probabilities, it might be argued, also lie in the direction of lower rates of physical crimes against the person in the USSR than in the United States, as a proportion of all crimes in each nation. Statistics here, as elsewhere, are a somewhat indifferent guide. Some students have come to see American violence as rooted partly in a long cultural tradition of self-reliance, aggressive individualism, and a "frontier ethic," [2] and questions concerning general cultural components in the style of crime in a particular society have therefore become a matter of concern. Russian history is scarcely poor in evidence of mass violence but gives little evidence of "aggressive individualism" or many other elements of the nineteenth-century American ethos. However, although this is a matter of exceeding interest, it involves issues so broad and historical questions so deep, as well as beyond the author's competence, that it seems better simply to note its existence and not to engage in an idle pursuit of it.

We have written here of similarities between Soviet deviance and that in the United States and other industrial societies. It has generally been the position of Soviet criminologists commenting on crime in the (capitalist) West that the behavioral similarities of the socialist and capitalist deviant are *only* that: that the deep-lying causes of such behavior are quite different and vary according to the "system." The merit or lack of merit of such a position can only be determined by a final examination of Soviet theory.

SOVIET THEORIES AND SOVIET REALITIES

The persistence of high rates of deviant behavior in societies where substantial time and manpower has been devoted to explaining, predicting, and controlling deviance (most notably, perhaps, in the United States) underscores the difficulty of assessing the "adequacy" of theoretical explanations, whatever their source. Measured by their immediate and long-term results, such enterprises have not, generally, been notably successful. In many ways, criminology (and the broader "sociology of deviance") today, as in the past, presents a Babel of voices, each offering and advocating a different theoretical perspective or a modification of some orientation accepted by a more-or-less large group of theorists. On many basic issues there is little consensus between competing schools of thought.

All this should serve to remind us that, in assessing the adequacy of Soviet theories of deviance, we must beware of employing criteria no society's theoretical output could satisfy. Conceivably, a theory may be "useful," productive of fertile hypotheses, yet have little impact on deviance because of the difficulty of translating its content into programs of prevention and/or correction. It is difficult to judge a theory by its practical results. Thus, what we shall be interested in here is not the practical success or failure of Soviet theories but rather the presence or absence of elements that *constrict* Soviet explanations, that limit the legitimate scope of inquiry and thus hamper theorists in taking into account important aspects of Soviet reality that have a possible impact on deviance.

Such constricting elements seem all too evident. As an officially decreed orthodoxy, Marxism-Leninism has had a profound effect on Soviet social sciences, criminology included. The victory of the "dialectical-materialist" camp in the late 1920s spelled the end, first of theoretical diversity in criminology, then of criminological research itself. The free debate that characterized criminology in the 1920s was not to be revived to anything like the same degree in the period beginning in the late 1950s, when criminology itself was restored.

Contemporary Marxism-Leninism, very much itself the product of the 1920s and 1930s, *has* postulated answers to some very basic questions, which in turn have left their mark on criminology. Crime, delinquency, and alcoholism are seen as *social* phenomena, for all practical purposes purely social in their causes.* Man is a social being; he bears the imprint of whatever social system he inhabits. He is malleable, plastic, adaptable—by implication he is, in a sense, "perfectible." This is already a heavy dose of doctrine. Even if each point *is* "true," the fact remains that information possibly dissonant with such truth is not processed: it tends to be sifted out, rejected. More important still is the most unshakable postulate that Soviet socialism is the "good society," here and now. While admittedly only a transitional phase in the construction of communism, socialism is, by the Soviet definition, *already* free of the characteristics that inevitably generate deviant behavior under capitalism. Hence, the socialist order at large cannot be responsible for the deviance that occurs within it. No Soviet criminologist viewing his society and culture could, consistently with this postulate, make the statement the American criminologist, Donald R. Taft, made with regard to American culture, that ". . . such a culture must expect considerable crime which can be attributed to its own inherent qualities. In this sense we get the criminals we deserve." [3] According to the orthodox view, Soviet socialism deserves no criminals at all.

The effects of conceiving of deviance as a socially caused phenomenon while simultaneously excluding basic "societal" factors from scru-

* The author himself, reflecting what is no doubt a combination of personal conviction and the results of a sociological training, would agree that these phenomena are at least basically social in causation. The main problem in the Soviet case, it seems, is that the position described above was reached by a process more political than intellectual (the victory of dialectical materialism in the disputes of the late 1920s) and that the nature of this victory has discouraged the speculative thinking Soviet criminology seems to need.

tiny as possible causes are evident in the level at which Soviet theory generally works: the level of the "middle-range," of the infrastructure. In a sense, it is the only level available. Personality-centered theories, which focus on individual characteristics, carry the taint of "psychologizing" or "biologizing." "Society" is itself defined as blameless. Hence, the causes of deviance are sought in the formation, socialization, and experiences of Soviet citizens, in those groupings and networks of interaction which are less than all-inclusive: taken together, they make up much of the society's infrastructure; separately, they constitute the "immediate environments" of individuals. Criminological research has been largely the search for and description of flaws in this infrastructure, points at which it is infected by socially communicable "survivals" of capitalist mentality. These points are located in both official and nonofficial groupings. The nuclear family, the adolescent peer group, the crowded communal apartment—these may all be so infected. Even in the low-level extensions of the official superstructure, the party cell, the Komsomol cell, the workers' *kollektiv*, those harmful and antisocial attitudes labeled as survivals may be encountered.

In a way, this is an "epidemiological" view of deviance. Were one to substitute "virus" for "survival," much of the rest of the language would still fit. The most important question, however, is what causes the infection to begin with—why are some immediate environments "infected" and not others? Here the answer is incomplete, and rather unsatisfying. Survivals persist long into the socialist period because of the "law of the lag of consciousness behind social existence." The law is accepted as a given. Helping to conserve survivals are "formal bureaucratic" attitudes manifested by some persons in responsible positions toward the legitimate needs and interests of citizens; the "objective difficulties" of war and postwar reconstruction, which placed heavy psychological as well as economic and physical burdens on the populace; and the ever-continuing attempts of the hostile bourgeois world to corrupt the minds and weaken the loyalty of Soviet citizens. From the whole-system standpoint, there is nothing self-critical or self-exploratory about this catalog of contributing factors. The official who demonstrates formal bureaucratic attitudes is himself seen as deviating from the ideal of socialist administration. War and its aftermath are seen as exogenous factors which socialism did not create and for which it is not responsible. The same is true of the influence of the capitalist world. Blame for deviance and the attitudes that foster it is internalized, but only at middle levels of the social structure, which cannot be controlled completely from the top, and "externalized" in time and space to historical forces beyond effective control and to the machinations of a hostile capitalist world. This is clear also in the one case where Soviet thought seems to encompass explanations beyond the middle range: the connection of alcohol problems with the traditional Russian drinking culture. Here the issue is one of a strong traditional element, resistant to uprooting, which has persisted with relatively minor modification into socialism. But it is "traditional," not "socialist": it is still viewed as rooted in a past whose effects socialism cannot eliminate all at once. Soviet society today is not held responsible for the continuing nature of alcohol problems.

Thus, the responsibility for deviance is deflected from any potentially blameworthy properties of the society itself onto history and imperfect immediate environments. The greatest cost of such deflection, with regard to the possibilities of explanation in Soviet theory, is that links between the large social structure and the "flawed" immediate .milieu are left unexplored. Yet the milieu mediates and refracts the impact of the general social structure on the individual: [4] whether "healthy" or flawed, it is linked to the general structure. Until such links are explored, a great deal of Soviet reality remains beyond the scope of inquiry.

In chapter 2, we wrote of "determinist," "interactionist," "neofunctionalist," and "voluntarist" emphases in theorizing about deviance. Obviously, it would be hard if not impossible to find a school of theory exemplifying only one of these. Much contemporary writing on deviance in the West seems to aim at an amalgam of determinist and interactionist perspectives, at least in the collection of data. Increasingly, inquiry into the characteristics, experiences, and acts of the offender is accompanied by studies of the backgrounds, behavior, and "ideologies" of police, judges, legislators, and corrections personnel—those who interact with the deviant at various stages in his career.

Taken as a whole, Soviet theory can be designated primarily as "social-determinist." The data that Soviet researchers assemble refer predominantly to social factors—education, occupation, residence, family background, etc.—that "shape" or determine the individual. These are the factors which, when of a certain quality, are viewed as producing antisocial attitudes and deviance. "Determinisms" of a biological or individual-psychological variety are generally rejected.

But for practical purposes, in the Soviet Union as elsewhere, to "explain" (even in a determinist way) is *not* to excuse. This determinism is "soft" enough to accommodate a voluntarist view of each deviant individually. The criminal and delinquent, corrupted as they may be by unfortunate environments, *decide* to act—they need not act. Their deviant acts are acts of the "will," for which they bear responsibility. Similarly, the alcoholic or habitual drunkard is one who, while frequently the victim of bad influences, is himself to blame, in the last analysis, for his problems. Contemporary Soviet writing in criminal law, with its emphasis on the deterrent effects of punishment on both the actual criminal and those prone to criminality, is far removed from the language of the 1920s, when "socially dangerous act" was made to serve for crime and the state's reactions bore the title "measures of social defense" rather than the bourgeois label of "punishment." The restoration of voluntarism brought to an end the type of "revolutionary" legal thought that saw law existing under socialism only until the point when it would, like the state itself, "wither away." [5]

Notable for its virtual absence from Soviet writing is any element of interactionism. One need not ponder long on why this is the case. The questions typically asked within an interactionist framework concern the motivations, interests, and prejudices of the social "controllers" themselves at least as much as, if not more than those of the deviants they control. As an enterprise, social control itself is transformed from a reaction to deviance into a separate, frequently autonomous species of *action*. The investigator who looks at social control through the filter of interactionism takes the role of a disinterested outsider, and sometimes even seems to adopt the perspective of the deviant underdog. None of this would be in any sense politically acceptable in the USSR. It suggests the possibility of a lack of unanimity between state and masses and of arbitrariness in defining what behaviors are deviant, when the official image is one of solidarity between the public and its leaders. None of this would contribute to the "struggle."

If there is an ideological strain in the interactionist perspective as it exists today, it seems to run in redefining much of what is now regarded as deviance as merely a manifestation of diversity in behavior.[6] In relatively open social systems, diversity may be viewed as a positive and useful, or at least neutral attribute, and bringing some types of deviance under this rubric may not be very difficult in a time of rapid change. It is otherwise in the USSR, a relatively closed system placing little on behavioral diversity and much more emphasis on predictability and control. The current boundaries of behavior are seen as valid, the existing diversity as sufficient, the deviant and not his controllers as the problem. Small wonder that Soviet writings on deviance show little if any trace of interactionist ideas.

It need scarcely be noted at this point that there is also little of neo-functionalism in Soviet thought on the causation of deviance. No writer suggests that the USSR needs its deviants, that it recruits and then deploys them in such manner as to make clear where the boundaries of acceptable behavior lie. No one argues that deviance is a resource: were someone to do so, how could such a position be squared with the commitment to the eradication of crime, delinquency, and alcoholism as "social phenomena" as a goal both reasonable and, ultimately, attainable? To look at things in a neo-functionalist way requires a degree of societal self-analysis that ideological requirements seemingly cannot permit. Whether such notions occur among Soviet criminologists is hard to say: it is clear that their expression would be too heterodox to be tolerated.

Yet, from the outside, much of the approach to deviance management in the USSR seems to fit neatly within the neo-functionalist frame. However recruitment occurs, the deviant is frequently "enlisted" to serve as exemplar of what undesirable behavior is in concrete terms. It would be hard to do without him. The habitual drunkard whose picture stares down upon his fellow workers from a "board of dishonor" or "window of satire" on the factory wall, the petty criminal tried by a comrades' court made up of and playing to an audience of his coworkers or residents in the same housing complex, the more serious offender whose criminal trial takes place before an audience of hundreds in an open session—all these, demonstrating the shapes "evil" can assume, are being *treated* as resources, are rendering service to the forces of social control. The emphasis in Soviet writings on the "educative significance" (*vospitatel'noe znachenie*) of such presentations of the deviant makes this clear.

The preceding discussion has brought us to two final questions. What are the functions, broadly conceived, that Soviet criminological and other thought on deviance perform beyond the "explanatory"? And what is the impact of the requirement that thinking and research on deviance be of practical utility and ideologically congruent with Marxism-Leninism? Much of what has gone before will suggest to the reader some of the answers to follow.

Soviet thought on the causation of crime, alcoholism, and delinquency, whatever its other functions are, serves also to exculpate the system itself (socialism in the contemporary USSR) of any blame for these phenomena. It incorporates expressions of complete confidence in the system with an optimistic view of the human individual (no individual is, because of any "innate" qualities, more deviance-prone than any other); and thus seeks the causes of deviance in immediate environments which are at variance with the overall blueprint of socialist society. In this sense, it can be said to be "conservative" in its implications. "Radical" criminological critiques of capitalist systems, locating the blame for crime and other evils in the nature of the capitalist economy, are hardly new, nor are they the sole property of Soviet writers. The Dutch criminologist W.A. Bonger advanced largely the same explanation in his *Criminality and Economic Conditions* (1916).[7] It is not surprising, given an economic-determinist frame of reference, that Soviet criminologists will blame crime in the West on capitalism itself and see it as an inevitable product of such an economic system, while viewing socialism as basically flawless in this regard. The two systems, after all, are seen as antithetical. Yet this does not alter the fact that such a position makes it impossible for Soviet criminologists to *think*, openly, of searching for criminogenic elements in the nature of the Soviet economy, the unequal distribution of power and other scarce goods, and other major aspects of the system. It has even made it difficult for Soviet researchers to come to grips with the possibility that some of the progress of the last fifty years—

industrialization and urbanization especially—may have had unde-sired consequences, even though carried out under socialism, an issue their Western colleagues have been grappling with for some time.

The demands for utility and congruence explain a great deal (though not all) of the conservative nature of Soviet explanations of deviance. Any "radical" critique of the present social system which attempted to pinpoint deviance-generating elements on the system level would be ideologically incongruent (since the system is, by defi-nition, free of such elements) and would also lack practical utility, since the system is not seen as needing basic changes. Of the two de-mands, congruence seems the more important, since it sets a limit on the scope of utility. It might, for example, be useful to examine the consequences of urbanization and industrialization in a critical man-ner, with an eye out for unanticipated consequences; but to so ap-proach these processes would be incongruent with the position that negative consequences flow from them only under capitalism, not under socialism. By and large, the Soviet view of criminology is one of an applied science; hence the demand for utility. It seems, how-ever, that in many cases the demand for congruence may reduce the overall utility achieved.

The sternest criticisms are reserved for those whose writings appear to meet neither the demands of congruence nor those of utility. The positions advanced by I.S. Noi, for example (see chapter 8), *were* in-congruent with prevailing ideology and its criminological interpreta-tion. While Noi launched no radical critique of society, his view of man was less optimistic than that of his colleagues. Its *utility* was al-so unclear: as Karpets asked, what sense would criminal law and criminal punishment (which are not viewed as dispensable) make, if criminal tendencies were "encoded" in many offenders? In a real sense, Karpets seems to have been correct in his criticisms of Noi, given the prevailing currents in Soviet criminology. But such an emphasis on utility limits the directions research may take.

This is not to say that Soviet thought on deviance causation is necessarily impervious to change. At sufficiently critical junctures, it can be "proven," if practicality takes precedence, that Marxism-Len-inism does accommodate a particular view. Noi and his supporters have tried to present themselves in this way. But the limits set by ideology make it comparatively difficult at present to accommodate or even accord a hearing to new views which smack of heterodoxy or, in criminology's case, a return to the 1920s.

Demands for utility and congruence need not be imposed directly to be effective. In the USSR, at least, control over the criminological enterprise is a relatively natural thing. Most of the important research takes place under the aegis of government research institutes. The rules of the game are clear to those who work there, who are, in effect, civil servants. Slightly less direct but similarly effective is the control over research and publication by criminologists who hold teaching positions on university faculties. These, after all, are state institutions too. (Yet, it seems that the "clearance" for access to statistical data enjoyed by university-located criminologists is not so high as that of their colleagues in institutes such as the All-Union one in Moscow, which is directly subordinated to the USSR Prokuratura.)

Control is self imposed as well. In the early stages of rebirth (the later 1950s) those who argued the value of empirical research on crime proposed it as something with practical value and argued in Marxist-Leninist terms the acceptability of the study of "concrete" data. At a time well before the term "criminology" came back into use, they were careful to connect the demise of concrete research itself to the "distortions" engendered by Stalin's personality cult. They accepted (and still do) the "verdict" of 1929, declaring that biological and bio-psychological orientations were false and harmful. The case for criminology was presented in the orthodox ideological terms its protagonists adopted as the best way to legitimate their activity.[8]

There is yet another element of indirect control, which focuses thought on the causes of deviance in an essentially conservative direction. This is the education and the total training experience of criminologists and others involved in the explanation and management of deviance. Marxism-Leninism, whether one accepts it or not, *is* a world-view. It is one way of organizing human history and contemporary reality into a comprehensible pattern. And It is the world-view in which virtually all Soviet criminologists have been raised. It has been presented to them as the only scientific view of reality, and its communication has not been jeopardized by giving "equal time" to contrary views. Though more intense, the experience seems roughly comparable to the education in "civics" Americans receive in junior high and high schools: the inculcation of a certain set of categories and of positive attitudes toward the set of social arrangements prevailing in one's own society. World-views, once internalized, resist change, especially when, as in the Soviet case, there is little opportunity to test them against the reality of societies other than one's own.

There is no real reason to assume, then, that many Soviet scholars engaged in the explanation of deviance do *not* accept as true the notions that deviance is a survival; that human history is comprehensible in terms of a progression, ascending in stages of feudalism to capitalism to socialism to communism, and that socialism harbors no "inevitable causes" of crime.* To some degree, social scientists everywhere work within the limits of some "conventional wisdom," whether "official" or not, and Soviet social scientists are no exception. For many of them, the conventional wisdom is a matter of conviction; for others, it is a required perspective, with which they may be dissatisfied but to which they have no alternative. For those who find it impossible to work within such terms, Soviet social science is an inhospitable enterprise, and one they are unlikely to enter.

Absent from Soviet criminology (at least to the degree it is present in much criminology in the West) is a critical, questioning attitude toward sanctions, as well as toward the belief that the same institutions can both punish and rehabilitate. This is not only a matter of the inadvisability of questioning the "unquestionable": it seems also to reflect the academic training of Soviet criminologists, which is overwhelmingly legal. (In this, the USSR reflects the general European pattern, where criminology is closely linked to criminal law, rather than the American, where its closest links seem to be with sociology.) The criminologists are part of the legal profession. Insofar as they criticize flaws in the practice of judges, prosecutors, and others, they do it mostly from the inside. Frequently enough, articles on the causes and prevention of crime and delinquency in the two "practi-

---

* One criminologist with whom the author has spoken offered the view that in the United States, in its present capitalist phase, some types of crime, especially in the rural South, give evidence of survivals of *feudalism*. Another, in response to a question about whether the "survivals" idea would come to play less of a role in explaining Soviet crime in the future, answered in the affirmative, because the survivals themselves were on the decline.

cal" journals—*Soviet Justice* and *Socialist Legality*—are written by judges and prosecutors rather than by research criminologists. Often, those with positions of importance in research—such as I.I. Karpets, who directs the All-Union Institute in Moscow—were practical workers for a long period before becoming criminologists. All this contributes not only to criminology's assuming less than an independent stance toward criminal law, but also to a tendency of criminologists to accept much of the definition of their work as practice-oriented, "applied" research: making criminal law work more "effectively." Under such circumstances, a conservative leaning can be expected; and it should be no surprise that, in their empirical research, criminologists are generally gatherers and analyzers of data, rather than testers of theoretically derived hypotheses.

The foregoing does not mean that the study of deviance in the USSR is at a standstill, or that no writers sound dissonant or innovative notes in their contributions. We have already seen the controversies surrounding the ideas of Sakharov and Noi. These are not yet completely resolved. Even within the orthodox framework, there are other examples of the diffusion of new ways of looking at specific deviance-related issues, if no examples of entire new frameworks.

Criminologists are asking new questions about the relationship between the individual and his immediate environment, as well as between the individual and the legal order itself. The questions are not radical in essence, and they provoke little acrimony. But they are becoming more subtle and thoughtful. They involve issues such as conformity to informal versus formal (i.e., legal) norms; the desirability, from a criminological viewpoint, of "principled" as opposed to "opportunistic" conformity to the laws (either type of conformity, on the surface at least, equals non-deviance); and the whole complex of questions surrounding the influence of reference groups on individual behavior.[9] It would be going too far to say that this is the trend in Soviet analysis of deviance. Such topics are dealt with by only a handful of writers, and their impact on their colleagues is as yet unclear. Only the future can tell whether the elements so strongly supporting orthodoxy, and resulting thus far also in relatively narrow limits on interpretation of phenomena, will prevail, or whether newer ways of looking at them will somehow be legitimated.

DEVIANCE AND THE NORMS:
CONSENSUS AND DISSENSUS

No social system, to be sure, provides all its members with equal shares of the sort of power it takes to determine that a type of behavior is deviant and that it is necessary to do something about it. In democratic systems, generally, legal definitions of deviance are enacted indirectly by legislators (and in common-law nations, expanded or contracted to a considerable degree by the judiciary) rather than by a plebiscite. Electoral control by constituents over their representatives is intermittent and influenced by constituent knowledge of and interest in the roles representatives play in the political process. In many cases, a legislator is free to vote his own convictions. Insofar as these may differ from those of a large number of his constituents, the definition of deviance becomes a work of specialists rather than of the public at large. The predominant social characteristics of legislators in the United States—generally middle-class, white, middle-aged— are the characteristics of only one subgroup of the population, one among many in a diverse society. While the "priorities" of legislators may in many instances dovetail with those of other segments of the population, there is no reason to expect that they always will. As Robert K. Merton noted,

Full or substantial consensus in a complex differentiated society exists only for a limited number of values, interests, and derived standards for conduct. We must therefore be prepared to find that the same social conditions and behaviors will be defined by some as a social problem and by others as an agreeable and fitting state of affairs.[10]

The question that interests us here is, is there a similar lack of "substantial consensus" in the USSR? Certainly, power is extremely centralized, and final decisions are made by a relatively narrow elite. For instance, when new legislative "principles" are formulated in the criminal-law field or in other areas, there *is* participation by legal "professionals"—but the ultimate power in determining the content of the law lies with the top state and party officials. Are their convictions, their views, their interests reflective of those of the masses? This is a critical question.

Ideology and political structure are both important in pointing toward the answer. Marxism-Leninism legitimates a view of elite and masses as unequal in the clarity of their perception of social reality. The leadership, with a monopoly over the interpretation of the ideology, has typically seen itself as the guide, the instructor, the educator of the masses. Evidence of dissent on the public's part is generally interpreted not as evidence of error on the part of the leaders, but as a reflection of inadequate "consciousness" or immaturity among the masses. Political structures which limit the expression of dissenting views also limit, to some degree, the ability of the state to gauge the presence or absence of dissent on nonpolitical issues of deviance-definition such as those that concern us here. These elements would generally lead us to expect some dissensus between state and public, though such an expectation is open to certain qualifications of its own, to be noted below.

The most marked dissensus arises in the area of alcoholic deviance. From the evidence, one has to conclude that the official anti-drink appeals find much of the population turning a deaf ear. The habitual problem drinker or alcoholic, however he views himself, is not a promising audience for anti-alcohol propaganda. More significantly, the working-class male population as a whole, from most indications, appears to hold the view that drinking is a manly, sociable thing to do and to view "excessive" drinking rather tolerantly. As well as being a part of the male style, drinking provides for some a convenient refuge from the problems of daily life. Complaints of insufficient intolerance toward drunkenness on the public's part underline the failure of the state to be convincing here; the fact that legal beverage alcohol production is a state monopoly can hardly add weight to the state's arguments. In short, deep-rooted pro-drink attitudes, as components of Russian culture, seem to mesh today with some strains of Soviet urban industrial life felt sharply by working-class males especially and render unlikely any rapid development of a state-public consensus on the evils of heavy drinking. (Chronic alcoholism may be another matter: Soviet writings fail to make fine distinctions between "alcoholic" and "drunkard," and thus complicate the separation of variations in the theme of alcoholic deviance.) State attitudes certainly have some support among those who for various reasons are abstainers and among women who, as wives, mothers, and sisters, have suffered from the ravages of alcohol on a male relative. But such support obviously does not suffice to tip the balance. Admissions about the grave nature of the "alcohol problem" and Soviet evidence on conflicts of attitudes between the public and the propagandists are clear enough in their indications that consensus here is still a long way off, if ever it is to be reached.

On juvenile delinquency, our evidence is much less clear. In the USSR, as in many other nations, "delinquency" encompasses criminal offenses by minors as well as violations which can only be committed by minors—truancy, running away from home, and the like. We have little indication of public-state conflict over the deviant *nature* of at least the more serious forms of juvenile misconduct, though when the members of the adult public involved are parents of the offender, their tendency is naturally to minimize the seriousness of the offense. Minor offenses of the sort handled by the Commissions rather than the courts may be a different matter. Here, it appears that many adults, not only parents of offenders, may feel that the mischievous behavior of male adolescents is something "natural" and to be expected—hence not to be treated as (seriously) deviant.[11] State and public show little evidence of division over the nature of violent offenses by juveniles; none, at least, can be easily perceived. But it is wise to tread lightly here: whatever the facts are, we still know too little about them.

There is some evidence of state-public dissensus on *how* serious a problem the delinquent presents in occasional complaints about the readiness of courts to sentence juveniles to terms in labor colonies, which some describe as too harsh a treatment, given the nature of many offenses.[12] But, at the time of this writing, nothing has yet emerged by way of systematic public opinion surveys aimed at developing information about how the adult public views the problem of delinquency, nor have we ready access to the public opinion of the juvenile population itself, whose members are eligible for the delinquency label.

Most complex of all is the place crime proper—offenses by adults —occupies in the collective mind of the state on one hand, the public on the other. Crime is of many varieties. The more heinous types, like murder and rape, are awarded relatively severe penalties in the law (though not so severe as in some Western countries); and there is no evident basis for arguing that the public is inclined to view them any more leniently than the state. These are, after all, crimes with clearly identifiable individual victims and irremediable consequences.

Crimes against personal property also have individual victims, and here it seems more likely that the public, composed as it is of potential victims of such offenses, may be relatively *more* harsh in its attitude than the state. Insofar as judgments can be based on criminal code provisions, however, it is crime against *state* property that systematically carries heavier punishments, across the whole gamut of acts (theft, robbery, extortion, damage) that can be committed against both types of property.[13] This is not surprising in a system where state or socialist ownership is regarded as a higher category than personal ownership. But one is entitled to wonder whether citizens, in their role of owners of personal property, agree.

We have little indication that Soviet citizens show the respect for socialist property they are supposed to. Though individual thefts of materials from factories may be petty, taken collectively they represent a great problem, not the least element of which, as we have seen, is the "tolerant" attitude coworkers who witness such thefts adopt. Most Soviet citizens, it seems, have not yet found it possible to apply universally the notion that state property is in fact their own—except insofar as they help themselves to shares of it on occasion. Many members of the rank and file engage in one or another form of cheating, corner-cutting, or minor skulduggery, their consciences assuaged by the knowledge that so many of their fellow-citizens act in like manner. This attitude, fostered also by perceptions of large (and annoying) gaps in living standards between the common man and the elite, is eloquently expressed in a Westerner's report of a conversation with a taxi driver, guilty herself of various minor illegalities.

The cheating's wrong, I know that. I hate it and I'd gladly stop it—I want to stop. But it would make no sense now. I cheat because everyone else does. The Party high-ups live like kings—on the people's money. Factory directors take a share of their plant's profits. Foremen take wage "kick-backs", workers smuggle out what raw materials they can under their coats, shop assistants water the wine. And we drivers fiddle the meter. That's the way it is. You know the proverb, *s volchami zhit', po-vol'chi vit.* [When in Rome, do as the Romans do; literally, when you live with wolves, howl like a wolf.] Cheating's the thing to do. The boss of my taxi park has made a fortune selling petrol and spare parts, and all the shift supervisors take their cuts too. Spare tyres on the black market, batteries and things. Why should I be a martyr? I would if it would help, but it wouldn't change a single thing.[14]

This is an attitude whose widespread character the author's experience and impressions also confirm.

Public tolerance for such offenses (and in the countryside for the illegal distilling which usually involves theft of grain from the collective warehouses) is not, however, matched by leniency toward the offenders when and if they are apprehended. Some examples provided by an observer of Soviet court practice may serve to make the point: for "petty theft of state property" (defendant, worker in a footwear factory, stole one pair of galoshes, valued at 4 rubles 10 kopeks), one year in a corrective labor colony; on the same charge (defendant, employed in cigarette factory, stole, over time, packs of cigarettes to a total value of 20 rubles), two years in a corrective labor colony.[15] Neither of these defendants was a "model" worker, both were drinkers, one had appeared before a comrades' court at his factory for petty pilferage before. Such offenses do not seem to provoke much public ire, except as it may be "orchestrated" in the court. While most would agree that such behavior is wrong, probably few support the type of punishments meted out. (A qualification is necessary here: as we shall see, some Soviet citizens apparently find the criminal a convenient and valid target for their general hostilities. For them, such penalties are too lenient.)

It does, then, seem arguable that there is dissensus between state and public at certain points where the seriousness of a particular variety of deviant behavior is at issue. This should not be surprising, for, accustomed as Soviet citizens may be to the leading roles of state and Party in determining which behaviors are good and which bad, a large sector of their private lives and opinions has remained unpenetrated by official thought over the last fifty years. In principle, and in outward expression, many would agree that the government should offer "moral leadership," that one's private behavior is not only one's own concern. But in practice, things are not so simple. As one criminologist noted, the view that *only* the behaviorally deviant are infected by survivals is an erroneous one—many citizens harbor them as attitudes,[16] whether they are "acted out" or not. The Soviet population, no less than the American, is a reservoir of subterranean values in conflict with, but just as much a part of the popular consciousness as, the approved or official values. They, too, affect the attitudes and behavior of the Soviet citizen.

On the whole, deviance probably is not as salient an issue to the public as it is to the state. The public is not told *how much* deviance there is and is not subjected to American-style alarmist accounts of the spread of criminality. Even were this not the case, the situation might show little change. There are more pressing problems in the daily life of the Soviet citizen than the persistence of deviance. Housing, a varied diet, the availability of consumer goods, and a host of private matters are much more central among his concerns. The state, with control as one of its main functions, is necessarily concerned with deviance; but the citizen, be he deviant or not, is more likely to be concerned with avoiding some of the more onerous manifestations of that control. The state's concern with punishing the more petty forms of deviance may strike him as misplaced.

Can the evidence of dissensus between state and public, as it shows itself in both attitudes and behavior, and of the differing salience of deviance for the two be placed within the context of differentiation along a "modern-traditional" continuum, as was suggested in chapter 2? Are we dealing here with a modern state imposing demands and priorities on a public with strong traces of traditionalism? Were somewhat different terminology employed in posing these questions, Soviet criminologists might answer them with a cautious "yes": for who is the bearer of survivals but an incompletely modernized individual, not yet fully accommodated to the realities of socialism?

For our own part, it may be said that there are points at which the modern-traditional dichotomy fits the facts reasonably well. For example, the typically rural manifestations of alcohol-connected deviance—illegal distilling and widespread prolonged drunkenness on holiday occasions or during special events—are patterns of activity with long histories. They have survived from the past, a past in which they were not perhaps viewed with favor by the government, but neither were they regarded as such retrograde phenomena as the relatively "modern" government of today sees them. Those of the rural public who participate seem to see these as natural occurrences, not as "deviant."

Another alcohol-linked example is that of the extraordinary amount of on-the-job drunkenness in urban, mechanized settings. Factory workers arrive at their places intoxicated, risking injury in work with fast-operating machinery. Construction workers returning to the job after a lunch that may include heavy doses of vodka risk injuries, perhaps fatal, from slowed reactions and dulled attention. Truck and taxi drivers, stopping when time allows for a quick drink, incur similar risks. Such drinking habits, while of no positive value, are much less dangerous when work is simple and manual—i.e., not mechanized. The slower pace and the different nature of traditional agricultural work accommodate better to such states of intoxication than does the mechanized urban work environment they fit so badly. Yet, the problem of on-the-job drunkenness is apparently among the most persistent in Soviet industry.

A final example is more general. Soviet sources themselves talk about the difficulties rural immigrants—predominantly male, unattached, relatively youthful—encounter in adjusting to city life. The expressed fear is that they will misapprehend the "true," progressive essence of urban culture, and instead act according to some distorted version thereof. Beyond reach of the more intimate social controls of the village, they may end as hooligans, petty thieves, or drunkards. Soviet Marxism-Leninism has inherited from Marx himself a pro-urban bias, a view of the city as the reservoir of progress and the countryside as the repository of tradition, ignorance, and parochialism. Given the view of such a gap, concern with the possible consequences of a move across it is not undue. Indeed, urbanization in the USSR and other East European countries has had many traumatic elements as rural populations accustomed themselves to the new demands for urban order, discipline, and life-style. One should not carry the argument too far (and Soviet writers deal with it in rather general terms), but neither should one fail to acknowledge that the problems of adjustment a young person from the countryside must face in the city have many possible ramifications. Deviance need not result simply from a mechanical acting-out, in an urban setting, of behavior patterns more acceptable in rural areas. The collision with the city may be a disorienting process, setting the individual adrift in a situation where positive behavioral guidelines are unclear. Of such situations, in many instances, is deviant behavior made.

These are only examples. They are not intended as a demonstration of any *overall* good fit of the modern-traditional dichotomy to state behavioral standards and the public's failure to meet them. Having examined deviance in this light, however, it seems worthwhile also to look at it from another angle: as a phenomenon which in the USSR has taken at least some of its contemporary shape from the *success* of modernization, rather than from the gap between the modern and traditional. In this way, much of what we have examined may be seen as a part of a legacy of coercive modernization. The USSR today is a relatively mature industrial society, despite the large portion of the population still engaged in agriculture, and a relatively modernized one, despite the underdeveloped regions in which industrial development and urban construction are still taking place.

All modernization, as we noted earlier, is coercive to a degree.[17] But the differences in degree, dependent as they are on the tempo and ultimate targets of the modernizers, as well as on the measure of their effective power in compelling compliance from the population, are themselves of extreme importance. On all three of these characteristics, Soviet modernization—the "second revolution" that commenced in 1928 with the launching of the first Five-Year Plan and accelerated soon after as the forcible collectivization of agriculture began—ranked high, and was correspondingly coercive.

Economic development focused on the construction of a heavy industrial base, aiming to insure a continued rapid growth of that base. The commitment of resources to the capital-goods sector was enormous and the share of the consumer sector relatively miniscule. Attention was concentrated on the attainment of societal goals, on overcoming a legacy of backwardness; the day-to-day concerns of citizens were of secondary or tertiary importance. The rapid growth of urban populations, as rural labor pools were ransacked for manpower to work in the industrial sector, was not matched by proportionate housing construction or the development of an adequate urban service sector. The bitter resistance to collectivization in the countryside was overcome, but at the cost of livestock slaughter, human deaths, and famine that have left their mark to the present day. Collectivization imposed a mode of organization on agricultural producers which, while it guaranteed a minimal food supply to the cities, has cost much in incentive and labor productivity. Agriculture remains the Achilles' heel of the Soviet economy, and diets—a basic component of any standard of living—reflect its shortcomings.

Standards of living declined after 1928 and began their modest rise again only in the 1950s. While today's living standards are better than most Soviet citizens had previously experienced, they are far lower than the norm for Western (and a good deal of Eastern) Europe. The economy is still geared overwhelmingly to heavy industry, and consumer goods, housing, and services run a poor second, making everyday life for the average Soviet citizen a drab and scarcity-ridden affair.

Modernization after 1928 also meant the thorough socialization of the economy. The period of the New Economic Policy (1921–1928) had seen an uneasy but economically productive coexistence between socialist control of the commanding heights of the economy and a substantial amount of private enterprise. When the NEP had completed its restorative task and productivity was once again at the pre-World War I level, the second revolution began. This saw the shift of what was virtually the entire economy to a socialist or collective basis. The vast majority of all factories, institutions, natural resources, and other fixed facilities then "belonged to the people." They still do today.

The political control aspects of modernization were coercive as well. The great purges of the later 1930s were the last step in the establishment of totalitarian control over the nation as a whole. Coercion was in evidence not only in the "polity" itself, but in the daily lives of the masses. Urban workers were subjected to harsh "labor discipline": changing jobs without permission became a criminal offense, criminal penalties were imposed on those who were repeatedly late to work, individual production quotas were high, and piece-rate wages threatened the meager livelihood of the weak, the unskilled, and the underproductive. In the countryside, compulsory deliveries of agricultural products to the state often left collective farmers with insufficient food for their own needs. More "surplus" was extracted via required fees for the services of the Machine Tractor Stations (MTS), which were the arms of political control and surveillance over the peasantry.

Much has changed in the post-Stalin era. But the major institutional outlines of the Soviet polity and economy remain those which developed after 1928, and the legacy of coercive modernization is a large element in contemporary Soviet life. If one examines the forms that crime, delinquency, and alcohol problems assume, one can see the legacy reflected there as well. It would be disingenuous to ignore the impact of low living standards, crowded housing, and the pressures of an urban environment on the drinking behavior of working-class males. To attribute all of this to a traditional drinking culture is not enough: alcohol is a widely employed escape mechanism, and many Soviet workers have as much, probably more, to escape from in their contemporary lives as do their counterparts in other societies.

The homicides and physical assaults that frequently take place in crowded communal apartments must be traced at least partly to the tensions generated by a lack of living space, the friction generated by close quarters which some persons certainly find unbearable. And the housing problem, a constant condition of Soviet life for so many years, is far from being solved.

Property offenses, which make up such a large proportion of all juvenile and adult crime, cannot be wholly attributed to Soviet "poverty." Such crimes exist in affluent societies as well, and they are not always perpetrated by the poor. Yet elements of coercive modernization's legacy also enter here. The petty thefts, the minor swindlings of adults and juveniles both, frequently involve consumer goods in short supply or priced beyond purchase ability. The fact that the modest luxuries of radios, tape recorders, and other items are frequent targets of juvenile thieves points to a general desire to upgrade one's level of enjoyment, to have things that make life "better." The taxi driver, the factory worker, the sales person who adds something to his income by illegal means refer in justification sometimes to the bare need to "get by," sometimes to the desire to get something a little beyond the bare minimum in a society where scarcity and depressed living standards are still part of everyday life and traceable at least in part to the form modernization took in the USSR.

The fact that Soviet modernization was of a socialist variety cannot be blamed, in itself, for these problems. Presumably, socialist modernization need not always be as rapid, intense, and coercive as it was in the USSR. But it would not do to ignore one of the apparent consequences of contemporary socialist ownership. Soviet citizens, as others elsewhere, probably find it easier to victimize large, amorphous, impersonal organizations through theft than to steal from each other. This applies no less to the managers and accountants who embezzle from their own organizations than it does to the factory worker who filches cigarettes or galoshes. Socialism is well established, but "socialist attitudes" toward property are not. Soviet citizens will generally express pride that theirs is a socialist rather than capitalist country, but the tangible rewards of socialism, in terms of better living and equality, have not been sufficient to convince them that in defrauding the state they are robbing themselves. Though they might not verbalize it thus, for many persons, that which belongs to all belongs to no one—and taking it oneself is no great matter.

The gap between official norms and the public's attitudes and behavior is wide at some points, narrower at others. Attributing some of this to survivals, to the lag of consciousness, as Soviet writers do, is not necessarily incorrect. The traditional and the modern confront each other at many points in Soviet life. But to ignore or minimize basic problems characteristic of contemporary Soviet life which owe their existence to the character of the USSR's modernizing experience, as well as to the ravages of World War II (a national trauma which cannot be ignored), is to miss another point. There are elements in that life, beyond "infected" environments, that encourage and provoke deviance. Some the USSR shares with other urban, industrial societies; socialism does not confer immunity. Other elements are more specifically Soviet. But all are real: and the degree to which Soviet theory comes to grips with them may, in the future, be one measure of the amount of that critical self-analysis which is a necessary component of any large-scale change in the USSR.

DEALING WITH THE DEVIANT

There is much in the preventive and corrective strategies and tactics applied to the Soviet deviant that resembles parallel activities in other societies, both socialist and capitalist. On the most general level, the USSR, like other nations, sees the basic task as adjusting the deviant to society, rather than accommodating the society to the diversity that deviance represents. Further, no civilized society talks today only of punishing the deviant. "Correction" and "rehabilitation" are the watchwords of modern penological theory, and this is true in the USSR. But the writ of the *lex talionis* has not yet run out: most societies manage to entertain notions of *both* punishment and correction. The Soviet Union is among these as well.

Despite the polyglot character of modern theories of deviance causation, the deviance-management systems of many nations still rely, in both prevention and correction, on an element whose roots are deep in "voluntarism": deterrence. Doing corrective works or a stretch in a labor colony, for adults or juveniles, is supposed to have a deterrent effect on the Soviet offender, as well as on those whose moral instability might make them deviate, were they not warned off by the penalties. In a sense, the various forms of aversion therapy for alcoholics, as well as the threat of a stay in a treatment-labor institution, also aim at deterrence. Here, too, there is more of the familiar than the exotic in the Soviet approach.

The concrete modes of handling offenders in the USSR show in their broad outlines relatively little that is innovative. Criminal courts, juvenile and adult institutions, incentives such as early release, suspended sentences, and probation, all can be observed in other societies. No really radical discoveries or innovations, such as universal in-society correction of offenders, have been produced by

Soviet experience. Isolation of many offenders is still one of the basic characteristics of the system.

Other aspects touched on in earlier chapters are more notable. The apparently wide application of conditional early release is one. Most (though not all) criminal-law writers and criminologists favor early release when it is practiced not "massively," but with discrimination. While this in part may account for the frequent use of the provision, it may well be that another factor plays some role—crowding beyond tolerable limits may threaten the operations of penal institutions, and the supply of institutions may not be adequate to the demand. In Soviet mental hospitals, to take another example, the length of average stay is relatively short, and release and readmission rates are both rather high. This again may be explained in part by the scarcity of facilities (basically, hospital accommodations), and the same may be true of penal institutions, where the threats to internal order posed by overcrowding may be severe.[18]

Within American penal institutions, one encounters relatively rarely the strategy of utilizing inmate organizations not only for the maintenance of order, but also in the corrections process itself. Enlisting convict support for reform, by developing group support for non-criminal attitudes and directing group pressure against adherents to criminal norms, is a rather "experimental" thing. Something of this sort, however, is at least theoretically very much a part of Soviet corrections. There is no notion in Soviet textbooks of making peace with the convict culture—rather, it is to be combatted through "independent inmate organizations." Enough has already been said about this strategy in earlier chapters to show the reader that, like other correctional strategies, it is neither an unqualified success nor an unmitigated failure. Much, it seems, depends on how well it is carried out and on the susceptibility or recalcitrance of its targets, the inmates themselves.

Most striking of all, however, is the emphasis on involving the public in the struggle with all manner of deviant behaviors. Though the enthusiasm of the early 1960s is now somewhat muted, and comrades' courts, *druzhiny*, public meetings, and the like are no longer presented as part of a grand design of "self-administration" as the USSR marches toward full communism, these correctional techniques deserve attention. In answer to the question raised in chapter 2 as to the degree of public responsibility for deviance control, it should be said that the public, by and large, functions as an auxiliary of formal social control agencies: it does not substitute for them. If anything, the 1960s witnessed increased formalization of official control over the comrades' courts and volunteer squads, which had too often produced unanticipated and unwanted consequences when "given their heads."

Another major problem is the disinterest of so many of the public in spending their free time in volunteer work, whether as members of comrades' courts, *druzhinniki,* or unpaid juvenile probation agents. Too often, the figures on public involvement in such work exist *only* on paper. As we have seen, the volunteers who present themselves for such work frequently have not, in fact, "volunteered" at all.

"Active" public involvement of this sort can be seen as potentially fulfilling three purposes: first, increasing the effectiveness of control and rehabilitation, simply by increasing personnel; second, activating anti-deviance and pro-conformity sentiments by drawing the public directly into the deviance-management process; and third, creating more social services without additional economic outlay—whatever aid volunteers render to professionals, it is unpaid. Such evidence as we have does not show that either of the first two functions has been satisfactorily fulfilled. There are few indications that effectiveness has increased markedly, and the frequent complaints show that public bodies have fallen short of expectations. Nor does involvement seem to have reached the point where society-wide intolerance for the deviant has been markedly intensified, although such involvement has provided mechanisms for some participants to settle personal grudges via the comrades' courts or to vent aggressive impulses on those who fall afoul of the *druzhiny.* With reference to the third function, such involvement has, of course, been free. Whether it has been very profitable to the state is another matter.

The public is summoned to aid the state in another way as well: as an audience for the deviant and his acts. This audience is not to be a collection of mere onlookers, but an active force, supporting and expressing the official line on deviance. It should be active both in the prevention of deviance and, when deviance occurs nonetheless, in the creation of an atmosphere of disapproval which will make the transgressor recognize the error of his ways. In the preventive phase, this means an activization of the spirit of *kollektivnost'*: coworkers, co-residents *should* concern themselves with the behavior of their colleagues and use their closeness and intimacy with the person who shows deviant tendencies as resources to persuade or, if necessary, pressure him to return to the correct path. *Kollektivnost'* implies not just group solidarity, but solidarity with officially supported, approved norms. Hence the aim appears to be a semi-formalization of primary-group relations, insuring support, at this most immediate level of social intercourse, for the "right" attitudes and behavior. However, as numerous examples of unconcern with the behavior of fellow workers and its consequences have shown, real *kollektivnost'* is hard to achieve.

After an offense is committed, the public again becomes an audience, either in the flesh, as at a comrades' court meeting, at a "visiting session" of the Peoples' Court held in a factory auditorium, or simply as viewers of the photographs and captions on a "board of dishonor," or vicariously through the media—a locally televised trial, or a long newspaper story of moral downfall and just deserts. In such contexts, the public is not shielded from deviance; it is given concrete examples of the shapes evil can assume and asked to draw the proper conclusions from the presentation. Here, indeed, the public itself is as much the target as is the deviant. These displays of deviance serve as mechanisms for the communication of moral lessons to the public and for the development of solidarity around the approved norms. (Most impressive, some argue, are the lessons learned when both Soviet society's justified intolerance of evil and its comradely concern for the fate of the offender are represented at a trial in the persons of the volunteer "public accuser" and "public defender," who are nonprofessional participants in the process.)

Such are the mechanisms. Do they produce the desired impact? The audience is a large one, and for some of its members, no doubt, they do. But it appears equally clear that for some others the outcome of such displays of the deviant is other than the one desired. To them the displays appear tasteless, needlessly cruel, and indeed evoke sympathy for the deviant—especially when the offense is minor. A case in point is a letter to *Pravda* from a reader in the city of Gorky, com-

menting on the photographs displayed in local streetcars, with appropriate commentary, of persons apprehended for riding without paying
the fare. The letter writer reports a woman who, looking at one of
the pictures, said, "I see someone who is suffering." "In fact, the photographs have given rise not to condemnation but to embarrassment
—not at all the reaction the authors of the posters had expected." [19]

In still other members of the audience, however, the presentation of
the deviant as one who has betrayed society's trust, as a legitimate
target, produces excessive reactions in the opposite direction. It stirs
up their tough-minded, punitive attitudes, evoking storms of abuse for
all lawbreakers and protestations that the "socialist humanism" of Soviet justice is *too* humane: by no means the outcome intended. Two
instances from the Soviet press in 1968 are particularly instructive.

Grigorii Medynskii, a novelist and essayist renowned among Soviet
readers for his writings on the experiences of the convict undergoing
correction (especially his 1964 book, *Trudnaia kniga*, or *A Difficult
Book*), was called upon to respond to readers' letters provoked by an
article he wrote for *Izvestiia*, in which he expressed doubts that intensification of punishment was a panacea for crime. Among his com-
batants, Medynskii notes, one

. . . even criticizes the formula stating that what counts is not the severity
but the inevitability of the punishment. "Nothing more harmful to the cause
of justice can be said," he remarks didactically, in blissful ignorance of the
fact that this formula is a highly important principle of our system of justice
and was expressed by Lenin himself.

Another disagreeing reader, troubled by theft,

. . . suggests a very simple means for achieving this security: "For theft:
deprivation of life." He is absolutely certain that this will help "to solve the
problem of crime once and for all." [20]

Boris S. Nikiforov, a senior member of the Institute of Criminology
in Moscow and one of the Soviet Union's most competent criminal
law scholars, was called upon to answer a reader's letter in *Literaturnaia gazeta*. The reader suggested a number of changes, among which
were (1) abandonment of the practice of setting the punishment to fit
the crime—however minor the offense, the *fact* of the offense should
entail harsh punishment; (2) no leniency of any sort for minors con-

victed of serious offenses; (3) "simplifications" of criminal legislation to remove lower and upper limits from terms of imprisonment (the term to be inflexible) and to extend the death penalty to bribery, embezzlement, theft, and some other offenses; and finally (4) an overhaul of the corrections system, to make penal institutions no longer places of "upbringing and reform" but of "isolation and punishment," with an abandoning of early release, application of measures including the death penalty for those who violate the rules, and no release (in effect, life imprisonment) for "incorrigibles."

Nikiforov sharply rejected these suggestions, noting in his response that the "science of law has one regrettable feature—it is completely unprotected from the onlooker's wish to reform." [21]

These letters to Medynskii and Nikiforov express sentiments not dissimilar to those many citizens in other societies express when perplexed by the failure of prevalent strategies and conventional wisdoms to banish from existence behavior they abhor. The sentiments may seem overstated, the proposals, all in all, somewhat far-fetched: but, as Nikiforov observed in his response, his critic was expressing "widely current notions."

Mobilizing public opinion in support of the state's priorities and preferences in dealing with deviance is an objective any government might pursue. The Soviet government, certainly, strives for this objective. But there are many "public opinions," even in the USSR, and their diversity guarantees that this is no easy task.

APPENDIX I PRISONER RIGHTS UNDER THE 1961 STATUTE AND THE 1969 PRINCIPLES *

	General (or "short") meetings per year		Personal (or "long") meetings per year		Number of packages, parcels in a year (up to 5 kilograms)		Number of letters that may be sent in a year	
	1961	1969	1961	1969	1961	1969	1961	1969
General-regime colony	6	3	4	2	6	Up to 3 per	Unlimited	Unlimited
Intensified-regime colony	4	2	2	2	4	year after	Unlimited	36
Strict-regime colony	3	2	1	1	—	service of ½	24	24
Special-regime colony	2	1	—	1	—	of sentence	12	12
General-regime prison	—	—	—	—	2	—	12	12
Strict-regime prison	—	—	—	—	—	—	6	6

* In addition, the 1961 statute specifies (but the 1969 Principles only set a 15-ruble ceiling on) the sum of earned money prisoners may spend per month in the colony or prison commissary:

General-regime colony	not more than 10 rubles
Intensified-regime colony	not more than 7 rubles
Strict-regime colony	not more than 5 rubles
Special-regime colony	not more than 3 rubles
General-regime prison	not more than 2 rubles
Strict-regime prison	not more than 2 rubles

APPENDIX II DAILY NUTRITIONAL NORMS FOR PRISONERS * (1961)

Prisoners in colonies:

1) working prisoners in general — 2413 calories

2) working prisoners in "hot shops, ore-mining, timber and peat industries" — 2828 calories

3) prisoner-invalids of groups I and II — same norm as working prisoners in similar colony

4) prisoner-invalids of group III — shall work and receive same food as other working prisoners

5) prisoners put into colonies' punishment cells, who
   - work — 2090 calories
   - "maliciously refuse" to work or fail to fulfill work norms — 1324 calories

Prisoners in prisons:

1) those under arrest, under investigation, having sentences reviewed, awaiting entry of their sentences into legal force, and those in transit — 2143 calories

2) general-regime prisons (for those who work, an extra 100 grams of bread each 24 hours) — 1937 calories

3) strict-regime prisons (with reduction of bread norm by 100 grams per 24 hours) — 1937 calories

4) prisoners placed in punishment cells for disciplinary reasons † — same norms as similar prisoners in colonies (apparently 1324 calories)

5) prisoners engaged in service activities in the prison — same norms as working prisoners in colonies

Other classes:

1) sick prisoners under treatment in *colony* facilities   2476

2) sick prisoners in *prisons*   2190

3) tubercular prisoners in colonies   3115
   tubercular prisoners in prisons   2600

4) children in "mothers' and childrens' houses"   1849

5) pregnant and nursing prisoners (in colonies and prisons)   3357

° *Source:* "Sutochnye normy pitaniia zakliuchennykh v ispravitel'not-rudovykh uchrezhdeniiakh Ministerstva vnutrennykh del RSFSR" (appendix to the 1961 *Polozhenie,* from a photocopy available in the library of the Moscow University Law Faculty).

† "Order of feeding: hot food, according to the established norm, is given every other day; on [alternate days] only bread according to the norm, hot water, and salt are given out."

NOTES

Due to the large number of Russian-language sources cited and the frequency with which certain journals appear in the notes, some modifications on standard practice have been adopted here. Second and succeeding references to the same article or monograph within a chapter are indicated by the author's last name and a shortened version of the title. Works in Russian which are available in English translations are cited fully in Russian the first time, with the source of the translation indicated, and subsequent references refer to the pagination of the translation.

Frequently cited journals have had their titles put into initials (though this rule may not be applied where doing so would lead to confusion) according to the following scheme:

Sovetskoe gosudarstvo i pravo	*SGIP*
Sovetskaia iustitsiia	*S.Iu.*
Sotsialisticheskaia zakonnost'	*SZ*
K novoi zhizni	*KNZ*
Current Digest of the Soviet Press	*CDSP*

Space limitations have made the inclusion of a systematic bibliography inadvisable. The interested reader, however, will find comprehensive bibliographic information, up to the year 1968, in Peter H. Solomon, Jr., "A Selected Bibliography on Soviet Criminology," *Journal of Criminal Law, Criminology, and Police Science*, LXI (1970), pp. 393–432.

Chapter 1
INTRODUCTION

1. Robert K. Merton, "Social Problems and Sociological Theory," in Robert K. Merton and Robert A. Nisbet, eds., *Contemporary Social Problems* (2d. ed.; New York, Harcourt, Brace & World, 1966), pp. 808–11.

2. Bernard Rosenberg and Harry Silverstein, *The Varieties of Delinquent Experience* (Waltham, Mass., Blaisdell, 1969), p. 12.

3. This assertion is based on various conversations with university-based Soviet criminologists. In 1967, a well-known criminologist noted that much data existed which was inaccessible to jurist-scholars and argued that the time had come to resolve both the question of access to these data within reasonable limits and that of their partial publication. See S. S. Ostroumov, "Statisticheskie metody v kriminologii," *SGIP*, No. 7 (1967), p. 75.

4. See, e.g., David Matza and Gresham M. Sykes, "Juvenile Delinquency and Subterranean Values," *American Sociological Review*, XXVI (October, 1961), 712–19.

5. See Frederick J. Fleron, Jr., ed., *Communist Studies and the Social Sciences* (Chicago, Rand McNally, 1969), and Roger E. Kanet, ed., *The Behavioral Revolution and Communist Studies* (New York, Free Press–Macmillan, 1970).

Chapter 2
ISSUES AND QUESTIONS

1. David Matza, *Delinquency and Drift* (New York, Wiley, 1964), p. 12. Matza discusses the determinist view in detail, using the term "positive" instead of "determinist," in *ibid.*, pp. 1–32.

2. Edwin M. Lemert, "Social Structure, Social Control, and Deviation," in Marshall B. Clinard, ed., *Anomie and Deviant Behavior* (New York, Free Press, 1964), p. 83.

3. For representative examples of the interactionist approach, see Howard S. Becker, *Outsiders: Studies in the Sociology of Deviance* (New York, Free Press, 1963), and, edited by the same author, *The Other Side: Perspectives on Deviance* (New York, Free Press, 1964); see also Earl Rubington and Martin S. Weinberg, eds., *Deviance: The Interactionist Perspective* (New York, Macmillan, 1968), and Edwin M. Lemert, *Human Deviance, Social Problems, and Social Control* (Englewood Cliffs, N.J., Prentice-Hall, 1967).

4. Becker, *Outsiders*, p. 25.   5. Lemert, "Social Structure," p. 82.

6. On "moral entrepreneurs" see Becker, *Outsiders*, pp. 147–63.

7. See Richard D. Schwartz and Jerome H. Skolnick, "Two Studies of Legal Stigma," in Becker, ed., *The Other Side*, pp. 103–17.

8. See Kai T. Erikson, "Notes on the Sociology of Deviance," *Social Problems*, IX (Spring, 1962), 307–14; Robert A. Dentler and Kai T. Erikson, "The Functions of Deviance in Groups," *Social Problems*, VII (Fall, 1959), 98–107; and Kai T. Erikson, *Wayward Puritans: A Study in the Sociology of Deviance* (New York, Wiley, 1966).

9. Erikson, *Wayward Puritans*, pp. 3–5.   10. *Ibid.*, pp. 10–11.

11. *Ibid.*, pp. 13–14.

12. Some theorists, however, have explored the utility of notions of "will" in an explanatory framework, notably David Matza. See *Delinquency and Drift*, pp. 181–91.

13. These demands are discussed in greater detail as "instrumentality" and "compatibility" in Peter Solomon's "Soviet Criminology: The Effects of Post-Stalin Politics on a Social Science" (unpublished M.A. thesis, Columbia University, 1967).

14. Allen Kassof, "The Administered Society: Totalitarianism Without Terror," *World Politics*, XVI (July, 1964), 559.

15. Alex Inkeles, Eugenia Hanfmann, and Helen Beier, "Modal Personality and Adjustment to the Soviet Socio-Political System," *Human Relations*, XI (1958), 16. See also Henry V. Dicks, "Observations on Contemporary Russian Behavior," *Human Relations*, V (1952), 111–75.

16. Inkeles, Hanfmann, and Beier, "Modal Personality," p. 15.

Chapter 3
HISTORICAL BACKGROUND

1. This account of the dynamics of crime is drawn from three sources on the period 1917–1935: the relevant sections in the textbook *Kriminologiia* (Moscow, "Iuridicheskaia literatura," (1st ed., 1966, pp. 62–72 and 2d ed., 1968, pp. 106–15), and from another work by the author of the textbook sections, N.F. Kuznetsova, *Prestuplenie i prestupnost'* (Moscow, Izdatel'stvo Moskovskogo universiteta, 1969), pp. 184–90.

2. Kuznetsova, *Prestuplenie*, p. 185.

3. Ibid., p. 185, citing *Statistika osuzhdennykh v SSSR 1923–1924 gg.* (Moscow, Izdatel'stvo Tsentral'nogo statisticheskogo upravleniia SSSR, 1927), pp. 8–9.

4. Kuznetsova, *Prestuplenie*, p. 186.

5. For an extended account of the response to the delinquency problem, see G.M. Min'kovskii, "Osnovnye etapy razvitiia sovetskoi sistemy mer bor'by s prestupnost'iu nesovershennoletnikh," *Voprosy bor'by s prestupnost'iu*, vyp. 6 (1967), 37–74.

6. Kuznetsova, *Prestuplenie*, p. 187, citing *Prestupnost' i repressii v RSFSR* (Moscow, Izdatel'stvo Tsentral'nogo statisticheskogo upravleniia RSFSR, 1930).

7. *Ibid.*   8. Kuznetsova, *Prestuplenie*, p. 188.

9. *Ibid.*, p. 188, citing *Prestupnost' i repressii*, p. 27.   10. Ibid., p. 189.

11. *Ibid.*   12. *Ibid.*   13. *Kriminologiia* (1st ed.), p. 71.

14. Kuznetsova, *Prestuplenie*, p. 190.

15. In this account, detailed reporting of the scattered statistics available in the Soviet sources has been avoided, as they add little, in the author's estimation, to

an understanding of the period. The interested reader is directed to the sources indicated in note 1.

16. The account which follows is based in large part on three Soviet sources: Iu. P. Kasatkin, "Ocherk istorii izucheniia prestupnosti v SSSR," in *Problemy iskoreneniia prestupnosti* (Moscow, "Iuridicheskaia literatura," 1965), pp. 187–225; material by the same author in *Kriminologiia* (2d ed.), pp. 71–83; and L.V. Il'ina, "Iz istorii razvitii sovetskoi kriminologii," *Voprosy bor'by s prestupnost'iu*, vyp. 7 (1968), pp. 29–41. It is essentially an "official" history of the controversies of the 1920s and reflects the viewpoint of the winners of the 1929 confrontation, whose position is largely that of official Soviet criminology today. However, it is also frank, if brief, on the virtual destruction of criminology that came about gradually after 1930. While history may sound very different from winners on the one hand and losers on the other, and while some distortions may be inevitable, the value of these brief accounts for understanding some of the controversies in contemporary Soviet criminology is considerable.

17. *Kriminologiia* (2d ed.), pp. 71–72.   18. Kasatkin, "Ocherk," p. 194.

19. *Prestupnyi mir Moskvy* (Moscow, "Pravo i zhizn'," 1924).

20. Space and the main focus of this book preclude extended treatment of criminology in pre-Revolutionary Russia. The interested reader should see S.S. Ostroumov, *Prestupnost' i ee prichiny v dorevoliutsionnoi Rossii* (Moscow, Izdatel'stvo Moskovskogo universiteta, 1960).

21. It would be hard to overestimate the impact of this struggle between two "Marxisms." At issue were fundamental questions about the individual's role in society, the malleability of individuals, and the nature and boundaries of social change. The relevance of these questions to practical political issues of the time is unmistakable, and politics played a great role in the triumphs that the voluntarist brand of Marxism began to win in 1929 and continued to win until the victory was consolidated in the mid-1930s. The best source on this period, touching on the fields of philosophy, law, economics, psychology, and education, is Raymond A. Bauer, *The New Man in Soviet Psychology* (Cambridge, Harvard University Press, 1952), esp. pp. 13–102. Of the arenas in which the debate was carried on, the one with the greatest implications for the future development of Soviet social and economic institutions was that of economic development. On this, see the works of Alexander Erlich, "Preobrazhensky and the Economics of Soviet Industrialization," *Quarterly Journal of Economics*, 64 (February, 1950), and *The Soviet Industrialization Debate, 1924–1928* (Cambridge, Harvard University Press, 1960).

22. Bauer, *New Man*, p. 50.   23. See Il'ina, "Iz istorii," pp. 31–32.

24. See *ibid.*, pp. 33–34, and Kasatkin, "Ocherk," p. 198.

25. E.g., V. Brailovskii, "O vegatativnoi nervnoi sisteme ubiits," *Voprosy izucheniia prestupnosti na Severnom Kavkaze*, vyp. 2 (Rostov-na-Donu, "Sevkavkniga," 1927), and the same author's "O biologicheskikh korniakh prestupnosti," *Sbornik po psikhonevrologii* (Rostov-na-Donu, 1928); N.P. Brukhanskii, *Sudebnaia psikhiatriia* (Moscow, 1929).

26. The Moscow office for the study of crime moved, it appears, in this direction. A collective volume published in 1926, *The Criminal and Crime*, or *Prestupnik i prestupnost'* (Moscow, Moszdravotdel, 1926), consisted largely of contributions from medical psychiatrists. The Saratov office, established in 1921, included medical specialists, psychiatrists, pedagogues, jurists, and sociologists, but, according to Kasatkin ("Ocherk," p. 203), almost "all the published works referred to psycho-neurological researches. . . ."

27. E.g., A.A. Zhizhilenko, *Prestupnost' i ee faktory* (Moscow, "Mir znanii," 1922). Followers of this and other sociological and legal tendencies regarded as "bourgeois" were also to be condemned in 1929 and the years afterward. M.N. Gernet, who is credited today as one of the early leaders in the collection and analysis of criminal statistics, is also criticized for flirtation with the factor theory approach and for not considering, along with numerical data, "the distribution of class forces and the course of the class struggle" (Kasatkin, "Ocherk," pp. 208–209).

28. Il'ina, in her account ("Iz istorii," p. 35) seems to assign a large role to "practical workers," as opposed to scholars, in the rise of objections to the "psycho-biological" orientation.

29. Very few scholars seem to have been entirely free of some "negative" taint, according to Kasatkin ("Ocherk," p. 211): "Only a few of the criminologists felt, at the time, the necessity of a deep study of Marxist-Leninist theory of state and law and the whole heritage of the founders of Marxism-Leninism."

30. Among their works, see: A.A. Gertsenzon, "Bor'ba s prestupnost'iu v RSFSR," *Sovetskoe pravo*, No. 3 (1929), pp. 96–117; "Obshcheugolovnaia prestupnost' i klassovoi nachalo v ugolovnoi politike SSSR," *Sovetskoe pravo*, No. 6 (1926), pp. 41–45; and "Osnovnye cherty sovremennoi prestupnosti v RSFSR," *Revoliutsiia prava*, No. 4 (1929), pp. 52–70; V.I. Kufaev, *Iunie pravonarushiteli* (Moscow, "Novaia Moskva," 1924); D.P. Rodin, "Gorodskaia i sel'skaia prestupnost'," *Pravo i zhizn'*, Nos. 2–3 (1926), pp. 94–101; M.N. Gernet, *Moral'naia statistika* (Moscow, Tsentral'noe Statisticheskoe Upravlenie, 1922), and *Prestupnost' i samoubiistvo vo vremia voiny i posle nee* (Moscow, Tsentral'noe Statisticheskoe Upravlenie SSSR, 1927).

31. See Erlich, *Soviet Industrialization Debate*.

32. Bauer, *New Man*, pp. 24–31.   33. *Ibid.*, pp. 36–37.

34. *Ibid.*, pp. 63–64.

35. S. Ia. Bulatov, "Vozrozhdenie Lombrozo v sovetskoi kriminologii," *Revoliutsiia prava*, No. 1 (1929).

36. M.M. Grodzinskii, "Disput k voprosu ob izuchenii prestupnosti v SSSR v sektsii prava i gosudarstva," *Revoliutsiia prava*, No. 3 (1929), pp. 47–78. Resistance evidently continued, since the journal published further articles condemning various proscribed orientations. See G.I. Volkov, "Krizis sotsiologicheskoi shkoly i freidizm v ugolovnom prave," *Sovetskoe gosudarstvo i revoliutsiia prava*, No. 6 (1929), and P.V. Kuz'min, "Noveishii revizionizm v ugolovnom prave," *Revoliutsiia prava*, Nos. 8 and 9 (1930).

37. Kasatkin, "Ocherk," pp. 213–14, and *Kriminologiia* (2d ed.), pp. 78–79.

38. Kasatkin, "Ocherk," p. 215. Some criminological work continued, but the rate of publication declined greatly.

39. *Ibid.*

40. One unsuccessful attempt was made to revive criminology in 1945. Gernet, Gertsenzon, and Khlebnikov wrote articles for a collective volume, arguing that the criticism of erroneous orientations in the criminology of the 1920s had led, not to the correction of "errors," but to an almost complete cessation of research on crime. See *Problemy izucheniia prestupnosti* (Moscow, Iurizdat, 1945). However, nothing came of this, many jurists being, as Kasatkin notes ("Ocherk," p. 217), convinced that the concepts of "survivals of the past in the consciousness of people and the hostile activity of the bourgeoisie from abroad" provided sufficient knowledge about crime.

41. For criminologists, especially those who had studied Soviet penal policy, the late 1930s were difficult years, when such work ". . . was far from safe. Many prominent Soviet authorities in the area of criminal policy were repressed without cause." I.S. Noi, *Voprosy teorii nakazaniia v sovetskom ugolovnom prave* (Saratov, Izdatel'stvo Saratovskogo universiteta, 1962), p. 20.

42. "Ukreplenie sotsialisticheskoi zakonnosti i iuridicheskaia nauka," *Kommunist*, No. 11 (1956), p. 17.

43. See, e.g., V.N. Roshchin and M.P. Lashin, "K voprosu ob izuchenii prestupnosti," *SGIP*, No. 7 (1960), pp. 168–72. This institute, now the "All-Union Scientific Research Institute for Preservation of Public Order of the USSR MVD," is occupied, *inter alia*, with studies of penal institutions and policy. Much of its output remains relatively classified, and a great number of the publications of its staff appear in the journal *K novoi zhizni*, which is not available to the Soviet public, as is, for example, *Sovetskoe gosudarstvo i pravo*.

44. *Voprosy metodiki izucheniia i preduprezhdeniia prestuplenii* (Moscow, Gosudarstvennoe izdatel'stvo iuridicheskoi literatury, 1962).

45. A.B. Sakharov, *O lichnosti prestupnika i prichinakh prestupnosti v SSSR* (Moscow, "Iuridicheskaia literatura," 1961).

46. *Voprosy bor'by s prestupnost'iu*. The first 4 issues were published under a different title, *Problems of Crime Prevention* (*Voprosy preduprezhdeniia prestupnosti*).

Chapter 4
ALCOHOL PROBLEMS

1. Ye. Korenevskaia, "Fighting Alcoholism," *Soviet Life* (June, 1965), p. 23.

2. *Alkogolizm—put' k prestupleniiu* (Moscow, "Iuridicheskaia literatura," 1966), p. 95.

3. See *Bol'shaia meditsinskaia entsiklopediia*, Vol. 1 (Moscow, 1956), col. 727, fig. 1 for a graphic presentation.

4. See Y. Mironenko, "The Fight Against Alcoholism in the USSR," *Bulletin of the Institute for the Study of the USSR* (Munich), XIV (September, 1967), 28. Mironenko makes his estimates from the same official data, but while he notes that "over 60 percent" of ethyl alcohol production goes to technical uses, he uses only 60 percent as his base. His per capita estimates are hence somewhat higher and less conservative than mine, which are based on an assumed 65 percent of ethyl alcohol production unavailable for beverage use.

5. *Alkogolizm—put' k prestupleniiu*, p. 84.   6. *Ibid.*, pp. 21–23.

7. See N.N. Kondrashkov, "Analiz raionnoi statistiki prestupnosti," *Voprosy preduprezhdeniia prestupnosti*, vyp. 4 (1966), p. 43.

8. B.M. Segal, *Alkogolizm: Klinicheskie, sotsial'no-psikhologicheskie i biologicheskie problemy* (Moscow, "Meditsina," 1967), p. 267.

9. V.M. Banshchikov, *Alkogolizm i ego vred dlia zdorov'ia cheloveka* (Moscow, 1958).

10. *Pravda*, April 6, 1969, p. 3; translated in *CDSP*, April 23, 1969, p. 19. See also *Pravda*, January 13, 1969, p. 3; translated in *CDSP*, January 29, 1969, pp. 18–19.

11. V.E. Rozhnov, *Po sledam zelenogo zmiia* (Moscow, Voennoe izdatel'stvo Ministerstva Oborony SSSR, 1969), p. 36. See also Iu. M. Tkachevskii, *Prestupnost'i alkogolizm* (Moscow, "Znanie," 1966), p. 8, and Iu. Levin, "O vrede alkogolia," in *Za kommunisticheskii byt* (Leningrad, "Znanie," 1963), p. 243.

12. Levin, "O vrede," p. 254.   13. Segal, *Alkogolizm*, p. 521.

14. L. Bogdanovich, *Zhizn' nachinaetsia segodnia* (Moscow, "Moskovskii rabochii," 1967), p. 56; Rozhnov, *Po sledam*, p. 60.

15. Bogdanovich, *Zhizn'*, p. 49.

16. See the instance in *Izvestiia*, February 25, 1964, p. 4.

17. See Robert F. Bales, "Cultural Differences in Rates of Alcoholism," *Quarterly Journal of Studies on Alcohol*, VI (1946), 480–99. On particular groups, see Donald D. Glad, "Attitudes and Experiences of American Jewish and American-Irish Male Youth as Related to Difference in Adult Rates of Inebriety," *Quarterly Journal of Studies on Alcohol*, VIII (1947), 406–72; Robert F. Bales, "Attitudes Toward Drinking in the Irish Culture," pp. 157–87 in David J. Pittman and Charles R. Snyder, eds., *Society, Culture, and Drinking Patterns* (New York, Wiley, 1962); Charles R. Snyder, *Alcohol and the Jews* (Glencoe, Ill., Free Press, 1958); and Giorgio Lolli et al., *Alcohol in Italian Culture* (Glencoe, Ill., Free Press, 1958).

18. *Literaturnaia gazeta*, May 13, 1970, p. 13.

19. David J. Pittman, "Drinking Patterns and Alcoholism: A Cross Cultural Perspective," in David J. Pittman, ed., *Alcoholism* (New York, Harper and Row, 1967), p. 5.

20. Iu. M. Tkachevskii, *Prestupnost' i alkogolizm* (Moscow, "Znanie," 1966), p. 7.

21. See Segal, *Alkogolizm*, pp. 47–48, 298.

22. It would be interesting and valuable to have parallel data on the familial attitudes in the backgrounds of those who are "moderate" drinkers and abstainers, but such are unfortunately unavailable.

23. An American study, which included a control group, showed no significant relationship between parental approval or disapproval of drinking, and later alcoholism of male offspring. William McCord and Joan McCord, *Origins of Alcoholism* (Stanford, Stanford University Press, 1960), p. 42.

24. *Izvestiia*, July 14, 1965, p. 4.

25. *Sovetskaia Rossiia*, February 12, 1958, p. 2; translated in *CDSP*, April 9, 1958, pp. 30–31.

26. Ia. E. Gurvich, *P'ianstvo gubit cheloveka, nanosit vred obshchestvu* (Moscow, "Znanie," 1958), p. 1.

27. *Nedelia*, July 24–30, 1966, p. 2.

28. *Literaturnaia gazeta*, March 11, 1970, p. 12.

29. See Gurvich, *P'ianstvo*, pp. 4–5.

30. In this connection, it is interesting to note an indication of mounting concern. The first (1966) edition of the official criminology textbook, while it frequently mentions drunkenness among crime's causes, does not devote a full chapter to it. The second (1968) edition does. *Kriminologiia* (Moscow, "Iuridicheskaia literatura," 1966, 1968).

31. *Izvestiia*, March 3, 1965, p. 3; translated in *CDSP*, March 24, 1965, p. 24.

32. *Izvestiia*, March 2, 1958, p. 4; translated in *CDSP*, April 9, 1958, p. 29.

33. Banshchikov, *Alkogolizm*, p. 32.   34. Gurvich, *P'ianstvo*, p. 30.

35. L. Vaisberg and Sh. Taibakova, "Alkogolizm i prestupnost' nesovershennoletnikh," in U. Dzhekebaev, ed., *Voprosy bor'by s prestupnost'iu nesovershennoletnikh* (Alma-Ata, "Nauka" Kazakhskoi SSR, 1968), p. 101.

36. Ia. E. Stumbina, "O prichinakh prestuplenii nesovershennoletnikh," in *Preduprezhdenie pravonarushenii nesovershennoletnikh* (Riga, 1963), p. 54.

37. See, e.g., A.B. Sakharov, "Alkogol' i prestupnost' nesovershennoletnikh," *S.Iu.*, No. 16 (1965), pp. 22–23.

38. A.B. Sakharov, *O lichnosti prestupnika i prichinakh prestupnosti v SSSR* (Moscow, "Iuridicheskaia literatura," 1961), p. 235.

39. *Ibid.*, p. 231.   40. *Ibid.*, p. 232.

41. *Alkogolizm—put' k prestupleniiu*, p. 6, citing *Problemy sudebnoi psikhiatrii*, vyp. IX (1961), p. 372.

42. For selected data on other nations, see Marvin E. Wolfgang, *Patterns in Criminal Homicide* (New York, Science Editions, Wiley, 1966), pp. 134–67.

43. Sakharov, *O lichnosti prestupnika*, p. 217.·   44. *Ibid.*, p. 215.

45. Kondrashkov, "Analiz raionnoi statistiki prestupnosti," p. 44.

46. See Stephen P. Dunn and Ethel Dunn, *The Peasants of Central Russia* (New York, Holt, Rinehart and Winston, 1967), p. 29.

47. Sakharov, *O lichnosti prestupnika*, pp. 239–40.

48. *Nedelia*, July 24–30, 1966, p. 2.

49. *Sovetskaia Rossiia*, March 26, 1964, p. 4. Polish research suggests a similar pattern in that country. A study of six factories in Lodz showed high rates of absenteeism and lowered output on Mondays, days after holidays, and especially after paydays, all apparently connected with alcohol. See Tadeusz Grzeszczyk, "Społeczno-ekonomiczne aspekty alkoholizmu: Próba badan w województwie Łódzkim," *Przegląd Socjologiczny*, XIV (1960), 110–17. (Summary in English, pp. 204–205.)

50. Rozhnov, *Po sledam*, p. 97.   51. Banshchikov, *Alkogolizm*, p. 8.

52. "Intensification" of the struggle with illegal distilling is reflected in the 1960 and 1961 RSFSR decrees on the subject. See *CDSP*, March 2, 1960, p. 21, and June 7, 1961, p. 22. See also N.F. Kuznetsova, *Ugolovnoe pravo i moral'* (Moscow, Izdatel'stvo Moskovskogo universiteta, 1967), pp. 16–17.

53. *Pravda*, March 29, 1969; translated in *CDSP*, April 16, 1969, pp. 28–29.

54. The original letter appears in *Izvestiia*, June 17, 1965, p. 3; translated in *CDSP*, July 28, 1965, p. 10. "Follow-up" letters are printed in *CDSP*, July 28, 1965, pp. 10–17.

55. See, e.g., Bogdanovich, *Zhizn'*, pp. 52–56, and Rozhnov, *Po sledam*, pp. 56–57.

56. The most complete discussion of this topic is in Segal, *Alkogolizm*, pp. 126–32.

57. See Bogdanovich, *Zhizn'*, pp. 17–22 for an account of teenage drinking parties.

58. Rozhnov, *Po sledam*, p. 61.

59. For a brief review of some of the problems and patterns of Soviet leisure, see Paul Hollander, "The Uses of Leisure," *Survey* (July, 1966), pp. 40–50.

60. *Literaturnaia gazeta*, December 13, 1967, p. 12; translated in *CDSP*, January 3, 1968, pp. 3–4.

61. *Pravda*, March 29, 1969; translated in *CDSP*, April 16, 1969, pp. 28–29.

62. See, e.g., Rozhnov, *Po sledam*, pp. 106–16, and Bogdanovich, *Zhizn'*, pp. 23–31.

63. Banshchikov, *Alkogolizm*, p. 3.

64. "Alkogolizm," *Bol'shaia meditisinskaia entsiklopediia*, Vol. 1, col. 731, and Gurvich, *P'ianstvo*, p. 7.

65. *Izvestiia*, June 4, 1958, p. 4; translated in *CDSP*, July 9, 1958, pp. 37–38.

66. See, e.g., Bogdanovich, *Zhizn'*, pp. 48–49.   67. Segal, *Alkogolizm*, p. 300.

68. Morris E. Chafetz and Harold W. Demone, *Alcoholism and Society* (New York, Oxford University Press, 1962), p. 133.

69. *Izvestiia*, June 23, 1965, p. 4.

70. *Izvestiia*, August 21, 1965, p. 4; translated in *CDSP*, September 15, 1965, pp. 22–23.

71. *Sovetskaia Rossiia*, March 26, 1964, p. 4. See also I. Lukomskii, *Lechenie khronicheskogo alkogolizma* (Moscow, 1960), p. 37.

72. Chafetz and Demone, *Alcoholism*, p. 134.

73. *Sovetskaia Rossiia*, March 26, 1964, p. 4.

74. *Izvestiia*, October 12, 1965, p. 4.

75. *Sovetskaia Rossiia*, March 26, 1964, p. 4.

76. See Chafetz and Demone, *Alcoholism*, pp. 52–56 for a discussion of the view of alcoholism as "learned behavior."

77. L.A. Lerman, "Meditsinskie rabotniki i protivoalkogol'naia propaganda," *Sovetskoe zdravookhranenie*, No. 11 (1958), p. 4.

78. Banshchikov, *Alkogolizm*, p. 12.

79. See A.R. King and M.H. Hand, "Observations in Russia on the Alcohol Problem," *Quarterly Journal of Studies on Alcohol*, XXIV (December, 1963), 725.

80. Banshchikov, *Alkogolizm*, p. 15.

81. This position, when presented to the public in popularized form, often fails to convince, as anti-alcohol propagandists complain. In slightly different form, however, there is support for such a view. Study of American drinkers of various ethnic backgrounds shows that, while cultural and attitudinal factors connected with ethnicity influence the likelihood of a drinker moving from "moderate" to "heavy" (but not alcoholic) drinking, "heavy" drinkers of whatever ethnic background have an equally high likelihood of becoming alcoholics. See Lee N. Robins, William M. Bates, and Patricia O'Neal, "Adult Drinking Patterns of Former Problem Children," in Pittman and Snyder, eds., *Society, Culture, and Drinking Patterns*, pp. 403–404. Considering the "drinking culture" described earlier, many male Russian drinkers would, it seems, fit the "heavy" description, and their frequent progress from this phase to diagnosable alcoholism must impress many Soviet physicians as evidence of a general tendency for drinkers to increase their dosage and progressively lose control. This would be especially probable if (though we cannot state this with certainty) "heavy" drinking were the *modal* pattern among Russian drinkers.

82. See, e.g., McCord and McCord, *Origins*, pp. 54–72.

Chapter 5

ALCOHOLISM: THERAPY AND PREVENTION

1. *Izvestiia*, March 29, 1961, p. 6; translated in *CDSP*, April 26, 1961, p. 27.

2. *Izvestiia*, January 11, 1962, p. 4; translated in *CDSP*, February 7, 1962, p. 37.

3. Iu. A. Povorinskii, "K voprosu o patogeneticheskiobosnovannoi terapii alkogolizma," *Voprosy psikhiatrii*, No. 7 (1961), pp. 285–92, cited in *Quarterly Journal of Studies on Alcohol*, XXIV (December, 1963), 754–55.

4. "Alkogolizm," *Bol'shaia meditsinskaia entsiklopediia*, Vol. 1 (Moscow, 1956), cols. 756–57.

5. Succeeding descriptions are from *ibid.*, cols. 756–57.

6. In connection with mental illness, see Mark G. Field, "Soviet and American Approaches to Mental Illness—A Comparative Perspective," in S.N. Eisenstadt, ed., *Comparative Social Problems* (New York, Free Press, 1964), pp. 105–28.

7. G.V. Zenevich and S.S. Libikh, *Psikhoterapiia alkogolizma* (Leningrad, 1965), p. 134.

8. See also Ralph G. Winn, ed., *Psychotherapy in the Soviet Union* (New York, Grove Press, 1962), pp. 129–40.

9. Zenevich and Libikh, *Psikhoterapiia alkogolizma*, p. 32.   10. *Ibid.*, p. 33.

11. *Ibid.*   12. *Ibid.*   13. *Ibid.*, p. 34.   14. *Ibid.*, p. 35.   15. *Ibid.*

16. *Ibid.*, p. 37.

17. *Ibid.*, and S.N. Andreichkov, "Opyt organizatsii i raboty narkologicheskogo dispansera," *Zhurnal nevropatologii i psikhiatrii imeni S.S. Korsakova*, LIX (1959), 761–63.

18. Andreichkov, "Opyt organizatsii," pp. 761–63.   19. *Ibid.*

20. See I. Lukomskii, *Lechenie khronicheskogo alkogolizma* (Moscow, 1960), p. 73.

21. *Meditsinskii rabotnik*, July 18, 1958, p. 2.

22. Zenevich and Libikh, *Psikhoterapiia alkogolizma*, pp. 34–35.

23. Lukomskii, *Lechenie*, p. 72.   24. *Ibid.*, p. 73.   25. *Ibid.*

26. Zenevich and Libikh, *Psikhoterapiia alkogolizma*, p. 134.

27. N.M. Shirshov and I.K. Smolovik, "Itogi individual' nogo metoda lecheniia khrr nicheskogo alkogolizma v usloviiakh somaticheskogo statsionara," *Sovetskaia meditsina*, No. 11 (1961), pp. 122–23, cited in *Quarterly Journal of Studies on Alcohol*, XXIV (June, 1963), 352–53.

28. B.M. Segal, *Alkogolizm: Klinicheskie, sotsial'no-psikhologicheskie i biologicheskie problemy* (Moscow, "Meditsina," 1967), p. 533.

29. Criminal Code of the R.S.F.S.R., Article 62. This provision, in pre-1967 form, appears in *Soviet Criminal Law and Procedure: The RSFSR Codes*, with introduction and analysis by Harold J. Berman (Cambridge, Harvard University Press, 1966), pp. 176–77.

30. *Vedomosti Verkhovnogo Soveta RSFSR*, No. 15 (April 13, 1967), pp. 329–30; translated in *CDSP*, May 3, 1967, p. 11.

31. Segal, *Alkogolizm*, p. 538.

32. The RSFSR decree refers to the "Statute on Treatment-Labor Medical Insti-

tutions of the MVD," but the statute itself is not published. Nonpublication of the Statute parallels similar procedure in the cases of the statutes which regulate the internal order of corrective-labor colonies and prisons for criminals.

33. See Iu. M. Tkachevskii, *Prestupnost' i alkogolizm* (Moscow, "Znanie," 1966), p. 70.

34. See *Izvestiia*, October 1, 1968, p. 5; translated in *CDSP*, October 23, 1968, p. 19.

35. *Pravda*, March 18, 1968, p. 6; translated in *CDSP*, April 1, 1968, p. 24.

36. See N. Bondarenko, "Otvetstvennost' za pobeg iz lechebno-trudovogo profilaktoriia," *Sotsialisticheskaia zakonnost'*, No. 9 (1968), pp. 39–40.

37. V. Samsonov and N. Beliakin, "Lechebno-trudovye profilaktorii v bor'be s alkogolizmon," SZ, No. 4 (1968), pp. 28–29. At the time of this article's publication, the RSFSR *profilaktorii* were presumably still by and large in the process of being organized. Some other republics, however, have had such institutions for some time. A 1964 decree of the Kazakh Republic Supreme Soviet may have operated as a trial balloon for the 1967 RSFSR decree, containing virtually the same provisions except that the period of confinement was six months to one year. See *Kazakhstanskaia pravda*, October 31, 1964, p. 3; translated in *CDSP*, December 16, 1964, p. 16.

38. Segal, *Alkogolizm*, pp. 537–38.

39. L.V. Orlovskii, "K metodike antialkogol'noi propagandy," in I. Lukomskii, ed., *Alkogolizm i alkogol'nye psikhozy* (Moscow, 1963), p. 418.

40. L.A. Lerman, "Meditsinskie rabotniki i protivoalkogol'naia propaganda," *Sovetskoe zdravookhranenie*, No. 11 (1958); p. 5.

41. "Zlodeika snakleikoi." Vera Efron notes this in "The Soviet Approach to Alcoholism," *Social Problems*, VII (Spring, 1960), 307–15. The reference is to the (vodka) bottle (*butylka*), feminine gender in Russian. Nicknames are frequently employed in the titles of pamphlets as well, as in the mixed-metaphor *In the Steps of the Green Serpent*. V.E. Rozhnov, *Po sledam zelenogo zmiia* (Moscow, Voennoe izdatel'stvo Ministerstva Oborony SSSR, 1969).

42. See, e.g., V.M. Banshchikov, *Alkogolizm i ego vred dlia zdorov'ia cheloveka* (Moscow, 1958), pp. 32, 34–35.

43. See, e.g., Lerman, "Meditsinskie rabotniki,"; Banshchikov, *Alkogolizm*, p. 12; and *Sovetskaia torgovlia*, May 12, 1959, p. 4.

44. *Meditsinskaia gazeta*, July 16, 1963, p. 2.

45. See Rozhnov, *Po sledam*, pp. 62–72, for a presentation of the argument that alcoholism does have a direct physical impact on progeny.

46. An example is Segal, who notes this possibility and remains far from unqualified acceptance of the "heredity" argument (*Alkogolizm*, pp. 132–33). To what degree Segal's position represents the convictions of other Soviet alcoholism specialists with medical training cannot be determined, but it suggests that acceptance of the "heredity" idea is far from total.

47. *Ibid.*, p. 546.

48. *Pravda*, August 7, 1964, p. 4; translated in *CDSP*, September 2, 1964, p. 32.

49. Orlovskii, "K metodike," p. 422.

50. *Meditskinskaia gazeta*, July 16, 1963, p. 2.

51. Orlovskii, "K metodike," p. 422.   52. Segal, *Alkogolizm*, p. 546.

53. At least one Russian authority, B.M. Segal, also doubts their utility. *Ibid.*, p. 546.

54. "The arousal of fears, implied warnings, or threats as to what will happen if one drinks too much have been noted to provoke avoidance reactions towards further propaganda. There also seems to be unwillingness of audiences to particularize such propaganda. This is very apt to be true if the educational materials are pointed to alcoholism as an end result of drinking." Edwin Lemert, "Alcohol, Values and Social Control," in David J. Pittman and Charles R. Snyder, eds., *Society, Culture, and Drinking Patterns* (New York, Wiley, 1962), p. 563.

55. "Alkogolizm," *Bol'shaia meditsinskaia entsiklopediia*, Vol. 1, col. 734; Segal, *Alkogolizm*, p. 542; and Iu. Levin, "O vrede alkogolia," in *Za kommunisticheskii byt* (Leningrad, "Znanie," 1963), p. 246.

56. The economics of the present state monopoly on alcohol, as well as the desire to avoid "bourgeois sanctimoniousness," provide at least part of the answer. The income from alcohol is large and expenditures absorb much of the population's buying power.

57. *Izvestiia*, June 27, 1965, p. 6; *Izvestiia*, July 9, 1958, p. 3. Latter translated in *CDSP*, August 13, 1958, pp. 26–27. See also *Pravda*, March 29, 1969; translated in *CDSP* April 16, 1969, pp. 28–29.

58. *Komsomol'skaia pravda*, October 9, 1964, pp. 2, 4; translated in *CDSP*, December 16, 1964, pp. 16–18.

59. Some writers refer to the severe alcohol problems of the immediate postwar years (see Segal, *Alkogolizm*, p. 267) when the standard of living hit a low point; others, recognizing this, argue that today's drunkards lack the excuses of poverty and deprivation. While it seems that alcoholism leads to a decline in personal standard of living (Segal, *Alkogolizm*, p. 105), those studies including control groups to test the relationship of income, education, and occupation to drinking habits have been inconclusive (*ibid.*, pp. 298–300), mainly due to the difficulty of securing a "representative" control group.

60. The authoritative *Alkogolizm—put' k prestupleniiu* (Moscow: "Iuridicheskaia literatura," 1966), a collective work of the All-Union Institute for the Study of Causes and Elaboration of Preventive Measures of Crime, recommended that such a society be established. Little more was heard on this until 1969, when the March 29 *Pravda* carried an article by Iu. M. Tkachevskii, a Moscow University criminal law professor, which proposed a new organization. On May 27, *Izvestiia* picked up the theme with a similar article by Professor A.A. Gertsenzon, the *doyen* of Soviet criminologists and the editor of the collective volume noted above. Since then, others have joined in such proposals (see *Pravda*, January 31,

1970, p. 3). The author spoke with Gertsenzon shortly after his *Izvestiia* article appeared, but the latter said at that time that he did not know whether such a society might be established in the then near future.

61. Banshchikov, *Alkogolizm*, p. 38.

62. Ia. E. Gurvich, *P'ianstvo gubit cheloveka, nanosit vred obshchestvu* (Moscow, "Znanie," 1958), p. 16.

63. *Izvestiia*, August 29, 1965, p. 4; translated in *CDSP*, September 22, 1965, pp. 32–33.

64. *Ibid.*   65. *Ibid.*

66. *Komsomol'skaia pravda*, October 9, 1964, pp. 2, 4; translated in *CDSP*, December 16, 1964, pp. 16–18.

67. *Ibid.*

68. H. Muller-Dietz, "Der Alkoholismus und seine Bekampfung in Der Sovjetunion," *International Journal of Alcohol and Alcoholism*, 2 (1957), pp. 34–39, cited in *Quarterly Journal of Studies on Alcohol*, XVIII (December, 1957), 689–90.

69. *Izvestiia*, March 2, 1958, p. 4; translated in *CDSP*, April 9, 1958, p. 29.

70. *Komsomol'skaia pravda*, September 10, 1961, p. 4; translated in *CDSP*, October 4, 1961, pp. 15–16.

71. *Vecherniaia Moskva*, September 20, 1963, p. 4.

72. Gurvich, *P'ianstvo*, p. 18.   73. *Izvestiia*, July 14, 1965, p. 4.

74. *Komsomol'skaia pravda*, September 10, 1961, p. 4; translated in *CDSP*, October 4, 1961, pp. 15–16.

75. *Ibid.*   76. *Komsomol'skaia pravda*, January 9, 1970, p. 4.

77. *Sovetskaia Estoniia*, January 9, 1970.

78. *Alkogolizm—put' k prestupleniiu*, pp. 151–52.

79. See, e.g., *Komsomol'skaia pravda*, January 6, 1970, p. 4.

80. *Sovetskaia Rossiia*, January 24, 1970, p. 2.

Chapter 6
JUVENILE DELINQUENCY

1. N. Alimov, "O roli narodnykh sudov v preduprezhdenii pravonarushenii nesovershennoletnikh," in *Voprosy bor'by s prestupnost'iu nesovershennoletnikh* (Alma-Ata, "Nauka" Kazakhskoi SSR, 1968), pp. 95–96.

2. E. Kairzhanov, "Naznachenie nakazaniia po delam nesovershennoletnikh," in *ibid.*, pp. 153–54.

3. See *Kriminologiia* (1st ed.; Moscow, "Iuridicheskaia literatura," 1966), pp. 24–25 for a brief Soviet periodization of stages in the delinquency problem.

4. See A. Shliapochnikov, "Prestupnost' i repressiia v SSSR (kratkii obzor)," in *Problemy ugolovnoi politiki*, book 1 (Moscow, 1936), p. 75 ff., and I. Averbakh and S. Bulatov, "Zakon 7 aprelia 1935 g. i bor'ba s prestupnost'iu nesovershennoletnikh," in *Problemy ugolovnoi politiki*, book 2 (Moscow, 1936), pp. 34, 37.

5. For instance, Soviet figures for the period show "escalation" of a punitive approach to convicted juveniles. Of those convicted of hooliganism in 1934, only 16.9 percent were sentenced to deprivation of freedom. For the first half of 1938, this figure had climbed to 66.2 percent. See John N. Hazard, "Trends in the Soviet Treatment of Crime," *American Sociological Review*, V (August, 1940), 575–76, citing *Sovetskaia iustitsiia*, No. 12 (1939), p. 25.

6. See, e.g., O.I. Morozov, N.I. Gukovskaia, V.I. Ivanov, and V.F. Statkus, "Opyt kompleksnogo obsledovaniia prichin i uslovii, sposobstvuiushchikh soversheniiu prestuplenii podrostkami," *SGIP*, No. 9 (1963), pp. 110–16.

7. For a short description of the tasks, "clientele," and mode of operation of the Commissions on Juvenile Affairs (*Komissii po delam nesovershennoletnikh*: this may also be rendered as "Commissions on Juvenile *Cases*" but, since the tasks of the commissions are not limited to coping with lawbreakers, the term "Affairs" shall be used here) see A.M. Beliakova, D.S. Karev, and V.S. Orlov, *Pravovaia okhrana detstva* (Moscow, "Znanie," 1968), pp. 92–104. For greater detail, see V.S. Pronina, *Kommentarii k polozheniiam o komissiiakh po delam nesovershennoletnikh* (Moscow, "Iuridicheskaia literatura," 1968). Article 10 of the Criminal Code of the Russian Republic (and corresponding articles in other union republic codes) specifies the offenses (homicide, assault, rape, robbery, theft, etc.) for which criminal responsibility begins at age 14 rather than 16. See *Soviet Criminal Law and Procedure: The RSFSR Codes*, introduction and analysis by Harold J. Berman, translation by Harold J. Berman and James W. Spindler (Cambridge, Harvard University Press, 1966), pp. 147–48.

8. See the data on commission practice in Krasnopresnensk district, Moscow, in Ye. V. Boldyrev, *Mery preduprezhdeniia pravonarushenii nesovershennoletnikh v SSSR* (Moscow, "Nauka," 1964), p. 145.

9. Boldyrev, *Mery*, pp. 136–37.

10. Ye. V. Boldyrev, "Primenenie komissiiami po delam nesovershennoletnikh mer vozdeistviia k pravonarushiteliam i ikh roditeliam," in *Preduprezhdenie prestupnosti nesovershennoletnikh* (Moscow, "Iuridicheskaia literatura," 1965), pp. 148–49. See also V.V. Ustinova and E.T. Iakovlev, "Nekotorye rezul'taty izucheniia effektivnosti primeneniia prinuditel'nykh mer vospitatel'nogo kharaktera," in *Voprosy bor'by s prestupnost'iu*, vyp. 9 (1969), p. 143.

11. See Ustinova and Iakovlev, "Nekotorye," p. 143, and A.V. Sadovskii, "Deiatel'nost' komissii po delam nesovershennoletnikh," in *Preduprezhdenie pravonarushenii sredi nesovershennoletnikh* (Minsk, "Nauka i tekhnika," 1969), p. 77.

12. G.M. Min'kovskii, "Nekotorye voprosy izucheniia prestupnosti nesovershennoletnikh," in *Preduprezhdenie prestupnosti nesovershennoletnikh*, p. 29; also M.M. Babaev, *Individualizatsiia nakazaniia nesovershennoletnikh* (Moscow, "Iuridicheskaia literatura," 1968), p. 89.

13. Babaev, *Individualizatsiia*, p. 90.

14. G.M. Min'kovskii, "Voprosy izucheniia prichin i uslovii, sposobstvuiushchikh soversheniiu prestuplenii i drugikh pravonarushenii podrostkami," *Uchenye zapiski* (Latviiskii gosudarstvennyi universitet, Riga), LVI (1964), 97. See also Min'kovskii, "Nekotorye voprosy," p. 40.

15. Min'kovskii, "Nekotorye voprosy," p. 29.

16. V.S. Karasev, "Nekotorye dannye, kharakterizuiushchie primenenie mer ugolovnogo nakazaniia k nesovershennoletnim prestupnikam," in *Preduprezhdenie prestupnosti nesovershennoletnikh*, p. 225.

17. Ye. V. Boldyrev, "The Study and Prevention of Juvenile Delinquency," *Soviet Review*, May, 1961; translated from *SGIP*, No. 2 (1960), p. 22.

18. L.K. Zaitsev and Iu. V. Shabanov, "Prichiny i usloviia protivopravnikh deistvii nesovershennoletnikh," in *Preduprezhdenie pravonarushenii*, p. 9. See also the data presented in V. Fursov, "Nekotorye voprosy sostoianiia i struktury prestupnosti nesovershennoletnikh v Kazakhskoi SSR," in *Voprosy bor'by s prestupnost'iu nesovershennoletnikh*, p. 20.

19. Illegitimacy and the problems of unwed mother and "fatherless" children were discussed at length in the Soviet press both before and after publication of the new draft principles of marriage and family legislation (*Izvestiia*, April 10, 1968, p. 4; translated in *CDSP*, May 8, 1968, pp. 3–6), which went some way toward "de-stigmatizing" illegitimacy but not so far as some wished. In the Estonian SSR in 1969, according to the Procurator-General's office, 26.6 percent of that year's delinquents were children of unmarried mothers. *Rahva Hääl*, January 28, 1970, p. 4, cited in *Soviet Studies Information Supplement* (Glasgow), No. 26 (April, 1970), p. 37.

20. See, on 1966, "Statisticheskie materialy," *Vestnik statistiki*, No. 11 (1967), p. 93. For 1967, see *Vestnik statistiki*, No. 2 (1969), p. 92.

21. Fursov, "Nekotorye voprosy," p. 23.

22. See the study of a group of young pre-delinquents in F.R. Filippov, "O dinamike i prichinakh pravonarushenii nesovershennoletnikh v usloviiakh promyshlennogo goroda," in *Voprosy bor'by s prestupnost'iu*, vyp. 7 (1968), 22–28.

23. "Employee," for example, can cover relatively highly paid persons at one end of the spectrum, and low-paid and low-prestige service and sales personnel at the other. A skilled worker or foreman in a priority industry will enjoy an income exceeding by far the earnings of the low (and indeed, in some cases, the middle) range of the "employee" category.

24. Kirov *raion* has been a subject of relatively intensive study, by sociologists as well as those interested in delinquency. See M.N. Rutkevich, ed., *The Career Plans of Youth*, translated by Murray Yanowitch (White Plains, N.Y., International Arts and Sciences Press, 1969) This is a translation of the original large-scale study of Sverdlovsk youth undertaken by sociologists at Sverdlovsk University: *Zhiznennye plany molodezhi* (Sverdlovsk, Izdatel'stvo Ural'skogo universiteta, 1966). Compared to other districts in Sverdlovsk, itself a heavily industrial city, Kirov is relatively nonindustrial, and the percentage of its popula-

tion who are workers is probably below the national average for urban areas. The nonetheless high percentage of Kirov district delinquents from workers' families thus takes on added significance, since it points toward possible overrepresentation of adolescents of a particular social origin (i.e. worker) among delinquents.

25. M. Kovalev, "Izuchenie prestupnosti nesovershennoletnikh i ee preduprezhdenie," *S.Iu.*, No. 3 (1966), p. 16.

26. *Itogi vsesoiuznoi perepisi naseleniia 1959 goda: RSFSR* (Moscow, Gosstatizdat, 1963), p. 154.

27. We do, however, have information about Kirov *raion* which may be of help in unraveling the problem of social origins in relation to delinquency. The social composition of Kirov *raion* is rather heavily weighted in favor of specialist and intelligentsia families and school enrollments reflect a heavy concentration of the children of such families in the district's adolescent population. Educational and research institutes apparently make up the main "business" in Kirov district; there is little industry. Hence, the 73.0 percent share of all delinquents claimed by those of worker origin may reflect a substantial overrepresentation of this group. See M. Tkach, "Career Plans of Graduates of Complete Secondary Schools" in Rutkevich, ed., *Career Plans*, pp. 57–58.

28. Fursov, "Nekotorye voprosy," p. 24.

29. *Itogi vsesoiuznoi perepisi naseleniia 1959 goda: Kazakhskaia SSR* (Moscow, Gosstatizdat, 1962), p. 63.

30. T.E. Chumakova, "Rol' sem'i v vospitanii u nesovershennoletnikh pravosoznaniia," in *Preduprezhdenie pravonarushenii*, pp. 50–51. More striking is a study by L.M. Ziubin of "best learners" and delinquents by educational levels of parents. Children of unskilled-worker parents made up only 3 percent of the former contingent but were an impressive 43 percent of the latter, while children of "employees" with at least secondary education made up 60 percent of the "best learners" but only 12 percent of the delinquents. See "Psikhologicheskii aspekt problemy perevospitaniia pedagogicheski zapushchennykh detei i nesovershennoletnikh pravonarushitelei," *Voprosy psikhologii*, No. 3 (1969), p. 139.

31. *Kriminologiia* (2d ed.; (1968), p. 347. A study in the city of Taganrog, in the Crimea, involving a sample of 428 working minors (55 of whom turned out to be lawbreakers) showed, however, relatively small differences in parental educational levels between delinquents alone and the entire sample (including the delinquents). In fact, a larger percentage of the total parental sample fell into the "less than four years of school" category than among parents of delinquents. (This was not, obviously, a strict use of "controls," and the disparity in size between the groups only 55 delinquents and 373 presumed nondelinquents—might more than account for some of the variations.) See A.F. Troshin and V.V. Ustinova, "Nekotorye rezul'taty izucheniia sotsial'noi sredy lichnosti pravonarushitelei iz chisla rabotaiushchikh podrostkov," in *Voprosy izucheniia i preduprezhdeniia pravonarushenii nesovershennoletnikh*, vol. 1 (Moscow, Vsesoiuznyi institut po izucheniiu prichin i razrabotke mer preduprezhdeniia prestupnosti, 1970), p. 123. It should be noted as well that this study, unlike most, concerned itself only with working youth and their backgrounds.

32. Boldyrev, "Study," p. 33.   33. *Kriminologiia* (2d ed.), p. 342.

34. See, e.g., Fursov, "Nekotorye voprosy," pp. 25–26; L.A. Andreeva, "O neko-torykh obstoiatel'stvakh, sposobstvuiushchikh polovym prestupleniiam nesover-shennoletnikh, i merakh ikh preduprezhdeniia," in *Voprosy bor'by s prestup-nost'iu*, vyp. 10 (1969), p. 108 (on juvenile sex offenders). Also see V.S. Orlov, *Podrostok i prestuplenie* (Moscow, Izdatel'stvo Moskovskogo universiteta, 1969), p. 83; A. Kuznetsov, "O formakh raboty po preduprezhdeniiu prestupnosti neso-vershennoletnikh," *SGIP*, No. 8 (1964), p. 93; M. Kovalev, "Izuchenie prestupnosti nesovershennoletnikh i ee preduprezhdenie," *S.Iu.*, No. 3 (1966), p. 15; G. Akh-medzianova and N. Gukovskaia, "Bol'she vnimanie rabote po delam o prestuple-niiakh nesovershennoletnikh," *SZ*, No. 3 (1966), pp. 62–63.

35. *Kriminologiia* (2d ed.), p. 342.   36. *Ibid.*

37. Sadovskii, "Deiatel'nost' komissii," p. 77.   38. *Ibid.*

39. Kovalev, "Izuchenie prestupnosti," p. 16.

40. Min'kovskii, "Nekotorye voprosy," p. 41.

41. Ustinova and Iakovlev, "Nekotorye," p. 143.

42. The same appears to be true of the trade schools, which serve to some degree as a dumping ground where school administrators can rid themselves of problem adolescents. Given this fact, the higher rate of delinquency among trade school students is not surprising. See Orlov, *Podrostok*, p. 131.

43. *Kriminologiia* (2d ed.), p. 342.

44. See, e.g., Karasev, "Nekotorye dannye," p. 227, and E.I. Kharshak, "Osoben-nosti sovmestnoi prestupnoi deiatel'nosti nesovershennoletnikh," in *Voprosy bor'by s prestupnost'iu*, vyp. 9 (1969), p. 134.

45. For a treatment of juvenile gangs as something less than cohesive, well-orga-nized groups, see Lewis Yablonsky, "The Delinquent Gang as a Near-Group," *Social Problems*, VII (Fall, 1969), 108–17.

46. "Antiobshchestvennye iavleniia, ikh prichiny i sredstva bor'by s nim," *Kom-munist*, No. 12 (1966), pp. 58–68; translated in *CDSP*, September 28, 1966, p. 9.

47. *Kriminologiia* (1st ed.), pp. 287–88.

48. On family policy, see Kent Geiger, *The Family in Soviet Russia* (Cambridge, Harvard University Press, 1968). For a short summary, see William Petersen, "The Evolution of Soviet Family Policy," *Problems of Communism*, 5 (September–October, 1956), 29–35.

49. *Komsomol'skaia pravda*, April 17, 1963, p. 4.

50. *Izvestiia*, May 22, 1964, p. 3; translated in *CDSP*, June 17, 1964, pp. 29–30.

51. *Izvestiia*, June 6, 1964, p. 3.

52. G.M. Min'kovskii, "Nekotorye prichiny prestupnosti nesovershennoletnikh v SSSR i mery ee preduprezhdeniia," *SGIP*, No. 5 (1966), pp. 84–93; translated in *CDSP*, August 17, 1966, p. 10.

53. Orlov, *Podrostok*, p. 64.   54. *Ibid.*, p. 70.

55. *Izvestiia*, June 17, 1965, p. 3.

56. M. Gritskevich, "Bor'ba s prestupnost'iu nesovershennoletnikh," SZ, No. 3 (1958), pp. 30–31.

57. Boldyrev, "Primenenie," p. 148.

58. S.S. Ostroumov, "Opyt provedeniia konkretnogo sotsiologicheskogo issledovaniia pravonarushenii sredi nesovershennoletnikh," *Vestnik Moskovskogo universiteta* (series XII, law), No. 2 (1967), p. 32. Seventy percent of the divorces in the Lenin *raion* of Moscow, according to Ostroumov, involved couples with children.

59. Orlov, *Podrostok*, pp. 74–75.

60. Min'kovskii, "Nekotorye prichiny," p. 11.

61. *Izvestiia*, September 18, 1964, p. 4.

62. Orlov, *Podrostok*, p. 76.   63. *Pravda*, July 4, 1965, p. 6.

64. A.A. Sokolov, "Profilaktike pravonarushenii nesovershennoletnikh—bol'she vnimaniia," *SGIP*, No. 5 (1964), p. 89.

65. Orlov, *Podrostok*, p. 90.

66. A. Troshin, "Rabota komissii g. Kieva po preduprezhdeniiu pravonarushenii nesovershennoletnikh," SZ, No. 6 (1964), pp. 53–54.

67. Ye. V. Boldyrev, "Sovershenstvovat' sistemu mer preduprezhdeniia pravonarushenii nesovershennoletnikh," *SGIP*, No. 1 (1966), p. 104.

68. Min'kovskii, "Nekotorye prichiny," p. 11.

69. G.M. Min'kovskii, V.S. Pronina, and Ye. V. Boldyrev, "Nekotorye voprosy izucheniia i preduprezhdeniia prestupnosti nesovershennoletnikh," *SGIP*, No. 9 (1964), p. 126.

70. See P.G. Volodarskii, *Prakticheskoe posobie dlia komissii po delam nesovershennoletnikh* (Moscow, "Iuridicheskaia literatura," 1964), pp. 44–45.

71. For the procedure under the new provisions, see Pronina, *Kommentarii*, pp. 33–34 and ff.

72. Ye. V. Boldyrev, "Soveshchanie v prezidiume Verkhovnogo Soveta RSFSR o rabote komissii po delam nesovershennoletnikh," SZ, No. 10 (1962), p. 43.

73. See, e.g., Orlov, *Podrostok*, p. 134.   74. *Ibid.*, p. 133.

75. *Pravda*, January 11, 1963, p. 2.

76. V.S. Tikunov, "Polnoe iskorenenie beznadzornosti i prestupnosti nesovershennoletnikh—vazhneishaia zadacha organov okhrany obshchestvennogo poriadka," *SGIP*, No. 4 (1964), p. 30.

77. A. Troshin, "Trudoustroistvo nesovershennoletnikh—uslovie preduprezhdeniia ikh beznadzornosti i prestupnosti," SZ, No. 7 (1965), pp. 25–27.

78. *Izvestiia*, June 26, 1965, p. 3.

79. N. Gus'kov and N. Gukovskaia, "Ustranit' prichiny pravonarushenii nesovershennoletnikh," SZ, No. 5 (1963), p. 9.

80. V.A. Dinevich, "Obshchestvennyi kontrol' za sobliudeniem rezhima i uslovii raboty nesovershennoletnikh," *Uchenye zapiski* (Latviiskii gosudarstvennyi universitet, Riga, 1964), 131, 134.

81. M.N. Rutkevich, "Social Requirements, the Educational System, and Career Plans of Youth," in Rutkevich, ed., *Career Plans*, p. 10.

82. Beliakova, Karev, and Orlov, *Pravovaia okhrana*, pp. 41–42.

83. Orlov, *Podrostok*, pp. 120–21.

84. A study of 476 adolescents in factories in Sverdlovsk *oblast'* who expressed dissatisfaction with their jobs revealed that 35 percent cited as a reason the lack of opportunity to increase their skills (the largest single category) while 20 percent cited inadequate wages. See A.A. Kostenko, B.I. Livshits and V.A. Mishchenko, "The Problem of Realization of Career Plans of Working Youngsters," in Rutkevich, *Career Plans*, p. 76 (table 3).

85. *Ibid.*, p. 74.

86. The world in which Soviet managers operate is detailed in Joseph S. Berliner, *Factory and Manager in the U.S.S.R.* (Cambridge, Harvard University Press, 1957). See also David Granick, *The Red Executive* (Garden City, N.Y., Doubleday, 1960).

87. Orlov, *Podrostok*, p. 125.   88. *Izvestiia*, February 25, 1964, p. 4.

89. V. Kloskov, "Nesovershennoletnim—osoboe vnimanie," *S.Iu.*, No. 21 (1963), p. 11.

90. Min'kovskii, "Nekotorye prichiny," p. 11.

91. *Nedelia*, October 10–16, 1965, pp. 8–9; translated in *CDSP*, December 8, 1965, pp. 14–15.

92. *Ibid.*

93. See, e.g., *Nedelia*, October 30–November 6, 1965, p. 20; translated in *CDSP*, December 8, 1965, pp. 15–16.

94. *Pravda*, April 19, 1958, pp. 1–3; translated in *CDSP*, June 4, 1958, p. 19.

95. On the operations of the youth organizations and the difficulties of simultaneously combining the functions of mobilization and control of youth, see Allen Kassof, *The Soviet Youth Program* (Cambridge, Harvard University Press, 1965).

96. *Komsomol'skaia pravda*, November 2, 1958, p. 3.

97. *Izvestiia*, June 2, 1963, pp. 2–3.   98. Orlov, *Podrostok*, p. 132.

99. One of the major themes is the "influence of the capitalist world." Annual influxes of Western tourists, the occasional movies from abroad shown in theaters, Western short-wave radio stations—all are blamed for the contaminating effect they have on "unstable" youth. See Orlov, *Podrostok*, pp. 34–43, and Beliakova, Karev, and Orlov, *Pravovaia okhrana*, pp. 58–61.

100. For a summary of such views, see John M. Martin and Joseph P. Fitzpatrick, *Delinquent Behavior* (New York, Random House, 1964), pp. 46–73.

101. For a summary of the position Soviet writers have taken, see Walter D. Connor, "Deviant Behavior in Capitalist Society: The Soviet Image," *Journal of Criminal Law, Criminology and Police Science*, LXI (December, 1970), 554–64.

102. A notable example is B.S. Vorontsov, N.I. Gukovskaia, and E.B. Mel'nikova, "O prestupnosti nesovershennoletnikh v gorode i sel'skoi mestnosti," *SGIP*, No. 3 (1969), pp. 103–108; translated in *CDSP*, May 21, 1969, pp. 9–13. The authors analyze a number of factors differentiating urban and rural life in the USSR which are presumably relevant to differences in delinquency rates. Rural youth begin work earlier and have less leisure. Participating in relatively clear-cut agricultural production, they can begin assuming responsibility for simple but necessary tasks earlier than youth in urban industrial areas. "Every stage of the work goes on before [their] eyes." The tighter-knit everyday life of the village facilitates the operation of informal social controls that are weakened by the anonymity of u ban life. Parents and other adults see more of their children and participate with them in more joint tasks in the rural areas, creating a greater degree of social supervision. Finally, the density of adolescent populations is much lower in rural than in urban areas, and the authors argue that less inter-adolescent contact reduces the chances of "bad influences." Results of a survey showed that 14.3 percent of the urban youth questioned knew someone who had been convicted of delinquency in court or who had been processed by a commission, while only 4.2 percent of the rural youth had such acquaintances.

103. *Kriminologiia* (1st ed.), p. 280.　　104. Babaev, *Individualizatsiia*, p. 13.

105. A.B. Sakharov, "Vozrastnye osobennosti psikhiki nesovershennoletnikh pravonarushitelei," *SZ*, No. 6 (1965), p. 14.

106. *Ibid.*, pp. 14–15.

107. U. Dzhekebaev, "O kriminologicheskikh aspektakh psikhologicheskogo vzaimovlianiia liudei v protsesse obshcheniia," in *Voprosy bor'by s prestupnost'iu nesovershennoletnikh*, p. 57.

108. Babaev, *Individualizatsiia*, p. 17.

109. G. Bochkareva, "Psikhologiia podrostkov-pravonarushitelei," *S.Iu.*, No. 22 (1967), pp. 15–16; translated in *CDSP*, February 14, 1968, p. 9. For a treatment of problem youth in a somewhat similar vein, see L.G. Sagatovskaia, "Opyt sotsial'no-psikhologicheskogo obsledovaniia gruppy 'trudnykh' podrostkov," *Voprosy preduprezhdeniia prestupnosti*, vyp. 4 (1966), pp. 139–46.

110. Sakharov, "Vozrastnye osobennosti," pp. 15–16.　　111. *Ibid.*, p. 15.

112. Babaev, *Individualizatsiia*, pp. 14–15.

113. L.A. Kliuchinskaia and L.A. Bergere, *Nesovershennoletnie i ugolovnyi zakon* (Riga, Izdatel'stvo "Zinatne," 1967), p. 74.

114. Babaev, *Individualizatsiia*, p. 13.

Chapter 7
DELINQUENCY: PREVENTION
AND CORRECTION

1. *Kriminologiia* (1st ed.; Moscow, "Iuridicheskaia literatura," 1966), pp. 291–93.

2. G.M. Min'kovskii, "Nekotorye prichiny prestupnosti nesovershennoletnikh v SSSR i mery ee preduprezhdeniia," *SGIP*, No. 5 (1966), pp. 84–93; translated in *CDSP*, August 17, 1966, pp. 9–10.

3. *Kriminologiia* (1st ed.), p. 293.   4. *Ibid.*, pp. 293–94.   5. *Ibid.*, p. 294.

6. A. Shchedrina, "Uchastie obshchestvennosti v preduprezhdenii prestupnosti nesovershennoletnikh," *S.Iu.*, No. 1 (1964), pp. 20–21.

7. *Ibid.*

8. I. Korchak, "Preduprezhdenie pravonarushenii nesovershennoletnikh," SZ, No. 6 (1964), p. 52.

9. Z. Samoshina and N. Osipenko, "Rol' obshchestvennosti v preduprezhdenie prestuplenii nesovershennoletnikh," *S.Iu.*, No. 2 (1962), pp. 17–19.

10. *Ibid.*

11. G.M. Min'kovskii and E. Mel'nikova, "Shefstvo nad trudnymi podrostkami— put' k preduprezhdeniiu prestupnosti nesovershennoletnikh," SZ, No. 1 (1966), pp. 25–29.

12. *Ibid.*, p. 26.   13. *Ibid.*, p. 28.

14. *Vedomosti Verkhovnogo Soveta RSFSR*, No. 51 (December 22, 1967), pp. 949–52; translated in *CDSP*, January 24, 1968, pp. 28–29.

15. V. Fofanov and S. Berezovskaia, "Obshchimi usiliami borot'sia s pravonarusheniiami nesovershennoletnikh," SZ, No. 10 (1964), pp. 51–52.

16. D. Karev, "Rol' partiinykh organizatsii v bor'be s pravonarusheniiami nesovershennoletn'·h," SZ, No. 5 (1966), p. 57.

17. *Ibid.*

18. Article 392, RSFSR Code of Criminal Procedure (hereafter, CCP). The RSFSR codes are readily available in *Soviet Criminal Law and Procedure: The RSFSR Codes,* with Introduction and Analysis by Harold J. Berman, translation by Harold J. Berman and James W. Spindler (Cambridge, Harvard University Press, 1966). Subsequent references to the codes of criminal procedure (CCP) and criminal law (CC) will be made to pagination in Berman and Spindler, *Codes.*

19. For a Soviet treatment of their roles, see N.I. Gukovskaia, *Deiatel'nost' sledovatelia i suda po preduprezhdeniiu prestuplenii nesovershennoletnikh* (Moscow, "Iuridicheskaia literatura," 1967).

20. T.E. Chumakova, "Rol' sem'i v vospitanii u nesovershennoletnikh pravosoz-

naniia," in *Preduprezhdenie pravonarushenii sredi nesovershennoletnikh* (Minsk, "Nauka i tekhnika," 1969), p. 52.

21. See *Pravda*, July 4, 1965, p. 6; translated in *CDSP*, July 29, 1965, pp. 18–19. See also *Pravda*, July 26, 1965, p. 4; translated in *CDSP*, August 18, 1965, p. 29.

22. M. Milovanova, "Vnimanie: podrostki!" in *Po mestu zhitel'stva* . . . (Moscow, "Moskovskii rabochii," 1967), p. 96.

23. Min'kovskii and Mel'nikova, "Shefstvo," p. 28.

24. A. Kuznetsov, "O formakh raboty po preduprezhdeniiu prestupnosti nesovershennoletnikh," *SGIP*, No. 8 (1964), p. 97.

25. V.S. Orlov, *Podrostok i prestuplenie* (Moscow, Izdatel'stvo Moskovskogo universiteta, 1969), p. 172.

26. *Ibid.*, p. 173.

27. Current views on "professionalization" of social service personnel, admittedly, are diverse, and (especially in the area of delinquency prevention and control) arguments have been made that nonprofessionals—the public—represent an untapped source of workers for such causes. See, e.g., the discussion of the Chicago Area Project in Solomon Kobrin, "The Chicago Area Project—A Twenty-five Year Assessment," *Annals of the American Academy of Political and Social Science*, 322 (March, 1950), 20–29. A major Soviet problem seems to be a lack of *any* "professionalization" in the Western sense, including the lack of any useful training for public volunteers when they make themselves available.

28. Min'kovskii and Mel'nikova, "Shefstvo," p. 29.

29. While allowance must certainly be made for differences between the societies, the unpaid volunteer exercising probation and parole functions in the USSR may resemble in some ways his paid American counterpart. Matza has argued that probation work with juveniles in the USA is a "marginal profession," marginality being the result of failure to synthesize the elements of "calling," or vocation, and "job" in a stable manner. While a calling, such as that of judge, permits one to preach, probation work has too much of the job about it to allow incumbents access to pedestals. Probation work is not highly rewarded in terms of either prestige or salary. Juveniles know this and refuse to recognize any right of the probation worker to pontificate or to "flaunt moral superiority." If, as Soviet sources note, so many "volunteers" prove incompetent in their work, it would not be surprising to find that their juvenile charges view them and their work with little awe or respect. See David Matza, *Delinquency and Drift* (New York, Wiley, 1964), pp. 144–47.

30. G. Bakharov, "Iskoreniat' usloviia, sposobstvuiushchie pravonarusheniiam nesovershennoletnikh," *SZ*, No. 10 (1965), pp. 11–12.

31. Ye. V. Boldyrev, M. Tokareva, and A. Troshin, "Rabota sudov po preduprezhdeniiu prestupnosti sredi nesovershennoletnikh," *S.Iu.*, No. 19 (1964), p. 23.

32. G. Akhmedzianova and N. Gukovskaia, "Bol'she vnimaniia rabote po delam nesovershennoletnikh," *SZ*, No. 7 (1966), p. 63.

33. Boldyrev, Tokareva, and Troshin, "Rabota sudov," p. 23.

34. A.M. Beliakova, D.S. Karev, and V.S. Orlov, *Pravovaia okhrana detstva* (Moscow, "Znanie," 1968), p. 111.

35. Article 10, CC RSFSR. Berman and Spindler, *Codes*, p. 148.   36. *Ibid.*

37. Article 8, CCP RSFSR. Berman and Spindler, *Codes*, p. 255.

38. Article 10, CCP RSFSR. Berman and Spindler, *Codes*, p. 256. However, one study of several commissions shows that remand from a People's Court is an atypical way for a case to reach the commission. Data collected by V.V. Ustinova of the Institute of Criminology in Moscow show "50 to 60 percent" of cases being referred directly by police agencies, including investigators, 15 to 20 percent by organs of the *Prokuratura*, and some from schools, public organizations, housing blocks, and private citizens. Remands from the courts "are encountered rarely." See V.V. Ustinova, "Rassmotrenie komissiiami po delam nesovershennoletnikh del o pravonarusheniiakh podrostkov," in *Voprosy izucheniia i preduprezhdeniia pravonarushenii nesovershennoletnikh*, Vol. 2 (Moscow, Vsesoiuznyi institut po izucheniiu prichin i razrabotke mer preduprezhdeniia prestupnosti, 1970), p. 48.

39. See G.M. Min'kovskii, "Nekotorye voprosy izucheniia prestupnosti nesovershennoletnikh," in *Preduprezhdenie prestupnosti nesovershennoletnikh* (Moscow, "Iuridicheskaia literatura," 1965), p. 24; V.S. Karasev, "Nekotorye dannye, kharakterizuiushchie primenenie mer ugolovnogo nakazaniia k nesovershennoletnim prestupnikam," in *Preduprezhdenie prestupnosti nesovershennoletnikh*, p. 225, n. 1.

40. Boldyrev, *Mery*, p. 135.

41. See L.A. Kliuchinskaia and L.A. Bergere, *Nesovershennoletnie i ugolovnyi zakon* (Riga, Izdatel'stvo "Zinatne," 1967), p. 57. The index numbers they give show a significant rise in the absolute numbers of juvenile cases terminated with remand to a commission or to the public and suggest that, unless the total number of juvenile cases almost doubled between 1961 and 1965, the percentage of remanded cases among all cases must have approached 50 percent in 1964–1965.

42. Min'kovskii, "Nekotorye voprosy," p. 29.

43. Article 21, CC RSFSR. Berman and Spindler, *Codes*, p. 151.

44. M.M. Babaev, *Individualizatsiia nakazaniia nesovershennoletnikh* (Moscow, "Iuridicheskaia literatura," 1968), p. 84.

45. *Ibid.*, p. 89.   46. *Ibid.*, p. 88.

47. Article 24, CC RSFSR. Berman and Spindler, *Codes*, p. 153.

48. Article 55, CC RSFSR. Berman and Spindler, *Codes*, pp. 172–73.

49. See Kliuchinskaia and Bergere, *Nesovershennoletnie*, pp. 177–78; also Iu. Solopanov, A. Natashev, Iu. Gerbeev, V. Marchenko, and L. Zakharov, "Pochemu maloeffektivnyi TKN," *K novoi zhizni*, No. 10 (1967), p. 23.

50. "Sistema perevoda iz trudovykh kolonii dlia nesovershennoletnikh dolzhna byt' izmenena," *S.Iu.*, No. 4 (1968), p. 22.

51. Kliuchinskaia and Bergere, *Nesovershennoletnie*, p. 168. The small size of the

sample is obviously unsatisfactory, and the results must be viewed in this light. Undersized samples in this study and others were criticized by a noted scholar in the corrections field. See I. Shmarov, "Metodika sotsiologicheskikh issledovanii v ITU," *K novoi zhizni*, No. 12 (1966), p. 57. Also, a study conducted in Leningrad in December, 1964, of juveniles released from TKN's during 1963 showed that only three percent of those released had served their full sentences. See N.P. Grabovskaia, "Ob effektivnosti mer, primeniaemykh k nesovershennoletnim pravonarushiteliam," in *Vosprosy izucheniia* (Vol. 2), p. 73.

52. Solopanov et al., "Pochemu," p. 22.   53. *Ibid.*

54. A recent detailed work on the structure and operations of labor colonies refers to the practice of massive early release and gives the impression that it is practiced almost automatically. See Z.A. Astemirov, *Trudovaia koloniia dlia nesovershennoletnikh,* hereafter *TKN* (Moscow, "Iuridicheskaia literatura," 1969), pp. 91–93.

55. See *ibid.,* pp. 6–24, for a short historical review of the development of Soviet institutions for juveniles.

56. From 1935 on, the colonies functioned successively under five different statutes. In 1956, a new statute, more detailed in character it seems, was adopted but remained unpublished. This statute was superseded by the 1968 published statute. *Ibid.,* pp. 19, 22.

57. *Vedomosti Verkhovnogo Soveta SSSR,* No. 23 (June 5, 1968), pp. 313–25; translated in *CDSP,* July 3, 1968, pp. 3–7. Referred to hereafter as *Statute.*

58. Before 1968, four types of colony existed: TKN's of a "standard type" for males convicted of less serious offenses; TKN's of "standard type" for males convicted of serious offenses; TKN's for female offenders, and TKN's "with a strict regime" for males who committed serious crimes or maliciously violated the regime rules in the standard TKN's.

59. The statute also permits, if circumstances warrant, the establishment of special colonies for older juveniles. Article 11, *Statute,* p. 3.

60. Astemirov, *TKN,* p. 26.   61. Article 3, *Statute,* p. 3.

62. Article 4, *Statute,* p. 3.   63. Astemirov, *TKN,* p. 46.

64. One finds it necessary to qualify rather carefully any statements about actual life within the TKN's, since problems of gaining access to these and other penal institutions are so great. Foreigners have gained access, but only rarely. It is the author's strong impression that access becomes more probable when (1) the visitor does not speak Russian; (2) when his stay in the USSR is of relatively short duration; and (3) when he can present himself not as one especially interested in *Soviet* correctional practice, but as having a general interest in the field. (The author himself, during an extended stay in the USSR, made application to visit either a juvenile or adult colony. The application was rejected) For the observations of foreign visitors, see John P. Conrad, *Crime and Its Correction: An International Survey of Attitudes and Practices* (Berkeley and Los Angeles, University of California Press, 1967), pp. 166–68; Harriett Wilson, "A Visit to the U.S.S.R.: Some Observations on a Visit to an Educational Colony, a Labour Col-

ony, and a Remand Home for Young Delinquents," *British Journal of Criminology*, I (July, 1960), 69–73.

65. Astemirov, *TKN*, p. 48.   66. *Ibid.*, pp. 55–56.

67. Article 30, *Statute*, p. 5.   68. Astemirov, *TKN*, pp. 56–57.

69. Article 4, *Statute*, p. 3.

70. Astemirov, *TKN*, p. 75. Anton S. Makarenko (1888–1939) gained fame through his writings on education and child-rearing, and his organization, in the years following the Civil War, of homes ("communes," "colonies") for homeless and delinquent children. A great deal of the emphasis on the *kollektiv*, the individual's place in it, and its use as an instrument of socialization proceeds from his writings, some of which are available in English. See *The Road to Life* (3 vols., Moscow, Foreign Languages Publishing House, 1955); *Learning to Live* (Moscow, Foreign Languages Publishing House, 1953). For a general study of his ideas and works, see James Bowen, *Soviet Education: Anton Makarenko and the Years of Experiment* (Madison and Milwaukee, University of Wisconsin Press, 1962).

71. Astemirov, *TKN*, p. 80.   72. *Ibid.*, p. 70.   73. *Ibid.*, p. 71.

74. *Ibid.*, pp. 72–73.   75. *Ibid.*, p. 82.   76. *Ibid.*, p. 83.

77. *Ibid.*, pp. 57–58.

78. One of the most interesting aspects of this Soviet idea is its similarity to some American thought on the same topic. Using inmates as active agents in the reform of other inmates is a common element. Where Soviet sources are less informative is on their ideas of what happens to such an "agent"—is he already presumed well on the road to reform, or will his experience as reformer result indirectly in changes in his own attitudes in a reform direction. The American version favors the latter idea: inmate A, in attempting to reform inmate B, will *himself* be the more affected, and B will be more affected as he participates in attempts to reform inmate C. This is, of course, a very general statement of the ideas involved. For fuller exposition of the ideas and their application, see Donald R. Cressey, "Changing Criminals: The Application of the Theory of Differential Association," *American Journal of Sociology*, LXI (September, 1955), 116–20; and Lamar T. Empey and Jerome Rabow, "The Provo Experiment in Delinquency Rehabilitation," *American Sociological Review*, XXVI (October, 1961), 679–95.

79. Considerations of space and the main focus of the description have precluded any lengthy consideration of the structure of colony administration in the text. Descriptions may be found in the official corrective-labor law textbook, published under the auspices of the Higher School of the RSFSR Ministry for the Maintenance of Public Order (MOOP—since renamed MVD, Ministry of Internal Affairs), *Ispravitel'no-trudovoe pravo* (Moscow: "Iuridicheskaia literatura," 1966), pp. 241–45. Additional information appears in Astemirov, *TKN*, pp. 87–90.

80. Astemirov, *TKN*, p. 59.

81. *Ibid.* At one point, Astemirov writes that "3–4" divisions make up a detachment; at another on the same page, that it takes "4–5."

82. In the TKN near Leningrad which Conrad visited, the commandant gave a figure of 391 inmates, in four detachments of 100 each. Each detachment was broken down into units of around 25. This is in line with Soviet descriptions in general, and suggests that Astemirov's figures (note 81 above) should be "averaged" to four divisions per detachment. Conrad, *Crime and Its Correction*, p. 166.

83. Astemirov, *TKN*, pp. 62–63.

84. *Ibid.*, p. 65. Kliuchinskaia and Bergere, in *Nesovershennoletnie*, p. 138, make this clear. "Candidates for commission membership are selected by the *vospitately*, teachers and instructors in production training together with the division councils of inmates. These candidates are recommended by the division meetings for selection to the general meeting of colony inmates."

85. Astemirov, *TKN*, p. 64.   86. "Sistema perevoda," p. 22.

87. L. Perov, "Malye gruppy v sledstvennom izoliatore," *K novoi zhizni*, No. 10 (1968), p. 58.

88. Astemirov, *TKN*, pp. 47–48.   89. *Ibid.*, p. 61.   90. *Ibid.*

91. See Solopanov et al., "Pochemu," pp. 22–23.

92. Complete turnover was reported in a colony in Cheliabinsk *oblast'* in the 1964–1965 school year. See *ibid.*, p. 23. Turnover in one Latvian colony reportedly reached 90 percent. Kliuchinskaia and Bergere, *Nesovershennoletnie*, p. 134.

93. See Solopanov et al., "Pochemu," p. 23. From the authors' sample data, 14.8 percent of a group of inmates reaching 18 wished to be transferred to an adult colony. Of these, one-third elected this course in the hope of less "discipline"—including the hope that "they won't make me study."

94. I. Morgunov, "Trud v soedinenii s obucheniem—vazhnoe uslovie ispravleniia nesovershennoletnikh pravonarushitelei," *SZ*, No. 11 (1966), p. 53.

95. Solopanov et al., "Pochemu," p. 23.   96. Astemirov, *TKN*, pp. 72–73.

97. Kliuchinskaia and Bergere, *Nesovershennoletnie*, pp. 130–31.

98. "Sistema perevoda," p. 21.

99. *Pravda*, July 4, 1965, p. 6; translated in *CDSP*, July 28, 1965, pp. 18–19.

100. See, e.g., the article by the then RSFSR Minister for the Maintenance of Public Order, V.S. Tikunov, "Polnoe iskorenenie beznadzornosti i prestupnosti—vazhneishaia zadacha organov okhrany obshchestvennogo poriadka," *SGIP*, No. 4 (1964), p. 30.

101. Astemirov, *TKN*, pp. 113–14.   102. *Ibid.*, pp. 101–102.

103. *Ibid.*, pp. 102–103.

104. See, e.g., Iu. Gerbeev, "Nasushchnye problemy," *K novoi zhizni*, No. 7 (1965), p. 63, and Kliuchinskaia and Bergere, *Nesovershennoletnie*, p. 159.

105. *Ispravitel'no-trudovoe pravo*, p. 239.

106. Kliuchinskaia and Bergere, *Nesovershennoletnie*, p. 159.

107. N. Gus'kov, "Novoe polozhenie o trudovykh koloniiakh dlia nesovershennoletnikh," *SZ*, No. 9 (1968), p. 26. Astemirov, *TKN*, p. 68, does mention them.

It is possible that such colonies did not exist in all republics, since not all republics have the full range of institutions. *Ibid.*, p. 39.

108. See Astemirov, *TKN*, p. 68.   109. *Ibid.*, pp. 68–69.   110. *Ibid.*, p. 69.

111. Babaev, *Individualizatsiia*, p. 96.   112. Solopanov et al., "Pochemu," p. 22.

113. K. Prikhod'ko, "Trudovaia koloniia—a potom?" *S.Iu.*, No. 1 (1966), pp. 19–20.

114. L.A. Kliuchinskaia, "Rol' komissii po delam nesovershennoletnikh v preduprezhdenii povtornykh pravonarushenii," in *Uchenye zapiski*, vyp. LVI (Latviiskii gosudarstvennyi universitet, Riga, 1964), 148.

115. Kliuchinskaia and Bergere, *Nesovershennoletnie*, p. 170.

116. A.P. Safonov, "O retsidive prestuplenii, sovershennykh litsami, otbyvshimi lishenie svobody," *SGIP*, No. 3 (1967), p. 107.

117. Solopanov et al., "Pochemu," p. 23.

118. V.V. Stashis and A.V. Senchin, "Opyt obsledovaniia nesovershennoletnikh prestupnikov, otbyvaiushchikh nakazanie za povtornoe prestuplenie," *Voprosy bor'by s prestupnost'iu*, vyp. 10 (1969), p. 137.

119. Kliuchinskaia, "Rol' komissii," p. 156.

120. K. Prikhod'ko, "Uslovnoe osuzhdenie i preduprezhdenie retsidivnoi prestupnosti nesovershennoletnikh," *S.Iu.*, No. 10 (1967), p. 18.

121. Article 52, CC RSFSR. Berman and Spindler, *Codes*, pp. 169–70.

122. Prikhod'ko, "Uslovnoe osuzhdenie," p. 18.

123. K. Prikhod'ko, "Uluchshit' organizatsiiu sudebnogo kontrolia za perevospitaniem uslovno osuzhdennykh nesovershennoletnikh," *S.Iu.*, No. 16 (1968), p. 20. See also Stashis and Senchin, "Opyt obsledovaniia," p. 138. Of the latter's group, only 10 percent of the conditionally sentenced had been committed to public custody.

124. Prikhod'ko, "Uluchshit'," p. 20.

125. Lack of such aid is sorely felt, since many factory managers are understandably reluctant to hire young ex-cons. See *Izvestiia*, June 26, 1965, p. 3; translated in *CDSP*, July 21, 1965, pp. 30–31.

126. Prikhod'ko, "Trudovaia koloniia," pp. 19–20, and (editorial) "Komsomol i bor'ba s pravonarusheniiami," *S.Iu.*, No. 19 (1968), p. 3.

127. Article 13, *Statute*, pp. 3–4.

128. Kliuchinskaia and Bergere, *Nesovershennoletnie*, p. 175.

129. Wilson, "A Visit to the U.S.S.R.," p. 72.

130. See, e.g., Astemirov, *TKN*, pp. 34–35.

Chapter 8
CRIME AND THE CRIMINAL OFFENDER

1. Provisions of the RSFSR Criminal Code covering "economic crimes" can be found in Berman and Spindler, *Codes* (see chapter 7, note 18), pp. 204–10. For "official crimes," see *ibid.*, pp. 210–13; for crimes against the system of justice, pp. 213–17; and for crimes against the system of administration, pp. 217–23.

2. *Kriminologiia* (2d ed.; Moscow, "Iuridicheskaia literatura," 1968), p. 117. If the table is a complete one with regard to all types of crime, then the categories (listed in the RSFSR Code) of state crimes, military crimes, and crimes "constituting survivals of local customs" must be included in the "other crimes" category. Whether this is in fact the case, we cannot tell.

3. N.N. Kondrashkov, "Analiz raionnoi statistiki prestupnosti," *Voprosy preduprezhdeniia prestupnosti*, vyp. 4 (1966), 39. In Lida *raion*, Grodno *oblast'*, in the Belorussian SSR, in 1963, "illegal distilling" made up more than one-third of all registered crimes.

4. See, e.g., I.I. Karpets, *Problema prestupnosti* (Moscow, "Iuridicheskaia literatura," 1969), p. 125.

5. A.A. Gertsenzon, *Ugolovnoe pravo i sotsiologiia* (Moscow, "Iuridicheskaia literatura," 1970), p. 77.

6. L.A. Andreeva and G.A. Levitskii, "Obstoiatel'stva, sposobstvuiushchie khishcheniiam (Opyt vyiavleniia obschchestvennogo mneniia)," *SGIP*, No. 11 (1969), p. 105.

7. See S.S. Ostroumov and V.E. Chugunov, "Izuchenie lichnosti prestupnika po materialam kriminologicheskikh issledovanii," *SGIP*, No. 9 (1965), pp. 93–102; translated in *Soviet Review*, VII (Summer, 1966), p. 15 for the Black Earth region data. In 1966, according to data from the Institute of Criminology in Moscow, men made up 87.8 percent of all those convicted of crimes. S.S. Ostroumov, *Sovetskaia sudebnaia statistika* (Moscow, Izdatel'stvo Moskovskogo universiteta, 1970), p. 141.

8. *Kriminologiia* (2d ed.), pp. 414–15.

9. V.N. Roshchin and M.P. Lashin, "K voprosu ob izuchenii prestupnosti," *SGIP*, No. 7 (1960), p. 169.

10. *Kriminologiia* (2d ed.), p. 407.   11. *Ibid.*, p. 442.   12. *Ibid.*, p. 429.

13. *Ibid.*, p. 383.

14. See Roshchin and Lashin, "K voprosu," and I.S. Noi, *Teoreticheskie voprosy lisheniia svobody* (Saratov, Izdatel'stvo Saratovskogo universiteta, 1965), p. 11.

15. I.M. Gal'perin, "Ob ugolovnoi otvetstvennosti retsidivistov v svete nekotorykh kriminologicheskikh pokazatelei effektivnosti bor'by s retsidivnoi prestupnost'iu,"

in B.S. Nikiforov, ed., *Effektivnost' ugolovnopravovykh mer bor'by s prestup-nost'iu* (Moscow, "Iuridicheskaia literatura," 1968), p. 244.

16. M.I. Kovalev, "Issledovanie obrazovatel'nogo urovnia prestupnikov," *SGIP*, No. 2 (1968), p. 91.

17. See Ostroumov and Chugunov, "Izuchenie lichnosti prestupnika," *passim.*

18. *Ibid.*, p. 17.   19. *Kriminologiia* (2d ed.), p. 410.

20. Noi, *Teoreticheskie voprosy*, p. 18.   21. *Ibid.*, p. 19.

22. Reported in S.S. Ostroumov, *Sovetskaia sudebnaia statistika* (3d ed.; Moscow, Izdatel'stvo Moskovskogo universiteta, 1962), p. 268.

23. *Kriminologiia* (2d ed.), p. 116.

24. See *Izvestiia*, May 19, 1966, p. 5, and *Sovetskaia Rossiia*, May 21, 1966, p. 2.

25. For an interesting attempt which clearly demonstrates the formidable problems in making such estimates see H. Kent Geiger, "Tables for 'Statistical Aspects of Crime and Delinquency in the USSR' " (Presented at Midwest Slavic Conference, March 25–26, 1966. Mimeographed.) For an estimate of the number of criminal cases tried in court in a single year (1964) see Robert Conquest, ed., *Justice and the Legal System in the USSR* (New York, Praeger, 1968), p. 133 n.

26. The discussion which follows is based largely on Karpets' contributions to *Kriminologiia* (2d ed.), pp. 120–24, and his *Problema prestupnosti*, pp. 51 ff.

27. Karpets, *Problema prestupnosti*, p. 52.   28. *Ibid.*, p. 65.

29. *Ibid.*, p. 66.

30. See, e.g., I.S. Noi, "Lichnost' prestupnika i ee znachenie v izuchenii prestupnosti v usloviiakh sotsialisticheskogo obshchestva," in Saratovskii iuridicheskii institut, *Uchenye zapiski*, vyp. XVI (Voprosy ugolovnogo i ispravitel'no-trudovogo prava, ugolovnogo protsessa i kriminalistiki, Saratov, 1969), 8–10.

31. *Kriminologiia* (2d ed.), p. 124.

32. V.N. Kudriavtsev, "K voprosu ob izuchenii prichin prestunosti," *SGIP*, No. 5 (1964), pp. 12–18.

33. S.S. Ostroumov, "Chto takoe kriminologiia?," *Vestnik vysshei shkoly*, No. 5 (1965), p. 47.

34. For more treatment of these and related issues, see Robert J. Osborn, "Crime and the Environment: The New Soviet Debate," *Slavic Review*, XXVII (September, 1968), 395–410.

35. Karpets, *Problema prestupnosti*, p. 53.

36. See, e.g., A.S. Shliapochnikov, "O klassifikatsii obstoiatel'stv, sposobst-vuiushchikh soversheniiu prestuplenii," *SGIP*, No. 10 (1964), pp. 91–100, and the comment on it in Osborn, "Crime and the Environment," pp. 398–99.

37. V. Zvirbul', V. Kudriavtsev, A. Mikhailov, R. Rakhunov, and N. Iakubovich, *Vyiavlenie prichin prestupleniia i priniatie predupreditel'nykh mer po ugolov-nomu delu* (Moscow, "Iuridicheskaia literatura," 1967), p. 6.

38. *Kriminologiia* (2d ed.), p. 127.

39. *Ibid.*, p. 128. 40. *Ibid.*, p. 128. 41. *Ibid.*, p. 126.

42. Karpets, *Problema prestupnosti*, p. 55.

43. "Antiobshchestvennye iavleniia, ikh prichiny i sredstva bor'by s nim," *Kommunist*, No. 12 (1966), pp. 58–68; translated in *CDSP*, September 28, 1966, pp. 9–11.

44. *Kriminologiia* (2d ed.), p. 130.

45. E.B. Mel'nikova, *Prestupnost' nesovershennoletnikh v kapitalisticheskikh stranakh* (Moscow, "Iurdicheskaia literatura," 1967), p. 145.

46. For a general review of Soviet evaluations of Western criminological theories, and their application to crime in the capitalist countries see Walter D. Connor, "Deviant Behavior in Capitalist Society—The Soviet Image," *Journal of Criminal Law, Criminology, and Police Science*, LXI (December, 1970), 554–64.

47. M.M. Babaev, "Kriminologicheskie aspekty migratsii naseleniia," *SGIP*, No. 9 (1968), p. 89.

48. *Ibid.*, p. 89. 49. *Ibid.*, p. 90.

50. See, e.g., I. Shmarov, Iu. Utevskii, and I. Iakovlev, "Izuchenie lichnosti prestupnika i naznachenie nakazaniia," *SZ*, No. 10 (1958), pp. 14–16; M. Korshik, "Izuchenie lichnosti obvinaemogo na predvaritel'nom i sudebnom sledstvii," *SZ*, No. 11 (1958), pp. 11–14; and S. Stepichev, "Formy i metody izucheniia lichnosti prestupnika," *SZ*, No. 8 (1960), pp. 76–79.

51. A.B. Sakharov, *O lichnosti prestupnika i prichinakh prestupnosti v SSSR* (Moscow, "Iuridicheskaia literatura," 1961).

52. *Ibid.*, pp. 174–75. 53. *Ibid.*, p. 174, n. 1. 54. *Ibid.*, p. 176.

55. *Ibid.*, pp. 178–79. 56. *Ibid.*, p. 180. 57. *Ibid.*, p. 183.

58. *Ibid.*, p. 181. 59. *Ibid.* 60. *Ibid.*, pp. 184–88. 61. *Ibid.*, p. 190.

62. *Ibid.*, p. 189.

63. N.S. Leikina, "Vlianie lichnostnykh osobennostei na prestupnost'," *SGIP*, No. 1 (1967), p. 103.

64. A.A. Gertsenzon, *Vvedenie v sovetskuiu kriminologiiu* (Moscow, "Iuridicheskaia literatura," 1965), p. 133.

65. Personal conversation with Gertsenzon (1969).

66. See A.M. Iakovlev, "Sotsial'naia effektivnost' ugolovnogo zakona," *SGIP*, No. 10 (1967), pp. 55–63; A.M. Iakovlev, "Sotsial'naia psikhologiia i protivopravnoe povedenie," *SGIP*, No. 7 (1968), pp. 50–59, and K.E. Igoshev, "Kriminologicheskoe znachenie protivorechii v formirovanii lichnosti," *SGIP*, No. 9 (1969), pp. 49–58.

67. See Sakharov's "Teoreticheskie voprosy izucheniia o lichnosti prestupnika," *SZ*, No. 7 (1967), pp. 26–30.

68. A.B. Sakharov, "Uchenie o lichnosti prestupnika," *SGIP*, No. 9 (1968), p. 66.

69. See, e.g., Karpets, *Problema prestupnosti*, pp. 83 ff.

70. I.S. Noi and L.G. Krakhmal'nik, "K voprosu o perevospitanii i ispravlenii

zakliuchennykh," in *Nauchnaia konferentsiia po voprosam sovetskogo ispraviteľ no-trudovogo prava, tezisy dokladov i soobshchenii* (Saratov, 1958), p. 2, cited in L.V. Il'ina, "Iz istorii razvitiia sovetskoi kriminologii," *Voprosy bor'by s prestupnost'iu*, vyp. 7 (1968), p. 29.

71. "Voprosy profilaktiki prestupnosti v SSSR" (Conference report), *SGIP*, No. 7 (1960), p. 184. Noi, along with L.G. Krakhmal'nik, was criticized at this conference (held in Leningrad) by V.N. Kudriavtsev and M.D. Shargorodskii, the former arguing that the causes of crime were "of a social, and not biological, character," and rejecting the idea that persons whose psyches "deviated from the norm," could be seen as having "reduced responsibility." *Ibid.*, pp. 185–86.

72. L.G. Krakhmal'nik and I.S. Noi, "O profilaktike prestuplenii psikhopatov," in *Sbornik nauchnykh rabot Saratovskogo otdeleniia Vsesoiuznogo obshchestva sudebnykh medikov i kriminalistov*, vyp. 3 (1961), 261–62.

73. *Ibid.*, p. 262, citing N.P. Brukhanskii, *Sudebnaia psikhiatriia* (Moscow, 1928), p. 279.

74. *Ibid.*, cited V.M. Gakkebush and I.A. Zalkind, *Sudebnaia psikhopatiia* (Kharkov, 1928), p. 358.

75. *Ibid.*, citing A.M. Iakovlev, "Perevospitanie opasnykh retsidivistov," in *Voprosy ispraviteľno-trudovogo prava: Sbornik statei*, II (Moscow, 1958), 176.

76. *Ibid.*, citing N.S. Khrushchev, *Sluzhenie narodu—vysokoe prizvanie sovetskikh pisatelei* (Moscow, "Gospolitizdat," 1959), p. 19. Sakharov also used a similar statement by Khrushchev, presumably to add validation to his choice of subject matter from an "authoritative" source. *O lichnosti prestupnika*, p. 173, n. 1.

77. I.S. Noi, *Voprosy teorii nakazaniia v sovetskom ugolovnom prave* (Saratov, Izdateľ'stvo Saratovskogo universiteta, 1962), pp. 137–40.

78. Il'ina, "Iz istorii," p. 30.

79. I.S. Noi, V.A. Shabalin, and Iu. A. Demidov, "O rasshirenii nauchnoi osnovy izucheniia lichnosti prestupnika," in *Tezisy dokladov i soobshchenii na mezhvuzskoi konferentsii po teoreticheskim i metodologicheskim problemam pravovoi nauki* (Kishinev, 1965), p. 214, cited in N.S. Leikina, "Vlianie lichnostnykh osobennostei na prestupnost'," *SGIP*, No. 1 (1967), p. 104.

80. *Ibid.*, p. 215, cited in V.N. Kudriavtsev, "Sotsial'naia obuslovlennost' prestupnogo povedeniia i rol' biologicheskikh faktorov," *SZ*, No. 6 (1967), p. 46.

81. *Ibid.*, p. 215, cited in N.A. Struchkov, "O mekhanizme vzaimnogo vliianiia obstoiatel'stv, obuslovlivaiushchikh sovershenie prestuplenii," *SGIP*, No. 10 (1966), p. 113.

82. I.I. Karpets, "O prirode i prichinakh prestupnosti v SSSR," *SGIP*, No. 4 (1966); translated in *Soviet Law and Government*, V (Summer, 1966), 53.

83. Reported in "Voprosy profilaktiki" (Conference report), p. 185.

84. Kudriavtsev, "Sotsial'naia obuslovlennost'," pp. 46–47.

85. "Vo vsesoiuznom institute po izucheniiu prichin i razrabotke mer preduprezhdeniia prestupnosti," *SGIP*, No. 5 (1964), pp. 148–49.

86. *Izvestiia,* January 26, 1967, p. 4.

87. See, e.g., V. Ledashchev, "Protiv biologizatsii prichin prestupnosti," *S.Iu.,* No. 1 (1968), pp. 13–14.

88. Struchkov, "O mekhanizme," p. 113.

89. *Literaturnaia gazeta,* November 29, 1967, p. 12; translated in *CDSP,* December 27, 1967, pp. 3–5.

90. *Izvestiia,* July 18, 1968, p. 5; translated in *CDSP,* August 7, 1968, pp. 24–25.

91. Karpets, *Problema prestupnosti,* pp. 30–31.   92. *Ibid.,* p. 33.

93. I.S. Noi, "Lichnost' prestupnika i ee znachenie v izuchenii prestupnosti v usloviiakh sotsialisticheskogo obshchestva," in Saratovskii iuridicheskii institut, *Uchenye zapiski,* vyp. XVI (Voprosy ugolovnogo i ispravitel'no-trudovogo prava, ugolovnogo protsessa i kriminalistiki, Saratov, 1969), 10. A somewhat similar complaint, about the "vulgar sociologization of the personality," had come from K. Platonov, a psychologist who deals with correctional problems (and one of those Noi claims as a supporter of his views). See "Lichnost' i nakazanie," *K novoi zhizni,* No. 5 (1966), p. 52.

94. Noi, "Lichnost' prestupnika," p. 17.   95. *Ibid.,* pp. 14–15.

96. *Ibid.,* p. 23.

97. In Italy and some Latin American countries, the idea of criminals as distinct physical types still has some currency. In the United States in (relatively) recent times, research along "morphological" lines has been conducted by Ernest A. Hooton (*Crime and the Man* [Cambridge, Harvard University Press, 1939]); William H. Sheldon (*Varieties of Delinquent Youth* [New York, Harper, 1949]); and Sheldon and Eleanor T. Glueck (*Physique and Delinquency* [New York, Harper, 1956]). In more recent times, little such work has been done—although recent attention to human chromosomes and their potential effects shows that interest in the linkage between biology and criminality is not entirely dead. See Stephen Schafer, *Theories in Criminology* (New York, Random House, 1969), pp. 191–94.

98. Karpets, *Problema prestupnosti,* pp. 38–39.

99. See report of Kudriavtsev's remarks in "Genetika cheloveka, ee filosofskie i sotsial'no-eticheskie problemy," *Voprosy filosofii,* No. 8 (1970), p. 131.

100. Donald R. Cressey, "Crime," in Robert K. Merton and Robert A. Nisbet, eds., *Contemporary Social Problems* (2d ed., New York, Harcourt, Brace & World, 1966), p. 163.

101. See Karpets, *Problema prestupnosti,* p. 32, and Ledashchev, "Protiv biologizatsii," p. 14. See also N.S. Leikina, *Lichnost' prestupnika i ugolovnaia otvetstvennost'* (Leningrad, Izdatel'stvo Leningradskogo universiteta, 1968), pp. 19–20.

102. Karpets, *Problema prestupnosti,* p. 81.

103. Ledashchev, "Protiv biologizatsii," p. 14.

104. On the principles of Soviet forensic psychiatry, see Harold J. Berman, *Justice in the U.S.S.R.* (Cambridge, Harvard University Press, 1963), pp. 312–29.

105. *Kriminologiia* (1st ed.; 1966), p. 90.

Chapter 9
CRIME PREVENTION AND
CRIMINAL CORRECTION

1. *Kriminologiia* (1st ed.; Moscow, "Iuridicheskaia literatura," 1966), pp. 113–14.

2. See *ibid.*, pp. 114–19, and *Kriminologiia* (2nd ed., 1968), pp. 170–78. A detailed summary of crime prevention activities and agencies is available in P.P. Mikhailenko and I.A. Gel'fand, *Preduprezhdenie prestuplenii—osnova bor'by za iskorenenie prestupnosti* (Moscow, "Iuridicheskaia literatura," 1964).

3. Article 63, CC RSFSR. Berman and Spindler, *Codes*, pp. 177–78 (see chapter 7, note 18).

4. *Kriminologiia* (1st ed.), p. 117.

5. For a brief summary of the subdivisions of the militia, see Robert Conquest, ed., *The Soviet Police System* (New York and Washington, Praeger, 1968), pp. 30–32.

6. *Ibid.*, p. 75.   7. *Ibid.*, pp. 62–63.   8. *Ibid.*, p. 64.

9. Robert Conquest, ed., *Justice and the Legal System in the USSR* (New York and Washington, Praeger, 1968), p. 121, citing *Partiinaia zhizn'*, No. 20 (1965), p. 20.

10. *Izvestiia*, April 21, 1966.

11. Soviet books and pamphlets for and about the *druzhinniki* give more detail on expectations and demands imposed on them. See, e.g., the handbook *Spravochnik druzhinnika* (Moscow, Gosudarstvennoe izdatel'stvo iuridicheskoi literatury, 1961); B.N. Tsvetkov, *Eto nuzhno znat' druzhinniku* (Leningrad, "Lenizdat," 1962); N.V. Dement'ev and G.M. Sergeev, *Tebe, tovarishch druzhinnik!* (Moscow, "Profizdat," 1961); A.I. Sokolov and Iu.M. Osipov, *Khoziaeva poriadka* (Leningrad, "Lenizdat," 1963). See also Dennis M. O'Connor, "Soviet People's Guards: An Experiment with Civic Police," *N.Y.U. Law Review*, XXXIX (June, 1964), 579–614.

12. As an institution, the *druzhina* is far from defunct: but official writings on law enforcement in the post-Khrushchev years have tended toward a greater emphasis on the role of professionals, and less on the role of auxiliaries. It seems very unlikely that the powers or operational scope of the *druzhinnik* will be notably expanded in the near future.

13. For a detailed treatment of the comrades' courts, see Albert Boiter, "Comradely Justice: How Durable Is It?" *Problems of Communism*, XIV (March–April, 1965), 82–92.

14. Conquest, ed., *Justice*, p. 117, citing *Sovetskaia Rossiia*, October 24, 1963.

15. One source complains of sessions "still" not taking place in auditoriums that can accommodate large numbers of people. Iu.A. Sokolov, *Uchastie trud-*

iashchikhsia v okhrane sovetskogo obshchestvennogo poriadka (Moscow, Gosudarstvennoe izdatel'stvo iuridicheskoi literatury, 1962), p. 155. General advice on how the work of the comrades' court should be conducted, its competence, etc. is given in K. Iudel'son, *Polozhenie o tovarishcheskikh sudakh: prakticheskii kommentarii* (Moscow, Gosudarstvennoe izdatel'stvo iuridicheskoi literatury, 1962). A more recent work is I.B. Mikhailovskaia, *Kommentarii k polozheniiu o tovarishcheskikh sudakh RSFSR* (Moscow, "Iuridicheskaia literatura," 1968).

16. The Western literature on the antiparasite laws is comparatively rich. See Leon Lipson, "The Future Belongs to . . . Parasites?" *Problems of Communism,* XII (May–June, 1963), 1–9; by the same author, "Hosts and Pests: The Fight against Parasites," *Problems of Communism,* XIV (March–April, 1965), 72–82. See also the series of articles by R. Beerman, all in *Soviet Studies* (Glasgow): "A Discussion of the Draft Law against Parasites, Tramps and Beggars," IX (October, 1957), 214–22; "The Law against Parasites, Tramps and Beggars," XI (April, 1960), 453–55; "The Parasites Law," XIII (October, 1961), 191–205; "Soviet and Russian Anti-Parasite Laws," XV (April, 1964), 420–29; and "The 'Anti-Parasite' Law of the RSFSR Modified," XVII (January, 1966), 387–88.

17. Lipson, "Hosts and Pests," p. 78.

18. Beerman, "Soviet and Russian Anti-Parasite Laws," p. 425.

19. See the Soviet Supreme Court's order of March 18, 1963 (No. 3): *Biulleten' Verkhovnogo Suda SSSR,* No. 3 (1963), translated in *Soviet Law and Government,* II (Winter, 1963–64), pp. 48–50.

20. *Komsomol'skaia pravda,* August 29, 1962, p. 4; translated in *CDSP,* September 19, 1962, p. 17.

21. *Vedomosti Verkhovnogo Soveta RSFSR,* No. 38 (September 23, 1965), pp. 737–39; translated in *CDSP,* November 24, 1965, p. 13.

22. Beerman, "Anti-Parasite Law . . . Modified," p. 388.

23. Article 10, CCP RSFSR. Berman and Spindler, *Codes,* p. 256.

24. Article 51, CC RSFSR. *Ibid.,* pp. 168–69. Also Article 7, CCP RSFSR. *Ibid.,* pp. 254–55.

25. Article 52, CC RSFSR. *Ibid.,* p. 169. Also Article 9, CCP RSFSR. *Ibid.,* pp. 255–56.

26. Article 21, CC RSFSR. *Ibid.,* p. 151.

27. Article 23, CC RSFSR. *Ibid.,* p. 152.

28. Article 44, CC RSFSR. *Ibid.,* pp. 164–65.

29. Article 43, CC RSFSR. *Ibid.,* p. 164.

30. N. Kondrashkov, "Mery nakazaniia v zakone i na praktike," SZ, No. 2 (1968), pp. 24–25. See also M.M. Babaev, *Individualizatsiia nakazaniia nesovershennoletnikh* (Moscow, "Iuridicheskaia literatura," 1968), p. 84.

31. Kondrashkov, "Mery nakazaniia," p. 23.   32. *Ibid.,* pp. 24–25.

33. Babaev, *Individualizatsiia,* p. 84.

34. A.S. Mikhlin et al., "Effektivnost' ispravitel'nykh rabot kak mery nakazaniia," in B.S. Nikiforov, ed., *Effektivnost' ugolovnopravovykh mer bor'by s prestupnost'iu* (Moscow, "Iuridicheskaia literatura," 1968), p. 109.

35. L.G. Krakhmal'nik, "Nekotorye voprosy pravovogo regulirovaniia ispravitel'nykh rabot bez lisheniia svobody," *SGIP*, No. 4 (1965), p. 130.

36. I.I. Karpets, "Nakazanie v sovetskom ugolovnom prave," *SGIP*, No. 9 (1967), p. 65.

37. See T.L. Sergeeva and L.F. Pomchalov, "Effektivnost' kratkosrochnogo lisheniia svobody," in Nikiforov, ed., *Effektivnost' ugolovnopravovykh mer*, p. 33, n. 1.

38. G.Z. Anashkin, "O zadachakh i tendentsiiakh razvitiia satsialisticheskogo pravosudiia," *Vestnik Moskovskogo universiteta* (series XII, law), No. 4 (1966), p. 6.

39. N.F. Kuznetsova, *Prestuplenie i prestupnost'* (Moscow, Izdatel'stvo Moskovskogo universiteta, 1969), p. 196. Kuznetsova reproduces Anashkin's figure for 1965, and *seems* to cite Anashkin for her 1960 and 1966 figures; but the latter two do not appear in Anashkin's article. (Nor, of course, *could* the 1966 figure appear, since Anashkin's article was published before the year was over.)

40. For a historical summary, see I.A. Bushuev, *Ispravitel'nye raboty* (Moscow, "Iuridicheskaia literatura," 1968), pp. 3–37.

41. Article 27, CC RSFSR. Berman and Spindler, *Codes*, pp. 156–57.

42. Mikhlin et al., "Effektivnost'," p. 99.   43. *Ibid.*, pp. 120–21.

44. Bushuev, *Ispravitel'nye raboty*, p. 80.

45. *Ibid.*, p. 81. As usual, the total number of cases studied is not given. Bushuev only notes that the materials are taken from "researches, conducted by scientific workers of the institute [the Institute of Criminology in Moscow], using official data of judicial statistics." P. 79, n. 2.

46. Article 24, CC RSFSR. Berman and Spindler, *Codes*, pp. 152–53.

47. Sergeeva and Pomchalov, "Effektivnost' kratkosrochnogo," pp. 28–29.

48. Mikhlin et al., "Effektivnost'," p. 109.

49. Sergeeva and Pomchalov, "Effektivnost' kratkosrochnogo," pp. 29–30.

50. Mikhlin et al., "Effektivnost'," p. 95.   51. See, further, *ibid.*, pp. 96–97.

52. Krakhmal'nik, "Nekotorye voprosy," p. 130.

53. *Ugolovnoe pravo—chast' obshchaia* (Moscow, "Iuridicheskaia literatura," 1966), p. 343.

54. See G.A. Odnoletknov and A.E. Natashev, "Primenenie nakazaniia v vide ispravitel'nykh rabot bez lisheniia svobody," *SGIP*, No. 4 (1965), p. 125; and M. Zhuravlev and P. Il'in, "Za pravil'noe primenenie i ispolnenie ispravitel'nykh rabot," *SZ*, No. 5 (1964), p. 45. This problem has been a persistent one in the administration of corrective works as a criminal punishment. See J.N. Hazard, "Trends in the Soviet Treatment of Crime," *American Sociological Review* V (August, 1940), 571–72.

55. See Krakhmal'nik, "Nekotorye voprosy," p. 131, and Mikhlin et al., "Effektiv-

nost'," pp. 100–101, for some comments and proposals on modifying the "two-type" structure of corrective works.

56. Mikhlin et al., "Effektivnost'," p. 126.   57. *Ibid.*, pp. 135–36.

58. Zhuravlev and Il'in, "Za pravil'noe primenenie," p. 46.

59. Mikhlin et al., "Effektivnost'," pp. 133–34.

60. Iu. Tkachevskii, "Primenenie ispravitel'nykh rabot bez lisheniia svobody," *S.Iu.*, No. 2 (1960), pp. 54–55.

61. Mikhlin et al., "Effektivnost'," pp. 107–108. For example, two courts in Chernigov *oblast'* sentenced defendants to corrective works frequently as punishments "below the limit"—61.3 percent and 46.4 percent of *all* their corrective works sentences fit this description.

62. Mikhlin et al., "Effektivnost'," pp. 143–45.

63. For a relatively systematic treatment, see Donald R. Cressey and Witold Krassowski, "Inmate Organization and Anomie in American Prisons and Soviet Labor Camps," *Social Problems,* V (Winter, 1957–1958), pp. 217–30.

64. See Anatoly Marchenko, *My Testimony* (New York, Dutton, 1969).

65. *Pravda* and *Izvestiia,* July 12, 1969, pp. 2–3; translated in *CDSP,* August 13, 1969, pp. 3–10. Hereafter cited as *Principles,* with pagination of *CDSP* given.

66. "Colonies" and "prisons" had existed from 1958 as the two major types of detention facilities. The present four regime types were introduced in 1961, with the adoption of that year's unpublished statute, *Polozhenie ob ispravitel'no-trudovykh koloniiakh i tiurmakh Ministerstva vnutrennykh del RSFSR* (ratified by the Presidium of the RSFSR Supreme Soviet, August 29, 1961), *Vedomosti Verkhovnogo Soveta RSFSR,* No. 37 (1961), p. 556. Little more than the announcement of ratification appears in *Vedomosti.* It is interesting that the copy of the document to which the author had library access gives a ratification date of September 9 rather than August 29. The discrepancy may have involved the additional ratification of norms for food rations in an appendix to the *Polozhenie.*

67. Article 14, *Principles,* p. 4. See also the textbook *Ispravitel'no-trudovoe pravo* (Moscow, "Iuridicheskaia literatura," 1966), p. 150. Hereafter cited as *ITP.*

68. For a discussion of the characteristics of the colony-settlements published shortly after their inception, see P.E. Podymov, "Novyi shag po puti sovershenstvovaniia sovetskoi ispravitel'no-trudovoi sistemy," *SGIP,* No. 8 (1964), pp. 99–105. For a later discussion of some of the problems involved in operating these institutions, see G. Rozhnov, "Koloniia-poselenie: Zaboty i problemy," *KNZ,* No. 10 (1967), pp. 51–53. An enumeration of the "special features" of the colony-settlements as of 1969 is available in Article 20, *Principles,* p. 5.

69. Article 34, *Principles,* pp. 7–8. See also *ITP,* p. 155 and pp. 173–74.

70. Article 19, *Principles,* p. 5.

71. For a textbook account, see *ITP,* pp. 168–71.

72. The statutory "norm" as of 1961 was 1.75 square meters of living space per inmate (1961 statute, article 51).

73. Article 36, *Principles*, p. 8.   74. Article 33, *Principles*, p. 7.

75. Article 34, *Principles*, pp. 7–8.

76. N.A. Beliaev, *Tseli nakazaniia i sredstva ikh dostizheniia v ispravitel'no-trudovykh uchrenzhdeniiakh* (Leningrad, Izdatel'stvo Leningradskogo universiteta, 1963), p. 153.

77. *ITP*, p. 231.   78. *Ibid.*   79. *Ibid.*, pp. 232–34.

80. Article 7, *Principles*, p. 3.

81. A.D. Glotochkin and V.F. Pirozhkov, *Psikhologicheskie osnovy rezhima* (Moscow, Vysshaia shkola MOOP SSSR, Nauchno-issledovatel'skii i redaktsionno-izdatel'skii otdel, 1968), pp. 11–15.

82. Generally, it is regarded as (also) an expression of the convict's continued claim on the "right" to work (though here, his exercise of the right is not free). Some writers take special note, however, of the commitment to use special-regime inmates at "heavy physical labor." See A.V. Kureev and N.A. Struchkov, "Sotsialisticheskii gumanizm sovetskogo ispravitel'no-trudovogo prava," *SGIP*, No. 8 (1966), p. 26.

83. On what inmate work "should" be like, see *ITP*, pp. 191–93.

84. Article 28, *Principles*, p. 6.   85. See *ITP*, pp. 206–207.

86. Article 29, *Principles*, p. 6.   87. *ITP*, pp. 200–201.

88. See *ibid.*, p. 210, for more detail on releases for study.

89. *Ibid.*, pp. 225–26, and article 31, *Principles*, p. 7.   90. *ITP*, p. 217.

91. Article 30, *Principles*, p. 7.

92. For an overview of all aspects of public participation, see *ITP*, pp. 123–45.

93. *Ibid.*, pp. 143 44. See also A.G. Volchenkov, "Rol' obshchestvennykh organizatsii v vospitanie osuzhdennykh," *SGIP*, No. 1 (1964), pp. 108–109, and A. Salmin and A. Kuznetsov, "Shefskaia rabota kollektivov trudiashchikhsia v ispravitel'no-trudovykh uchrezhdeniiakh," *SZ*, No. 12 (1959), pp. 23–29.

94. See, generally, *ITP*, pp. 130–34.

95. On the observation commissions, see *ibid.*, p. 84. On "legality" generally, see *ibid.*, pp. 79–86.

96. Limits of space preclude extended discussions of the peculiarities of the prisons, where confinement in cells limits both the level of inmate "organization" attainable and the execution of work and upbringing programs. The interested reader should see *ITP*, pp. 173–74.

97. See, e.g., I. Afanasiev and P. Trykin, "Vrednye 'eksperimenty,'" *K novoi zhizni*, No. 12 (1966), pp. 19–20. Hereafter cited as *KNZ*.

98. *Sovetskaia Rossiia*, August 27, 1960, pp. 2–3; translated in *CDSP*, October 26, 1960, p. 18. See also A. Kairialis, "Deiatel'nost' ispravitel'no-trudovykh uchrezhdenii Litovskoi SSR," *SZ*, No. 1 (1967), p. 65.

99. F.T. Kuznetsov, P.E. Podymov, and I.V. Shmarov, *Effektivnost' deiatel' nosti*

ispravitel'no-trudovykh uchrezhdenii (Moscow, "Iuridicheskaia literatura," 1968), pp. 156–57.

100. M. Melent'ev, "Ob effektivnosti trudovogo vospitaniia," *KNZ*, No. 2 (1968), pp. 62–64.

101. See G. Rozhnov, "Diagnoz—simuliatsiia," *KNZ*, No. 5 (1967), pp. 52–53.

102. Kairialis, "Deiatel'nost," p. 65.

103. Sergeeva and Pomchalov, "Effektivnost' kratkosrochnogo," pp. 40–41.

104. N. Ablizin and G. Avanesov, "Ob effektivnosti PKT," *KNZ*, No. 12 (1968), p. 64.

105. A. Dymerskii, "Khuliganstvo v ITU: prichiny i mery bor'by," *KNZ*, No. 7 (1967), p. 63. Kureev and Struchkov ("Sotsialisticheskii gumanizm," p. 26) also complain that "too few" of poorly educated inmates are compelled to take advantage of the ITK's general schooling facilities.

106. See *Sovetskaia Rossiia*, August 27, 1960, pp. 2–3; translated in *CDSP*, October 26, 1960, p. 19; and P. Ogorodnikov, "Oshibki ne dolzhni povtoriat'sia," *KNZ*, No. 7 (1965), pp. 61–62.

107. A.D. Glotochkin and V.F. Pirozhkov, *Psikhologiia kollektiva zakliuchennykh* (Moscow, Vysshaia shkola MOOP SSSR, Nauchno-issledovatelskii i redaktsionno-izdatel'skii otdel, 1968), p. 14.

108. *Ibid.*, p. 15.

109. A.D. Glotochkin and V.F. Pirozhkov, *Psikhicheskie sostoianiia cheloveka, lishennogo svobody* (Moscow, Vysshaia shkola MOOP SSSR, Nauchno-issledovatel'skii i redaktsionno-izdatel'skii otdel, 1968), pp. 29–30.

110. See Glotochkin and Pirozhkov, *Psikhologiia kollektiva*, p. 17. See also Iu. I. Vilkov, "Ob individual'nom podkhode v vospitatel'noi rabote," *Voprosy psikhologii*, No. 3 (1968), p. 134.

111. Vilkov, "Ob individual'nom podkhode," p. 134.

112. *Ibid.*, pp. 134–35, and Glotochkin and Pirozhkov, *Psikhologiia kollektiva*, p. 17.

113. Vilkov, "Ob individual'nom podkhode," p. 135.

114. K. Platonov and O. Zotova, "K teorii grupp i kollektivov pravonarushitelei," *KNZ*, No. 2 (1966), p. 51.

115. Vilkov, "Ob individual'nom podkhode," p. 135.

116. Glotochkin and Pirozhkov, *Psikhologiia kollektiva*, p. 18.

117. V.F. Pirozhkov, *Predmet sovetskogo ispravitel'no-trudovogo prava* (Moscow, Vysshaia shkola MOOP RSFSR, Nauchno-issledovatel'skii i redaktsionno-izdatel'skii otdel, 1966), p. 26.

118. Platonov and Zotova, "K teorii grupp," pp. 49–50.

119. Glotochkin and Pirozhkov, *Psikhologiia kollektiva*, p. 29.

120. *Ibid.*, pp. 6–7.   121. *Ibid.*, p. 13.   122. *Ibid.*, pp. 22–23.

123. Sometimes, even the extreme measure of sending an inmate out of the ITK for a period in prison is based on exceedingly minor misdeeds—such as smoking where prohibited, leaving the dining hall "out of formation," or playing cards. See V. Makienko, "Koloniia ili tiurma?" *KNZ*, No. 9 (1967), pp. 64–65.

124. Glotochkin and Pirozhkov, *Psikhicheskie sostoianiia cheloveka*, pp. 28–29.

125. Glotochkin and Pirozhkov, *Psikhologicheskie osnovy rezhima*, p. 8.

126. Glotochkin and Pirozhkov, *Psikhicheskie sostoianiia cheloveka*, p. 33.

127. *Ibid.*   128. Vilkov, "Ob individual'nom podkhode," p. 138.

129. See *ibid.*, pp. 138–39. Iu.'s behavior was "discussed" and condemned at a meeting, and it was unanimously demanded that he change his behavior. At the meeting, the vice-chairman of the observation commission, an "old Bolshevik," appeared and made a speech. He made further visits to the colony to talk with Iu., who "began to change his behavior and attitude toward work." Iu. finished the tenth grade and was granted early release. Vilkov reports that he "works well and lives honorably."

130. Some Soviet research on juveniles and their "legal consciousness" (*pravosoznanie*) provides interesting glimpses of how the law enforcement system may come to be viewed as vengeful. In a series of questions testing the legal knowledge and attitudes of samples of delinquents and nondelinquent minors, subjects were asked whether drunkenness while committing a crime is viewed in the law as a mitigating, aggravating or irrelevant circumstance, and also *their* feelings on how it should be regarded. Delinquents exceeded their non-delinquent peers in percentage of correct answers as to the law (drunkenness is an aggravating circumstance) but *also* "voted" much more heavily than non-delinquents that it should, in their opinion, be considered a mitigating circumstance. See A.I. Dolgova, "Pravosoznanie v mekhanizme prestupnogo povedeniia i ego defekty u nesovershennoletnikh pravonarushitelei," in *Voprosy izucheniia i preduprezhdeniia pravonarushenii nesovershennoletnikh*, Vol. I (Moscow, Vsesoiuznyi institut po izucheniiu prichin i razrabotke mer preduprezhdeniia prestupnosti, 1970), pp. 145–46.

131. Glotochkin and Pirozhkov, *Psikhologiia kollektiva*, pp. 22–23.

132. Article 53, CC RSFSR. Berman and Spindler, *Codes*, pp. 170–72. See the discussion of criteria for applying conditional early release in Z.A. Vyshinskaia and S.A. Shlykov, "Effektivnost' uslovno-dosrochnogo osvobozhdeniia ot nakazaniia," in Nikiforov, ed., *Effektivnost' ugolovnopravovykh mer*, pp. 181–92.

133. Article 363, CCP RSFSR. Berman and Spindler, *Codes*, p. 398.

134. Vyshinskaia and Shlykov, "Effektivnost' uslovno-dosrochnogo," pp. 185–86, 188.

135. *Ibid.*, p. 195.   136. *Ibid.*, p. 199.

137. *Ibid.*, p. 200. See also V. Baskov, "Uslovno-dosrochno osvobozhdat' tol'ko dokazavshikh svoe ispravlenie," *SZ*, No. 8 (1961), p. 17; and A.I. Vasil'ev, "Nekotorye voprosy uslovno-dosrochnogo osvobozhdeniia osuzhdennykh k lisheniiu svobody," *Pravovedenie*, No. 3 (1966), pp. 81–82.

138. Vyshinskaia and Shlykov, "Effektivnost' uslovno-dosrochnogo," p. 203.

139. Article 49, *Principles*, p. 10. Administrative supervision was "added" as a means of coping with recidivism in 1966. See N. Kondrashkov, "Novaia forma preduprezhdeniia retsidiva," SZ, No. 12 (1966), pp. 46–47.

140. G. Bulatov and L. Katserikov, "Administrativnyi nadzor organov militsii za litsami, osvobozhdennymi iz mest lisheniia svobody," SZ, No. 2 (1968), p. 37.

141. See *ibid.*, p. 38, and A. Ia. Edir, "Administrativnyi nadzor organov militsii za litsami, osvobozhdennymi iz mest lisheniia svobody," in *O merakh po usileniiu bor'by s narusheniiami obshchestvennogo poriadka* (Moscow, Vysshaia shkola MOOP SSSR, Nauchno-issledovatel'skii i redaktsionno-izdatel'skii otdel, 1967), pp. 107–108.

142. Edir, "Adminstrativnyi nadzor," p. 105.

143. A.M. Iakovlev, *Bor'ba s retsidivnoi prestupnost'iu* (Moscow, "Nauka," 1964), pp. 198–99.

144. V. Pirozhkov, "Gotovit' k zhizni na svobode," KNZ, No. 6 (1966), p. 38.

145. K. Platonov, "Lichnost' i nakazanie," KNZ, No. 5 (1966), p. 53.

146. V.I. Pinchuk and T.A. Kleimenov, "Iz opyta izucheniia prestupnikov-retsidivistov," SGIP, No. 5 (1965), pp. 102–103.

147. A.P. Safonov, "O retsidive prestuplenii sovershennykh litsami, otbyvshimi lishenie svobody," SGIP, No. 3 (1967), p. 112.

148. Article 47, *Principles*, p. 10.

149. Kuznetsov, Podymov, and Shmarov, *Effektivnost' deiatel'nosti*, p. 98. The three-year period, while not an unreasonable choice, may be a bit low. Several studies in the West indicate that almost all reconvictions after service of a sentence take place within five years after that sentence is completed. See Roger Hood and Richard Sparks, *Key Issues in Criminology* (New York, McGraw-Hill, World University Library, 1970), pp. 178–79.

150. See Mikhlin et al., "Effektivnost'," pp. 142–49. The same results are reported in Iu. Mel'nikova, "Za povyshenie effektivnosti ispravitel'nykh rabot," SZ, No. 3 (1968), pp. 9–13.

151. Mel'nikova, "Za povyshenie," p. 11.

152. Article 53, CC RSFSR. Berman and Spindler, *Codes*, pp. 170–72.

153. Mikhlin et al., "Effektivnost'," p. 148.   154. *Ibid.*, pp. 148–49.

155. Mel'nikova, "Za povyshenie," p. 11. The author notes that the 88-court study shows that almost one-fifth of all corrective-works sentences are given by way of "exception."

156. Safonov, "O retsidive prestuplenii," p. 107. The author's figures include, however, inmates of labor colonies for juveniles as well as inmates of the ITK's for adults.

157. Daniel Glaser, *The Effectivenss of a Prison and Parole System* (Indianapolis, Bobbs-Merrill, 1964), pp. 13–35.

158. *Ibid.*, p. 108.

159. A. Natashev and N. Ovsiannikov, "Opyt izucheniia retsidiva," *KNZ*, No. 3 (1967), p. 59.

160. M. Melent'ev, "Ob effektivnosti kolonii usilennogo rezhima," *KNZ*, No. 1 (1967), p. 65.

161. Safonov, "O retsidive prestuplenii," p. 111. See also A.E. Natashev, "Effektivnost' ispoleniia lisheniia svobody i preduprezhdenie retsidivnoi prestupnosti," *SGIP*, No. 3 (1967), p. 104.

162. Sergeeva and Pomchalov, "Effektivnost' kratkosrochnogo," pp. 46–47.

163. See the summary of findings and the citations to the relevant studies in Hood and Sparks, *Key Issues in Criminology*, p. 190. It is worth noting, however, that Soviet advocates of longer sentences sometimes base their arguments not on the effects of varied sentence lengths in the *same* type of institution, but on the lower recidivism rates reported for first offenders confined for generally longer terms in intensified-regime colonies, as compared to first offenders sent to standard-regime institutions.

164. *Ibid.*, p. 47.

165. Vyshinskaia and Shlykov, "Effektivnost' uslovno-dosrochnogo," p. 175.

166. Sergeeva and Pomchalov, "Effektivnost' kratkosrochnogo," p. 47.

167. See table in Vyshinskaia and Shlykov, "Effektivnost' uslovno-dosrochnogo," p. 174.

168. See President's Commission on Law Enforcement and Administration of Justice, *Task Force Report: Corrections* (Washington, D.C., U.S. Government Printing Office, 1967), pp. 60–62.

169. Safonov, "O retsidive prestuplenii," p. 109.

170. *Ibid.*, p. 110. On "specialization" see also Vyshinskaia and Shlykov, "Effektivnost' uslovno-dosrochnogo," pp. 178–79.

171. See Iakovlev, *Bor'ba s retsidivnoi prestupnost'iu*, p. 74. Citing data gathered by Ye.V. Boldyrev in a sample survey, Iakovlev finds that 61.8 percent of the sample of recidivists had committed their first crime before the age of 18. These figures are higher than some others: from a 450 person sample of "especially dangerous recidivists," other researchers found that 31.1 percent had been convicted of their first crime by age 18, and another 23.1 percent before age 19—54.1 percent in all before 19 years of age. See I.M. Gal'perin, "Ob ugolovnoi otvetstvennosti retsidivistov v svete nekotorykh kriminologicheskikh pokazatelei effektivnosti bor'by s retsidivnoi prestupnost'iu," in Nikiforov, ed., *Effektivnost' ugolovnopravovykh mer*, p. 245.

Chapter 10
DEVIANCE AND CONTROL IN
SOVIET PERSPECTIVE

1. See, e.g., note 102, chapter 6.

2. See, e.g., some writings on this theme in the reports submitted to the National Commission on the Causes and Prevention of Violence, collected in Hugh Davis Graham and Ted Robert Gurr, *Violence in America: Historical and Comparative Perspectives* (New York, Bantam, 1969).

3. Donald R. Taft, *Criminology* (3d ed., New York, Macmillan, 1956), p. 342.

4. See Robert K. Merton, "The Social-Cultural Environment and Anomie," in Helen L. Witmer and Ruth Kotinsky, eds., *New Perspectives for Research on Juvenile Delinquency* (Washington, D.C., U.S. Department of Health, Education, and Welfare, 1956), p. 26.

5. On radical legal thought in the 1920s, see Raymond A. Bauer, *The New Man in Soviet Psychology*, pp. 35–37, and Harold J. Berman, *Justice in the U.S.S.R.*, pp. 24–29.

6. On the theme of deviance and diversity, see generally David Matza, *Becoming Deviant* (Englewood Cliffs, N.J., Prentice-Hall, 1969), pp. 41–66.

7. William A. Bonger, *Criminality and Economic Conditions* (Boston, 1916).

8. On the "self-presentation" of criminologists during the period of revival, see Solomon, "Soviet Criminology," pp. 46–50.

9. Most notable in this regard are two articles by A.M. Iakovlev, "Sotsial'naia effektivnost' ugolovnogo zakona," *SGIP*, No. 10 (1967), pp. 55–63, and "Sotsial'naia psikhologiia i protivopravnoe povedenie," *SGIP*, No. 7 (1968), pp. 50–59.

10. Robert K. Merton, "Social Problems and Sociological Theory," in Robert K. Merton and Robert A. Nisbet, eds., *Contemporary Social Problems* (2d ed., New York, Harcourt, Brace & World, 1966), p. 786.

11. Exemplary evidence of a less-than-intense response to a comrades' court proceeding against a group of juveniles appears in George Feifer, *Justice in Moscow* (New York, Delta Books, 1965), pp. 121–25.

12. See *Literaturnaia gazeta*, July 19, 1967, p. 10.

13. The reader should compare articles 89–101 of the Russian Republic criminal code, which cover crimes against state ownership, with articles 144–151, which deal with personal ownership. Berman and Spindler, *Codes*, pp. 186–91 and 202–204 (see note 18, chapter 7).

14. "An Observer," *Message from Moscow* (New York, Knopf, 1969), p. 193.

15. Feifer, *Justice in Moscow*, pp. 32–46 and 56–57.

16. I.I. Karpets, *Problema prestupnosti* (Moscow, "Iuridicheskaia literatura," 1969), p. 53.

17. See, e.g., Barrington Moore, *Social Origins of Dictatorship and Democracy* (Boston, Beacon Press, 1966), pp. 506, for some remarks on the theme that populations have not freely "opted" for an industrial society.

18. With regard to mental illness, see Mark G. Field, "Soviet and American Approaches to Mental Illness: A Comparative Perspective," in S.N. Eisenstadt, ed., *Comparative Social Problems* (New York, Free Press, 1964), pp. 105–28.

19. *Pravda*, July 14, 1968, p. 2; translated in *CDSP*, July 31, 1968, p. 25. Combinations of mercurial responses and a certain amount of contempt from the audience at public proceedings are described in Feifer, *Justice in Moscow*, pp. 107–25. For a detailed description of a trial held in visiting session, see Peter Juviler, "Mass Education and Justice in Soviet Courts: The Visiting Sessions," *Soviet Studies*, XVIII (1967), 494–510.

20. *Izvestiia*, January 11, 1968, p. 3; translated in *CDSP* January 31, 1968, pp. 23–24.

21. *Literaturnaia gazeta*, July 24, 1968, p. 11; translated in *CDSP*, August 21, 1968, pp. 13–15.

INDEX

Absenteeism, and drunkenness, 78, 281n49

Academy of Sciences, 34

Adolescent personality, 95, 108–11, 254

Affluence, 191

Aktivs, 118–19, 121

Alcohol: consumption of, 36, 36T; in high proof forms, 37, 41; public attitudes toward, 52; stockpiling of, 78n; *see also* Ethyl alcohol, Beer, Wine

Alcohol, production of, 37T, 37–38, 52, 78, 253, 285n56

Alcohol, sale of, 38, 52, 76–77, 105, 193; to minors, 117

Alcohol pathology, 41

Alcoholics, 35, 36n, 40, 66, 146, 192, 245, 253; statistics on, 35, 36n; women, 40–41, 42, 42n; socioeconomic background of, 44, 44n; and crime, 47; types of, 55, 60–61

Alcoholism, 38, 57–58, 147, 185; as escapism, 45, 261; social costs of, 45–50; theories of causation of, 50–58; early socialization and, 51–52, 280n22; medical viewpoint on, 53–54, etiology of, 54–55, 282n81; public attitudes toward, 57, 253–54; socioeconomic patterns of, 57, 285n59; effect on family of, 97; family

attitudes to, 280n23; effect on offspring of, 284n46, 285n53

Alcoholism, treatment of, 56, 60–68; medical approaches to, 60–68; institutions for, 61–62 (*see also* Treatment-labor institutions); compulsory, 61n, 65–68; public involvement in, 65; costs of, 65, 68; success of, 65, 68

Alkogolizm—put' k prestupleniiu (Alcoholism—Path to Crime), 78

All-Union Council of Anti-Alcohol Societies, 73

All-Union Institute for the Study of the Causes and Elaboration of Preventive Measures of Crime (Institute of Criminology), 149n, 153, 159, 174, 184, 251; founding of, 33; recommendations on alcohol problems of, 78, 285n60; access to statistical data of, 249

All-Union Institute of Legal Sciences, 34

All-Union Scientific Research Institute of Criminalistics, 33

Anti-alcohol measures, 44, 59–60; propaganda as, 68–73, 253, 285n51; effectiveness of, 71–73, 79; social pressures as, 73–76; regulation of trade as, 76–79